Microsoft® Windows Server® 2012 Administration

Instant Reference

Microsoft® Windows Server® 2012 Administration

Instant Reference

Matthew Hester

Chris Henley

SYBEX®

A Wiley Brand

Acquisitions Editor: Mariann Barsolo
Development Editor: Mary Ellen Schutz
Technical Editor: Scott Pearson
Production Editor: Dassi Zeidel
Copy Editor: Kathy Grider-Carlyle
Editorial Manager: Pete Gaughan
Production Manager: Tim Tate
Vice President and Executive Group Publisher: Richard Swadley
Vice President and Publisher: Neil Edde
Book Designer: Maureen Forys, Happenstance Type-O-Rama
Proofreader: Amy J. Schneider
Indexer: Ted Laux
Project Coordinator, Cover: Katherine Crocker
Cover Designer: Ryan Sneed
Cover Image: © iStockphoto.com / kycstudio

Dear Reader,

Thank you for choosing *Microsoft Windows Server 2012 Administration Instant Reference*. This book is part of a family of premium-quality Sybex books, all of which are written by outstanding authors who combine practical experience with a gift for teaching.

Sybex was founded in 1976. More than 30 years later, we're still committed to producing consistently exceptional books. With each of our titles, we're working hard to set a new standard for the industry. From the paper we print on, to the authors we work with, our goal is to bring you the best books available.

I hope you see all that reflected in these pages. I'd be very interested to hear your comments and get your feedback on how we're doing. Feel free to let me know what you think about this or any other Sybex book by sending me an email at nedde@wiley.com. If you think you've found a technical error in this book, please visit http://sybex.custhelp.com. Customer feedback is critical to our efforts at Sybex.

Best regards,

Neil Edde
Vice President and Publisher
Sybex, an Imprint of Wiley

To Deb, the best wife, mother, and friend I could have ever asked for,
Your love amazes me each and every day. Thank you for everything
you do for me, and I love you. To Nicole, Mitchell, and Caitlin, you
three truly are amazing blessings in my life, and I am honored to be
your father. I love you all!
—*Matthew Hester*

To Julie, my best friend, thanks for seeing my potential and helping me
realize it! All that I am I owe to you!
To Megan, Nicholas, and Lauren, thanks for helping me remember
that all things have been done in the wisdom of him who knoweth all
things. It is my pleasure to be your father!
—*Chris Henley*

Acknowledgments

I would like to thank all the wonderful editors and staff at Sybex; thank you for giving Chris and me a chance to write this book. Lastly, and most importantly, I want to acknowledge one of the best coauthors I could ask for, Chris Henley. Thanks for doing this project with me, and I look forward to more from H&H productions.

—Matthew Hester

The production team at Sybex deserves a huge thank-you for taking a chance on me and bringing me patiently through the process of getting this book to the presses. Thank you! I also would like to acknowledge the efforts of Matt Hester—a great coauthor, mentor, peer, and friend. Thanks for a great opportunity to work together! I look forward to many more successful projects together!

—Chris Henley

About the Authors

M att Hester is a seasoned IT Professional Evangelist for Microsoft and has been involved in the IT Pro community for more than 20 years. In his role at Microsoft, Matt has presented to audiences nationally and internationally as large as 5,000 people and as small as 10. Prior to joining Microsoft, Matt was a highly successful Microsoft Certified Trainer for more than eight years. Matt has also published several articles for *TechNet* magazine and runs a successful blog at http://aka.ms/matthester. In his spare time, Matt is a movie buff with a massive collection. He also runs marathons and dreams of joining the PGA tour. Matt cites his father as his role model: "The older I get, the smarter he gets." Funny how that works. Follow Matt on Twitter at @matthewhester.

C hris Henley is a Microsoft IT Professional Evangelist at Veeam focused on technologies related to Windows Server and Hyper-V. He is a published author and a regular speaker and presenter at user groups and major technology conferences around the world. He is fun and energetic in his style of communication and has a way of making technical concepts easy to understand. He loves talking about what technology can do. He loves speaking to audiences of all sizes and says, "There is no other experience that can compare with speaking to a large audience and helping them understand the possibilities that a new piece of technology can avail them." Chris loves to spend time in the outdoors with his wife and three children. Camping, fishing, hiking, skiing, biking, and chocolate are his favorite pastimes. Follow Chris on Twitter at @NerdyLikeThat, @HyperVBear, or @Veeam.

Contents at a Glance

Contents

Introduction

Administering and maintaining servers can sometimes appear daunting. In fact, a lot of industry studies say a majority of IT resources (such as budget, personnel, and time) are spent just maintaining existing servers and infrastructure. As administrators, we do not always have the time to learn how new technologies can improve our day-to-day tasks, and we often rely on the status quo the server can provide.

Although this book is not designed to dig deeply into the details behind Windows Server and server technologies, it will provide you with a quick and easy reference to many of the tasks you perform daily. This book will also get you quickly up to speed with many of the new features in Windows Server 2012 as well as show you how Windows Server 2012 can improve your daily administrative tasks.

You will notice that the book is organized specifically to help you find information quickly. It is organized into parts that categorize chapters into major topics. Then each chapter deals with a specific subject. At the beginning of each chapter, you will see what the chapter will cover and where you will find it in the pages. This method of organization is designed to assist you in finding the information that you need to solve immediate problems or begin a process as painlessly as possible. Ideally, this book will become part of your everyday toolbelt, something you can pick up whenever you need a quick reference or a reminder.

We hope you enjoy this book.

Who Should Read This Book

This book is designed for anyone who administers a Windows server environment. It is for experienced and new administrators alike. This book is also for administrators looking to learn how to use many of the new enhancements Windows Server 2012 can bring to their existing networks. This book will show administrators how to improve many of the day-to-day tasks of server administration.

This book will provide guidance for many common server tasks, such as setting up Group Policy and backing up and recovering your server.

This book will also show you many of the new and improved features built into Windows Server 2012 to help you improve server administration and management.

How to Contact the Authors

We welcome feedback from you about this book or about books you'd like to see from us in the future. You can reach us by writing to Matt at raid78@msn.com or to Chris at cj.henley@hotmail.com. You can also contact us via our blogs:

```
http://blogs.technet.com/matthewms/
http://www.veeam.com/blog/author/chris-henley
```

Sybex strives to keep you supplied with the latest tools and information you need for your work. Please check its website at http://www.sybex.com/go/winserver2012instantref, where we'll post additional content and updates that supplement this book if the need arises.

PART I

Getting Started

IN THIS PART ▶

1

Getting Started with Windows Server 2012

IN THIS CHAPTER, YOU WILL LEARN TO:

E very release of Windows Server has offered numerous features and functionality to assist administrators and companies with their day-to-day tasks. Each new release has offered plenty of new functionality but has also increased the administrative burden for the servers. Windows 2000 Server laid the foundation for Active Directory. Windows Server 2003 became the first dedicated server platform from Microsoft. Windows Server 2008 sought to offer server flexibility by providing role-based deployment including streamlined new roles such as Server Core.

Windows Server 2012 is a revolutionary release of the operating system. While Windows Server 2012 continues to build on prior releases, it delivers improvements to the Microsoft Windows Server platform. From the game-changing Hyper-V addition of shared-nothing live migration (you will learn more about that in Chapter 14, "Maintaining Your Virtual Servers") to better server management capabilities (you can now easily manage multiple servers from one console) and improvements designed to work with Windows 8, Windows Server 2012 has a lot to offer.

However, even with the addition of all these capabilities, Windows Server 2012's true benefits still are for administrators and were designed to improve the day-to-day tasks of administrators.

Before you begin to dig into the day-to-day improvements of administrative tasks, you should understand how the server was built so you can properly administer it. Do you need to install a new server? Do you need to perform an in-place upgrade? Do you migrate existing services such as DNS, Active Directory, or printers? These vital questions need to be answered so you can start to take advantage of the administrative improvements in Windows Server 2012. This chapter will take a brief look at planning, installing, and upgrading to Windows Server 2012. You will also learn about installing the migration tools.

Plan for Windows Server 2012

You have probably heard this phrase a thousand times (well, make this a thousand and one): "If you fail to plan, you plan to fail." Having a solid idea what role the server will play is important to the health of IT as well as to your sanity. Some of the decisions you make during the planning process can impact the installation phase. If your planning is off, your installation will be off. Although fixing most installation problems can be straightforward, some can become quite complex to fix, if not completely irreversible. Everyone has done the "FDISK, format, reboot" dance of destruction at least once to fix the wrong decisions.

In this section, you will look at the hardware requirements and recommendations for a Windows Server 2012 server installation. You will also learn about the roles and features that a Windows Server 2012 server can perform. In addition to the resources mentioned in this chapter, Microsoft offers several free tools to assist you in your planning process. These assessment tools are included in the Microsoft Assessment and Planning (MAP) Toolkit:

```
http://technet.microsoft.com/en-us/solutionaccelerators/
dd537566.aspx?SA_CE=NOT-MAPBETA-SITE-TNETWINSVR-20090615
```

Understand Hardware Requirements

Like its predecessors, Windows Server 2012 offers numerous roles and editions of the server operating system. Just like Windows Server 2008 R2, Windows Server 2012 will be released only in *64-bit versions*. This means before you even start, you need to have the proper hardware to support the operating system. This requirement will also dictate upgrade and migration paths. Table 1.1 shows the base hardware requirements for Windows Server 2012.

Table 1.1: Windows Server 2012 Minimum Hardware Requirements

Resource	Requirement
Processor	1.4GHz x64 processor
Memory	512MB RAM
Drive space	32GB
Drive	DVD-ROM
Display and others	Super VGA 800 × 600 or higher Keyboard and mouse

These recommendations are the bare minimum needed to get the server up and running. See Table 1.2 for additional recommendations for processor memory and hard drive space. They will offer a base system with solid performance and flexibility for additional functions.

Table 1.2: Additional Hardware Recommendations

Resource	Recommendation
Processor	2GHz x64 dual-core processor
Memory	4GB RAM
Drive space	100GB

You should always look at the base requirements as the bare minimum to get the server operating system up and running. Generally speaking, these minimum requirements do not take into account the workload you will be placing on the server. You should always consider the roles and applications that will be loaded on the server. You should consider the recommendations and requirements for those applications as additional resources to those listed in Table 1.1. This will allow you to have servers that will perform satisfactorily and meet your needs, while having a little room to grow.

If the server is going to be used for virtualization workloads, ensure you have enough RAM and processor cores to support the Windows Server 2012 operating system as well as the virtual servers running on the server. How many servers, what types of servers, and what types of applications are all factors you need to review carefully when you're planning a virtualization server. One last note of concern for a virtualization server: Whether you choose VMware or Hyper-V virtualization technologies, make sure your processor hardware supports hardware-assisted virtualization. Either AMD Virtualization (AMD-V) or Intel Virtualization Technology (Intel VT) will work. These technologies typically also need to be enabled in the BIOS because they are generally not enabled by default. Enabling the virtualization normally requires a full hard reboot to take effect. Make sure you enable these technologies before installing your virtualization technology. In Chapter 14, you will learn more about Hyper-V.

Understand Windows Server 2012 Editions and Roles

Windows Server 2012 streamlined the number of editions to four. This book focuses on the Datacenter and Standard editions. One important note is that both editions (Datacenter and Standard) are technically the same; they both provide the full technical capability of the Windows Server 2012 platform. The difference between the Datacenter and

Standard editions involves licensing virtual operating systems. (We will cover those in the "Consider Your Licensing Options" section in this chapter.) Table 1.3 gives an overview of the Windows Server 2012 editions.

Getting Started

PART I

Table 1.3: Windows Server 2012 Editions

Edition	Overview
Datacenter	Designed for large-scale highly virtualized infrastructures. Ideal for public, private, and hybrid cloud deployments.
Standard	Designed for nonvirtualized environments where physical server deployment is preferred. Great for smaller infrastructures or branch offices.
Essentials	Geared toward small business environments. Includes built-in configurations to connect to cloud-based services. Limited to 25 users.
Foundation	Provides general-purpose Windows Server functionality. Limited to 15 users.

Once you have chosen the right edition for your needs, you need to look at the services the server will provide for your infrastructure. These services come in the form of *roles*. Windows Server 2012, like Windows Server 2008 R2, provides several server roles that can be installed on the server. A role is a set of software features and functions that provides services for your server and infrastructure. Some of these roles require additional planning to provide a stable and reliable environment.

Table 1.4 describes the server roles.

Table 1.4: Windows Server 2012 Server Roles

Role	Function
Active Directory Certificate Services (AD CS)	Allows for the creation of certificate authorities. This role allows you to host your own Public Key Infrastructure (PKI) on the server.
Active Directory Domain Services (AD DS)	Provides single sign-on (SSO) capabilities for your network and network services. This allows for the creation of objects (users, groups, computers, and so on) for use with network authentication and authorization.
Active Directory Federation Services (AD FS)	Provides single sign-on capabilities across multiple forests and domains. Additionally, this role provides web single sign-on.

Table 1.4: Windows Server 2012 Server Roles *(continued)*

Role	Function
Active Directory Lightweight Directory Services (AD LDS)	Commonly referred to as ADAM, this role is a lightweight version of AD DS. It allows for the storage of a base directory used for specific applications.
Active Directory Rights Management Services (AD RMS)	Allows you to provide authorization and verification services to users to access protected content.
Application Server	Provides the ability to have high-performance distributed applications (mainly applications that use the .NET Framework).
DHCP Server	Provides automatic TCP/IP address services for your network.
DNS Server	Provides name and service resolution services for TCP/IP networks. This is a core component for AD DS, and it is highly recommended you use this built-in service for your domain controllers.
Fax Server	Allows basic fax functions to be hosted on the server, such as sending, receiving, and reporting.
File and Storage Services	Provides many services for the file system, including replication, managing shares, and faster file searches. This role also provides services for UNIX clients to access files on the server.
Hyper-V	Provides the ability to create, manage, and perform live migration of virtual machines. Virtual machines operate on the host machine and are servers without the hardware.
Network Policy and Access Services	Provides resources for routing and remote access. This service also provides the framework for Network Access and Protection (NAP) and DirectAccess. Included in this service are two core components: Health Registration Authority and the Host Credential Authorization protocol.
Print and Document Services	Provides the ability for a centralized print server as well as management for printers. This service also installs the necessary Group Policy Objects (GPOs) for printer management through Group Policy.
Remote Access	Provides remote access services for your clients, from always-on Direct Access to traditional VPN. Additionally Remote Access provides routing capabilities such as Network Address Translation (NAT).

Role	Function
Remote Desktop Services	Provides the ability for your users to access the Remote Desktop Services on your server. These services provide presentation virtualization for your thin clients. Formerly called Terminal Services.
Volume Activation Services	Provides the server capability to manage licensing in your organization for Key Management Services or Directory Based Activation.
Web Server (IIS)	Provides the core infrastructure for a web server.
Windows Deployment Services	Installs the services for deploying Windows operating systems across the network.
Windows Update Services (WSUS)	Provides the management framework for Microsoft updates. This service allows you to deploy updates in a variety of options across your network.

Getting Started

PART I

NOTE   Table 1.4 gives brief explanations of all the services available to Windows Server 2012. For more details, please take a look at Chapter 2, "Adding Server Roles and Functionality." You can also get a more thorough explanation of the roles at http://technet.microsoft.com/en-us/windowsserver/default. aspx. In Windows Server 2012, some of the roles and features have been changed under the covers.

Understand Server Core

Windows Server 2012 Server Core is another installation option that is worth further mention. As in Windows Server 2008 and Windows Server 2008 R2, Windows Server 2012 Server Core is a very streamlined version of Windows Server. In Windows Server 2012, Server Core is now the default installation option. Server Core has limited functionality and runs a subset of the roles provided by Windows Server 2012. Server Core does not have a GUI. This means that all the administration is performed remotely or via a command prompt. Most importantly, the Server Core option is no longer a permanent installation-time decision; you can add the GUI back later if you want. Unlike Windows Server 2008 R2 (where you had to reinstall the server to remove the GUI), with Windows Server 2012 you can add and remove the GUI management tools easily.

This by no means implies that Server Core does not have usefulness in the network. The Server Core role provides a nice addition to your network without the overhead of a traditional server. This lowers the overall maintenance and security risks for the server. Server Core can also reduce the amount of patching that is required to keep the server up-to-date, and it is the Microsoft preferred installation for Windows Server 2012. The server provides support for these thirteen roles:

- DNS Server
- DHCP Server
- Active Directory Domain Services (AD DS)
- Active Directory Lightweight Directory Services (AD LDS)
- File Services (including File Server Resource Manager)
- Print and Document Services
- Web Server (IIS, including a subset of ASP.NET)
- Streaming Media Services
- Windows Server Update Server
- Active Directory Rights Management Server
- Active Directory Certificate Services (AD CS)
- Hyper-V
- Routing and Remote Access Server and the following subroles:
  - Remote Desktop Services Connection Broker
  - Licensing
  - Virtualization

Server Core is one of the two choices during installation, the other being a Full GUI installation. Additionally, you have a new option called Minimal Server Interface. The Minimal Server Interface provides graphical management tools and infrastructure for a hybrid management alternative.

Also in Windows Server 2012, if you install the full GUI, you can add additional desktop components via the Desktop Experience feature. In Table 1.5, you can see the components included in each of these choices.

Table 1.5: Windows Server 2012 Feature Availability by Installation Option

Feature	Server Core	Minimal Server Interface	Server with GUI	Desktop Experience Feature
Command Prompt	Available	Available	Available	Available
Windows PowerShell/ Microsoft .NET	Available	Available	Available	Available
Server Manager	N/A	Available	Available	Available
Microsoft Management Console (MMC)	N/A	Available	Available	Available
Control Panel	N/A	N/A	Available	Available
Control Panel applets	N/A	Some	Available	Available
Windows Explorer	N/A	N/A	Available	Available
Taskbar	N/A	N/A	Available	Available
Notification area	N/A	N/A	Available	Available
Internet Explorer	N/A	N/A	Available	Available
Built-in help system	N/A	N/A	Available	Available
Themes	N/A	N/A	N/A	Available
Windows 8 Shell	N/A	N/A	N/A	Available
Windows Store and support for Windows Store apps	N/A	N/A	N/A	Available
Windows Media Player	N/A	N/A	N/A	Available

In the "Perform a Windows Server 2012 Server Core Installation" section, you will see how to install these different options.

Consider Your Licensing Options

When you install Windows Server 2012 into your environment, you have to take into account the licensing. Windows Server 2012 for Standard and Datacenter are licensed per physical processor; each license covers two processors. For example, if your hardware comes with four processors, you will need two licenses to properly license the server. Every Windows Server 2012 requires two types of licenses. First, you need a server license for the rights to run the operating system, and second, you need a client access license (CAL) to allow your clients to access the server. CALs come in two flavors:

- The *device* CAL allows access for one device for any user.
- The *user* CAL allows access for one user on any device.

Depending on your existing licensing, you may already be covered for Windows Server 2012. If Windows Server 2012 is solely used for virtualization servers, you do not need to have CALs for the host operating system. However, you will still need CALs for the guest operating systems running on the server. There is only one difference between the Windows Server 2012 Standard and Datacenter editions, and this is in regard to how you use virtualization technologies inside your network. Depending on which edition you have chosen (Standard or Datacenter), you may not need to purchase server licenses for your virtualized instances of Windows Server 2012. If you are using Windows Server 2012 Standard edition, you are allowed to run two virtualized instances of Windows Server 2012 under your server license. If you are using Windows Server 2012 Datacenter, you are allowed to run unlimited virtualized instances of Windows Server 2012 under your server license. For more details and specific license questions and pricing, contact your Microsoft reseller.

Install Windows Server 2012

After you plan your environment, it will be time to install Windows Server 2012. The installation process is fairly straightforward. This is mainly because of the role-based nature of Windows Server 2012. You will learn more about installing roles in Chapter 2.

Perform a Windows Server 2012 Full Installation

In this section, you will take a step-by-step look at the installation process for a Windows Server 2012 full installation. We'll cover the key decisions you need to be aware of as you install the operating system.

1. Insert the DVD media into the drive and reboot the system. Make sure your DVD is in the proper boot priority order so the DVD boots first. Upon reboot you will see the screen shown in Figure 1.1.

NOTE The DVD-ROM should hold boot priority over the HDD in this instance.

Figure 1.1: Selecting your language

2. Select your chosen language, time/currency, and keyboard method, and then click Next. You will see the screen shown in Figure 1.2.

Figure 1.2: Starting the installation

This screen provides the option to install Windows Server 2012 by clicking the Install Now button. The Repair Your Computer option takes you to the repair and diagnostics functions of Windows Server 2012. To continue the installation, click the Install Now button.

3. The next window you see (Figure 1.3) provides you with the choice to install your edition of Windows Server 2012. You can choose to install the Server with a GUI or the Server Core version. Select your version, and click Next. Here is the screen for the trial version of Windows Server 2012.

Figure 1.3: Selecting your Windows Server 2012 version

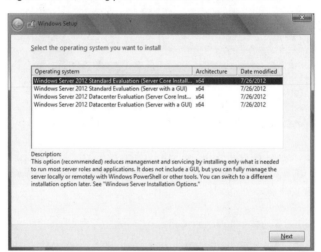

NOTE   Depending on the version of Windows Server 2012 you are installing, you may not see the screen in Figure 1.3 initially. You may see a screen prompting you for a product key. After you type in the product key, you will see your installation options based on the key you entered.

4. Clicking the Next button takes you to the License Agreement screen. This screen, shown in Figure 1.4, allows you to read, print, and agree to the license terms. Select the check box on the bottom left of the dialog box to agree to the license terms, and click Next to continue.

Figure 1.4: Licensing terms

5. The screen shown in Figure 1.5 provides you with the choice between performing an upgrade or custom installation of Windows Server 2012. To perform a new installation, click Custom, and you will be taken to the next step.

Figure 1.5: Upgrading or customizing

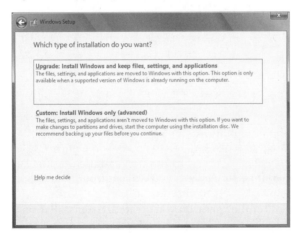

6. The next screen, displayed in Figure 1.6, allows you to choose the location for your Windows Server 2012 installation. This screen also allows you to load drivers for your SCSI hard drives.

If you are installing on a hard drive connected to a SCSI control-ler, select Load Driver, and insert the media with the drivers on it. You also have a full set of drive partitioning and formatting options, as shown in Figure 1.6. When you click the installation drive and click Drive options (advanced) for Windows Server 2012, you are presented with the options to create new partitions or delete, format, or extend existing partitions. Choose the appropriate option for your system, and click Next. If you do not select a partition and the only option you have is unallocated space, the Windows Server 2012 installation will create a parti-tion on that drive by taking all the unallocated space and format-ting it for you automatically with NTFS. Windows Server 2012 will also automatically make a system partition of 200MB in size during this step. The 200MB partition is not assigned a drive and will not be visible in the OS. The partition holds the Windows boot files for the Windows recovery environment (winRE).

Figure 1.6: Selecting a drive and partition

7. When you select the partition you created, the installation will begin, and you will see a screen similar to Figure 1.7. The system may also reboot several times during this phase of installation.

Figure 1.7: Windows installation progress

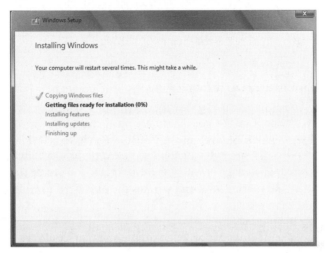

8. After the final system reboot, you will be asked to configure the administrator's password, and you will see a screen similar to Figure 1.8.

Figure 1.8: Initial change of password logon

Set your administrator password. The password needs to be complex. This means the initial password needs to meet the following requirements:

■   Cannot contain the user's account name or parts of the user's full name that exceed two consecutive characters

- Be at least six characters in length
- Contain characters from three of the following four categories:
  - English uppercase characters (A through Z)
  - English lowercase characters (a through z)
  - Base 10 digits (0 through 9)
  - Nonalphabetic characters (for example, !, $, #, or %)

There is also an option for you to create a password reset disk. By clicking this option, you can create a recovery disk, which allows you to create a new password for the user ID. You create this disk only once, no matter how many times the password for the account changes.

9. After you set the password, you will see a screen similar to Figure 1.9.

Figure 1.9: Logon window

After you have set the password, the Windows Server 2012 installation will complete, and you will see a new screen with the new version of Server Manager, as shown in Figure 1.10.

Figure 1.10: Server Manager

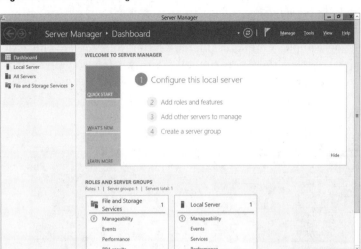

Perform a Windows Server 2012 Server Core Installation

Installing Windows Server 2012 Server Core follows a process similar to the previous steps. The only difference comes in step 3; here you would select Server Core Installation instead of Server with a GUI for your edition of Windows. You will learn how to add roles in Chapter 2.

Use *sconfig* to Configure Your Windows Server 2012 Server Core

After you install Windows Server 2012 Server Core, you need to configure the basics of the server, such as the network settings, computer name, domain membership, and so on. In prior versions of Windows Server, you had to be familiar with the netsh commands in configuring these aspects of Server Core.

Although you can still configure the Server Core installation with netsh commands as you may have done in the past, by default PowerShell is installed on a Windows Server 2012 core installation and you can begin your management with PowerShell. We will take a look at PowerShell in Chapter 3, "Automating Administrative Tasks with Windows Server 2012." You can also leverage Server Configuration. Server Configuration is a DOS-style menu configuration system that provides simple commands for configuring your server. This tool allows you to complete these common tasks easily. After you log on to Server Core, type **sconfig**. You will see a screen similar to Figure 1.11.

Figure 1.11: Server Configuration tool

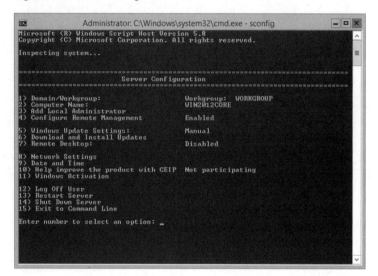

As you can see, this tool is very easy to follow. For example, if you want to change the network settings after you have launched sconfig, press the 8 key to configure the settings. Then you will just need to follow the menu screens to finish the configuration.

If you do not want to use sconfig, PowerShell, or the command prompt, you can add the GUI management components. Adding the GUI management components provides an easy and familiar way to add and remove server roles and features. What makes Server Core great in Windows Server 2012 is that you can add the GUI, configure the server, and then easily remove it.

To start a PowerShell on a Server Core, type **PowerShell** at the command prompt. To install the GUI features, you will first need to mount the installation files:

1. Make a mount directory for the installation files. From within a PowerShell session, type **Mkdir c:\mount**.

2. Mount the source files, In this example, the files are mounted from the Windows Server 2012 installation in the D: drive. By default, you can use index 1:

```
Mount -WindowsImage -ImagePath d:\sources\install.wim
-Index 1 -Path c:\mount -readonly
```

Once you have mounted the files, you can use one of the two commands to install the GUI components:

- To Install the full Windows Server 2012 GUI, run the following PowerShell command:

```
Install-WindowsFeature Server-Gui-Mgmt-Infra,
Server-Gui-Shell -Restart -Source c:\mount\windows\winsxs
```

- To Install the Minimal Server Interface, run the following PowerShell command:

```
Install-WindowsFeature Server-Gui-Mgmt-Infra
 -Restart -Source c:\mount\windows\winsxs
```

Likewise, if you have installed a full server GUI, you can also remove the GUI and convert your installation to a Windows Server Core installation. You do that by using the Remove Roles and Features Wizard. To remove the GUI, follow these steps:

1. Open Server Manager from the Start screen.

2. Click Manage on the top toolbar.

3. Click Remove Roles and Features.

4. Click Next on the default page.

5. Select the local server from which you want to remove the GUI and click Next.

6. On the Server Roles page, click Next.

7. On the Features page, find User Interfaces and Infrastructure.

8. Expand the User Interfaces and Infrastructure.

9. To remove the full server GUI, deselect Graphical Management Tools and Infrastructure and Server Graphical Shell and then click Next.

10. Verify the information on the Confirm installation selections screen and then click Remove.

11. Verify the results and then click OK. Your server will need to be restarted to complete the conversion to Server Core.

Activating Windows Server Core

When you install Windows Server 2012 on a server with a GUI installation or Server Core, you must activate the operating system to ensure you have a valid product. Activation also enables your copy of Windows Server 2012 to function properly. On a full server installation, the Activate Windows Wizard is located in the Control Panel. This simple wizard takes you step-by-step through the process. However, there is no wizard in a Server Core installation of Windows Server 2012, so you will have to run one of the following two commands to activate the operating system.

- If you entered the product key for your Server Core installation during the install process, run this script:

```
cscript C:\windows\system32\slmgr.vbs -ato
```

- If you did not enter the key during the install process, run the following command:

```
cscript C:\windows\system32\slmgr.vbs -ipk <product key>
```

When the script finishes execution, run this command to activate Windows:

```
cscript C:\windows\system32\slmgr.vbs -ato
```

Upgrade to Windows Server 2012

Upgrading to Windows Server 2012 can require some additional planning and consideration because Windows Server 2012 is released only in 64-bit versions. You cannot upgrade an x86-based system to Windows Server 2012. You can only perform a migration, which will be covered in the next section. Your current operating system and edition will determine the proper path for your upgrade. However, when you perform an upgrade, the process is really an in-place migration under the covers. Table 1.6 shows the paths you can take. If your current operating system is not listed, it is not supported.

Table 1.6: Upgrade Paths

Existing Windows Operating System	Windows Server 2012 Upgrade Options
Windows Server 2008 Standard with SP2 or Windows Server 2008 Enterprise with SP2	Windows Server 2012 Standard, Windows Server 2012 Datacenter
Windows Server 2008 Datacenter with SP2	Windows Server 2012 Datacenter
Windows Web Server 2008	Windows Server 2012 Standard
Windows Server 2008 R2 Standard with SP1 or Windows Server 2008 R2 Enterprise with SP1	Windows Server 2012 Standard, Windows Server 2012 Datacenter
Windows Server 2008 R2 Datacenter with SP1	Windows Server 2012 Datacenter
Windows Web Server 2008 R2	Windows Server 2012 Standard

Performing an in-place upgrade is a destructive process in a sense. You are replacing the existing server operating system with the new one—and this is a one-way street. If the upgrade process goes awry, you will incur downtime until you resolve the issue and restore your system. Before you perform any upgrade or migration, back up your existing server operating system and data. To perform an in-place upgrade, follow these steps:

1. Insert the DVD media into the drive. The screen shown in Figure 1.1 displays.

2. When you click Install Now, you will be presented with a couple of choices, as shown in Figure 1.12. You can choose to partici-pate in the Microsoft Customer Experience program by selecting I Want To Help Make Windows Installation Better. This pro-gram helps Microsoft identify trends for successful and unsuc-cessful installations and determine which updates are needed. Choosing to participate is strictly optional. You can learn more about the program by clicking What Information Will Be Sent To Microsoft?

Figure 1.12: Installation updates

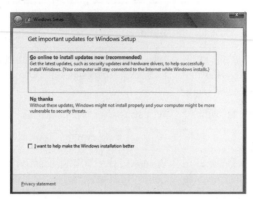

You will also be presented with a choice to upgrade your installation files. You should always choose to update them; the following updates are included in this choice:

- Installation updates

- Driver updates

- Windows updates

- Microsoft Windows Malicious Software Removal Tool updates

If you choose to go online and update your installation, you will see a screen similar to Figure 1.13 while downloading the updates. After you're done downloading them, or if you choose not to update the installation, you will proceed to the next step.

Figure 1.13: Update installation progress

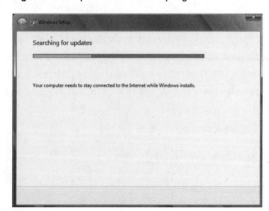

3. The next step provides you with the choice to install the edition of Windows Server 2012. You can choose to install the full edition of Windows Server 2012 or the Server Core version. Select your version, and click Next.

4. When the License Agreement screen appears, you can read, print, and agree to the license terms. Select the check box on the bottom left of the dialog box to agree to the license terms, and click Next to continue.

5. The next step offers you the choice between performing an upgrade or custom installation of Windows Server 2012. To proceed to the next step of the upgrade, you need to choose the upgrade option.

6. The Windows Server 2012 installation will perform a compatibility check, and you will see a screen similar to Figure 1.14. The report will be saved to your desktop, and you will see what devices will be affected by the Windows Server 2012 upgrade. Click Next to continue.

Figure 1.14: Compatibility report

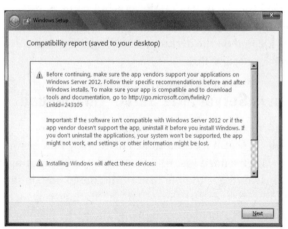

7. The Windows Server 2012 upgrade will continue to the next step, and you will see a screen similar to Figure 1.15. During this phase

of installation, all the necessary files, settings, and programs needed for the upgrade will be collected and analyzed. The system may also reboot several times during this phase of installation.

Figure 1.15: Upgrading Windows progress

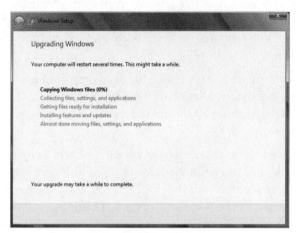

8. After the final system reboot, the upgrade will be complete, and you will be presented with a Login screen. Log in, and you will finish the upgrade. You can also review the compatibility report again; it is located on the desktop. The file will be called Windows Compatibility Report.htm.

Install Windows Server 2012 Server Unattended

You can also perform an unattended installation of Windows Server 2012. This provides a useful method to rapidly deploy new servers in your environment. Unattended installs are completed by creating an answer file. The answer file is the file containing the main configurations for the Windows Server 2012 installation. Settings can include application configuration, such as configuring the home page in Internet Explorer and controlling the desktop look-and-feel settings. To create an answer file, you first need to install the Windows Automated Installation Kit (WAIK). The WAIK is available in the MDT Toolkit, located here:

http://www.microsoft.com/en-us/download/details.aspx?id=25175

After you download the MDT, install the tool by clicking the MSI file and step through the wizard, accepting the defaults.

Install the WAIK

The WAIK is a flexibility utility tool that allows you to customize your Windows Server installs. You can also create the necessary files to assist with configuration and deployments. To install the WAIK, you need to install the .NET framework feature. You can find it in the Add Roles and Features Wizard in Server Manager.

1. Open Server Manager.

2. Click Dashboard.

3. Click Add Roles And Features.

4. Click Next on the default page.

5. Select Role-based or feature-based installation and click Next.

6. Select the local server and click Next.

7. On the Server Roles page, click Next.

8. On the Features page, find .NET Framework 3.5 Features.

9. Expand the .NET Framework 3.5 Features.

10. Select .NET Framework 3.5 Features (includes .NET 2.0 and 3.0) and click Next.

11. Verify your selection on the Confirm installation selections screen and click Install.

12. Verify the results and click OK. The server may need to be restarted to complete the installation.

After you have installed the MDT, go to the Start screen, begin typing **Deployment Workbench**, and then click the Deployment Workbench icon in the results.

Where's the Start Menu?

You might have noticed that Windows Server 2012 has no Start menu. When you press the Windows key on your keyboard, a screen similar to the one shown here appears.

Although you probably will not use the Start screen very frequently, you might have to venture into it. If you do, my advice is to just type what you want to find. The Start screen has built-in search capabilities and, when you start typing, you'll get a list of applications installed on the server. For example, if you are looking for the Administrative Tools group, just start typing **administrative tools** and see what happens. Alternatively, type `cmd` and see what happens. You will find the Start screen is useful, but for server management, you probably will not need to look any further than the new Server Manager. (You'll learn about Server Manager at the end of this chapter. You're going to love it!)

1. In the Navigation pane of DeploymentWorkbench, expand the Deployment Workbench and then expand the Information Center.

2. Select Components and then select Windows AIK from the Components pane.

3. Click Windows AIK to download the files. After the files (approximately 1GB) are downloaded, you should see a screen similar to Figure 1.16. Click Install.

Figure 1.16: Welcome to WAIK

4. Click Next on the Welcome screen.

5. Click Next after you accept the license agreement.

6. Pick a drive and directory for the tools. (The tools require about 1.2GB of drive space.) Then click Next.

7. Click Next to begin to the installation, and click Close on the final screen.

Create an Answer File

After you have installed the WAIK tools, your next step is to create an answer file. The file contains configuration settings for Windows and provides the settings to your preferred desktop. To create an answer file, you will use the Windows System Image Manager (SIM). Before you create an answer file, you will need to load the install.wim file from the Windows Server 2012 DVD. The file is located in the sources directory. Copy the file to a local directory—for example, c:\source.

1. Start Windows SIM by going to the Start screen and typing **Windows System Image Manager**, and select it when it appears in the results list.

2. In Windows SIM, select File ➢ Select Windows Image, and navigate to the directory that contains the install.wim file.

3. After you select the `install.wim` file you located in step 2, you will be presented with the dialog box shown in Figure 1.17. Choose the edition of Windows Server 2012 for which you are creating the answer file and click OK.

Figure 1.17: Windows image selection

4. After you select the edition, you will be asked to create a catalog file; click Yes. This process can take several minutes.

5. Choose File ➢ New Answer File, and your screen will look similar to Figure 1.18.

Figure 1.18: WAIK

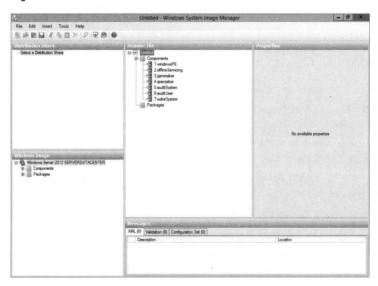

6. You will need to add and configure the many settings that fit your needs. For more information on configuring the settings, see the help file that comes with the WAIK toolset (waik.chm).

7. When you are done modifying settings in the answer file, you will need to save the file. Select File ➤ Save Answer File. During the save process, the SIM tool will start a validation process. The Validation tool ensures that your answer file is correctly formatted and the settings are properly configured. Before you save, you can also validate the file by selecting Tools ➤ Validate Answer File.

8. Save the answer file with the name **Autounattend.xml**.

Install Windows Server 2012 Unattended

After you have an answer file, it is time to install Windows. The previous process is good for single-server deployments. However, the WAIK tools also provide resources for many deployment methods. The WAIK toolset provides many tools to quickly deploy multiple servers via a variety of sources. You will learn the DVD method to deploy Windows Server 2012 unattended.

1. Copy your answer file (Autounattend.xml) to a disc or USB flash drive (UFD).

2. Insert your UFD and your Windows Server 2012 DVD into the server you want to install.

3. The Windows Server 2012 setup program automatically checks the removable media for a file called Autounattend.xml.

4. After the installation is complete, make sure your settings were properly installed.

5. Lastly, you need to *reseal* the system by running this command:

```
c:\windows\system32\sysprep\sysprep.exe /oobe /
generalize /shutdown
```

Resealing the system removes hardware-specific and unique system information. This is required if you plan to redeploy the image and properly ready the system for users.

Migrate to Windows Server 2012

Performing a server migration instead of an in-place upgrade has some advantages you should consider. Performing a migration does require two servers; however, this is one of the advantages. On the server you will be migrating to, you will perform a clean install of Windows Server 2012, and clean installations exhibit more stability than upgraded servers. Migrations also reduce the risk of downtime in your server environment and offer a fallback plan. During migration, the server being migrated from is still running, and if the migration fails, you can start all over with the new server without impacting your environment. Lastly, migration allows you to do performance and benchmark testing prior to fully completing the migration.

Windows Server 2012 migration can be used successfully in these three scenarios:

x86 to x64 scenarios   As mentioned earlier, Windows Server 2012 is available only in 64-bit. Migration is the only method for the x86 hardware.

Virtual server to physical server and physical server to virtual server   If you are looking to virtualization for some of your server components in your current environment, then migration is the way to go. Likewise, if you are looking to move some of your virtual servers to the physical systems, migration offers another great pathway for you.

Core Server to full server and full server to Core Server   As mentioned in Table 1.6, you can perform this type of upgrade only on Windows Server 2012 servers. Migration is the only way to move from a Server Core installation to a full installation of Windows Server 2012. You can also turn a full server into a Server Core through this process. However, make sure the roles on the full server are supported by Server Core.

Migration can be from x86 or x64 systems and supports the following source operating systems:

- Windows Server 2003
- Windows Server 2003 R2
- Windows Server 2008 (full server only)
- Windows Server 2008 R2 (full server or Server Core)

NOTE Windows 2008 Server Core is not supported for migration because Server Core has no .NET Framework support. Additionally, the system language on both the source and the target have to be the same. For example, if the source server's system language is English and the target server is in Spanish, then the migration tools will not work.

Migration can be performed for the following roles, features, settings, and data:

- Active Directory Domain Services (AD DS)
- DNS
- DHCP
- File Services
- Print Services
- BranchCache
- IP configuration
- Local Users and Groups

Prior to performing the migration, you need to install the Windows Server 2012 migration tools.

Install Windows Server 2012 Migration Tools

The migration tools are new and provide a much improved resource for successfully migrating your environment. You will install the migration tools first on the target Windows Server 2012 server and then on the source server. Prior to installing the migration tools, make sure the source servers meet the system requirements listed in Table 1.7, and verify you are, at the minimum, a member of the Administrators group on both the target and source servers.

Table 1.7: Migration Tool System Requirements

Source Server OS	Requirements
Windows Server 2003 or Windows Server 2003 R2	25MB free drive space, .NET Framework 2.0, Windows PowerShell 1.0 or later
Windows Server 2008, 2008 R2, or 2012	23MB free drive space, Windows PowerShell or the Server Manager command-line tool (`ServerManagerCmd.exe`)

First, install the migration tools on the Windows Server 2012 target server. After the tools are installed on the target server, create deployment folders on the target server for the source server. Lastly, to complete the installation, register the Windows Server migration tools on the source servers. You will see how to install the tools via Server Manager:

1. Open Server Manager (you can also install the tools via PowerShell if you are running Windows Server 2012 Server Core) on the target server, click Dashboard and select Add Roles And Features.

2. Click Next on default page.

3. Select Role-based or feature-based installation and click Next.

4. Select the local server and then click Next.

5. On the Server Roles page, click Next.

6. On the Features menu, you may need to scroll down to select Windows Server Migration Tools. You will see a screen similar to Figure 1.19. After you select Windows Server Migration Tools, click Next.

Figure 1.19: Migration features

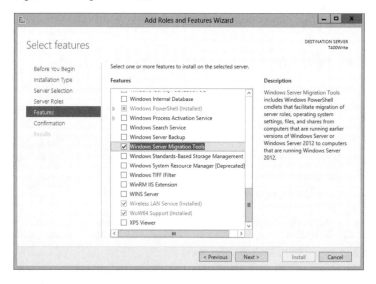

7. Verify the Confirm installation selections screen and click Install. You will see a screen similar to Figure 1.20.

Figure 1.20: Windows Server Migration Tools confirmation

8. Verify the results and click OK. The server may need to be restarted to complete the installation.

9. After the tools are installed, create the deployment folders on the target computer. To do this, first you need to open an administrator command prompt. Move your mouse to the lower left of the screen and right-click. You will see a menu similar to Figure 1.21. Select Command Prompt (Admin).

Figure 1.21: Selecting Command Prompt (Admin)

10. Create a deployment folder on the target computer to hold the migration tools; the following examples use `c:\migration`. This folder can also be a network path.

11. In the Command Prompt window, change to the Server Migration Tools directory. The directory by default is located at `c:\windows\system32\ServerMigrationTools\` (if you installed to the default directory on the C: drive). To get there quickly, you can enter the command `cd %windir%\system32\servermigrationtools\` and press Enter.

12. Depending on what architecture and operating system your source system is running, you will need to run one of the following commands. The command creates a directory with the migration tools in it, as in Figure 1.22, which shows a directory created for a 64-bit version of Windows 2003 with the name of `SMT_ws03_amd64`.

Figure 1.22: Windows migration directory

- If your server is 64-bit Windows Server 2003, type the following command and press Enter:

```
SmigDeploy.exe /package /architecture amd64 /os WS03 /
path c:\migration
```

- If your server is 64-bit Windows Server 2008, type the following command and press Enter:

```
SmigDeploy.exe /package /architecture amd64 /os WS08 /
path c:\migration
```

- If your server is x86 Windows Server 2003, type the following command and press Enter:

```
SmigDeploy.exe /package /architecture X86 /os WS03/path
c:\migration
```

- If your server is x86 Windows Server 2008, type the following command and press Enter:

  ```
  SmigDeploy.exe /package/ /architecture X86 /os WS08 /
  path c:\migration
  ```

- If your server is Windows Server 2008 R2, type the following command and press Enter:

  ```
  SmigDeploy.exe /package /architecture amd64 /os WS08R2 /
  path c:\migration
  ```

13. Copy the folder created in step 10 to a local directory on the source computer so you can register the tools with the source server.

14. On the source server, open a command prompt. If the server is Windows Server 2003, just run the command. However, if the source server is Windows Server 2008 or 2008 R2, you will need to run an elevated command prompt. To do that, select Start ➢ All Programs ➢ Accessories, right-click Command Prompt, and select Run As Administrator.

15. Change to the directory to which you copied the files in step 13.

16. Type **.\Smigdeploy.exe**, and press Enter to register the tools. When this command is complete, you will see a status message, and a Windows PowerShell window will open. You will see a screen similar to Figure 1.23.

Figure 1.23: Windows migration install

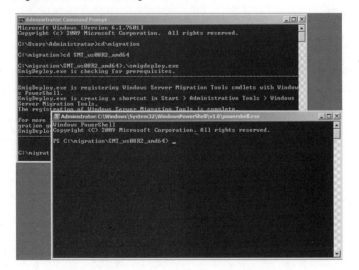

After you install the migration tools, it will be time to perform the migration.

Migrate to Windows Server 2012

Regardless of the feature or role you will be migrating to Windows Server 2012, you will follow three general steps after you install Windows Server 2012 on the new target server:

1. Export the settings from the source server to temporary storage.

2. Import the settings to the target server from temporary storage.

3. Transfer any data and shares from the source server to the target server.

A New Server Manager

One of the new tools you will first see in your Windows Server 2012 installations is Server Manager. This tool will change not only how you manage your local server but all of the servers in your infrastructure. Throughout this book, you will see Server Manager in action; in this section, you will get a brief tour of the tool.

One of the first things you will notice about the new Server Manager is the Dashboard. The Dashboard is where you can get a quick glimpse of your server environment. You can see an example in Figure 1.24.

Figure 1.24: Server Manager

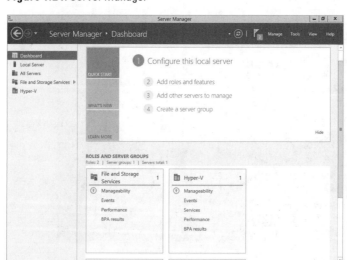

In the Dashboard, you see the status of all the servers and their respective installed roles. This is designed to save you time and administrative effort. If the category in the Roles and Server groups is green, then all systems are normal. If the category is red, then you most likely have some issues. From the Dashboard, you can quickly jump to the status of the roles by clicking the role (or by clicking the role name on the left-hand navigation tree). You then will be taken to a screen that will show you events, best practice analyzer results, a listing of servers running the role, performance counters, and even a snapshot of the services that support the role. You can see an example of the Hyper-V role in Figure 1.25. Also from the Dashboard, you can quickly configure the local server, add roles and features, add servers to manage, and create groups to manage your server right from the Dashboard.

Figure 1.25: Hyper-V in Server Manager

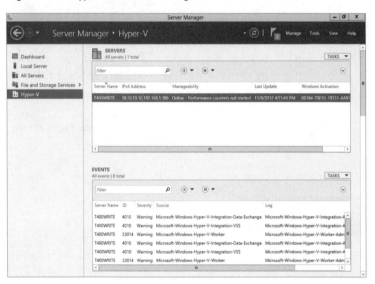

Let's take a look at managing some of the aspects of your local server. When you click Local Server on the Navigation pane or Configure Local Server on the home page of the Dashboard, you will see a screen similar to Figure 1.26.

Figure 1.26: Configure Local Server

As you can see, all the common tasks for server management are listed and have links to quickly manage those aspects. From changing the name of your server or configuring the IP address to a quick overview of the hardware, this central location allows you to quickly manage the server.

One very important aspect of the Server Manager is the top-right menu bar shown in Figure 1.27.

Figure 1.27: Server Manager menu bar

This menu bar provides three menus that offer the key to successfully managing your servers. The first menu, represented by the flag icon, is the Action Center. Click the icon to display a list of recent events, such as a successful installation or additional steps taken after a role installation. You might also see potential issues here.

The next menu item is labeled Manage. From this menu, you can add and remove server roles and features, add servers, create a server group, and configure basic properties of the server manager.

The last menu item, Tools, is probably going to be one of your favorites. Click Tools to access all of the available administrative tools. Essentially, the Tools menu is the Administrative Tools group from previous server environments.

Now, with Server Manager, you can manage multiple servers. To do that, you need to add the servers you want to manage. (Make sure you have administrative privileges on the servers you add.) You can add servers using any of the three following methods:

- Active Directory

- DNS

- Import

  - To add a server, you can either right-click All Servers or click the Manage menu and select Add Servers. When you have done so, you will see a screen similar to Figure 1.28.

Figure 1.28: Add Servers Via DNS

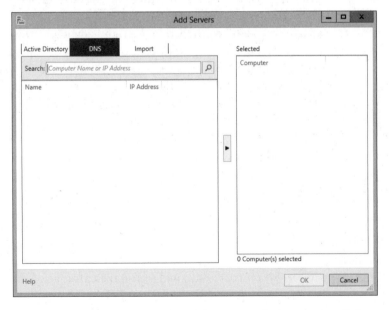

Then choose the appropriate method for your infrastructure, click OK, and the server will be added to the server list. One of Server Manager's hidden gems is that once the server is added to the list, you have a great shortcut menu to manage the server, When you right-click the server, you will see a screen similar to Figure 1.29.

Figure 1.29: Server Management shortcut menu

Not only can you add and remove roles and features remotely, you can also open a remote desktop connection to the server. You can create groups that will allow you to organize your servers. By going to the Manage menu on the menu bar, you can also select Create Server Group to create a group of servers you can easily access and manage. After you create the server group you can then add all the servers you want to manage; they will be grouped in the right-side navigational tree.

In this section, you just took a quick tour of the Server Manager. Do not be afraid to explore the different options as you add roles or additional functionality to your server. Throughout the rest of this book, you will see the Server Manager in action and learn how this tool provides access to all of your server management needs.

2

Adding Server Roles and Functionality

IN THIS CHAPTER, YOU WILL LEARN TO:

O nce you have installed your Windows Server 2012 server, your job is just beginning, even though installing the Windows Server 2012 operating system can be a fairly straightforward process. More than likely, you had a purpose in mind for the server. Unlike earlier server operating systems from Microsoft where there were quite a few preinstalled roles and servers, no additional roles or features are installed as a part of the base operating system in a Windows Server 2012 installation. You have a blank slate for the server in which to create your environment.

As an administrator of a Windows Server 2012 server, you get to choose the roles and features you want to install on the new server installation. Additionally, when you install the needed functionality on the server, Windows Server 2012 will install only the components necessary for the functionality to properly run. Because unnecessary components are not installed, the performance of the server is increased. This role-based installation methodology has the added benefit of reducing the potential attack surface of your server.

Role-based installation also offers some great flexibility; however, this will add time to your planning process. It also means that when the server operating system first boots up, some things might not work as you expect. This generally is a result of a role or feature that has not been installed yet and is usually not indicative of a bigger problem or server error.

Although there are many roles and services that can be installed on a Windows Server 2012 server, this chapter will focus on just a few. Each role you install on the server can have numerous considerations for installation and planning. The roles selected for this chapter are based on the most common elements in many infrastructures.

Knowing how to properly plan, install, and migrate the roles to Windows Server 2012 are key factors to working with your server. In this chapter, you will learn about planning, installing, and migrating the more common roles you can install on a Windows Server 2012 server. This chapter will discuss both a Windows Server 2012 full installation and the Server Core version.

Plan for Windows Server 2012 Roles

Before you can install any roles, you need to plan. Some roles (such as the Fax server role) require minimal planning, but others (like the

Active Directory roles) require a great deal of planning. In this section, we'll cover some of the planning decisions for these common roles:

- Active Directory–related roles
- Hyper-V
- Remote Desktop Services

Plan for Active Directory

One of the most common functions installed on a Windows Server 2012 server is Active Directory (AD). AD governs authentication and access to your network applications and resources. AD provides the directory services that allow you to organize and secure your network infrastructure. Before you begin to plan the AD environment, you need to understand some of the common terminology used in a typical AD deployment:

Forest   This is the main and first logical structure for your directory structure. The forest is the main security boundary and will contain all the objects for your directory, starting with domains. Domains inside a single forest will automatically have a two-way transitive trust with all the other domains in the forest. The forest also defines several things for all the domains in the forest. First, the forest defines the schema for the AD structure. The schema contains the definition and attributes for all the objects in the forest. The schema is extremely important to the AD structure because it defines the various objects such as the users and groups. It will also define what properties make up those objects; an example of a property would be a last name or phone number. Also, with some enterprise-wide applications, such as email, the schema will get extended to support any new objects or properties needed by the new application. Some applications need to extend the schema to provide the proper objects for the application to function. Second, the forest also contains the replication information for the directory to properly function. Lastly, it holds the global catalog, which provides search capabilities for the forest.

Domain   Domains divide the forest into logical units. Domains are created to help control data replication and are instrumental in allowing your directory structure to scale. The domain contains all the security principals (for example, users and groups are stored here) for your organization. The domain also handles the authentication for your network and, through this, provides the base for securing your resources. The domains also help manage trusts. The domain is considered one of the main security boundaries for your network. Domains not only allow you to quickly segment resource access for users but also provide a tool to delegate administrative tasks.

Trees   Inside forests you have trees; they are where your domains reside. A tree is where domains share a common namespace as well as a security context for sharing the many resources located in a domain. Any domains you install underneath the first domain become child domains and get a new DNS name. However, the name inherits the parent domain name. For example, if a parent domain is called admin.com and you install a new child domain called server, the child domain's DNS name would be server.admin.com.

Trusts   Trusts allow the domains to authenticate resources not natively stored in the domain. Trusts can be one-way or two-way. Typically, trusts are two-way. For example, if a two-way trust exists between domain A and domain B, users from either domain could log on and be authenticated regardless of physical location. Inside a single tree in a forest, all the domains automatically have a two-way transitive trust between one another, making the flow of information much easier. You can control and configure the trust relationships to meet your needs. Additionally, when you create a new forest, no trust relationship is created between the two forests, but you can, however, create one.

Organizational unit (OU)   This provides logical organization to a domain. Without the use of OUs, the domain is just one giant bucket of unorganized objects, making administration a headache. OUs offer the ability to logically organize the objects in your directory. (Objects are generally user or group accounts.) Although there are several objects you can find in a domain, the main objects you will use on a day-to-day basis are user and group accounts. This organization provides several administrative benefits. Being able to find users and edit properties of a group of users is easier with OUs. You can also delegate administration to the OUs, which allows you to have multiple administrators without having to grant them access to the entire domain. Lastly, OUs are used in the deployment of group policies. Group Policy provides you with the tools to centrally manage and control your clients. Chapter 5, "Directory Management and Replication," discusses Group Policy.

User   The user is the account to which you grant access to log on to your network. This is one of the main objects inside your domain environment.

Group This is another important AD object. Providing another way to organize your users, groups are invaluable resources when you're granting secure access to your network resources, such as file shares, printers, or applications. Groups can have scopes that range from local to the domain to the entire forest.

Domain controller (DC) This is the main server (or servers) holding your domain objects (users, groups, and so on). The domain controller is also responsible for replicating the directory structure to other DCs, as well as for providing support for search capabilities.

Read-only domain controller (RODC) This is a variation of the domain controller and holds only read-only copies of the directory. Traditional DCs can receive and deliver changes to other DCs in the directory structure, but RODCs can receive only replication updates. Normally, these servers are used in branch-office scenarios but could also be used for other reasons, such as web applications.

Sites When you're designing Active Directory domains, OUs, and the many other objects that offer logical containers to help organize your structure, an important physical element of Active Directory is the site. Sites allow you to control the physical structure of your network. Sites help govern three important functions in your environment: replication, authentication, and service location. Sites allow you to define boundaries of your network via IP addresses and subnets, and they give you a mechanism to control traffic. For example, when a user logs on to the network, the site determines which domain controller will handle the request. The site containing the same IP subnet as the system the user is logging in from will be where the request will be directed. Any domain controllers in the site will then proceed to authenticate the user.

For more information on working with Active Directory, please review the planning guide located here:

http://technet.microsoft.com/en-US/library/hh831484.aspx

When you start planning your AD structure, you start at the top with the forest and domains. Typically, most organizations will have one forest, but it is not uncommon to have more than one forest. For example, you may have a forest for testing and research purposes. This forest is normally, logically, and physically segmented from the rest of the network. A typical scenario for this type of forest would be when you are testing applications, such as Microsoft Exchange, that extend the schema.

When you install your first domain controller, this becomes the root domain and the beginning of your forest. Server Core cannot be installed as the first domain controller in your forest; the first DC must always be a full install of Windows Server 2012. Additional domain controllers may be installed under the root domain, becoming child domains or installed off the root of the forest, which will become new trees with new namespaces.

The domains are logical units inside the forest that help you organize all the directory objects and define the namespace for the rest of the domains in the forest. You define the DNS namespace for your entire forest when you install the first domain controller in AD; typically, this is your company's public-facing DNS name. However, it does not have to be. Remember, these are logical structures, and you can call them whatever best suits the needs of your organization. It is important to note, however, that you should have your DNS name well thought out and planned before you install your first domain controller. Changing your DNS name can have wide-ranging impact not only on your Active Directory forest but on any applications that leverage the directory, such as email or other line-of-business applications.

For example, if your first domain is called corp.com, all the domains installed as part of the parent domains tree will share that namespace of corp.com. Take a look at Figure 2.1 for a quick picture of what a logical structure of Active Directory would look like.

Figure 2.1: In this Sample Active Directory design, triangles represent domains, circles are OUs, and trusts are represented by arrows.

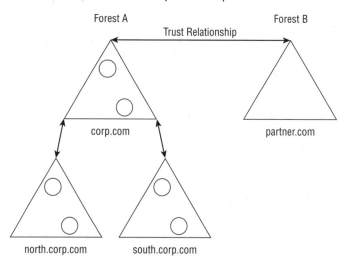

Inside the domain, you create organizational units to further create logical organizational structure for the domain. When you create OUs, there is no right or wrong way to set them up, as long as they add efficiency and organization to your directory structure. You may choose to organize the OUs alphabetically by last name (the least common way) or align them by business units (the most common way). There are any number of other ways, but the main point is that you want to make your life easier as an administrator.

Plan for Hyper-V

Growing in demand is the use of virtualization technologies to leverage underutilized resources to help with server consolidation and flexibility. Windows Server 2012 Hyper-V is built on the hypervisor technology. Hypervisor allows virtual systems to access server hardware efficiently. Unlike other virtualization technologies, Hyper-V does not place any third-party drivers in the hypervisor layer. The drivers that are leveraged by the virtualized systems are placed in the parent partition (the host operating system). All other virtual machines you install will be placed in child partitions.

Deciding to have your server handle virtualization workloads might seem straightforward, but this role does require additional planning. You need to take a look at which server workloads will be virtualized on the server and what additional hardware resources, if any, will be needed on the server, should you virtualize open-source (Linux) systems. With all of these questions you need to answer, you may be inclined to start looking at your performance logs and application logs to determine workloads. Fortunately, you can take advantage of a resource that Microsoft provides called the Microsoft Assessment and Planning (MAP) Toolkit. You can download this utility from `http:// technet.microsoft.com/en-us/library/bb977556.aspx`.

You can take advantage of several reporting and analysis functions that the MAP Toolkit makes available. Specifically for Hyper-V planning, there is a report that can help you make those server consolidation decisions. MAP Toolkit can generate both application and server recommendations for your network to help you determine the most optimal candidates for virtualization. This tool can dramatically reduce the amount of Hyper-V planning time. If you plan correctly, you can discover the potential for reducing your physical servers.

Understand Remote Desktop Services

In Windows Server 2008 R2, Terminal Services was renamed to Remote Desktop Services (RDS). The functionally of Remote Desktop Services is similar to the functionality of Terminal Services in Windows Server 2008. You can use these services to provide presentation virtualization to your environment. Planning for presentation virtualization follows similar methodologies of server virtualization. In addition to traditional terminal services, RDS provides capabilities for Virtual Desktop Infrastructure (VDI), which allows you to virtualize your desktop infrastructure workload onto servers in your data center. VDI allows you to take your typical desktop applications, data, and even the operating system itself and provide it on your thin clients. The systems those users work on use the Remote Desktop Protocol to connect to the back-end server. When installing RDS, the general rule of thumb is to install the applications that will be used on the RDS server after you install RDS so you avoid any potential issues or reinstallations of applications. In most cases, the applications have special terminal-server-friendly installation instructions. (You'll find more about virtualization in Chapter 13, "Managing Server Remote Access.")

Another planning consideration is security. How will clients authenticate against your server and with what level of security? You have two choices:

- Require network-level authentication
- Do not require network-level authentication

Your decision can impact the type of clients and the level of security provided by your RDS server. The decision also controls when the authentication of clients occurs during the logon process. If you choose to require network-level authentication, the user is authenticated before the remote desktop connection is established. This method provides a higher level of security. However, this method also requires your remote desktop clients to be using at least version 6.0 of the Remote Desktop client, and the Windows client needs to support the Credential Security Support Provider (CredSSP) protocol. CredSSP is built into Windows Vista and comes with Service Pack 3 for Windows XP, as well as Windows 7, Windows 8, Windows Server 2008, Windows Server 2008 R2, and Windows Server 2012.

If you choose to not require network-level authentication, you will allow any version of the remote desktop client software to connect. However, this will lower the security because the user authentication occurs late in the connection process.

When planning Remote Desktop Services, you need to understand the core services. Table 2.1 describes them.

RDS and Active Directory Services

We do not recommended placing RDS on a server running AD services. There are two reasons for this. First, RDS can create the potential for security risks on the AD services. Second, depending on RDS workload in your environment, the RDS services can degrade your server's performance.

Table 2.1: Remote Desktop Services Functions

Function	Description
Remote Desktop Session Host	This provides two services for the server to host for your environment; this server can host Windows-based applications or a full Windows desktop. This is the core component for RDS.
Remote Desktop Licensing	This server manages and monitors the usage of RDS client access licenses (CALs). CALs are required for connections to the remote desktop server. This server is also a required component when you install RDS.
Remote Desktop Connection Broker	This function is for remote desktop server farms. This service helps load balance the connections to the server.
Remote Desktop Gateway	This allows your users to connect to the remote desktop server over the Internet, without the need to be connected directly to the corporate network.
Remote Desktop Web Access	This allows users to connect to the remote workspaces configured on the RDS server via a web browser; this service also provides configuration settings that can be placed on the Start menu of the client computer. The website provides access to applications or desktops you have authorized for web access.
Remote Desktop Virtualization Host	This enables the RDS server to provide desktop virtualization services. This role service requires the Hyper-V role to be installed on the server.

Required Windows Server 2012 Features for RDS Services

Two RDS roles, Remote Desktop Gateway and Remote Desktop Web Access, require more services to be installed for the RDS roles to properly function.

If you install the Remote Desktop Gateway service, you must install Web Server, Network Policy and Access Services, RPC over HTTP Proxy, and Remote Server Administration Tools.

If you install Remote Desktop Web Access, you must install Web Server and Remote Server Administration Tools.

Understand Windows Server 2012 Features

Windows Server 2012 provides an additional set of functions to the server called *features*. These features were part of Windows Server 2008, but there are also some new features in Windows Server 2012. Some of these features are required for certain roles to function, while other features will add reliability to your server, as in the clustering feature. Some will just add aesthetics, such as the desktop experience feature. When planning your server OS, you might need to install some of these features to achieve the desired configuration. In most cases, you will not need to install the necessary features to support a role. Required features will generally be installed when you install the role. To install a Windows Server 2012 feature, open Server Manager and go to Add Roles and Features. Table 2.2 provides a quick review of the features.

Table 2.2: Windows Server 2012 Features

Feature	Description
.NET Framework 3.5	Provides the necessary application programming interfaces for applications to work. The framework is needed for a variety of the roles.
.NET Framework 4.5	Is the next generation of the .NET framework. In addition to previous versions, it provides the platform for a variety of applications from desktops to smartphones to cloud-based applications.

Feature	Description
Background Intelligence Transfer Service (BITS)	Provides an asynchronous transfer service for files. This can help with the download of files in the background. If interrupted, BITS continues a download from the point where it was interrupted; it does not start over.
BitLocker Drive Encryption	Provides drive encryption in case the drive is lost or stolen.
BitLocker Network Unlock	Enables a network-based service to unlock domain-joined system drives automatically. This enables administrators to work on systems during off hours when the users are not available to unlock the drives.
BranchCache	Helps reduce bandwidth consumption for clients located in branch-office scenarios The clients need to be Windows Server 2008, Windows Server 2008 R2, or Windows Server 2012 servers or Windows 7 clients.
Client for NFS	Provides client connectivity for UNIX NFS shares.
Data Center Bridging	A suite of IEEE standards that provides hardware-guaranteed bandwidth and reliable transport. Helps to enforce bandwidth allocation.
Enhanced Storage	Provides support for accessing functions on enhanced storage hardware and devices.
Desktop Experience	Includes common desktop components, such as a Media Player, visual effects (Windows Aero), and other common desktop applications. Even though these features are installed, they still need to be enabled manually.
Failover Clustering	Provides failover capabilities by clustering multiple servers together to act as one server.
Group Policy Management	Installs the MMC snap-in so you can manage Group Policy Objects.
Ink and Handwriting Services	Provides support for services typically needed for tablet-style systems. Also includes a useful tool called the Snipping tool, which allows you to create snapshots of Windows screens.

Table 2.2: Windows Server 2012 Features *(continued)*

Feature	Description
Internet Printing Client	Installs the necessary protocols for printing on the network or Internet.
IP Address Management (IPAM) Server	Provides the framework for managing IP address space and other services including Dynamic Host Configuration Protocol (DHCP) and Domain Name Service (DNS). IPAM manages trends, monitors, and provides other functions for both IPv4 and IPv6 address spaces.
Internet Storage Name Server (iSNS)	Provides the necessary services for discovering and supporting Internet Small Computer System Interface (iSCSI) storage area networks.
Lineprinter (LPR) Port Monitor	Enables the server to print to line printer daemons, which are commonly used on UNIX-based systems.
Management OData IIS Extension	Provides the necessary framework for PowerShell cmdlets through a web service running on IIS.
Media Foundation	Provides the subset of DirectShow to support application to transcode, analyze, and generate media files. The Desktop Experience feature requires this.
Message Queuing	Provides messaging support services between applications.
Multipath I/O	Coupled with Device Specific Module (DSM), provides support for multiple data paths to storage devices.
Network Load Balancing	Provides support for Transmission Control Protocol/Internet Protocol (TCP/IP) to distribute network traffic across multiple servers. This is very useful when your server is providing web services that need to scale as the load increases.
Peer Name Resolution Protocol	Provides name resolution for applications that can register with your computer so other systems can communicate with the applications.

Feature	Description
Quality Windows Audio Video Experience (qWave)	Provides a network platform enhancing the quality and reliability of AV applications, such as streaming media capabilities. This feature provides Quality of Service (QoS). Specifically, on Windows Server 2012, it provides rate-of-flow and prioritization services.
Remote Access Service (RAS) Connection Manager Administration Kit (CMAK)	Provides a tool to create Connection Manager profiles for remote connections like what is used in VPN scenarios.
Remote Assistance	Provides you and support personnel with the ability to view and share control of a user's desktop that needs support.
Remote Differential Compression	Provides the computation to minimize bandwidth utilization for transfers between two network resources.
Remote Server Administration Tools	Installs tools for remotely managing roles and features on your Windows Server 2012 server. With this feature, you can selectively install the roles or features for which you want to enable remote management.
Remote Procedure Call (RPC) over Hypertext Transfer Protocol (HTTP) Proxy	Used for client applications capable of relaying RPC traffic over HTTP. A common example is Outlook over RPC, which allows Outlook to leverage the HTTP protocol for communication to the email servers.
Simple TCP/IP Services	Provides backward-compatibility support for TCP/IP services and should not be installed unless an application requires any of the functions of a character generator, echo, or other simple services.
Simple Mail Transfer Protocol (SMTP) Server	Supports basic email transfer services for email messages and systems.
Simple Network Management Protocol (SNMP) Service	Installs agents for monitoring network activity.
Subsystem for UNIX-based Applications (Deprecated)	Provides the Windows Server 2012 server to run UNIX-based programs.
Telnet Client	Allows connections to Telnet servers.

Getting Started

PART I

Table 2.2: Windows Server 2012 Features *(continued)*

Feature	Description
Telnet Server	Provides remote command-line administrative capabilities for Telnet client applications.
Trivial File Transfer Protocol (TFTP) Client	Provides read and write capabilities to a remote TFTP server.
User Interfaces and Infrastructure	Contains the features for the full GUI installations, and minimal interface in the server's graphical shell. Additionally, the desktop experience is included in this feature.
Windows Biometric Framework	Installs the necessary support services for fingerprint devices, typically used to log on to the server.
Windows Feedback Forwarder	Allows your server to automatically send feedback to Microsoft via Group Policy settings and to join the customer experience improvement program. The service periodically collects and sends data to Microsoft.
Windows Identity Foundation 3.5	Is used to implement claims-based identity for applications that leverage claims-based authentication.
Windows Internal Database	Provides a data store for only Windows roles and features such as Active Directory Rights Management Services (AD RMS), Windows Server Update Services (WSUS), and Windows System Resource Manager.
Windows PowerShell	Provides a GUI window that allows you to run PowerShell commands. You can also test and create PowerShell scripts in this new utility. This feature includes the Integrated Scripting Environment (ISE) and PowerShell 2.0 engine. It also includes a new feature called Windows PowerShell Web Access, which provides a web gateway that provides remote access for remote administration via PowerShell.
Windows Process Activation Service	Removes the dependency on HTTP for Internet Information Services (IIS), allowing other applications to use non-HTTP protocols.
Windows Search Service	Provides fast file search for Windows Search Service compatible clients.

Feature	Description
Windows Server Backup	Provides backup and recovery tools for Windows Server 2012 for the operating system, applications, and data.
Windows Server Migration Tools	Installs the PowerShell cmdlets for migration; refer to Chapter 1, "Getting Started with Windows Server 2012," for how to install this feature.
Windows Standards-Based Storage Management	Allows you to connect and work with storage devices that conform to the SMI-S standard.
Windows System Resource Manager (Deprecated)	Provides administrator control over how CPU and memory resources are allocated and helps provide reliability to applications.
Windows TIFF Filter	Provides your Windows Server 2012 server with the ability to work with Optical Character Recognition (OCR) files. Specifically for TIFF 6.0 files, this feature will also allow the files to be properly indexed and searched.
Windows Remote Management (RM) ISS Extensions	Provides secure communication with local and remote systems using web services.
WINS Server	Is for NetBIOS name resolution for computers and groups on the network, used now primarily in backward-compatibility scenarios.
Wireless LAN Service	Installs the necessary services and configurations for wireless adapters to function properly on your Windows Server 2012 server.
WoW64 (Windows 32-bit on Windows 64-bit) Support	Includes the support to run 32-bit applications on Server Core installations and is a required component for full-server installs.
XPS Viewer	Installs the support for XPS documents.

Install Windows Server 2012 Roles

In this section, you will see how to successfully install the roles of a full installation of Windows Server 2012 as well as a Server Core installation. You will learn some of the differences between the two installation methods.

Install Roles on a Windows Server 2012 Full Server Installation

In this section, you'll learn how to install roles on a Windows Server 2012 full server installation. You will go through the installations for Active Directory, Hyper-V, and Remote Desktop Services.

One important new functionality built into Windows Server 2012 Server Manager is that you can install roles and features. You can use the Add Roles and Features Wizard to install on the local server, on remote servers (if you have administrative privileges), or on an offline virtual hard disk (VHD). When you install to a VHD, Server Manager injects the role or feature into the virtual hard disk and, when the server is started, the role or feature is installed. To use this feature, the VHD must be offline and must have the Windows Server 2012 operating system installed. When you select to install to a VHD file from the Add Roles and Features Wizard, you will see a screen similar to Figure 2.2.

Figure 2.2: Install to a VHD.

Install the Active Directory Role

As you'll see, you can install Active Directory Directory Services (DS) by adding the Active Directory DS role via Server Manager. After the role is installed, DCPromo starts. You then can use DCPromo to turn the Windows Server 2012 server into a fully functional domain controller (DC). Here are a few important notes you should consider:

- After you install the first DC, you should consider installing a second DC for redundancy. Having a second DC allows your users to log on in case of a server outage.

- Active Directory requires DNS services. Although you can leverage most existing DNS services, you should seriously consider utilizing Microsoft's DNS. It is made with AD in mind. Additionally, if no DNS server is installed in your network, DNS will be installed as part of the Active Directory installation.

- Installing AD also installs three necessary services required for directory replication:

  - Distributed File Services (DFS) namespaces

  - DFS replication

  - File replication

With this in mind, follow these steps:

1. Open Server Manager.

2. Click Open The Dashboard.

3. Click Add Roles And Features to begin the installation of Active Directory.

4. On the Add Roles and Features Wizard Welcome screen, click Next. (You can also select the Skip This Page By Default box on the Welcome screen to ignore that page for future role installations.)

5. On the Select Installation Type screen, select Role-based or Feature-based Installation and click Next.

6. On the Select Destination Server screen, select the server or VHD for the service and click Next. You will see a screen similar to Figure 2.3.

Figure 2.3: Selecting server roles

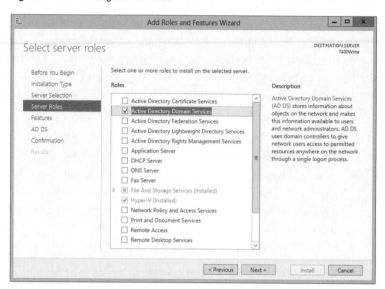

7. On the Select Server Roles screen, select Active Directory Domain Services. If you are prompted to add required services, review the services and click Add Features to continue the installation. Then, click Next.

Add Required Features

When you install certain roles and services, you might be required to install features or functions as part of the role installation. When this occurs, you will be presented with a dialog box for adding the required services. For example, when you install Active Directory Domain Services, that role requires the installation of the Group Policy management tools and the remote server administration tools. If those tools are not installed already, you will be prompted to install the services, as shown next.

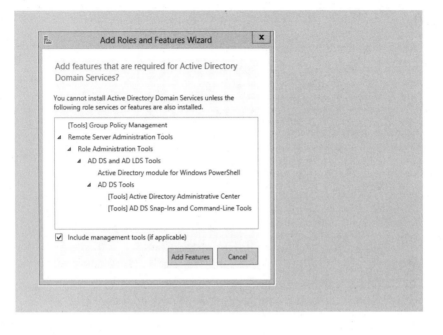

8. On the Select Features screen, click Next.

9. On the Active Directory Welcome screen, review the information and click Next.

10. You will be presented with a Confirmation screen; click Install to begin the installation of Active Directory.

11. After the role is installed, review the Confirm Installation Selections screen. You should see a message indicating the status of the installation on the server and then click Close.

12. To finalize the AD installation, you need to run the Active Directory Domain Services Installation Wizard (dcpromo.exe). To promote the server, in Server Manager click the Action Pane Notification flag. You will see a screen similar to Figure 2.4. Click Promote This Server To A Domain Controller.

Figure 2.4: Notification for ADDS install

Configure Your Existing AD Forest and Domain

If your Windows Server 2012 is joining an existing Active Directory, you need to take a couple of steps to prepare the schema. You need to prepare the forest and the domain before joining the existing forest and domain. When you prepare the forest, you extend the schema so that it can support the new functionality in Windows Server 2012. To prepare the forest, you need to be a member of the Enterprise Admins, Schema Admins, or Domain Admins group on the schema master. To prepare the domain, you need be a member of the Domain Admins group on the infrastructure master. You also need to copy the Adprep tools to the servers to run the commands. To do that, open your Windows Server 2012 DVD, and copy the contents of the \support\adprep folder to both the schema and infrastructure master servers, or run the commands directly from the DVD after you insert it.

To prepare the forest on the schema master, you need to run one of these commands from the adprep directory you copied to the server:

If you're installing a domain controller from the command prompt, run this command:

```
adprep /forestprep
```

If you're installing an RODC from the command prompt, run this command:

```
adprep /rodcprep
```

To prepare the domain on the infrastructure master, from the command prompt, run this command:

```
adprep /domainprep /gpprep
```

13. The Active Directory Domain Services Configuration Wizard will display the Deployment Configuration screen, as shown in Figure 2.5. Choose the appropriate installation path for your infrastructure. For this exercise, you will see a new forest and domain installation.

Figure 2.5: Joining or creating a new domain

14. In the Domain text box, enter the Fully Qualified Domain Name (FQDN) for your domain, and then click Next.

15. On the Domain Controller Options screen, shown in Figure 2.6, choose the appropriate level of functionality for your forest and domain based on your current infrastructure and the operating systems that are running your Active Directory services. For example, if you have Windows 2008 domain controllers, you would most likely set your forest functional level to Windows 2008. Make sure to read the notes and warnings as you choose your functional level because they differ from one functional level to the next. You also can add services and configure your domain recovery password; simply fill in the appropriate information and then click Next.

Figure 2.6: Setting the forest functional level

16. On the DNS Options screen, click Next. Depending on your existing DNS structure, you might have more actions presented in additional dialog boxes.

To Use Built-in DNS or Not

When you first install a new server, you should consider using the built-in DNS provided by Microsoft to support Active Directory services. Microsoft has optimized the DNS server to handle AD services and requests. Although there is nothing wrong with using a third-party DNS server, you need to perform a manual configuration to ensure your AD runs properly across the network.

17. Enter or verify the NetBIOS name, and click Next.

18. On the next screen, you will be asked to choose the installation location for your directory databases, log files, and sysvol folder. Choose the location for the files, and then click Next. Place the database and log files on separate volumes to provide better reliability and performance.

19. On the Summary screen, review the settings and click Next. If you are going to be performing unattended installs of Active Directory in the future, click the View Script button to review and save your settings file for future installs.

20. A prerequisites check will run, and you will see a screen similar to Figure 2.7. Review the information, verify that you meet the requirements, and then click Install.

Figure 2.7: Prerequisites screen

21. On the Results screen, click Finish. To finalize the AD installation, you will need to reboot the server.

Install Hyper-V

Hyper-V allows you to create virtual servers to handle workloads on your server. For all intents and purposes, virtual servers are just like any other server in your infrastructure, and installing the role is straightforward:

1. Open Server Manager.

2. Open the Dashboard.

3. Click Add Roles and Features to begin installing Hyper-V.

4. On the Add Roles and Features Welcome screen, click Next. (You can select the Skip This Page By Default check box on the Welcome screen to ignore that page for future role installations.)

5. On the Select Installation Type screen, select Role-based or Feature-based Installation and click Next.

6. On the Select Destination Server screen, select the server or VHD you want to install the service on and click Next.

7. On the Select Server Roles screen, select Hyper-V. If you are prompted to add required services, review the services and click Add Features to continue the installation. Then, click Next.

Hyper-V Processor Requirement

If your processor does not support hardware-assisted virtualization or it is not enabled, the problems will be explained on the Validation Results screen. If you see a warning similar to the one shown next, your current Windows Server 2012 installation will not be able to install the Hyper-V role until you enable hardware-assisted virtualization or obtain new hardware. If you need to enable hardware-assisted virtualization, the setting is located in the BIOS and the server requires a hard reboot—not a soft restart—for the setting to take effect.

8. On the Select Features screen, click Next.

9. On the Introduction Hyper-V screen, review the information, take note of the links to documentation, and then click Next.

10. On the Create Virtual Switches screen, shown in Figure 2.8, review the network adapters and virtual networks that will be created. You can choose to select a network adapter during this step or you can modify the network adapters from Hyper-V Manager after you complete the installation. After you finish reviewing the settings, click Next.

Figure 2.8: Creating virtual switches

11. From the Virtual Machine Migration screen, you can enable Live Migration, or you can choose to configure it later. When you finish reviewing the settings, click Next. (See Chapter 14, "Maintaining Your Virtual Servers," if you need more information to adequately review the settings.)

12. On the Configure Default Stores screen, you can control the default location for Hyper-V file storage. After you configure the location for your server, click Next.

13. Read the summary of the Confirm Installation Selections screen, and then click Install. You may notice the Restart The Destination Server Automatically If Required check box. This setting is useful if you are managing remote servers that will need to be restarted to complete the installation.

14. After the role installation completes, you will see the installation results windows, which might (depending on your current server configuration) ask you to restart the server. After you review the results, click Close. If you need to restart the server, make sure you save all of your changes before you click Yes to restart the server.

Install Remote Desktop Services

Remote Desktop Services (RDS) provides you with the ability to handle numerous workloads on the server using the Remote Desktop Protocol (RDP) to handle the requests. Although installing the RDS service through Quick Start requires the machine to be joined to the domain, you should be aware that, for security reasons, you cannot install Server 2012 RD Connection Broker on a domain controller. In some scenarios, you can use web browser protocols to accomplish these tasks.

1. Open Server Manager.

2. Open the Dashboard.

3. Click Add Roles and Features to begin the installation of Remote Desktop Services.

4. On the Add Roles and Features Welcome screen, click Next. (You can select the Skip This Page By Default check box on the Welcome screen to ignore that page for future role installations.)

5. On the Select Installation Type screen, select Remote Desktop Services installation. (You can choose Role-based or Feature-based Installation and install RDS individually. However, this new wizard makes the installation easier.) After you've made your selection, click Next.

6. On the Select Deployment Type screen (Figure 2.9), you can choose either Standard Deployment or Quick Start.

    Standard Deployment—Standard deployment takes you through a traditional installation of RDS and allows you to install the RDS across multiple servers or on a single server. In most RDS scenarios, this will be your choice.

    Quick Start—As the name implies, Quick Start allows you to install all of the RDS roles and services on a single server. It is a great way to get RDS up and running quickly.

    This exercise will take you through a standard deployment. Choose Standard Deployment and click Next.

Figure 2.9: RDS deployment type

7. On the Deployment Scenario screen, you can choose either Virtual Machine-Based Desktop Deployment (for VDI installations) or Session-Based Desktop Deployment (for session-based desktops). Either choice presents you with similar installation steps. One of the differences you will see is in configuring either the RD Virtualization host or RD Session host. In Chapter 13, you will see these features in more detail. For this exercise, choose Session-Based Desktop Deployment. After you have made your selection, click Next.

8. On the Review Role Services screen (Figure 2.10), you will see which RDS components will be installed. Review the features and click Next.

9. On the RD Connection Broker screen, double-click to select the server you want to install the service on and click Next.

10. On the RD Web Access screen, select the server(s) you want to install the service on and click Next.

11. On the RD Session Host screen, select the server(s) you want to install the service on and click Next.

12. On the Confirm Installation Selections screen (Figure 2.11), review your selections and any messages displayed. Select the Restart The Destination Server Automatically If Required check box. After you review your choices, click Deploy.

13. If the server requires a restart, after you log on you will see a View Progress screen similar to Figure 2.12. After the configuration is complete, click Close.

Figure 2.10: RDS role services

Figure 2.11: RDS confirmation

Figure 2.12: RDS installation progress

Install Roles on a Windows Server 2012 Server Core Installation

As mentioned in Chapter 1, Server Core, as in Windows Server 2008, is a very streamlined version of Windows Server. Server Core has limited functionality and runs a subset of the roles provided by Windows Server 2012. It provides a nice addition to your network without the overhead of a traditional server. This lowers the overall maintenance and security risks for the server. During your installation and planning process, you might determine Server Core servers will be part of your installation. Server Core servers can become an integral part of your environment and provide services similarly to full server installations. For the most part, when you install a role on a Server Core installation, the role will function the same as if it were on the full server. Because Server Core does not have a GUI or Server Manager, you need to perform the installation from the command prompt.

Install Active Directory on Windows Server 2012 on Server Core

Installing Active Directory on a Server Core installation can be done either by hand or with an answer file. Either command will start by running DCPromo on the Server Core. If you choose to run the command by hand, you will need to enter all the parameters by hand as part of the dcpromo command. This method can be tricky, and you should consider using an answer file. Creating an answer file is fairly straightforward; all you need to do is create a .txt file with the parameters already entered in the file. To create an answer file, create a new text document and put [DCINSTALL] at the top of the file. Following that, you just need to configure the parameters for the domain join. Table 2.3 describes the parameters.

Table 2.3: Domain Controller Parameters

Parameter	Description and Values
UserName	Username with domain administrative credentials.
UserDomain	Domain of the user.
Password	Password for the user.
ReplicaDomainDNSName	FQDN of the domain to join or create.
Replica or NewDomain	Replica for an additional domain controller. NewDomain for a new domain.
DatabasePath	Location of the ntds.dit file; this is a local folder with "" if no value is set. dcrpomo defaults to %systemroot%\ntds.
LogPath	Location of the log files; this is a local folder with "" if no value is set. dcrpomo defaults to %systemroot%\ntds.
SYSVOLPath	Location of the SYSVOL tree; this is a local folder with "" if no value is set. dcpromo defaults to %systemroot%\SYSVOL.
InstallDNS	Determines whether to install DNS on the domain controller; takes a yes or no value.
ConfirmGC	Determines whether the domain controller will be a global catalog server; takes a yes or no value.
SafeModeAdminPassword	Password for account for Directory Services Restore mode; make sure the password meets the password requirements for your domain.

Parameter	Description and Values
RebootOnCompletion	Determines whether the server reboots and if you are prompted; takes Yes, No, or NoAndNoPromptEither.
ApplicationPartitionsTo Replicate	Specify if you want application partitions to replicate.

Sample Answer File

The answer file shown here would join Server Core to the w2012.com domain using the administrator account ID with the password of P@ssw0rd. This server would not have DNS installed or become a global catalog server. It would be assigned a recovery password of P@ssw0rd. All of the databases would be installed in the default directories, and the server would automatically reboot at the end of the installation.

```
[DCINSTALL]
UserName=administrator
UserDomain=w2012
Password=P@ssw0rd
ReplicaDomainDNSName=w2012.com
ReplicaOrNewDomain=Replica
InstallDNS=no
ConfirmGC=no
SafeModeAdminPassword=P@ssw0rd
RebootOnCompletion=Yes
```

After you create the answer file, you need to drop it on the Server Core and run the dcpromo command with the unattend switch and a path to the answer file. After you run the installation, the passwords will be removed from the answer file. For example, the following command would install the domain controller with the answer file named dcunattend.txt from the root of the C: drive:

```
DCPROMO.exe /unattend:c:\ dcunattend.txt
```

During the install, you may see a screen similar to Figure 2.13.

Figure 2.13: Running dcpromo on Core Server

Install Other Roles and Features on Windows Server 2012 Server Core

Installing Active Directory is a unique role installation for Windows Server 2012 Server Core. If you want to install other roles or features on Server Core, you can run the dism (Deployment Image Servicing and Management tool) command. Alternatively, you can use PowerShell. The dism command allows you to add and remove roles and features during your Server Core installation. As when installing features through Server Manager, if you use the dism command to install a role that has prerequisite features, you will be prompted to install those features as well. Using the dism command, you can also install multiple features at the same time. Although we will not list all the roles and features you can install on Server Core, here are a few commands that you should learn:

dism /online /get-features lists the state for the installed features—either enabled or disabled—for the current server installation. The command also provides you with a list of the features (with the appropriate names) that can be installed on your Server Core installation.

dism /online /enable-feature is the base command for installing any new role or feature on the Server Core. You will add the /feature-name switch followed by the name of the feature you want to install. For example, to install Hyper-V on the Server Core, your command would look like this:

```
dism /online /enable-feature /featurename:Microsoft-
Hyper-V
```

`dism /online/disable-feature` is the base command for uninstalling any new role or feature on the Server Core.

PowerShell uses similar commands to install features during a Windows Server Core installation. To find out which features are installed and which are available to install, you can run the following command:

```
Get-WindowsFeature
```

To install features from PowerShell, use the `Install-WindowsFeature` cmdlet. For example, the following command would install the Windows Data Deduplication feature.

```
Install-WindowsFeature FS-Data-Deduplication
```

3

Automating Administrative Tasks with Windows Server 2012

Getting Started

PART I

IN THIS CHAPTER, YOU WILL LEARN TO:

I n Windows Server 2012, learning how to automate everyday tasks can save you a tremendous amount of time and will allow you to spend more time with other administrative tasks. In this chapter, you will get an overview of Windows PowerShell v3. If you already are familiar with Windows PowerShell, your knowledge still applies in this version. If you are not familiar with Windows PowerShell, you will learn the basic underpinnings of this extremely powerful and useful tool.

Windows PowerShell is a command-line utility that is built into Windows Server 2012 and allows you to perform virtually all the tasks you can complete in the graphical user interface (GUI). Windows PowerShell 3.0 is unlike any other scripting tool you might have used with prior versions of Windows Server, including PowerShell 2.0 in Windows Server 2008 R2.

At the core of PowerShell is a very powerful engine providing several key areas for automation. PowerShell is a command-line shell for running basic commands, it's a scripting language for common commands, and it provides the administrative platform for several Microsoft Server–based applications. For example, the Microsoft Exchange 2007 administrative GUI was made entirely from PowerShell. Although in this chapter we will not show you how to build the Exchange interface, you will get an introduction to the PowerShell language.

Windows PowerShell does have a learning curve, but this chapter will get you up and running quickly with this powerful administrative tool.

Understand the Basics of Windows PowerShell v3

In this section, you will learn the basic terminology of Windows PowerShell. You will also take a look at enabling and installing Windows PowerShell v3 on your systems. In addition, you'll learn to start working properly with basic commands.

Understand Windows PowerShell v3 Terminology and Structure

As you begin to learn Windows PowerShell, it is important to start with the terminology and the basic command structure. Learning the basics allows you to learn the syntax, so you can then go on to write your own scripts and commands. The syntax is consistent across the PowerShell engine and allows you to apply what you learn in numerous situations. Microsoft has worked hard with the PowerShell language to allow you to type commands in common sense language (for the most part), which really allows you to focus on typing what you think. Additionally, in PowerShell 3.0 they worked hard to make sure that what you learned from using previous versions of PowerShell still apply.

It is also important to note that PowerShell provides you with another way to administer your common tasks; if you find yourself repeating common tasks, you most likely will be able to create your own PowerShell script to perform the tasks for you automatically.

The basic building blocks for PowerShell scripts are called *cmdlets* (pronounced "commandlets"). All of the cmdlets you create will be in the common pattern of a verb with a noun. For example, Get-Service, Start-Service, and Format-Table all follow this pattern of verb-noun. In general, when you look at cmdlets, you should be able to figure out the general purpose of what they do based on this naming structure.

You can use the verbs and nouns in many combinations. For the example, you can use Service noun, with the Start, Stop, Set, and Suspend verbs:

```
Start-Service

Stop-Service

Suspend-Service

Set-Service
```

This pattern is the key to learning the cmdlet structure. It also provides you with an easy way to find and remember the commands you use on a regular basis.

You can also add useful functionality to most cmdlets by specifying *parameters* as part of the command-line syntax. For example, if you run Get-Service, you will see the status of all the services running on the local server, as shown in Figure 3.1.

Figure 3.1: Listing services

If you then add the -Name parameter to the Get-Service command, you can filter the results to a specific command about which you are particularly interested. For instance, you can run the following command to find the status of the Task Scheduler service, as shown in Figure 3.2.

```
Get-Service -Name Schedule
```

In this command, you see the -Name parameter used to narrow the results of the Get verb.

Figure 3.2: Get-Service with -Name parameter

Additionally, with the use of parameters, PowerShell provides you with the ability to use shortcuts via aliases. For example, the following command is the same command as the `Get-Service -Name Schedule` command you saw earlier:

```
gsv -n Schedule
```

Aliases allow you to abbreviate verb and parameter names for your cmdlets. You can create your own custom aliases with the `New-Alias` cmdlet. To learn how to do this, run this cmdlet (you will see later in this chapter how to work with other help functions):

```
Get-Help New-Alias
```

However, it is important to note not all cmdlets and parameters have an alias by default. To list the aliases currently on your Windows Server 2012 server, you can run the following command:

```
Get-Alias
```

As you might have noticed, quite a few aliases are built into the system, and some of the aliases may look familiar to you from other command-line shell programs. You might also notice there are a few aliases that have the same cmdlet assigned to them. For example, the next three aliases all have the same cmdlet assigned to them: `Set-Location`.

```
cd
chdir
sl
```

So, for example, if you typed any of the following commands in PowerShell, you would notice that they would all change your current directory location to `c:\windows`:

```
cd c:\windows
chdir c:\windows
sl c:\windows
Set-Location c:\windows
```

The goal of these aliases is to help ease the transition into learning the PowerShell scripting language.

One last shortcut provided for parameters is that most parameters are positional in nature, meaning you do not always need to use the name of the parameter if you know the proper order for your cmdlet. Although this method can save you some typing, this may also create an ounce of confusion if you are not very familiar with the commands you are running. Building on the previous examples, the following

Getting Started

PART I

command will also show the status of the Task Scheduler; notice there is no '-n' in the command:

```
gsv schedule
```

Functions are another feature of PowerShell you need to understand. You can see a list of the currently loaded functions by running this command:

```
Get-Command -Type Function
```

Functions in some cases are variations of aliases and provide some of the same basics of running commands. However, functions are typically used to extend PowerShell or provide additional abilities to PowerShell. Functions will also provide additional information for your verbs. You will see some of the functions later in this chapter.

Enable Windows PowerShell v3

Now that you have seen some of the common terms and syntax of installing PowerShell, it is time to take a look at how to get PowerShell up and running on your Windows Server 2012 server. Windows Server 2012 installs PowerShell by default. Go to the Start screen and click the PowerShell icon. This makes the basic PowerShell cmdlets available to you; however, you might not see all the cmdlets you could find useful. Additional cmdlets on your server are available to you when you load the appropriate module(s).

In Windows Server 2008 R2, you had to use the import-module cmdlet. For example, when you installed the IIS role and the scripting tools for IIS, you got the IIS PowerShell cmdlets. To load the PowerShell modules for IIS, you would run this command:

```
Import-Module WebAdministration
```

When you use the import-module cmdlet, you have to load each module individually as you need them. Windows Server 2012 with PowerShell v3 offers a new feature that allows you to leverage the modules on your server; PowerShell v3 now offers autoloading modules when you use PowerShell cmdlets that are not currently loaded when features are added.

Understand Security in Windows PowerShell

When you first run scripts in PowerShell, you may see the error message in Figure 3.3.

Figure 3.3: Disabled execution of scripts

Even though PowerShell is installed on Windows Server 2012 by default, the server does not allow the execution of unsigned scripts. This error message is by design and, fortunately, easy to correct. The cause of the error is most likely the restricted Execution Policy that by default does not allow you to run scripts on your server. The policy is in place to protect your servers from running unauthorized scripts that aren't digitally signed. Digitally signed certificates are all about providing you with the assurance that you are running valid scripts.

Normally, when you run scripts locally, they are scripts you have created by hand and are generally scripts you trust. However, whenever you see this message after you have downloaded a script from the Internet or from a friend, you should always take the time to review it. Although it is common to allow locally unsigned scripts to run, you should never enable the remote execution of unsigned certificates. You want to ensure that you do not accidentally infect your own servers.

To enable your server to run local unsigned scripts while preventing remote scripts from running without review, you need to change the Execution Policy. After your first install of Windows Server 2012 and when you are initializing the Windows PowerShell modules, you will need to turn this policy off. To do this, follow these steps:

1. Set the Remote Execution Policy with this PowerShell command from the PowerShell interface:

   ```
   Set-ExecutionPolicy RemoteSigned
   ```

   When you run this command, you will see the warning message in Figure 3.4.

   Figure 3.4: Execution Policy warning message

2. That message informs you of the possible security risks by enabling this policy on your server. After you have reviewed the warning, press Y for yes.

3. To verify that the command executed properly, you can view the Remote Execution Policy of your server with this command:

   ```
   Get-ExecutionPolicy
   ```

   The command should return "RemoteSigned."

Learn to Help Yourself to PowerShell

After you have installed PowerShell, you need to learn some simple and basic commands that will prove invaluable for working with PowerShell. The commands in this section show you how to leverage the extremely powerful built-in help system.

Learn How to Help Yourself

You have probably heard the phrase "Give a man fish and he will eat for a day, but teach a man to fish and he will eat for a lifetime." To be successful with Windows PowerShell, you need to learn how to fish for yourself. Fortunately, PowerShell provides some very good tools to help you fish. There are two commands that you can use to find more information about commands and, more important, information about how to use them.

The following two cmdlets allow you to access PowerShell's built-in help system:

```
Get-Command
Get-Help
```

All Mixed Up: PowerShell Cmdlets and Case

When you begin to work with PowerShell cmdlets, you will notice a variety of ways in which cmdlets are written. Some are uppercase, some are lowercase, and some are all mixed up. For example, these three cmdlets provide the same results:

```
GET-COMMAND
get-command
Get-Command
```

The default standard for PowerShell is mixed case with each word being capitalized in the cmdlet—for example, Get-Command. Bottom line: Unless specifically noted for a particular cmdlet, PowerShell cmdlets *are not* case-sensitive, and you can use the case that is most convenient for you.

As mentioned earlier, when you run the Get-Command cmdlet, you will see a list of the currently loaded cmdlets and functions on your Windows Server 2012 server. However, you can also run Get-Command to learn about which particular commands will work against certain objects.

For example, you might want to use PowerShell to work with the services on Windows Server 2012, but you are not sure what cmdlets are available for doing this. To find out, use the following command:

```
Get-Command *-Service
```

You will see all the commands you can use on the services running on your Windows Server 2012 server, as shown in Figure 3.5.

Figure 3.5: Get-Command *-Service

So, now that you know what commands you can use against the Service object, you might be wondering what the proper syntax is for those commands. This is where the Get-Help cmdlet comes to save the day. By itself, the Get-Help cmdlet by default will give you a generic help listing on how to use Get-Help—in other words, it's help on help.

However, the true benefit of the Get-Help cmdlet is when you run it in context. You can get the context you need when you run cmdlets, such as the cmdlet from the earlier Service example. When you use the Get-Command and Get-Help cmdlets in conjunction, you can unlock virtually any information you need to learn PowerShell, as well as get the proper syntax and usage needed to work with PowerShell cmdlets.

Let's return to the previous example for Windows Server 2012 services. Let's say you want to learn how to properly stop a service. To find this out, run the following cmdlet:

```
Get-Help Stop-Service
```

This cmdlet will give you the general information about what the cmdlet will do, how to use it, and any possible parameters that can be used with the cmdlet. You might need more information on the command or even examples of the cmdlet in action. There's no need to go search the Internet just yet. The PowerShell help system can provide you with even more information with the four following switches you can apply to your cmdlets.

If you learn by viewing examples, run the following cmdlet to see a list of examples of the cmdlet in action:

```
Get-Help Stop-Service -Examples
```

If you want to see even more detailed information about the cmdlet you are considering, run this cmdlet:

```
Get-Help Stop-Service -Detailed
```

If you want to see more technical information about the cmdlet you are running, run the following cmdlet. This cmdlet also shows you all the additional parameters and how they are used with the cmdlet. The -Full switch really provides an exhaustive explanation of the cmdlet:

```
Get-Help Stop-Service -Full
```

If you want to see an online article that is equivalent to the -Full parameter, you can run the following cmdlet:

```
Get-Help Stop-Service -Online
```

The -Example, -Detailed,-Full, and -Online switches can be used with virtually all of the cmdlets inside PowerShell. This provides a consistent approach for learning to use PowerShell. However, depending on the command, sometimes the results for the detailed and example switches will be identical.

PowerShell provides various other ways to get even more information about how to run commands. For example, you could use the following cmdlet to learn more about the Service keyword:

Get-Help Service

Although the results for this cmdlet may look similar to the Get-Command *-Service cmdlet you saw earlier, this cmdlet actually provides other areas that you can investigate with the help system. Additionally, the help system allows you to query based on the topic that interests you. Several help files are built into the PowerShell interface. They are traditional-style help files you can quickly access. To get a full listing of the available topics, run this cmdlet:

Get-Help About

Exploring one of the about topics that interests you is just a matter of asking PowerShell. For example, if you want to learn more about parameters and how they are used in PowerShell, you can run this cmdlet:

Get-Help About_Parameters

That last cmdlet offers a great example of working with the help system inside PowerShell. Normally, when you start looking at the information contained in the About help files, several screens of information will be generated when you access the file. This requires you to scroll back up through the window to see all the information. Fortunately, the help system has an alternative to viewing multiple pages. If you want to have a break at each page so you can read the information before you move to the next page, you simply use the Help command instead of the Get-Help cmd.

Help About_Parameters

When you use the Help command, you may be required to press any key to move to the next page of information. For example, notice the difference in behavior between the Get-Help cmdlet and the Help cmdlet shown in Figure 3.6.

Figure 3.6: Scrolling pages with help

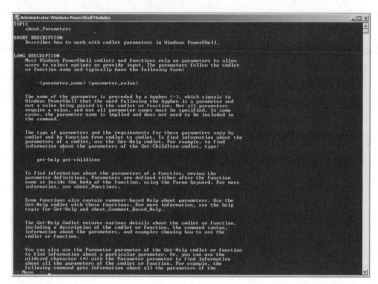

You can also get help with various levels of detail about the cmdlets and parameters that interest you. For example, if you run the following cmdlet, you will learn more about the ComputerName parameter used in the Get-Service cmdlet, as shown in Figure 3.7.

```
Get-Help Get-Service -Parameter ComputerName
```

Figure 3.7: Parameter help example

As you have seen, the help system is extremely useful and provides you with the information you need to begin working with PowerShell. The examples you saw around services can be virtually duplicated for any of the commands.

One last cmdlet you may use is the Get-Member cmdlet. This cmdlet lets you find out the properties of and any operations for a particular object. The properties can provide additional information about the object you are interested in, such as the status of the object, how long a process has been running, and the required services that need to be running.

To fully utilize the Get-Member cmdlet, you need to have a quick briefing on *variables* for PowerShell. Using variables allows you to take a PowerShell cmdlet, abbreviate it for other functions, and store information for later use in your scripts. For example, instead of typing **Get-Service -Name Bits**, you could create a variable to assign to this command, a bit of shortcut. (BITS is the Background Intelligent Transfer Service.) To assign the variable $bits to the command string Get-Service -Name Bits, type this command in PowerShell:

```
$bits = Get-Service -Name Bits
```

Then you can simply type **$bits** to run the assigned cmdlet. Variables also allow you to use the Get-Member cmdlet more effectively. To view all the currently loaded variables, you can run the Get-Variable cmdlet. For example, if you want to find all the properties and operations for a service using the previous variable, then all you need to type is this cmdlet:

```
Get-Member -i $bits
```

The -i represents the parameter input object used by the Get-Member cmdlet. Figure 3.8 shows an example of what Get-Member returns for results.

Figure 3.8: Get-Member

To see the required services for the BITS service, use the following cmdlet:

```
$bits.RequiredServices
```

It is important to note these variables are temporary to your currently running PowerShell session, meaning that when you close your PowerShell window, the variables will be cleared from memory.

You have seen how to generally work with services with PowerShell, which can prove to be very handy, especially when using remoting with PowerShell (discussed later in this chapter). Another useful way to use Get-Member is when you are looking for information about a particular process running on your Windows Server 2012 server. You can determine fairly easily how long a process has been running on your system and whether you need to terminate the process.

For example, you can create a variable to track a process. Start Paint by typing **MSPaint** in your PowerShell session. To create the variable, type the following:

```
$process = Get-Process -name mspaint
```

This will create a variable called $process to follow the mspaint.exe process. To see what other processes are running on the system, you can run the Get-Process cmdlet.

After you assign a variable to a process, you can see the start time of the process by running this command:

```
$process.StartTime
```

You then can use the environment variable to determine how long the process has been running using the Now system variable. The results of the following cmdlet will look similar to Figure 3.9:

```
[DateTime]::Now - $process.StartTime
```

Figure 3.9: Running time of a process

You then can stop the process using the variable again with the `Kill()` method used in this cmdlet:

```
$process.Kill()
```

Tab Completion: Discover the Power of the Tab

One of the last things you can utilize in PowerShell is tab completion. This feature of PowerShell will make sure you get the right names when you type in cmdlets. To use tab completion you simply need to hit the Tab key as you begin to type in your cmdlet.

For example, after you open PowerShell, type the `Get` verb, and press Tab, PowerShell will begin to cycle through all the different nouns you can use with the `Get` verb. If you press the Tab key again, you will see the next possible noun in alphabetical order. You can also type in partial spellings, or use wildcard characters for your commands. If you type **ge** or **ge*** and press Tab, you will cycle through the commands as well. Tab completion can save you time when typing cmdlets.

Take the Next Step

When you start working with PowerShell, you are going to want to control the output from the various cmdlets and commands you will run to make sure you get the information that most interests you most. In a sense, you want to control the objects and their data. You can do this fairly easily with several built-in PowerShell commands that allow you to work with multiple objects. Table 3.1 describes some of the common commands that will work with and manipulate multiple objects at the same time.

Table 3.1: Working with Objects

Command	Description
Compare	Compares two sets of objects. For example, you might want to compare the previous state of a service to the current state.
Group	Splits a set of objects into groups. For example, you might want to group the types of documents in a current file directory.
Measure	Measures some property on a set of objects. For example, you might want to count the number of files in a particular directory.

Table 3.1: Working with Objects *(continued)*

Command	Description
Select	Selects one or more properties from a set of objects. This allows you to control the type of data output. For example, you might want to see the name and ID of the currently running process.
Sort	Sorts a set of objects by one or more properties. There are several parameters you can use to control the sort, including the descending or ascending parameters.
Tee	Makes a copy of a set of objects. This command allows you to save the results of a command to a file or a variable.
Where	Filters a set of objects based on their properties and conditions. For example, you could use this command to discover the running services on your server.
ForEach	Provides a looping mechanism that allows you to act on every object meeting certain criteria. For example, you might want to stop a set of processes or services that meets a certain criterion.

You may also choose to export the information created from your cmdlets for documentation and reporting purposes. PowerShell provides several commands for outputting your information whether you are formatting the output on the screen or whether you want to create a file. PowerShell provides commands that allow you to convert objects into useful formats. Table 3.2 describes the common outputting commands.

Table 3.2: Output Formats

Command	Options	Description
Format	Custom List Table Wide	Converts objects into formatting records in a variety of choices. List formats the objects into a list for each property. Table formats the object in a table, with the selected properties taking a column in a table. Wide creates a table for an object with only one property displayed for each object. Custom allows you to use predefined views; you can find examples of predefined views in the *format .PS1XML files located in the Windows PowerShell directory.

Command	Options	Description
Out	File Printer String GridView	Sends the output of your commands into different formats. File and Printer are straightforward. The host will output the commands into the command line. String will send the output to the host system as a series of strings. GridView will send the output into an interactive table created in a separate window. Note that GridView requires the .NET Framework 3.51 and the Windows PowerShell Integrated Scripting Environment (ISE) to be installed.
Export/ Import	CliXML CSV	Converts objects into and out of common file formats. CSV is a comma-separated file, typically used for spreadsheet programs. CliXML will send the file into an XML file representation of the command.
ConvertTo	CSV HTML XML	Converts objects into other objects or formats; once again used to view data in a different manner.

To effectively use any of these commands, you will make a lot of use out of the built-in variable $_, which will always reference the current object being used in your cmdlet. You will also need to learn to use the | (pipe symbol). The | is used to combine one or more cmdlets into one line. The output of the first cmdlet is used as the input of the second cmdlet, and so forth.

Here are some useful examples of those commands to help you really work with PowerShell. You will see how many of the previous commands work very effectively when combined.

If you want to list all the services currently started on your server, you can use the Where-Object cmdlet to get the information, as shown in this example:

```
Get-Service | Where-Object { $_.Status -eq "Running" }
```

Alternatively, you could also see the stopped services by replacing the -eq parameter value with stopped. You could also use the and clause to see all the services as well as their dependent services.

```
Get-Service | Where { $_.Status -eq "Running"    -and
    $_.DependentServices.Count -gt 0}
```

Notice that the previous command does not list the actual services that are dependent on each other. This is where you can use the sort and `format` commands to display the information you want to find. As you can see in the following, those two commands were added to produce the desired results, and this would look like Figure 3.10.

```
Get-Service |
where { $_.Status -eq "Running"
-and $_.DependentServices.Count -gt 0 } |
sort Name |
format-table Name,DisplayName,DependentServices -auto
```

Figure 3.10: Dependent Services table

Another useful example using the sort and select properties can help determine why a particular server may not be performing well. You can quickly find the processes that are taking up the most CPU. The following command will list the top five processes taking up most of the CPU on the local machine:

```
Get-process | Sort-Object -Property CPU -Descending |
Select-Object -First 5
```

You can also execute commands on multiple objects at a time by using the `ForEach-Object` command, which will allow you to execute a script on every object. So, if you wanted to start all the services currently stopped that have dependent services, you would use `ForEach` to make this task easier to accomplish. You will notice for the previous commands there is a variable created called `$services`, which will allow you to effectively use the `ForEach` command.

The following command will create the variable:

```
$services = Get-Service |
Where { $_.Status -eq "Stopped" -and $_.DependentServices
.Count -gt 0 }
```

Then you can quickly start those listed services by running the following command. Now, this command will most likely fail on your

Windows Server 2012 servers because the proper roles and features might not be currently installed.

```
Get-Service |
ForEach { if ($_.Status -eq "Stopped" -and
$_.DependentServices.Count -gt 0)
{ $_.Start() } }
```

You can also list the individual objects in your command string that you want to perform actions on in the ForEach loop. For example, if the Calculator and Notepad are running on your server but you want to stop them, you can use the following command:

```
Get-Process -Name calc,notepad | ForEach-Object { $_.Kill() }
```

Another powerful tool you can use with processes is Out-Gridview. This will create a nice interactive table to use with the output of the commands. You can click the column headers to quickly sort, and this command even has a built-in filtering mechanism to filter the data you want to see. For example, if you run the following command, you will create an interactive table, as shown in Figure 3.11:

```
Get-Process | Out-Gridview -Title "Processes Local Server"
```

Figure 3.11: Out-Gridview

You can also use the Compare-Object to see previous states of objects through PowerShell. For example, what if you want to see whether a certain service had been recently stopped? Here you will see two variables used to make the comparison command work effectively. Remember, variables are created at a point in time, so they can be used quite effectively in the Compare commands. If you create a variable like the following:

```
$services = Get-Service
```

and then stop a service either in PowerShell or the Services Control Panel and then create another variable like the following:

```
$updatedServices = Get-Service
```

then it is simply a matter of comparing the two variables and using some properties to generate some basic data with the following command:

```
Compare $updatedServices $services -Property Name,Status
```

Figure 3.12 shows a sample of the results.

Figure 3.12: Compare in action

These are just some of the basics; now you will see how to take some of the objects and leverage the Export/Import commands. The Export/Import commands will allow to you to work with objects in different file formats. How you are going to use the files will determine whether you choose to use XML or CSV files. What makes using these commands effective is that regardless of what file format you choose, the command will largely remain the same for either file format.

If you want to save a list of all the services currently on your server to a CSV file, you can use this command:

```
Get-Service | Export-Csv services.csv
```

Figure 3.13 shows you what the exported file will look like.

Figure 3.13: PowerShell CSV file

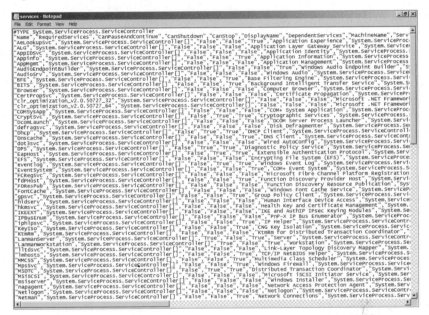

Alternatively, if you want to save the list to a CliXML file, you can change the CSV switch to CliXML and change the filename to reflect the different file format. You can also use the ConvertTo command to transform the output objects to HTML. The HTML format has the added benefit that you can format the HTML file inside your PowerShell commands. The following command will show some basic information about the Internet Explorer process.

```
Get-Process iexplore | ConvertTo-Html > processes.htm
```

Figure 3.14 shows what the file looks like.

Figure 3.14: HTML outputted

This is not very nice looking, but if you apply a little formatting to your HTML reports with the following command, you will get the results you see in Figure 3.15.

```
gps iexplore |
Select Name, id, handles |
ConvertTo-Html -Title "Iexplore"
-Body "<H1>Info about Internet Explorer</H1>" > processes.htm
```

Figure 3.15: HTML formatted

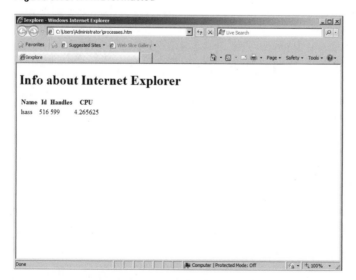

Use PowerShell Remoting

Windows Server 2012 PowerShell v3 improves remoting. The remoting infrastructure enables any PowerShell command or script to be run on remote servers.

Once the servers have Windows PowerShell v3 installed locally and remoting has been enabled, you can run PowerShell commands on remote servers. You can even write configuration scripts or a script that starts services—all from your local computer.

What makes remoting a powerful feature on Windows Server 2012 server is that you do not need any major network infrastructure configuration. Once you know the script or command you want to run, it is then just a matter of executing the script on any number of computers without any knowledge of the underlying network and how it functions. In the end, PowerShell takes care of all the details of the network connection. Remoting allows you to run any number of PowerShell commands on any number of computers simultaneously.

The remoting functions are all built on WMI remoting, and this allows you to both execute commands on and work interactively with remote PowerShell sessions.

Enable PowerShell Remoting

Before you can use PowerShell v3 remoting, you have to enable it on the Windows Server 2012 servers on which you want to run remote PowerShell sessions. In this brief section, you will now see how to enable remoting on your Windows Server 2012 server installations.

When you enable remoting on your server, it will do a few things for you:

- Start or restart the WinRM service, if it is currently running
- Set the WinRM service to start automatically
- Create a listener to accept requests on any IP address
- Enable the firewall exception for WS management traffic

To enable remoting, follow this procedure on either a Windows Server 2012 full server or Server Core installation:

1. Open your PowerShell window from the Tools menu in Server Manager.

2. Run the following cmdlet:

    ```
    Enable-PSRemoting
    ```

Getting Started

PART I

3. Press Y (or A) and press Enter to continue the process. If you press Y, you will be prompted before each change is made to the system and will need to approve each one individually. If you press A, your answer is "Yes to All"; you may see a screen similar to Figure 3.16.

Figure 3.16: Enabling remoting

4. After you review the changes being made to your server, press Y and then press Enter to continue.

Run Remote Commands

In this section, you will see how to use remoting to run your PowerShell commands. To do this, you will run the same commands that you would normally run locally. However, now you will use the Invoke-Command (ICM) to begin the process, followed by your PowerShell cmdlet, and ending with the ComputerName parameter. The ComputerName parameter can except host names, fully qualified domain names (FQDNs), and IP addresses.

Trusted Hosts Error

If you see the following error message (or the message pictured next), it could be for a few reasons:

Enter-PSSession: Connecting to remote server failed with the following error message: The WinRM client cannot process the request. If the authentication scheme is different from Kerberos, or if the client computer is not joined to a domain, then HTTPS transport must be used or the destination machine must be added to the TrustedHosts configuration setting. Use winrm.cmd *to configure TrustedHosts. You can get more information about that by running the following command:* winrm help config.

If you are using host names or FQDNs and you have a name resolution error, you will see this error. One way you can verify whether you are having an issue with name resolution is to insert the IP address of the system on which you want to run the remote commands. If the IP address works, you had a name resolution error.

Another reason for this error is the inability to configure your WinRM trusted hosts. To see the trusted hosts that are currently configured, you can run this command:

```
winrm Get winrm/config/client
```

To configure the trusted hosts, you can run the following command:

```
Set-Item WSMan:\localhost\Client\TrustedHosts
<computername> -force
```

Note that if you use the * wildcard, this will enable remote con-nection for all computers where you have security privileges.

Running commands is a matter of using the parameters covered ear-lier. For example, if you wanted to see all the running services on the remote server, your PowerShell command would look like the following, and your results would look like Figure 3.17 for a server named WIN-NGKN55U121R. Notice that the PSComputerName column is now listed.

```
icm {Get-Service | Where {$_.Status -eq "Running"}}
-ComputerName <computername>
```

Figure 3.17: Remote service listing

As you can see, the command is identical to a command you saw earlier in this chapter with three changes:

- The statement begins with icm.

- The command is wrapped in braces {}.

- The statement ends with the -ComputerName parameter.

Remote commands on servers with remoting enabled will more than likely follow this syntax. This allows you to quickly reuse your scripts and apply the knowledge you've gained by working with PowerShell locally to remote systems. For example, you can assign a variable to the previous command by using the following one. Here, the output variable (OV) is used to save the results into a variable called sv:

```
icm -Session $s {Get-Service | Where {$_.Status -eq
"Running"}} -OV sv
```

As you can see, you can work remote objects as you would any other objects. You can even get more information with the get-member command using the following:

```
$sv | Get-Member
```

Or you can continue to manipulate the objects with the following command:

```
$sv | Select * | Out-GridView
```

As you read this book, you will see many more examples leveraging the basic knowledge covered in this section to help build your PowerShell knowledge.

Understand PowerShell Integrated Scripting Environment (ISE)

One of the powerful tools in Windows Server 2012 is the PowerShell Integrated Scripting Environment (ISE). The PowerShell ISE provides some great components. Specifically, it is the component required for the Out-Gridview output format. This component provides a GUI front end for PowerShell and is a nice tool to use to create and validate your PowerShell scripts.

NOTE   PowerShell ISE is a GUI-based tool; it is not available on Server Core.

Work with the PowerShell ISE

The PowerShell ISE is enabled by default on a Windows Server 2012 GUI installation. Working with the PowerShell ISE is just a matter of loading it:

1. Go to the Server Manager.

2. Click Tools.

3. Click PowerShell ISE or PowerShell ISE (86), and you will see a screen similar to Figure 3.18.

Figure 3.18: PowerShell ISE

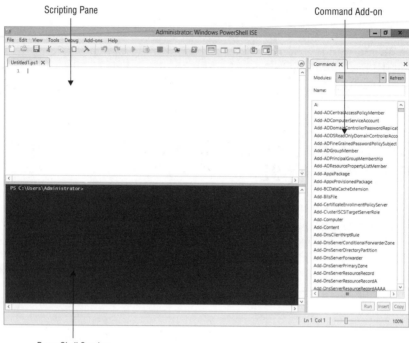

The PowerShell ISE is broken into three panes. In the top pane, you can create and edit scripts. The bottom pane is the PowerShell Scripting window where you can enter and execute commands, just as you would in a Command Prompt window. The third pane is the Command Add-on pane and is new to Windows Server 2012.

The true power of the PowerShell ISE tool is its ability to chain several of your PowerShell cmdlets together. All you need to do is type in your commands as you normally would, and then execute the script by pressing your F5 key. The Windows PowerShell ISE also gives you some minimal debugging tools to set breakpoints in your PowerShell script.

The Command Add-on pane is a new pane; it allows you to quickly find and create PowerShell cmdlets in a dialog box–style interface. The pane should be visible by default. If it is not, you can open the Command Add-on from the View menu in the PowerShell ISE. With the Command Add-on, you can filter commands by category and scroll through the list until you find the cmdlet you need. When you select cmdlet, you can then click Show Details and see all the parameters for that cmdlet. You can see an example in Figure 3.19.

Figure 3.19: Command Add-on

You can then fill in all the values for the parameters in the cmdlet. When you're done, you can click either Insert or Copy. If you click Insert, the completed cmdlet will be inserted in the command prompt area and you can then execute the cmdlet. If you click Copy, the cmdlet will be placed on the Clipboard; from there, you can paste it into the Script pane or some other PowerShell editing tool. This exposes all the parameters for cmdlets and helps ensure that PowerShell does all it can for you.

The PowerShell 3.0 ISE has two more powerful additions that make writing PowerShell scripts easier and faster. The first is IntelliSense, something developers and IT Pros wanted for years. This feature is very similar to the drop-down support in Visual Studio and assists you in writing properly formatted PowerShell commands. In Figure 3.20, you can see an example of IntelliSense in action. IntelliSense provides support for properties, methods, cmdlet names, function names, and even parameters—all via a drop-down list as you type in your cmdlets.

Figure 3.20: IntelliSense

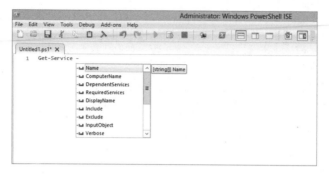

The second addition to the ISE is the Integrated Script Snippets feature (snippets for short). Snippets are stored in the Integrated Scripting Environment (ISE) and were designed to help you learn PowerShell as well as write proper scripts. When you access the snippets, you can select from a list of script templates, select the appropriate template, and have a partially completed script inserted into the Script pane. The snippets are easy to access from within the ISE; press Ctrl+J or select Start Snippets from the Edit menu. Figure 3.21 shows the Snippets list box with information about scripting.

Figure 3.21: Integrated Script Snippets

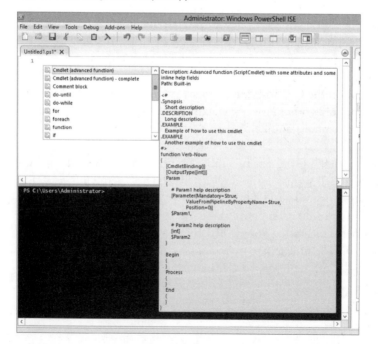

To view and learn more about a snippet, click a cmdlet name, and you will see a script along with a description. To insert the snippet, either double-click the cmdlet name or, with the cmdlet name selected, press Enter.

By default, the ISE ships with several script snippets to make it easier to create the commonly used programming syntax patterns. Here are the default built-in snippets:

- `Cmdlet` (advanced function)
- `Cmdlet` (advanced function) – complete
- `Comment block`
- `do-until`
- `do-while`
- `for`
- `foreach`
- `function`
- `if`
- `if-else`
- `switch`
- `try-catch-finally`
- `try-finally`
- `while`
- `Workflow` (advanced)
- `Worflow` (simple)
- `Worflow ForEachParallel`
- `Workflow InlineScript`
- `Workflow Parallel`
- `Workflow Sequence`

The built-in snippets are just one of three possible types of snippets available to you in the PowerShell 3.0 ISE. You can find snippets in modules, and you can even create them yourself (user-defined snippets). Some modules you may load in the future may have snippets in them that were created by the developers of the modules. You can import them with the Import-IseSnippet cmdlet.

PowerShell 3.0 now provides a comprehensive platform to help you manage server roles and automate management tasks where you can accomplish virtually anything now with PowerShell. There is no better time than now to learn PowerShell.

PART II

Manage Active Directory and Local Users

IN THIS PART ▶

4

Maintaining Users and Groups

Manage Active Directory and Local Users

PART II

I n this chapter, you'll take a look at working with your users and groups and maintaining them. You will also look at the local users and groups on a system, and a majority of the chapter will focus on the Active Directory (AD) users and groups.

AD users and groups really are the cornerstone of your infrastructure. Knowing how to properly maintain and leverage them is vital to a healthy network. Learning how to work with your users and groups not only offers agility to your network infrastructure but is also key to your enterprise-wide applications such as email.

Effectively managing your users and groups will help you perform your job easier and will ensure the integrity and security of your network infrastructure.

Understand Local Users and Groups

Even if you are leveraging Active Directory, you still need to understand how local users and groups work. Local users and groups provide a key role not only for maintenance but also for central administration.

In this section, you will see how to manage local users and groups on both Windows Server 2012 full server installations and Server Core installations. You will also learn about the default local users/groups, the default settings on these servers, and how those settings impact your infrastructure.

Learn Default Local Users and Groups

Whether you are working with a Windows Server 2012 full installation or with Server Core, managing local groups offers some great similarities. Starting with the default installations, both systems have the same default users and groups installed.

On your Windows Server 2012 server, by default two user accounts are created, Administrator and Guest.

- *Administrator* is the default built-in account for administering the local machine. The Administrator account is by default the only account that is enabled.

- *Guest* is the default built-in account for guest access to the system; however, the account is disabled by default.

Table 4.1 describes several other local and remote server groups installed by default that you need to know.

Table 4.1: Default Local Groups

Group	Definition and Usage
Access Control Assistance Operators	This group can check for authorization attributes and permission remotely for the local server.
Administrators	This group has unrestricted access to the local computer. This account is the main account to accomplish any task on a server. By default, the Administrator account is the only member of this group.
Backup Operators	This group, as the name suggests, is designed for the backup and restoration of files on the server.
Certificate Service DCOM Access	This group is allowed to connect to certificate authorities for enrollment in your preferred Public Key Infrastructure (PKI).
Cryptographic Operators	This group is allowed and authorized to perform cryptography operations on your server. These settings include the crypto settings in the IPsec Policy of the Windows Firewall, among other settings.
Distributed COM Users	This group can activate and launch DCOM objects on the server. DCOM objects are used for the communications of the applications.
Event Log Readers	This group can work with and read the local event logs on the server.
Guests	Users of this group, by default, have the same access as the Users group, except for the Guest account, which is further restricted. By default, the only account in this group is the disabled Guest account.
Hyper-V Administrators	This group has unrestricted access to all of the functionality of Hyper-V.
IIS_IUSRS	This is the default group account for use with Internet Information Services.
Network Configuration Operators	Users in this group have some administrative privileges over managing the configuration of networking features on the server.
Performance Log Users	This group allows its users to schedule the logging of performance counters, enable trace providers, and collect event traces for the local server. The tasks can be performed locally or remotely.
Performance Monitor Users	This group can access the local performance counter data either locally or through remote administration.

Manage Active Directory and Local Users

PART II

Table 4.1: Default Local Groups *(continued)*

Group	Definition and Usage
Power Users	This group has limited administrative capabilities on the system and is primarily included for backward compatibility with previous operating systems.
Print Operators	These users can work with and administer printers on the local server system.
RDS Endpoint Servers	This is a Remote Desktop Services (RDS) server group, and the servers in this group run virtual desktops and RemoteApp programs. The group is designed to contain servers that are running the RD Connection Broker, RD Session Host, and RD Virtualization Host.
RDS Management Servers	This is an RDS server group. Servers in this group perform the administrative functions for the RDS servers. This group is designed to contain all the servers in the RDS deployment. The RDS servers running the RDS Central Management service need to be in this group.
RDS Remote Access Servers	This is an RDS server group. Servers in this group allow RemoteApp and virtual desktops to access resources. If your RDS deployment is Internet-facing, these servers are deployed on the edge network. This group is designed to contain RD Gateway, RD Connection Broker, and RD Web Access servers.
Remote Desktop Users	Users in this group are given the right to log on remotely to the server.
Remote Management Users	Users in this group can access WMI resources over management protocols on the server.
Replicator	This group is designed for file replication.
Users	These users have limited access to the system to prevent members from inadvertently making changes that can cause system-wide changes; however, users in this group can run and access most applications.
WinRMRemoteWMIUsers_	Users in this group can access WMI resources over management protocols on the server. This group allows members to see file permissions remotely.

Placing user accounts in these local groups will grant those users access to the proper permissions and responsibilities for the groups. The basic concept behind using groups allows you to assign permissions just once to the group, thereby granting permissions to all the members in the group. This provides an easy way for you to delegate administration for your server. For example, if you want to have a user perform a daily backup of your server, you would simply need to add them to the Backup Operators group, and they would be granted the necessary rights to perform backup and restore operations. Later in this chapter, you will see the impact of joining the domain to these local groups.

Administer Local Users and Groups

Managing local user groups on your server is just a matter of loading the correct snap-in for the Microsoft Management Console (MMC). You can manage either a Windows Server 2012 full server installation or a Server Core installation. However, if you want to manage the local users and groups on your Server Core installation with the MMC, you will need to do that remotely. There are system commands that allow you to manage Server Core locally, and you will see those commands later in this section. To access the local user groups, you can go to the Control Panel to manage the accounts, or you may prefer a more thorough look at the users. You will see the Local Users and Group management tools in action for both a server with a GUI installation and a Server Core installation in the following steps.

1. Go to the Start screen, type **MMC** and select the MMC console. (Alternatively, you can press the Windows key+R key combination. In the Run dialog box, type **MMC** and press Enter.) This loads a blank MMC, as shown in Figure 4.1.

Figure 4.1: Blank MMC

2. To perform work in any blank MMC, you need to load the appropriate snap-in. To load snap-ins, select File ➤ Add/Remove Snap-In. This loads the Add or Remove Snap-Ins dialog box, as pictured in Figure 4.2.

Figure 4.2: Adding snap-ins

3. To manage local users and groups, select the Local Users and Groups snap-in and click the Add button. This will open the Choose Target Machine dialog box, as pictured in Figure 4.3.

Figure 4.3: Target machine

4. In the Choose Target Machine dialog box, you can either select the local computer to manage the users on the machine from which you're running the console or select the Another Computer radio button and enter either the IP address or the name of the computer you want to manage. This option allows you to manage the local users and groups on a remote server, such as Server Core, if you have the appropriate permissions. After you make your selection, click Finish to return to the Add or Remove Snap-Ins dialog box.

NOTE   The Local Groups snap-in referenced here cannot be used on a domain controller (DC).

---

5. In the Add or Remove Snap-Ins dialog box, click OK to load the snap-in into your MMC. Figure 4.4 shows a Local Users and Group MMC.

Figure 4.4: Managing local users and groups

6. After you have loaded the snap-ins into the MMC, you can save your customized MMC for future use. To do so, select File ➤ Save.

After you have loaded the MMC to manage local users and groups, you can easily work with your users and groups. Creating user IDs and groups, changing passwords, and changing other properties can all be done easily with the interface.

Create a Local User Account

When you create a local user account, you grant the account access to the local server, which is a straightforward process:

1. Inside the Local Users and Group MMC you created in the previous procedure, right-click the Users folder.

2. Select New User, which will display the New User dialog box, as shown in Figure 4.5.

Figure 4.5: New User dialog box

3. Enter the username, full name, and optional description, as well as the password. The password by default must follow the password complexity requirements listed in the "Default Password Requirements" sidebar. Additionally, you can mark the account disabled, if you know the account will not be in use for a period of time. You also have the following options regarding the setting of the initial password:

User Must Change Password At Next Log On   This is the default setting, and you should consider keeping this check box enabled when you create a new user account. The only time you should clear this check box is when the account you are creating will be a service account for an application. This setting allows the user to set their own personal password when they log on to the system the first time. All you need to do as the administrator is set an initial temporary password for the user. You may want to know the passwords for your users in case a user leaves the company or is on vacation. In reality, as long as you know the administrator password, you have the administrative right to reset a password temporarily and gain access into an account. Although it is good to have this ability, you should exercise it with caution and only when the situation warrants it.

User Cannot Change Password   By default this setting is grayed out and becomes available only when you clear the User Must Change Password At Next Log On setting, mentioned previously. This allows you to make sure the password for the account does not change. This is also good for service accounts for applications loaded on your server. This setting will also bypass any local machine Password Policy. Default password policies will be covered later in this chapter.

Password Never Expires   By default this setting is also grayed out, and like the previous setting, it becomes available only when the User Must Change Password At Next Log On setting is cleared. The setting, as the name implies, locks down the password. This setting bypasses any local machine Password Policy.

4. After you fill out the form, click Create to create the account. If your password does not meet the requirements for password complexity, you will see the screen in Figure 4.6.

Figure 4.6: Password complexity error

Manage Active Directory and Local Users

PART II

Default Password Requirements

The default password requirements are the same for both the local user accounts and the Active Directory user accounts you will see later in this chapter. The default password requirements for a Windows Server 2012 server are as follows:

- Cannot contain the user's account name or parts of the user's full name that exceed two consecutive characters

- Be at least six characters in length

- Contain characters from three of the following four categories:

  - English uppercase characters (A–Z)

  - English lowercase characters (a–z)

  - Base 10 digits (0–9)

  - Nonalphabetic characters (for example, !, $, #, and %)

5. If you have no more local user accounts to create, click Close. Otherwise, repeat steps 3 and 4 to continue creating local accounts on your server.

Create a Local Group

After you create user accounts, you will most likely want to create groups for those users. Groups, as you may know, are used to grant access permissions generally to files or printers located on the Windows Server 2012 server. These local groups can be granted rights and permissions to resources only on the local server.

1. Inside the Local Users and Group MMC you created earlier, right-click the Groups folder.

2. Select New Group to display the New Group dialog box, as shown in Figure 4.7.

Figure 4.7: New Group dialog box

3. Enter the name of the new group and a description. To immediately add members to the group, click the Add button at the
bottom of the screen. Clicking the Add button displays the Select
Users dialog box, as shown in Figure 4.8.

Figure 4.8: Select Users dialog box

4. To add users, type the usernames in the Enter The Object Names
To Select text box. To verify the spelling, click Check Names. The
Advanced button expands the dialog box to let you view a list of
all the user accounts on the system. The Find Now option on the
expanded dialog allows you to quickly list all the users on the
system. If you click Find Now, you will see a screen similar to
Figure 4.9.

Figure 4.9: Advanced selecting users

5. After you click Find Now, you will see a list of users on the system, as well as local system user and group accounts. Select the user or users you want in your group. To select multiple users, you can hold down the Ctrl key on your keyboard as you click. You could also select a list by using the Shift key. If you click the top item of your list, hold down the Shift key, and click the bottom item on your list, you will select all the items between and including your top and bottom selection.

Special Identity Groups

When you add users to your group, you may notice accounts and groups that you did not create. These are special identity groups, and you cannot control the membership of these groups. Users become members of these groups through the course of actions they perform on your servers or the way they access servers; membership in these groups is temporary and changes based on the way the user works with the system. System groups can be used to help set permissions based on how users access or interact with the server. Table 4.2 lists a few of the system groups you might encounter as you work with a server.

Groups that are not listed in the table are typically system groups that are reserved for the use by the operating system and the services running on a Windows Server 2012 server. In particular, you need to pay particular attention to one special identity account, the SYSTEM account. The SYSTEM account represents the Windows Server 2012 operating system. As you work with the files on your server and the user rights, you might encounter the SYSTEM account—leave this account unmodified. If you make a change to the permissions or rights the SYSTEM account has on a server, you could disable the server, which may result in you reinstalling the operating system or performing a system restore from backup.

Table 4.2: Special Identity Groups

Group	Description
Anonymous Logon	Users in this group did not use credentials of any kind to access the system.
Authenticated Users	Users are automatically placed in this group when they log on locally to the system. Leveraging this group is a great way to make sure only valid, authenticated users can gain access to resources.
Creator Owner	When a user creates an object, such as a file or folder on the server, they are put into the Creator Owner group for that object. Generally speaking, the Creator Owner user has full control over the created object.
Dialup	When a user connects to the server via a dial-up connection, such as a remote VPN connection, they are added to this group.
Everyone	Every user is a member of this group regardless of how they accessed the server.
Interactive	When a user has physical access to the server and physically logs on to the server, that user is placed in this group.
Network	When a user accesses the server remotely over a network connection, such as when they connect to a file share, that user is placed in this group.
Remote Interactive Logon	When a user accesses the server remotely with a local user ID and actively logs on to the system to perform remote tasks, such as when an administrator logs on to the server from a remote workstation, that user is placed in this group.

Table 4.2: Special Identity Groups *(continued)*

Group	Description
System	This is the account group ID used by the Windows Server 2012 operating system.
Terminal Server User	When users access the server using Remote Desktop Services, they are automatically placed in this group.

Manage Local Users and Groups

After you are done creating user groups, you will need to maintain and manage the local accounts. To begin managing local groups, just right-click the user or group you want to manage. They share some common tasks. When you right-click a user or group, you can delete, rename, open help, or view the unique properties for the object.

When you right-click a user, you can set a new password for that user. The only time you should set the password for an existing account is when the user has forgotten or lost their password. When you perform the reset, the user loses access to information such as encrypted files, stored Internet passwords (although the user can re-create these with the new password), email that was encrypted with the user's public key, and any stored certificates (again, new certificates can be issued to still grant access). Data in files that were encrypted by the encrypted file system (EFS) is also at risk. If you backed up the recovery keys, you will be able to retrieve the data; if you did not, no one will be able to access the data.

When you right-click a user account, you will be presented with the choice to set the password. If you select that option, you will receive the warning shown in Figure 4.10.

Figure 4.10: Setting password warning

After you click Proceed, you will be prompted to provide and confirm a new password for the user account. Once that process is complete, right-click a group and select the Properties option. (If you select Add, the process for adding members to a group that you used in the previous procedure when you created the group starts.) Now, you can modify a variety of properties for the user account, as shown in Figure 4.11.

Figure 4.11: User properties

The properties here are part documentation and part account configuration. The tabs allow you to configure a username, enter description information, and assign group membership. You can also set properties for Remote Desktop Services connection information, user profiles, home directory information, and dial-in access, as well as a variety of other properties you will see later in this chapter and throughout this book as the respective topics come up.

Manage Local Users and Groups on Server Core

If you did not install the minimal interface, you might not have access to a Microsoft Management Console, and you may need to make modifications to the local users and groups on a Windows Server 2012 Server

Core installation. You can add, delete, and modify all aspects of the local users and groups via the command prompt. Use the net command to work with users and groups directly on Server Core. (The net command also works on a Windows Server 2012 full server installation.)

The net command has many functions, including starting and stopping services and configuring the IP address on the server. This section explains how to use the net command to manage local users and groups.

All of the net commands begin with net; for users this will be followed by user, and for local groups it will be followed by localgroup. For example, to see the current list of local users or local groups, type one of the following straightforward commands and press Enter:

- Use net user to see a list of local users.

- Use net localgroup to see a list of local groups.

To add a user or local group to the system, the commands follow similar syntax. The commands will include the /add switch. For example, to add a user named Mitchell with a password of pass@word1 to the system, use the following command:

```
net user Mitchell pass@word1 /add
```

To add a local group called Writers to your server, use the following command:

```
net localgroup Writers /add
```

To add Mitchell to the Writers group, use the following command:

```
net localgroup Writers Mitchell /add
```

To see the current membership for the local group Writers, use the following command:

```
net localgroup Writers
```

The commands are straightforward and fairly intuitive. To learn more about commands for working with local users and groups, just use the built-in help system:

- Use net user /? to learn more about working with users.

- Use net localgroup /? to learn more about working with local groups.

Understand Local User Rights

You might be thinking that granting users permissions on a server is as easy as adding the user to the right group. Well, in part, you are correct; however, you need to understand what truly grants users the ability to work on a Windows Server 2012 server. Those abilities are called *rights* on a server. Local rights are assigned to individual users or groups. When you add a user to a group, that user automatically is granted the rights that are built into the group. For example, among the rights automatically granted to users in a Backup Operators group are the rights to Backup Files and Directories and to Restore Files and Directories.

View the Local User Rights

To see a list of the local rights on a server, you need to open the Local Security Policy MMC on the system. The Local Security Policy allows you to look at the local user rights and shows account policies, Windows Firewall, and other important security settings on your server. To view the Local Security Policy, you need to be an administrator for the server.

1. Open Server Manager.

2. From the Tools menu, select Local Security Policy, and you will see a screen similar to Figure 4.12.

Figure 4.12: Local Security Policy MMC

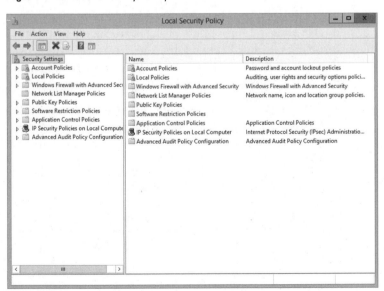

Manage Active Directory and Local Users

PART II

3. In the Local Security Policy MMC, expand Local Policies in the console tree.

4. Click User Rights Assignment to view the currently assigned rights on the system, as shown in Figure 4.13.

Figure 4.13: Local user rights

5. To see the currently assigned rights for the local users, simply double-click the appropriate object in the right pane. For example, if you double-click Backup Files And Directories, you will see that by default two local groups, Administrators and Backup Operators, have been granted that right.

WARNING   When you first look at the Local Security Policy, you will see that several user rights are already assigned to various local built-in groups and special identities. If you're not sure what the user right is designed to accomplish, you should avoid making any changes to the default assignments on your server. In general, it is OK to make additions to the assigned local rights but not deletions from the default policies. Making the wrong deletion could prevent your server from functioning properly and could cause you to have to reinstall the server or perform a system restore.

Even though you can make changes to the user rights, try to avoid doing so. If you need to grant users rights to perform actions on a server, check to see whether any of the built-in groups can accommodate your needs.

6. If you want to add users or local groups you created on the server to a user right, simply double-click the right to view its properties.

7. Click Add and use the wizard. It should be familiar; you used a similar wizard to add users to a group. The only difference is that during this wizard, you will see both users and groups.

Rights or Permissions

A common area that can cause confusion is the distinction between rights and permissions. Even though they are similar, in a Windows Server 2012 environment, they are used for different purposes. Understanding the difference will help you maintain your systems more efficiently. This concept of rights and permissions will follow you through all the work you do regarding secure access to Windows Server 2012 servers, even when you work with the Active Directory domain infrastructures.

Rights   One way you can think of rights, as discussed in the previous examples, is that they grant user abilities on the server. These abilities are special and usually give your user extra access to a server.

Permissions   These grant the user the ability to access Windows Server 2012 resources, such as printers, files, and shares. Permissions will determine the level of access to an object, such as a file, or whether a user or group can change the object or just read it. Permissions are assigned to the object. You will learn more about permissions in Chapter 7, "Configuring Folder Security, Access, and Replication."

Work with Local Account Policies

You will need to manage the local account policies on your servers. They are designed to protect the integrity of your users and the passwords they use. Local policies have the same impact whether you are using a stand-alone server or an Active Directory domain for logon access. They also help lock out the accounts if there are too many invalid attempts to access a given user account. Before you look at how to manage your server's account policies, you need to understand the importance of passwords and how the account policies can protect you.

A Word on Passwords

As you most likely know, there is nothing more important to the security of your environment than the passwords used by you and your users. Keeping passwords protected is critical to any environment. Always enforce password complexity and length to make sure your users' passwords are hard to guess and can't be hacked.

You may have heard this before:

> "Passwords are like bubble gum. They are strongest when fresh, should only be used by individuals and not a group, and if left lying around can create a sticky mess."

This is a fantastic way to think of passwords. What it means in a technical sense for you as an administrator is this: Make sure you expire passwords on a regular basis to force users to regularly change them. This goes hand-in-hand with monitoring password history and making sure that users cannot revert to old passwords. If you do not keep track of password history, when their passwords expire, users may change their password to a new password, and then change the password right back to their former password. Expiring passwords and tracking password histories will help keep passwords fresh and secure.

If you have shared workstations in your network and multiple users using a workstation, it is well worth your time to create individual accounts for each user. Not only will this help protect the security of your environment, but it will also provide you some flexibility when administering the users on the workstation.

Lastly, you may have seen or heard about users using sticky notes with the passwords written on them stuck to the monitor of their workstation. As you can imagine, this potentially opens your environment up to having user passwords stolen. It is worth your time to occasionally patrol the hallways of your business to make sure this is not happening.

While on patrol, you might also notice unlocked desktops, which is another avenue for attack. One way you can protect systems is by using group policies to set screensaver policies to lock the desktop after a predetermined amount of idle time. (You will learn more about group policies in Chapter 6, "Maintaining and Controlling the Centralized Desktop.") If you're feeling a bit more nefarious, you can provide your users with a teachable moment when you find an unlocked desktop— send the user an email from themselves. You would not need to send the message to anyone other than the user who left their desktop unlocked. It might look something like this:

From: Unlocked User

To: Unlocked User

Subject: Lock Your Desktop

Message: Just think, this message could have gone to your boss. A virus, malware, or spyware could have been loaded on your system. Files could have been stolen.
Please, lock your desktop whenever you step away from your workstation.

Sincerely,
Your friendly neighborhood administrator

Now, this is more than likely prohibited by your employer, and we do not recommend actually sending a message, but we do recommend that you think about the potential dangers of unlocked desktops in your organization.

A Look at Account Policies

You can find the local account policies in the Local Security Policy for your server. The account polices are broken into two areas. One is the Password Policy, as shown in Figure 4.14, and the other is the Account Lockout Policy, as shown in Figure 4.15.

Manage Active Directory and Local Users

PART II

Figure 4.14: Password Policy

Figure 4.15: Account Lockout Policy

Your Password Policy allows you to control password settings. Table 4.3 describes those settings and the default values. To change any of the settings on your server, you can use Group Policy or modify the settings by double-clicking them when you're viewing them in the Local Security Policy MMC.

Table 4.3: Password Policies

Policy	Description	Default Setting
Enforce Password History	This determines the number of unique new passwords associated with the users on the system and can be set to any number from 0 – 24. Depending on your setting, this requires your users to keep their passwords fresh.	0 for stand-alone servers 24 for domain controllers
Maximum Password Age	Determines how many days a password can remain unchanged on a system and can be set to any number from 1 – 999. If you set this policy to 0, then the passwords never expire.	42 days until passwords expire
Minimum Password Age	Determines how many days a password has to be used before the user can change it and can be set to 0 – 998. You should change this value on your stand-alone servers. If the value is set to 0, users can change the password immediately after a change.	0 days for stand-alone servers 1 day for domain controllers
Minimum Password Length	Determines the minimum number of characters for a valid password.	0 for stand-alone servers 7 for a domain controller
Password Must Meet Complexity Requirements	This determines whether the password has to meet complexity requirements. If the minimum password length is set to 0, the complexity requirement of six characters will supersede the minimum password length setting; otherwise, the minimum password length setting wins.	Enabled
Store Passwords Using Reversible Encryption	This determines whether the passwords will be stored using a reversible encryption algorithm. This is akin to storing your passwords in plaintext and should never be enabled unless you have an application or system that requires this to be enabled.	Disabled

Manage Active Directory and Local Users

PART II

Working with account lockout policies allows basic control over failed logon attempts to your server. When an account is locked out, it effectively becomes disabled and cannot be used until the account is unlocked by an administrator or a preset amount of time has passed. All of those settings can be changed from within Group Policy, or you can modify the settings by double-clicking them when you're viewing them in the Local Security Policy MMC. Table 4.4 describes the Account Lockout Policy settings and the default values.

Table 4.4: Account Lockout Policy

Policy	Description	Default Setting
Account Lockout Duration	Determines the amount of time the account will remain locked out before unlocking automatically. It can be set from 0 to 99,999 minutes. If the policy is set to 0, the account will remain locked out until an administrator explicitly unlocks the account. The setting has no pertinence until the Account Lockout Threshold Policy is set.	None
Account Lockout Threshold	Determines the number of failed logon attempts before the account is locked out and can be set to 0 – 999 attempts. If this policy is set to 0, the account will never be locked out. Failed attempts include errors detected during the main logon following a Ctrl+Alt+Del restart, a locked desktop logon, and logons from a password-protected screensaver.	0 invalid logon attempts
Reset Account Lockout Counter After	Each failed attempt to log on counts against the threshold counter. However, you can set a period of time so that the counter is reset when the specified period of time passes. The setting can be a period of time from 0–99,999 minutes. The setting has no pertinence until the Account Lockout Threshold Policy is set. If the Threshold Policy is set, this setting needs to be less than or equal to the Account Lockout Duration setting.	None

Understand Active Directory Users and Groups

When working with Active Directory users and groups, you should follow some of the same basic guidelines you have already seen in this chapter. However, Active Directory does add some layers of complexities because of the nature of how applications and other functions of the directory are handled. In this section, you will see some of the added complexity introduced for groups and by the extended properties users have by default in a domain environment.

Learn Active Directory Users and Groups Terminology

When you create users in AD, they are very similar to local users; however, AD users have extended properties, and the ability to log on to the domain from any workstation in your infrastructure.

AD groups, on the other hand, have some additional capabilities and complexity. Understanding how groups work is key to working with permissions, rights, and even applications in a domain environment. Before creating groups in an AD environment, you must understand the basic terms and concepts. Make sure you understand the differences in the group types and group scopes listed in Table 4.5 and Table 4.6.

Table 4.5: AD Group Scopes

Group	Definition and Usage
Domain local	Domain local groups can be assigned permissions only to resources in the domain in which the group was created. Members in these groups can be global groups, universal groups, other domain local groups from the same domain, and local user accounts. These groups are primarily used to control access to resources in the local domain.
Global	Global groups are used to control access to resources in the domain in which they are created. Using global groups is preferred over using other groups because they generate less replication traffic when you have groups with frequent changes. Members of this group can be only other groups and user accounts located in the same domain in which the global group was created. This group is also the default group type selection when a new group is created.

Manage Active Directory and Local Users

PART II

Table 4.5: AD Group Scopes *(continued)*

Group	Definition and Usage
Universal	Universal groups are groups that can travel across domain and forest boundaries, and they are used to assign members of the group access to resources outside their forest. Members of this group can be any accounts and groups from other domains or forests with the proper trusts (with the exception of domain local groups). You want to avoid making frequent changes to the membership of this group, because each change will cause replication of the entire membership to all the Global Catalog servers in the forest. You can avoid replication traffic by nesting global groups in this group. Nesting groups can be useful for managing resource permissions across multiple domains.

Table 4.6: AD Group

Group	Definition and Usage
Security	Security groups are used to assign permissions or user rights in order to quickly grant the members of the group access to resources or abilities in your network. These groups can also be used for email distribution, much like the distribution group mentioned next.
Distribution	Distribution groups are used only for your email applications, such as Exchange Server, Lotus Notes, or Outlook. These groups are not security enabled and cannot be assigned access to resources.

Organize Your Users and Groups

As you begin to create users, groups, and computer accounts in AD, you are going to want to organize the AD environment into logical containers. In AD, these logical containers are called *organizational units* (OUs). OUs are the way you can easily organize the various users, groups, computer accounts, and so on, in your AD infrastructure. You create OUs to provide a logical structure, and you can design them in a variety of ways. You can create an OU structure following the business functions of your business. For example, you could create OUs for marketing, sales, finance, and so on. This is probably the most common OU design structure. Another popular method is geographic; for example, you create OUs where businesses reside, such as North America, Asia, Europe, and so on. Additionally, you can nest OUs inside each other to logically represent your business. This logical design helps you organize your AD environment, delegate administration, and provide a key to working with your Group Policy design. You will learn more in Chapter 6.

Computer Accounts

Before you begin to learn how to work effectively with AD groups and users, you need to understand computer *accounts*. Computer accounts are the objects that represent the client computers and servers in your domain. If a server or client desktop does not have a computer account, the system cannot be managed by the domain, and users cannot log on to the domain from the system. Having computer accounts in your domain allows additional auditing capability and network authentication services. You manage, delete, reset, add, and do other administrative tasks for computers similar to users. As you work with domain users and groups, you will see computer accounts in your Active Directory structure.

Join an Active Directory Domain as a Member

Before your users can log on and work in your AD domain, you need to join them to your domain. Each server or client system in your domain requires a computer account in your domain. To join a domain, all you need to do is configure the system.

1. Open Server Manager.

2. Select Local Server from the left-hand navigation tree.

3. In the Local Server Properties pane, click the name of the workgroup, which by default is WORKGROUP.

4. In System Properties on the General tab, click Change.

5. Select the radio button for Domain, type in your domain name, and click OK.

6. Type in your administrative account ID and password.

7. In the Welcome To Domain box, click OK.

8. Click OK to acknowledge the reboot is required.

9. Click OK to exit System Properties, and click OK to reboot the system.

When the system reboots, you will be able to log on with your domain credentials.

Manage Active Directory and Local Users

PART II

Work with Active Directory and Local Groups

You might be confused about which groups to use and about the best way to work with groups and manage them. More importantly, you might be wondering about the best way to quickly grant access to user rights or permissions to the many objects in your infrastructure. You will want to know the interrelationship between your AD groups and the local groups on your servers that have resources.

The preferred process can be summed up in a one-word acronym, UGLY:

U is for users.

G is for global groups.

L is for local groups (where the resource resides).

Y is for your permissions on the local resources.

You might be thinking that this sums up the confusion, but learning this process will provide you with an efficient and effective way to quickly manage and control access to resources in your domain. When you access a resource in the same domain, this is how UGLY can be applied:

1. Place your users in the global group for the domain on which they both reside.

2. Place the global group in the local group on the system with the resource.

3. Grant the local group your desired permissions, and grant members access to the resource.

If the resource is in another domain, you will have one more step, and the acronym changes a little. UGLY becomes UGULY, but the basic premise is still the same:

1. Place your users in the global group for the domain in which they both reside.

2. Place the global group in the universal group in the same domain.

3. Place the universal group in the local group on the system with the resources.

4. Grant the local group your desired permissions, and grant members access to the resource. The reason you nest the global groups into the universal groups is to avoid replication traffic that can

occur when universal groups change. This way, you can modify the global groups, and only those groups are changed, which will allow the nested members to gain access to resources.

For example, if you want a user in your single domain to back up a client desktop or member server in the domain, after you create the user, you would create a global group, called something like Global Backup. You would place the user in Global Backup and place Global Backup into the local group Backup Operators. In this case, you are using the built-in Backup Operators group, which has already been assigned the necessary rights and permissions to perform the backup on the system.

Manage Users and Groups in Active Directory

To manage users and groups, you can use a number of tools built into Windows Server 2012. Two tools allow you to work with Active Directory users and groups:

- Active Directory Users And Computers
- Active Directory Administrator Center

You can find both tools under the Tools menu in Server Manager and in the Administrative Tools group on the Start screen, as shown in Figure 4.16.

Figure 4.16: Administrative Tools group

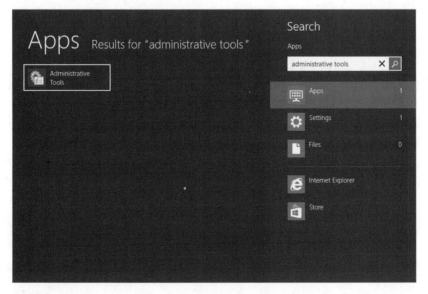

When you want to work with the AD Users and Groups, load either tool, and you will be able to see the AD Users and Groups. If you open AD Users and Computers, you will be taken directly to working with your AD objects. To load the Active Directory Users and Computers:

1. Open Server Manager.

2. Click Tools.

3. Click Active Directory Users And Computers.

4. Expand the domain name and click Users to begin managing your AD users and groups. Your screen should look like Figure 4.17.

Figure 4.17: AD user management

Once you have opened your chosen Administrative console, it is just a matter of creating the groups and other objects you need.

Create Organizational Units

Once you have loaded the console, you can start creating AD objects. OUs are one of the first objects you may create for organizational purposes. To create an OU, follow these steps:

1. Right-click the level of domain where you want to create the OU.

2. Select New.

3. Select Organizational Unit.

4. Type a name for your OU. You will also notice a default check mark for Protect Container From Accidental Deletion. This will prevent administrators from accidentally deleting the object.

Create Users

Creating users is similar to creating local users in a nondomain environment. To create a user, follow these steps:

1. Right-click the domain folder or organizational unit within the domain where you want to create the user.

2. Select New.

3. Select User. You will see a screen similar to Figure 4.18.

Figure 4.18: New AD user

4. Fill out the form, assign a logon name to the new user, and click Next.

5. Set the default password information for the user, and click Next.

6. Review the summary, and click Finish to create the user.

Just as with users on a local machine, after you create the user, you can right-click and view all the properties for the user. You will notice there are several more properties for the AD users. After you create a user, you can later move that user by simply dragging and dropping the user into the appropriate OU.

Create Groups

To create groups, follow these steps:

1. Right-click the folder for the domain where you want to create the group.

2. Select New.

3. Select Group, and you will see a screen similar to Figure 4.19.

Figure 4.19: New AD group

4. Fill out the form, and make the appropriate selections for the group type and scope.

5. Click OK to finish creating the group.

After you create the group, you can add members to the group by right-clicking the group, selecting Properties, and clicking the Members tab. You can then simply click Add. The Find Users dialog box that opens will function similarly to the one for local users. Also while in the Properties window, you can change the group's existing group type and scope.

Viewing Advanced Features

When you first view the default containers and properties of objects inside an AD, you will not see the whole picture. There will be several other AD objects, and a Security tab will become visible in the properties for the various AD objects. To see these additional objects and tabs, you just need to view the advanced features. To view the advanced features, when you're managing AD users and groups, go to the View menu and select Advanced Features. If you do not want to see the advanced features anymore, simply go back to the View menu and deselect the Advanced Features option.

Active Directory Administrator Center

The improved Active Directory Administrator Center (ADAC) tool in Windows Server 2012 makes your life easier when working with objects inside the AD. Using this tool, you can search, reset passwords, and perform other administrative tasks. You can also create users and groups. To load the tool, select Tools from Server Manager and then select Active Directory Administrator Center. Figure 4.20 shows the ADAC.

Figure 4.20: ADAC

Manage Active Directory and Local Users

PART II

The tool is intuitive; it's task-based and quite easy to run. The ADAC consists of customizable panels that represent the most common tasks you can perform. You can add and remove panels and customize the overview page to enable you to quickly get to the tasks you perform most often.

A good use for the ADAC is for searching an AD for various objects. Similar to saved queries in the AD Users And Computers, it is a quick way to find objects that interest you. In the Overview pane on the right side, you'll see Global Search. Type in your search parameter, and click the magnifying glass icon. Your results should look similar to Figure 4.21.

Figure 4.21: ADAC search

Fundamentally, to create new users and groups, you can follow the same guidelines mentioned in the previous sections. However, the ADAC provides a much more detailed interface that allows you to create users and groups more easily. To create a user, navigate to the folder or OU as you may have done in the past, right-click the folder, and select New User. You will see a new user form that allows you to populate all the needed properties for a user and much more. The interface highlights required fields with a red asterisk (*). Figure 4.22 shows the Create User screen.

Figure 4.22: New user in ADAC

Creating groups involves filling in a form-based interface similar to one for Create User. Figure 4.23 shows the Create Group interface.

Figure 4.23: New group in ADAC

When you view the properties of a user in ADAC, you will see a screen similar to Figure 4.24.

Figure 4.24: ADAC user properties

Whether you use the standard tools or the improved ADAC is up to you. Although they provide slightly different capabilities, both will take you to the same management place. With Windows Server 2012, you should get to know the ADAC, because it may provide a more intuitive interface to working with AD.

Automate User and Group Management

With PowerShell, you have a great tool to help you automate users and groups in your AD environment. In versions prior to Windows Server 2008, you could use PowerShell to manage objects, but it was cumbersome. In Windows Server 2012, you will find several improvements and additions for easy management with Windows PowerShell. Specifically, there are newly created PowerShell cmdlets and the AD Recycle Bin, which provides easier access to working with AD at a PowerShell level. You will see both of those in this section.

Load AD PowerShell Modules

Even though the PowerShell autoloads the Active Directory module to allow you to use cmdlets, there might be times when you need to load the cmdlets by hand. You can load the AD cmdlets in one of two ways:

1. From Server Manager, select Tools ➢ Active Directory Module For Windows PowerShell.

or

1. From a Windows PowerShell session, run this cmdlet:

```
Import-Module ActiveDirectory
```

2. Verify the module was loaded by running this:

```
Get-Module
```

If you want to see a list of all the commands available from managing AD objects and resources, you can run this command:

```
Get-Command *ad*
```

Work with Users and Groups in PowerShell

You can use the AD PowerShell cmdlets to manage your users, groups, and OUs, just as you can with the tools previously mentioned in this chapter. The reasons for using PowerShell are the same generally with any scripting tool. You might have a preference for using command-line and scripting tools. You might also find yourself repeating the same tasks over and over again; if so, PowerShell provides you with a consistent and repeatable approach to these tasks.

When working in AD PowerShell, you can also use directory-style commands to move around the AD structure. For example, you can run this command to get to the top of your AD structure:

```
cd AD:
```

When you run the command, the command prompt will change to the following:

```
PS AD:\>
```

The command prompt changes as you navigate through directories, and it always reflects your current location in the directory hierarchy. From the top of the directory structure, you can run dir to see the

Manage Active Directory and Local Users

PART II

objects at the root. To navigate to the actual domain, you will need to run a command similar to this:

```
cd "dc=yourdomainname,dc=com (or your FQDN ending)"
```

To change to an OU or container, after you have navigated to your domain structure, you can run this command:

```
cd cn=containername
```

If you want to switch to OU, the command is slightly different:

```
cd ou=Organizational Unit
```

Figure 4.25 shows an example of the previous commands and a dir command, which will show all the objects in the container.

Figure 4.25: Browsing the AD structure

Table 4.7 lists some of the common tasks for working with PowerShell with your users and groups. When you run the commands listed in the table, they run from the directory in which you are currently working. If you need more information, do not forget about the built-in help system. You can use get-help with any of the following commands to learn more.

Table 4.7: Common PowerShell AD Commands

cmdlet and example application	Description	Output
`Get-ADobject`	Lists multiple AD objects. As with users and groups, it works similarly to other `get` cmdlets.	This command lists all the objects in AD.
`Get-ADObject -Filter {name -like "*"}`	This command uses `filter`, `ldpafilter`, and `searchbase` to query the information. You can also combine this with the format and output switches of PowerShell to work with the command's output.	
`Get-ADuser`	Lists the AD users in the domain. This command uses `filter`, `ldpafilter`, and `searchbase` to query the information. You can also combine this with format and output switches to work with the command's output.	This command lists all the users at your current level of the AD hierarchy.
`Get-ADUser -Filter {name -like "*"}`		
`New-ADuser`	Creates a new user in your AD environment. You can also control most of the properties for this cmdlet. You will need to set a password and enable the account for use.	This command creates a user called John Smith in the Marketing OU in the `admin.com` domain, with display name and given name filled out.
`New-ADuser johnsmith -GivenName "Smith" -Surname "John" -Displayname "John Smith" -Path 'OU=Marketing,DC=admin,DC=com'`		

Table 4.7: Common PowerShell AD Commands *(continued)*

cmdlet and example application	Description	Output
Set-ADaccountpassword	Sets the password for an AD account. Depending on the nature of how you use this command, you may be presented with a series of prompts to set the password. When you run this command, you do not need to specify the OU or domain name if you are located in the OU that contains the user.	This command will reset the password of John Smith with a new password of p@ssw0rd: Set-adaccountpassword -identity johnsmith -reset -newpassword (ConvertTo-SecureString -AsPlainText "p@ssw0rd" -force).
Remove-ADuser Remove-aduser johnsmith	Removes a user from AD. When you run this command, you do not need to specify the OU or domain name if you are located in the OU that contains the user.	This command deletes John Smith.
New-ADgroup New-adgroup Accounting -groupscope global	Creates a new group. You can also modify the group type, scope, and other properties of the group.	This command creates a new global security group called Accounting.
Add-ADGroupMember Add-ADGroupMember -Member John Smith	Allows you to modify the membership of an AD group.	This command adds John Smith to the Marketing group in the admin.com domain.
New-ADOrganizationalunit New-ADOrganizationalUnit -Name "Finance" -Path "DC=admin,DC=com"	Creates a new AD organizational unit.	This command creates a new OU called Finance in the admin.com domain.

Use the AD Recycle Bin

At one time you may have deleted a user by accident. In previous versions of Windows, when an accidental deletion occurred, you had to implement AD disaster/recovery scenarios to recover the deleted object. This method, as you may know, was complex. Accidental deletions also became the number-one reason you may have implemented your AD disaster recovery scenarios. In Windows Server 2008 R2, the Recycle Bin was introduced as an additional part of your overall backup and recovery strategy; even though the Recycle Bin provides you with the ability to recover AD objects, you will still need to perform regular backups in your environment.

This is an optional tool that you can enable on your Windows Server 2012 domain controller. The Recycle Bin provides a tool for you to recover deleted users, groups, OUs, and so on. Upon recovery all attributes of the object are automatically restored, including the description, password, group membership, and managed by properties, as well as many of the other properties of the user objects, including the formerly problematic "linked attributes."

Enabling the Recycle Bin can increase the size of the Active Directory database file by about 5 to 10 percent when you install on a new DC. The amount of growth of the database really depends on the size and frequency of object deletions in your domain.

When you delete an object, that object will have a lifetime of 180 days by default before it is put into the normal tombstone and collection process in AD. You can modify the value manually by modifying the `msDS-deletedObjectLifetime` attribute. This applies only to newly deleted objects. Any object deleted before you enable the Recycle Bin will follow normal deletion properties.

Manage Active Directory and Local Users

PART II

WARNING The Recycle Bin requires your server to be in at least Windows Server 2008 R2 forest functional level or higher in Windows Server 2008 R2. This is required in order to ensure that all DCs preserve the attributes necessary to complete a successful object recovery.

Raising the functional level, in and of itself, really has no effect other than to allow optional features (such as the Recycle Bin) to be enabled. This allows you to raise the functional level with confidence.

Enable the AD Recycle Bin

To use the Recycle Bin, you need to enable the optional feature in your AD PowerShell:

1. Load AD PowerShell.

2. Type the following command, and press Enter to enable the Recycle Bin:

   ```
   Enable-ADOptionalFeature "Recycle Bin Feature"  -Scope
   ForestorConfigurationSet -Target 'your domain name'
   ```

3. Press Y to enable the feature.

4. Verify that the Recycle Bin has been enabled by running the following command and pressing Enter.

   ```
   Get-ADOptionalFeature -Filter *
   ```

Your screen will look similar to Figure 4.26.

Figure 4.26: Enabled Recycle Bin

Using the AD Recycle Bin

If you deleted a user and need to recover that user from the Recycle Bin, you can use PowerShell or, in Windows Server 2012, you can now use the ADAC.

If you want to recover the user using PowerShell, use the following steps:

1. Load AD PowerShell.

2. Type the following command to view the objects in the Recycle Bin:

```
Get-ADObject -SearchBase
 "CN=Deleted Objects,DC=your domain name,DC=Com"
-ldapFilter "(objectClass=*)"
-includeDeletedObjects | format-list
```

You could also use the out-gridview object to see a GUI of the deleted objects. Your results may look like Figure 4.27.

Figure 4.27: Recycle Bin

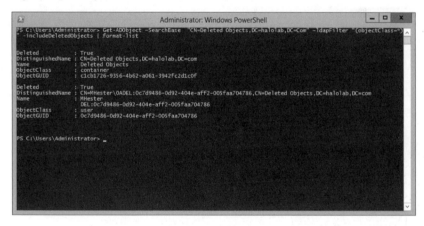

3. Write down or copy the ObjectGUID for the object you want to recover. This is the identity of the object you have deleted:

   - To copy text from a command prompt, right-click and then select Mark. Highlight the text to copy and then press Enter.

   - To paste, right-click and then click Paste where you want the ObjectGUID to be copied to.

4. Recover the object with the following command:

```
Restore-ADObject -Identity ObjectGUID from step 3
```

Manage Active Directory and Local Users

PART II

You can also use the ADAC to view and recover objects from the Recycle Bin. This is new functionality in Windows Server 2012, and it allows you to recover the users quickly through the GUI.

1. Load Server Manager.

2. Click Tools And Select Active Directory Administrative Center.

3. Expand your domain name, and you will see a screen similar to Figure 4.28.

Figure 4.28: Deleted objects in ADAC

4. Double-click Deleted Objects to see the contents of the Recycle Bin. Your screen will look similar to Figure 4.29.

Figure 4.29: Deleted Objects contents

5. Right-click the user you want to recover, and you will be presented with four choices:

Choose Restore to restore the object to the original location.

Choose Restore To to restore the object to an alternative location.

Choose Locate Parent to display the object's home location.

Choose Properties to display the GUID of the user; an example can be in seen in Figure 4.30.

6. Select Restore and the object will be restored to its original location.

The ADAC has one other addition in Windows Server 2012 that allows you to learn the PowerShell cmdlets. In the ADAC, you have the ability to view the PowerShell history of the cmdlets that were used as you worked inside the ADAC. At the bottom of the ADAC window, you click and expand the Windows PowerShell History to see what commands were executed. When you do so, you will see a screen similar to Figure 4.31.

Figure 4.30: Deleted user properties

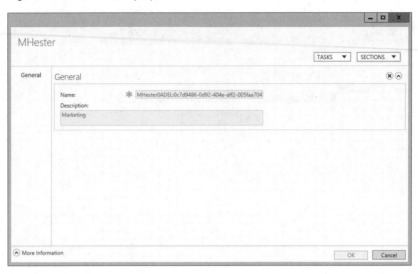

Figure 4.31: Windows PowerShell History

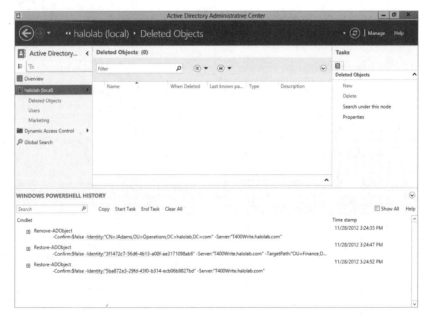

5

Managing and Replicating Active Directory

IN THIS CHAPTER, YOU WILL LEARN TO:

▷ **MANAGE THE ACTIVE DIRECTORY DATABASE (Pages 158 – 176)**

▷ **UNDERSTAND ACTIVE DIRECTORY
REPLICATION (Pages 177 –181)**

A n Active Directory database brings some tremendous benefits to a network of users and computers. Authentication, organization, permission controls, policy applications, resource management, and sharing are all key benefits. When you implement Active Directory, it is imperative to understand that it will indeed be "active." In other words, it will be exposed to changes on a regular basis. In addition, it is important that you understand the processes by which changes are made and shared with other domain controllers that have roles in maintaining the directory database. It is also essential that you take a proactive approach to managing and maintaining the directory database in order to prevent possible difficulties in database functionality or replication. This chapter will talk about key operations related to managing the directory database and replicating the database.

Manage the Active Directory Database

For all of its fanfare and cool functions, when you take off all the pretty interfaces and controls, Active Directory (AD) is at its core a database named NTDS.DIT. It has a defining schema, a set of partitions, and tables much like any other database. It shares the data contained within the database among a series of authoritative servers (that can write to the active directory database) and nonauthoritative servers (that cannot) called *domain controllers* (DCs) and *read-only DCs*, respectively. To maintain consistent performance, the directory database relies on the physical hardware on which it resides. If the hardware has significant limitations of speed, capacity, or other performance aspects, those limitations will be inherited by the directory database. In a like manner, if the physical hardware suffers failures, those failures will be perpetuated through the directory database. This section covers how to manage the directory database by managing the hardware on which the database resides.

So, how exactly should you do this? Here's how many successful clients have done it:

1. Install the operating system on a mirrored partition.

2. Install the NTDS.DIT database on a RAID 5 volume.

3. Install the log files associated with AD on a separate mirrored partition.

By distributing the processor and disk workload across multiple physical platforms, this straightforward implementation provides performance and fault tolerance to the operating system, directory database, and log files. It does take a fair number of disks to implement, but the resulting benefits in performance and fault tolerance are well worth it.

What about other installation options? Couldn't you install the OS, directory database, and log files on a single local drive? In short, yes, you could install them all on the same physical drive. Please don't do this, though. Doing so places too much of a workload on a single point of failure. When that drive fails (and it will), you will lose everything. Bite the bullet up front, and set up your directory for performance and fault tolerance. Once your directory database is happily running on its physical hardware, which you will be constantly monitoring to maintain its health and performance, then it's time to start considering some important topics.

Maintain FSMO Roles

Active Directory is stored in writable form on multiple DCs. This means more than one DC can have a writable copy of the AD database. Usually, having all these writable copies of the directory database is just fine. On rare occasions, it can be problematic—for example, when you create new domain objects, when you change the schema of the directory, or when you change a user's password.

To protect the AD database from potential overwrites, name duplications, object conflicts, time stamp differences, and infrastructure implementation conflicts, there are some key roles that exist only once per domain and once per forest. These roles are called Flexible Server Master Operations roles, or FSMO roles for short. These are the FSMO (pronounced "fizz-mo") roles:

Schema master   The schema master domain controller controls all updates and modifications to the schema. To update the schema of a forest, you must have access to the schema master. This role would be used in conjunction with the adprep or domainprep command. There can be only one schema master in the whole forest.

Domain naming master   The domain naming master domain controller controls the addition or removal of domains in the forest. There can be only one domain naming master in the whole forest.

Infrastructure master   The infrastructure master is responsible for updating references from objects in its domain to objects in other domains. It is also used in conjunction with `adprep` or `domainprep` and to update SID attributes and distinguished name attributes for objects that are referenced across domains. At any one time, there can be only one domain controller acting as the infrastructure master in each domain.

Relative ID (RID) master   The RID master is responsible for processing RID pool requests from all domain controllers in a particular domain. These RID pools are used to create new user accounts, computer accounts, or groups. At any one time, there can be only one domain controller acting as the RID master in the domain.

PDC emulator   The PDC emulator is a domain controller that advertises itself as the primary domain controller (PDC) to workstations, member servers, and domain controllers that are running earlier versions of Windows. It is also the domain master browser, and it handles password discrepancies and updates to user and computer account passwords. At any one time, there can be only one domain controller acting as the PDC emulator master in each domain.

TIP   See `http://technet.microsoft.com/en-us/library/cc754889(v=WS.10).aspx` for additional details on planning the placement of the FSMO roles.

The real questions begin when you start to consider that the initial DC that is built in each forest (referred to as the *forest root server*) will by default hold all five FSMO roles. Should they stay there when you add DCs? If not, how do you move them? What if, heaven forbid, the server that holds your FSMO roles crashes and burns? What do you do then?

On the day it is installed, the forest root server does in fact hold all five FSMO roles; while you are setting up your other DCs, that forest root server will likely do just fine holding all five roles. Roles come in two types: forest-wide roles, one per forest, and domain-wide roles, one per domain. Each forest will have a single schema master and domain naming master, regardless of the number of domains you create. These roles are just fine to stay on your forest root server. Each domain will have its own PDC emulator, RID master, and infrastructure master. As you create new domains in your directory database and add new domain controllers to manage those domain directory resources, the first DC created in each domain will take on the domain-based roles for that individual domain. This all proceeds quite nicely in an organized fashion as you build the infrastructure of your directory. Assuming that you are allocating sufficient server resources for each DC, you will not have any problems with FSMO roles.

It is possible to relocate the FSMO roles to another domain controller for reasons of personal preference, to handle the event of a failure by a current role holder, to avoid service interruption, or to balance server workloads. The circumstances surrounding the transfer of roles will determine the process of the role change. If all the DCs are still online and you are making a role change in a nice controlled environment, that's called a *role transfer*. If the server that holds the role is offline for any reason (for example, if it has failed), you will take the role from it in a process called *seizing* the role.

Although the absence of a FSMO role holder can have serious consequences, it is much more likely that the failure of a FSMO role holder can be tolerated in most situations for at least a limited amount of time, allowing you to "fix" whatever caused the DC to fail.

Transfer FSMO Roles

Ideally, you will be performing a nice planned transfer of roles from one operating DC to another. In this case, you have a couple of options:

- Use the graphical user interface (GUI) tools to view role ownership and initiate transfers. The graphical tools can be used only if the server that is the original role holder is still online. If the original role holder is not currently online, then the transfer of roles (seizure) can be performed using the command-line utilities only.

- Use the command-line utility called NTDSUTIL to script the transfer or seizure of roles.

The Active Directory Users And Computers tool is one of the GUI tools that can be used for viewing and transferring FSMO roles to work with the RID master, PDC emulator, and infrastructure master.

1. Open the Active Directory Users And Computers tool from the Tools menu in Server Manager.

2. Right-click Active Directory Users And Computers.

3. Choose All Tasks.

4. Choose Operations Masters.

You can click Change to change the role to another server, as illustrated in Figure 5.1.

Figure 5.1: The Active Directory Users And Computers tool shows the three domain-based FSMO roles.

You must be connected to the server to which you want to change. To change the domain naming master, use the Active Directory Domains And Trusts GUI tool to view the forest-wide tools.

1. From the AD Users and Computers snap-in, open the Active Directory Domains And Trusts tool.

2. Right-click Active Directory Domains And Trusts.

3. Choose Operations Master.

Figure 5.2 illustrates how you can view the role holder and change it to another computer.

Figure 5.2: The Active Directory Domains And Trust tool shows the domain naming master FSMO role holder.

The GUI tool for viewing the schema master role is a little trickier to use. By default, there is no built-in or enabled GUI tool that you can use to work with the schema master role. You need to both enable and add the Active Directory Schema snap-in to the Microsoft Management Console (MMC) in order to have GUI access to the schema master role. This tool is not enabled by default. To enable the Active Directory Schema snap-in, follow these steps:

1. Open Windows PowerShell and Type `CMD`.

2. Type `regsvr32 schmmgmt.dll`, and press Enter.

3. When the message appears confirming that DLLRegisterServer in `schmmgmt.dll` succeeded, click OK.

You are not done yet. Now that you have enabled the tool, you need to add it to the MMC in order to actually use it. To add the Active Directory Schema snap-in to the Microsoft Management Console, follow these steps:

1. Open Windows PowerShell.

2. Type `MMC`.

3. Select File ➤ Add/Remove Snap-In.

4. Select Active Directory Schema.

5. Click Add and then click OK to work with the snap-in.

6. Right-click Active Directory Schema, and select Operations Master.

Figure 5.3 shows how to view the schema master and change the server that hosts this role.

Figure 5.3: The Active Directory Schema snap-in shows the schema master FSMO role holder.

It is not always possible to use the GUI tools to work with FSMO role changes. What if the server from which you want to transfer a role is offline? Connecting to an offline server is not possible. You will have to take more drastic action. As is often the case when working with Windows Server 2012, you can access significantly more options by using the command-line tool NTDSUTIL. This utility allows you to transfer FSMO roles, and it can be used to seize these roles without the expressed permission of the original role holder.

NOTE   Once you have seized a role from the original role holder, you will need to make certain the original role holder is not brought back online in that network. Seizure does not remove the role from the original role holder. If the original role holder is brought back online, there will be a conflict between the two DCs.

Seize FSMO Roles with *NTDSUTIL*

Seizing FSMO roles is really a last resort and should be done only if you are certain your original role holder will never come back online. Once the role is seized, there is no going back. To seize roles using NTDSUTIL, you can follow these steps:

1. Open Windows PowerShell.

2. Type **ntdsutil**.

3. Type **roles**, and then press Enter.

4. Type **connections**, and then press Enter.

5. Type **connect to server** *servername*, where *servername* is the name of the domain controller to which you want to assign the FSMO role, and then press Enter.

6. At the server connections prompt, type **q** and then press Enter.

7. Type **seize** *role*, where *role* is the role that you want to seize. For a list of roles you can seize, type **?** at the fsmo maintenance prompt and then press Enter. For example, to seize the RID master role, type **seize rid master**. The one exception is for the PDC emulator role, whose syntax is seize pdc, not seize pdc emulator.

8. At the fsmo maintenance prompt, type **q** and then press Enter to access the ntdsutil prompt.

9. Type **q**, and then press Enter to quit the NTDSUTIL utility.

TIP   For more information on NTDSUTIL and FSMO roles, please review the article at http://support.microsoft.com/kb/255504.

Defragment the Directory Database

A directory database becomes fragmented as you add, change, and delete objects from your database. Like any file system–based storage, as the directory database is changed and updated, fragments of disk space will build up so it needs to be defragmented on a routine basis to maintain optimal operation. By default, Active Directory performs an online defragmentation of the directory database every 12 hours with the garbage collection process, an automated directory database cleanup. IT pros should be familiar with it. However, online defragmentation does not decrease the size of the NTDS.DIT database file. Instead, it shuffles the data around for easier access. Depending on how fragmented your database actually is, running an offline defragmentation process—which does decrease the size of the database—could significantly affect the overall size of your NTDS.DIT database file.

There is a little problem associated with defragmenting databases. They have to be taken offline in order to have the fragments removed and the database resized. Windows Server 2012 has a great feature that allows you to take the database offline without shutting down the server. It's called Restartable Active Directory, and it could not be much easier to stop and start your directory database than by using this feature. Figure 5.4 shows the Services tool and how you can use it to stop the Active Directory service.

Figure 5.4: You can use the Services tool to stop and restart Active Directory.

1. Start the Services tool from the Tools menu in Server Manager.

2. Right-click Active Directory Domain Services, and select Stop.

That's it! Now, when you stop Active Directory Domain Services, any other dependent services will also be stopped. Keep in mind that while the services are stopped, they cannot fulfill their assigned role in your network. The really cool thing about Restartable AD is that while the directory services and its dependent services are stopped, other services on the local machine are not. So, perhaps you have a shared printer running on your DC. Print services still run, and print operations do not stop. Nice!

Offline Directory Defragmentation

Now that you have stopped Active Directory services, it is time to get down to the business of offline defragmentation of the directory database:

1. Back up the database. This will be covered in more detail in Chapter 8, "Backing Up and Recovering Your Server."

2. Open Windows PowerShell, and type **NTDSUTIL**.

3. Type **ACTIVATE INSTANCE NTDS**.

4. Type **FILES**, and press Enter.

5. Type **INFO**, and press Enter. This will tell you the current location of the directory database, its size, and the size of the associated log files. Take a screen shot or write down all the information.

6. Make a folder location with enough drive space for the directory to be stored there.

7. Type **COMPACT TO DRIVE:\DIRECTORY**, and press Enter. The drive and directory are the locations you set up in step 5. If the drive path contains spaces, put the whole path in quotation marks, as in "C:\database defrag."

A new defragmented and compacted NTDS.DIT will be created in the folder you specified. If you are prompted to copy the database back to C:\Windows\NTDS\ntds.dit, do not do so at this time. Copying the database back to the original location will remove the old copy and replace it with the new one.

8. Type **QUIT**, and press Enter.

9. Type **QUIT** again, and press Enter to return to the command prompt.

10. If defragmentation succeeded without errors, follow the NTDSUTIL prompts.

11. Delete all log files by typing **DEL** *x*:**\pathtologfiles*.log** where *x* is the drive letter of the drive where the logs are stored.

12. Overwrite the old NTDS.DIT file with the new one. Remember, you captured its location in step 5. (The NTDS.DIT file location is also displayed after the defrag operation completes, so you can copy/ paste directly from the Defrag tool screen output and then press Enter).

13. Close the command prompt.

14. Open the Services tool, and start Active Directory Domain Services.

Depending on how long it has been since your last offline defrag, defragmenting your directory database using the offline NTDSUTIL process can significantly reduce the size of your database. The hard thing about offline defrag is that every network is different, so providing recommendations about how often to use the offline defrag process is somewhat spurious. Get to know your directory database. Monitor its size and growth. When you think it is appropriate to defragment offline, do it. A pattern will emerge for you, and you will find yourself using offline defragmentation on a frequency that works well for your network and your directory database. One of the cool things about offline defragmentation is that if an error happens to occur during the defragmentation process, you still have your original NTDS.DIT database in place and can continue using it with no problems until you can isolate and fix any issues.

Audit Active Directory Service

Windows Server 2012 not only allows you to audit changes to Active Directory but also allows you to see the actual values entered into the directory before the change was made and after the change is made. In Windows 2000 Server and Windows Server 2003, it was possible to audit directory service access to see whether a change had been made, but this auditing allowed you to see the results of the change only, not the "before and after" settings.

In Windows Server 2012, the Audit Directory Service Access setting policy is divided into four subcategories:

- Directory Service Access

- Directory Service Changes

- Directory Service Replication

- Detailed Directory Service Replication

When you want to see changes, implement the Directory Service Changes Policy. This policy will allow you to see the changes made by any security principal, including create, delete, modify, move, or undelete operations. This policy will record not only the new values but also the original values in the event of a modify or undelete operation. In the event of a move operation, the original location of the object will also be logged.

You can enable auditing in Windows Server 2012 through the use of three mechanisms. First, you can choose to enable a global audit policy for all the directory service subcategories mentioned previously. This setting is in the default domain controller policy on the Domain Controllers OU and is *not* enabled by default on Windows Server 2012 DC. Therefore, if you want to audit directory service changes, you will need to implement this setting.

Second, you can also enable auditing through the use of system access control lists (SACLs). The SACL of an object determines whether access to an object will or will not be audited. It determines which operations are to be audited and for whom. SACLs are controlled by those security administrators who have rights to the local system. The Administrators group holds this right by default. So, it is technically possible to edit the access control entry (ACE) of an object and remove the auditing requirement of the object even though Directory Services Changes has been enabled.

Finally, there is also a set of schema controls that you can use to create exceptions using search flag properties for what is being audited.

Enable Group Policy Auditing in Group Policy Management Console

To enable directory services auditing, you need to use Group Policy. Use the Group Policy Management Console (GPMC) to make the suggested changes.

1. Open Windows PowerShell and type **GPMC**.

2. In the console tree, double-click the name of the forest, expand Domains, expand the name of your domain, select Domain Controllers, right-click Default Domain Controllers Policy, and then click Edit.

3. Under Computer Configuration, expand Policies, expand Windows Settings, expand Security Settings, expand Local Policies, and then click Audit Policy (see Figure 5.5).

4. In the Details pane, right-click Audit Directory Service Access, and then click Properties.

5. Select the Define These Policy Settings check box.

6. Under Audit These Attempts, select the Success check box, and then click OK.

Figure 5.5: Auditing enabled in Group Policy Management Console

Enable Auditing Using the Command Line

Although you will most likely enable auditing using the Group Policy Management Console, as PowerShell becomes more and more prominent with scripted solutions for day-to-day tasks, you may prefer to use the command line. Here are the steps:

1. Open Windows PowerShell, and type **cmd**.

2. Type the following command, and then press Enter:

   ```
   auditpol /set /subcategory:"directory service changes"
   /success:enable
   ```

Configure Auditing in the Object SACLs

SACLs hold the real power in auditing. They define the permissions and functions for auditing on any given object or file location. It is possible to configure auditing of Active Directory on the SACL:

1. Open Active Directory Users And Computers from the Tools menu in Server Manager.

2. Right-click the organizational unit (or any object for which you want to enable auditing) and then click Properties.

3. Click the Security tab, click Advanced, and then click the Auditing tab. (If you do not see the Security tab, you may need to enable Advanced Features from the View menu.)

4. Click Add, and under Enter The Object Name To Select, type **Authenticated Users** (or any other security principal). Click Check Names to verify object and then click OK.

5. In Apply Onto, click Descendant User Objects (or any other objects).

6. Under Permissions, select the Successful check box for Write All properties.

7. Click OK.

Directory Service Changes auditing can add a powerful tool to your toolbox of management features in Windows Server 2012.

Use Fine-Grained Password Policy

Password policies provide you with a way to set strict enforcement of the length, age, and complexity of the passwords used in your network. In the Windows 2000 Server through Windows Server 2008 R2 versions of Active Directory, there was a single password policy that could be set, and it was created by default as part of the Default Domain Policy. If you had an environment where you wanted to implement another password policy, for whatever reason, you were stuck creating a new domain to get a new Default Domain Policy object wherein you could create your new password policy. It seems a little silly to create a new domain simply to get an additional password policy object, but that is how it was done. Windows Server 2012 will let you create more than one password settings object (PSO) per Active Directory domain. This means it is now possible to create multiple password policies and their corresponding lockout restrictions in a single-domain environment. This ability to create multiple password policies that have differing levels of impact on different users and groups has been termed *fine-grained password policies.*

To use these policies, Windows Server 2012 relies on two object classes in the Active Directory schema called Password Settings Container and Password Settings. The Password Settings Container object class is created by default in the System container in the domain. It is responsible for storing the PSOs for the domain. The Password Settings object class contains the list of attributes that must be contained for the PSO to be considered valid.

When you build a fine-grained password policy for your domain, there are some things to consider. First, although your domain is probably organized into organizational units, PSOs will need to be applied to security groups. This will mean that moving a user from one OU to another will require updating group memberships to meet password policy requirements. Why not just apply the PSO to the OU? There are several reasons:

- Groups are a lot more flexible for managing users than OUs are.

- You have already used a systematic set of groups in your Active Directory deployment in Domain Admins, Enterprise Admins, Schema Admins, Backup Operators, Account Operators, and so on. It works!

- Using groups makes deploying fine-grained password policies so much easier because you don't have to restructure OUs to match your password policy structure, which can really be a pain, not to mention that it can have negative side effects on the Group Policy inheritance you have worked so hard to get right.

Before you create your first PSO, there are some important rules to know:

- By default, only members of the Domain Admins group can create PSOs. They are the only ones who have write permissions to the PSO once it is created and, therefore, are the only ones who can tie the PSO to an object.

- PSOs apply only to user objects and global security groups. They *cannot* be applied to computer objects.

- You can delegate Read permissions to the default security descriptor of the PSO to any other group in the domain or forest. (For example, you might want to delegate Read permissions to your help-desk group.)

Create PSOs

Now that you are ready to build your own PSO, you actually have two tools that can be used to build it. You can build PSOs with the Active Directory Service Interfaces Editor (ADSI Edit) or LDAP Data Interchange Format Directory Exchange (LDIFDE.) Realistically, ADSI Edit is sufficient for the majority of cases in which you will create PSOs. For the purposes of this example, you'll use ADSI Edit:

1. Open ADSI Edit from the Tools menu in Server Manager.

2. If this is the first time you have run ADSI Edit on this machine, then in the ADSI Edit snap-in, right-click ADSI Edit, and then click Connect To.

3. In Name, type the fully qualified domain name (FQDN) of the domain in which you want to create the PSO, and then click OK.

4. Double-click the domain.

5. Double-click DC=<domain_name>.

6. Double-click CN=System.

7. Click CN=Password Settings Container, as shown in Figure 5.6.

Figure 5.6: Using ADSI Edit to create a password settings object

8. Right-click CN=Password Settings Container, click New, and then click Object.

9. In the Create Object dialog box, under Select A Class, click msDS-PasswordSettings and then click Next.

10. In Value, type the name of the new PSO and then click Next.

11. Continue with the wizard, and enter appropriate values for all must-have attributes, as shown in Table 5.1.

12. On the last screen of the wizard, click More Attributes.

13. In the Select Which Property To View menu, click Optional or Both.

14. In the Select A Property To View drop-down list, select msDS-PSOAppliesTo.

15. In Edit Attribute, add the distinguished names of users or global security groups to which the PSO is to be applied, and then click Add.

16. Repeat step 15 to apply the PSO to more users or global security groups.

17. Click Finish.

Table 5.1: PSO Attribute Values and Settings

Attribute	Description	Values	Sample Value
msDS PasswordSettingsPrecedence	Password Settings Precedence	Values greater than 0	7
msDS PasswordReversibleEncryptionEnabled	Reversible Encryption settings for User accounts	True/false	False (recommended)
msDS PasswordHistoryLength	Password History Length	0 through 1024	30
msDS PasswordComplexityEnabled	Password Complexity Requirement	True/false	True (recommended)
msDS MinimumPasswordLength	Minimum Password Length	0 through 255	8
msDS MinimumPasswordAge	Minimum Password Age	None or 00:00:00:00 through the msDS MaximumPasswordAge value	02:00:00:00 (2 days)
msDSMaximumPasswordAge	Maximum Password Age	msDS MinimumPasswordAge through (Never)	30:00:00:00 (30 days)
msDS LockoutThreshold	Lockout Threshold	0 through 65535	15
msDS LockoutObservationWindow	Lockout Observation Window	(none) or 00:00:00:01 through the msDS LockoutDuration value	00:00:15:00 (15 minutes)
msDS LockoutDuration	Lockout duration	None, Never, or any value between the msDS LockoutObservationWindows through (Never)	00:00:30:00 (30 minutes)
msDS PSOAppliesto	Links PSO to objects	Distingushed names of users or global security groups	"CN=user1, CN=users, DC=Server1, DC=xyz,DC=com"

Please note that as you create the values in the PSO, they must exactly match the syntax and formatting shown in Table 5.1, or you will not be successful in creating the object.

Once you have created your PSO and associated it to your user or group accounts, you are ready to go. (Be sure to give it a quick test to make sure it is behaving as you expect before you roll it out to the entire system.) Now what happens if you decide to apply this PSO to another group? Do you have to go back to ADSI Edit and reassociate the PSO to the group? You could do that, but an easier way would be to simply use Active Directory Users And Computers to associate the PSO to the group.

Associate a PSO to an Additional User or Group

To associate a PSO to an additional user or group, follow these steps:

1. Open the Active Directory Users And Computers tool from the Tools menu in Server Manager.

2. On the View menu, ensure that Advanced Features is selected.

3. In the console tree, navigate to Active Directory Users And Computers*domain node*\System\Password Settings Container.

4. In the Details pane, right-click the PSO and then click Properties.

5. Click the Attribute Editor tab.

6. Select the msDSPsoAppliesTo attribute, and then click Edit.

7. In the Multi-Valued String Editor dialog box, enter the distinguished name of the user or the global security group to which you want to apply this PSO, click Add and then click OK.

   To get the distinguished name of a global Security group, you can right-click the group and choose Properties. On the Attribute Editor tab, view the value of the Distinguished Name attribute.

PSOs can be managed in much the same way they were created using ADSI Edit. Let's say you want to delete a PSO for whatever reason. To do so, simply go back to ADSI Edit, locate the PSO, right-click, and choose Delete. If you want to change the settings of a PSO, use Active Directory Users And Computers to navigate to the Password Settings objects container. Right-click the object, and edit its attributes.

PSOs make it possible for you to have a flexible password policy, which in turn will help you enrich the security of your directory database.

Understand Active Directory Replication

Active Directory is a database. The really cool thing about Active Directory is that it has multiple points of authoritative input. Objects can be added, deleted, changed, and so on, from any domain controller (with the obvious exception of the read-only DC, which we will discuss later). This distributed database capability adds tremendous flexibility to Active Directory. It makes administration and management much easier and much more efficient. You might be wondering how a distributed database with write permissions at each DC can share those changes across a network to get true synchronization. The process is called *directory replication*.

Understand the Components of Replication

Remember that a directory database is really just a file called NTDS.DIT. It would seem like you could just pass around the most current copy of the NTDS.DIT file and make sure each DC had the most current copy and this whole process would be academic. That would be just fine if your directory database remained at its default size of around 15MB. The problem is that as you add more and more objects to your directory, it grows and grows and grows. Passing 15MB between DCs is not such a big deal. If the file is 10, 20, or 50 times that size, you have some real bandwidth issues with which to deal. You cannot feasibly pass full-size copies of the directory database around between DCs. You have to break the database down into smaller component parts and pass those parts around as updates to each domain controller.

Each directory database is broken down into three separate subsections called *partitions*, or naming contexts. The partitions are the schema partition, configuration partition, and domain partition.

The *schema partition* is replicated to all DCs in the directory forest. It contains the information about the directory schema, which provides definitions to all the objects in the directory.

The *configuration partition* is replicated to all DCs in the directory forest. It contains information about the physical structure of the actual directory.

The *domain partition* is replicated only to DCs within a single domain. Each domain in a directory forest will have its own unique domain partition information. This is where you would find the actual users, groups, computers, and other objects associated with the domain.

Manage Active Directory
and Local Users

PART II

Each of these partitions is replicated independently of the others. This allows partitions that have lots of changes, such as the domain partition, to have a limited effect on partitions that don't change very often, such as the schema partition.

Types of Updates

Each domain controller has the ability to write changes to the directory database. This means that when you think about replication, there are really two types of updates that can be made to a directory database. The update could be what is termed an *originating update*, meaning an object was created on this DC in the local copy of the database. It does not exist elsewhere on other DCs in the forest. Once the originating update has occurred, it needs to be sent to the other DCs in the domain. When the other DCs receive the update, they are not creating the original object. Instead, they are making what is termed a *replicated update*. They are replicating data from another DC.

Metadata

The question of how a DC knows whether it is making an originating update or a replicated update is significant. Each DC uses metadata to manage the replication of objects. This means that in addition to the objects themselves, the directory service also sends key bits of information about the DC where the object originated, when the change was made, and what update was made (where in the sequence of updates this one fits). All this metadata is used by the receiving DC to determine whether this update should be written and whether it should be sent to other partner DCs called *replication partners*.

Metadata items include the following:

- *Update sequence numbers (USN)*: These sequence numbers are specific to the DC. When a change is made to an object, the DC increments the USN by 1. Each DC maintains its own USN independent of the other DCs in the directory. The USN of a DC is shared with its replication partners.

- *High watermark vector (HWMV)*: This piece of metadata is used to help the DC limit the changes that are being sent across the wire at each replication.

- *Globally unique identifier (GUID)*: This piece of metadata identifies the remote DC and prevents possible confusion if the DC were to be renamed.

- *Up-to-dateness vector (UTDV)*: This piece of metadata is used to prevent the same replication changes from being sent out over and over again. This data is kept by each DC for each of the other DCs associated with each of the three directory partitions.

Through the use of these metadata controls, it is possible to get consistent and rapid replication updates throughout a directory forest without having to send the entire copy of the directory database at each replication attempt.

TIP For more information on advanced Replication and metadata used in replication with PowerShell, see http://technet .microsoft.com/en-us/library/jj574083.aspx.

Understand the Physical Constructs of Replication

As you learned earlier in this book, Active Directory has two types of constructs. There are *logical* constructs, such as forests, trees, domains, and organizational units, and there are *physical* constructs, such as sites and domain controllers. When replication is being discussed, we are concerned with the physical constructs of Active Directory. Replication is all about passing information about changes to objects in the directory database to each domain controller within and between the physical sites in the network topology.

By definition, a site is composed of one or more IP subnets connected by high-speed links. We like to define a high-speed link as one that has at least 512KB of "available bandwidth." This means that the bandwidth can be entirely dedicated to the directory service traffic of the site. If the IP subnets in your network are not connected by high-speed links, then generally you would create additional sites. One of the reasons you build sites is to provide a framework on which replication can be built. Replication comes in two flavors: replication within the same site, which is referred to as *intrasite* replication, and replication that occurs between sites, which is referred to as *intersite* replication.

Active Directory uses a set of standards in replication to make it as effective and efficient as possible. These standards are referred to as the *replication model* for Active Directory. In short, these standards mean that all replication in Active Directory will follow a multimaster replication model. Every domain controller can receive updates to data for which it is authoritative, and all replication is "pull-based," meaning DCs request changes rather than push or send them. This way, only desired changes arrive at the DC. Each domain controller communicates with a subset of all the DCs in the forest and "stores and forwards" changes, instead of having a single DC responsible for sending all updates. Finally, each DC tracks the state of replication updates through partner DCs using metadata to ensure synchronization while minimizing network bandwidth usage.

Latency in directory replication is always a concern. *Latency* refers to some delay in time between an originating update and its replication throughout the directory to the appropriate DCs. When all changes have been updated throughout the directory, the directory is said to have achieved *convergence*. The goal of replication is to build a topology where latency is minimized and you achieve convergence.

Now that the groundwork is laid, it is time to see how all of these components work together to build effective replication (and all of this is done without any help from us humans, thankfully!).

Knowledge Consistency Checker

The replication topology of your directory is generated by a built-in component of the directory service called the Knowledge Consistency Checker (KCC). The KCC runs locally on each domain controller; it reads configuration data and writes connection objects for DCs in the site. The KCC also writes local nonreplicated values that define the replication partners from which to request replication updates. This little application is the engine that defines and consequently drives the topology of directory replication. There is one designated KCC in each site that is responsible for writing the connections to other DCs in other sites. This KCC is given the title of Intersite Topology Generator (ISTG). Through defined connections within and between sites, metadata and actual updates are then passed to the DCs that make up a directory service replication topology.

The KCC uses a host of information about topology to build replication partnerships. In the case of the ISTG, much of that information is user-defined as you configure the information about the site objects and how those sites are to be connected and when (and using what method) replication should occur between sites.

Viewing Replication Data

Sometimes when working with Active Directory replication, you may want to see the replication topology of your network. You can use the built-in command-line tool called REPADMIN.exe to view and manage replication data in your directory.

Start REPADMIN by opening Windows PowerShell and typing **REPADMIN.exe**.

You will be presented with the supported commands that can be executed with REPADMIN. This tool is exceptional at reporting replication data. You might remember another Microsoft Tool called REPLMON that was included with Windows Server 2003. It was graphical-based, not command-line-based. It is not included with Windows Server 2012; but if you were to go to the Support Tools folder on a Windows Server 2003 DVD, you could install the REPLMON tool on a Windows Server 2012 machine, and it would work. Please keep in mind that it is *not* supported as a replication monitoring tool in Windows Server 2012. Use REPADMIN to be on the safe side.

Manage Active Directory and Local Users

PART II

6

Maintaining and Controlling the Centralized Desktop

IN THIS CHAPTER, YOU WILL LEARN TO:

▶ **UNDERSTAND GROUP POLICY** (Pages 184 – 197)

- Know the Difference Between Policy and Preferences (Page 186)
- Understand the Scope of Group Policy Management (Page 188)
- Understand and Control the Order of Precedence (Page 189)
- Learn Group Policy Processing (Page 191)

▶ **ADMINISTER GROUP POLICY** (Pages 198 – 213)

- Use the Group Policy Management Console (Page 198)
- Use the Group Policy Management Editor (Page 208)
- Automate Group Policy Administrator Tasks (Page 212)

▶ **TROUBLESHOOT GROUP POLICY** (Pages 213 – 219)

- Use the Group Policy Modeling Wizard (Page 214)
- Use Tools to See the RSOP (Page 216)

As you begin to manage the systems for your network, servers, or workstations, you will want to strive for consistency. In Windows Server 2012 Active Directory, as in previous versions of Windows Server, you have a tremendously powerful tool at your disposal called Group Policy.

Group Policy provides a great asset for controlling and maintaining your users' desktops. Group Policy can help you configure both the computers and the users in your Active Directory. By targeting a computer with Group Policy, you can maintain the desktop but also ensure that any user who uses the desktop will have a default configuration you mandate for your systems. When you target users with Group Policy, the policy will travel with those users. In other words, regardless of which system in your AD environment the user logs on to, the policies applied to the user account will apply.

Group Policy allows you to define your corporate desktop, and there are thousands of settings you can configure. For example, you can set what applications are installed, what the background is for the desktop, whether the user can use Control Panel applets, what the logon scripts are, and more. Group Policy also provides mechanisms to configure many security settings. This provides you with a tool not only for maintaining and configuring your infrastructure but also for protecting it.

Learning how to use Group Policy is a key benefit you can provide to your infrastructure. By providing you with a method to maintain and control your environment, an effective use of Group Policy can save you time and energy when working with the desktops and users in your environment. In this chapter, you'll learn some of the ins and outs of Group Policy and how to get started using it.

Understand Group Policy

Using Group Policy, you can easily deliver one-to-many management of users and computers. Group Policy allows you to enforce your IT policies, implement any necessary security settings, and implement a standard computing environment. Having a standard environment provides a consistent base and helps to alleviate support-desk calls. Group Policy will also help simplify your day-to-day administrative tasks and leverage your existing Active Directory environment.

Before you begin working with Group Policy, you need to be aware of some basic terms. Refer to Table 6.1 to get up to speed with some of the terminology behind this powerful tool. Then, you'll learn about the scope of policy management, as well how client systems process group policies.

Table 6.1: Group Policy Terminology

Term	Description
Group Policy Management Console (GPMC)	This is the main tool where you create your Group Policy objects. GPMC creates the links defining which objects the GPO will target and the three main scopes managed in GPMC: sites, domains, and OUs.
Group Policy Object (GPO)	GPOs are the objects that contain all the settings you want to apply to your users or computers. GPOs are also what you link to your organizational units (OUs), sites, or domains.
Group Policy Object link	The GPO link is what links the GPO to the portion of your Active Directory environment where you want the GPO to be applied. This is referred to as the *scope*, and there are three main levels you apply GPOs to: site, domain, and OU.
Group Policy Management Editor	This is the tool you use to modify the settings in the GPOs. The available settings are based on the administrative templates currently loaded.
Administrative template files (ADMX files)	These files have two purposes. One is to define the settings and configuration location (on the local system) for those settings. The second is to create the interface you use to modify the setting in the Group Policy Management Editor.
Group Policy preferences	Preferences provide an alternative to working with company-wide images to manage settings previously not easily configured in Group Policy. The settings initially set by the administrator reflect a default state of the operating system, so these settings are not necessarily enforced.
Resultant Set of Policy (RSOP)	RSOP is the set of policy settings applied after all the Group Policy processing is complete. This could be a combination of many levels of group policies.

Manage Active Directory and Local Users

PART II

Know the Difference Between Policy and Preferences

As you begin to work with Group Policy settings, you will notice that there are two ways to configure systems: policies and preferences. Both policies and preferences can modify user and computer objects; however, the reasons to use them are very different. The main difference is enforcement; policies are enforced, while preferences are not strictly enforced. In this section, you will see the difference between the two.

Policies

When you are working with policies, the settings and interface are based on administrative templates. Policies make changes to the Registry as directed by the administrative template. There are special sections in the Registry hives that are controlled by Group Policy. The Group Policy settings stored in these locations are known as *true policies*.

Specifically, Group Policy works with these two locations for computer settings:

- HKEY_LOCAL_MACHINE\SOFTWARE\policies (preferred location)
- HKEY_LOCAL_MACHINE\SOFTWARE\Microsoft\Windows\ CurrentVersion\policies

For the user settings, Group Policy works with the following two locations:

- HKEY_CURRENT_USER\SOFTWARE\policies (preferred location)
- HKEY_ CURRENT_USER\SOFTWARE\Microsoft\Windows\ CurrentVersion\policies

Every time a system processes a policy and gets the RSOP, these Registry hives (all the keys and values) are erased and rewritten with the new RSOP. This occurs only as long as a valid Group Policy is still being applied to the computer or user.

Lastly, you can also make your own policy settings by modifying one of the administrator templates or creating your own. This allows you to work with the entire Registry (except for the keys mentioned earlier). However, it is important to note these settings will "tattoo" the Registry. In other words, the settings are permanently set until you specifically reverse them in Group Policy. This means if you just delete your GPO, these types of settings do not go away; you must reverse them by hand.

Preferences

Introduced in Windows Server 2008, preferences provide an alternative to using scripts to perform common tasks. These tasks were traditionally not done easily—if at all—in Group Policy. Preferences allow you to modify local Registry settings, local users and groups, files and folders, printers, local services, mapped drives, and many other local settings. Because preferences are not enforced on local systems, users have the ability to make changes. Additionally, preferences are useful for non-Group-Policy-aware applications and system settings. However, even if a user decides to make changes, they most likely will not have the permission to make the change because a majority of the preferences require some kind of administrative credentials.

You can also target individual preference items through Group Policy filtering, which you will learn about later in this chapter. This is very different from true policies, in that you do not target individual settings inside Group Policy settings.

In Windows Server 2012, the targeting of preferences has been dramatically improved. You now can leverage the Targeting Editor, which is shown in Figure 6.1.

Figure 6.1: Targeting Editor

Manage Active Directory and Local Users

PART II

The Targeting Editor is a straightforward rules-based tool that allows you to create very specific targeting for a preference. You can target based on computer name, operating system (including version, service pack, 64-bit), RAM, CPU, and so on. This makes item-level targeting very flexible. To access the Targeting Editor, choose the Common tab while modifying a preference setting and select Item-Level Targeting, as shown in Figure 6.2. Later in this chapter you will see how to access the Targeting Editor.

Figure 6.2: Selecting item-level targeting

Understand the Scope of Group Policy Management

As you begin working with Group Policy, you'll start to see how an effective AD design provides the basis for managing Group Policy. You can apply group policies to the site, domain, and organizational unit levels. Table 6.2 describes the impact and recommendations for using the different levels to apply group policies.

Table 6.2: Scopes of Group Policy Management

Scope	Objects Impacted	Recommendation
Site	All the domains and the objects in the AD site are impacted; this is the largest scope of impact.	It is not recommended you use the site scope for a typical Group Policy setup. However, sites are useful when you are setting network security settings, such as a proxy server or IPsec policies. You also need to be an Enterprise Administrator to link GPOs at this level.
Domain	All the objects in the chosen domain are impacted.	This is also not a recommended scope for applying group policies. The domain scope is used for your password policies (length, complexity, expiration, and so on) and other security settings where you want to apply them consistently.
Organizational unit	All the objects in the chosen OU as well as any nested OUs and their objects are impacted.	This is the recommended scope for applying group policies. OUs provide the easiest-to-manage location for all of your Group Policy needs.

As mentioned in Table 6.2, organizational units are the recommended way you should apply Group Policy. One of the benefits of having a good OU design is that it can assist you in applying group policies by allowing you to target the unique needs for the users and computers in each OU.

Understand and Control the Order of Precedence

When you create group policies, you are not limited to just one GPO or one scope of management. By default, the RSOP is the culmination of all the scopes and all of the GPOs, and policies are cumulative. In other words, the RSOP could be the combination of multiple GPOs from multiple scopes. You could have an RSOP containing settings from the site, domain, and OU scopes. Typically, there is very little conflict when working with policies, and all the settings will apply as you go through the levels.

However, it is important for you to understand the default order of precedence. This becomes important when you have two or more group policies that have conflicting settings. The following is the general rule of thumb when working with multiple GPOs:

The GPO closest to the object (user or computer) wins.

The following is the default order of precedence:

1. Local policies

   Local policies live on the local system and are applied first, including multiple local policies on Windows Vista systems or later.

2. Site

3. Domain

4. Parent OU

5. Child OU

   Nested OUs are called *child* OUs, and they can have separate settings as well.

For example, if you have a setting to remove the run command at the domain scope and a setting to enable the run command at the object's OU, the setting at the OU level will "win," and the run command will be enabled.

With Group Policy, you also have the ability to link multiple GPOs per site, domain, or OU. When this happens, you need to understand link order. In Figure 6.3, you can see an OU with two GPOs linked to the OU. Link order determines the order in which policies are applied. The link with the highest order (with 1 being the highest order) is applied last and, therefore, has the highest precedence for a given site, domain, or organizational unit. So, in Figure 6.3, the run command would be disabled because it has a link order of 1 and is processed last. By changing the link order, you determine the order of processing. You can move a link up or down in the list to the appropriate location.

Figure 6.3: Link order

You can control how Group Policy is processed using two other ways: block inheritance and enforce (known as *no override* in server operating systems prior to Windows Server 2008 R2).

Block inheritance prevents GPOs from higher scopes from being inherited and, therefore, keeps them from being applied by the child scopes further down the chain. The only exception is if the GPO has been marked as enforced. Block inheritance is selected at either the domain level or the OU level. For example, if you did not want domain-wide policies applying to the child OUs, you could block inheritance at the OU level, and the domain policies would not be inherited.

Enforce is applied to the Group Policy link and marks the GPO to be processed last, regardless of where the policy falls in the scope of management. In other words, an enforced policy will always win unless another enforced policy is further down the scope of management. This also means that when you use an enforced policy, it will also override the block inheritance setting.

Learn Group Policy Processing

Understanding Group Policy processing is key to understanding how to apply settings and can really assist you in troubleshooting. Policy processing will also impact when you see the Group Policy settings take effect on your targeted systems and users.

You also need to understand that Group Policy is processed differently for computer settings and user settings. There is also a difference on the client operating system; specifically, the client operating system can affect how Group Policy is applied. We'll discuss this in the "Learn How Group Policies Process on the Client Side" section later in this chapter.

Computer settings are applied at two times: during startup of the operating system and during shutdown. User settings are applied when the user logs on to and logs off from the system. With the user settings being applied second, by default they take precedence over computer settings unless you have configured Loopback Processing mode.

When you make changes to Group Policy via the GPMC, they may not immediately take effect but may also not require any action by the user or computer. A background process controls the refresh of policies. Policies are updated in the background at various intervals; the intervals are also configurable via Group Policy settings. If the system is a domain controller, the policy is refreshed by default every 5 minutes. On all other systems, the refresh interval is by default 90 minutes plus a random interval of 0–30 minutes. The random interval prevents multiple computers from updating at the same time, so a policy could take up to 2 hours before the changes you made to the GPO are reflected on the targeting system.

Loopback Processing Mode

When you apply both computer and user settings via Group Policy, they are processed at separate times. With the user settings applied after computer settings, there is a potential that your computer settings will be overridden by the user settings. Even though there are only a few settings that can conflict in this way, ultimately this behavior may not be what you desire. You can control the order of processing of computer and user settings by configuring Loopback Processing mode. Loopback Processing mode enables the computer settings of the GPO to take precedence over the user settings in the GPO.

Loopback Processing mode is configured via the Group Policy Editor and is located under `Computer Configuration\Policies\ Administrative Templates\System\Group Policy`. The setting is Configure User Group Policy Loopback Processing Mode, as shown here.

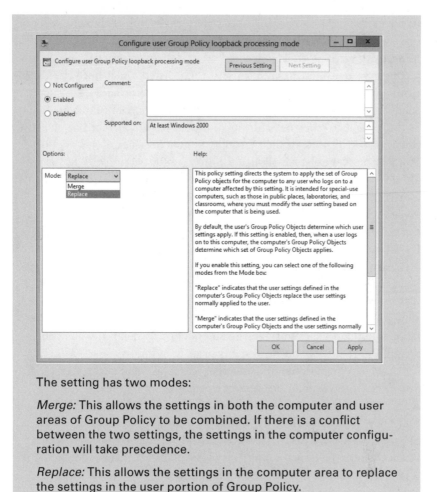

The setting has two modes:

Merge: This allows the settings in both the computer and user areas of Group Policy to be combined. If there is a conflict between the two settings, the settings in the computer configuration will take precedence.

Replace: This allows the settings in the computer area to replace the settings in the user portion of Group Policy.

Not all policies are processed in the background; by default, policies are not reapplied if the policy has not changed. Additionally, software installation, scripts, and folder redirection are not reapplied during background processing. Those policies are applied when either a computer restarts or a user logs off or logs back on. However, there is one exception to the order of processing for GPOs. If a GPO is in the startup or shutdown settings for computer objects or in the logon or logoff settings for user objects, those policies will process the next time the sequence occurs. In other words, if a policy is updated in the background and is in the startup settings, those policy changes will not take place until the next time the system is restarted.

Security settings are also treated separately from other Group Policy settings. Security settings are those settings listed under both the User Configuration and Computer Configuration under Windows Settings\ Security Settings. They include such things as Account Policies, Local Security Policies (such as Auditing and User Rights), Event Log size and retention settings, Restricted Groups, System Services, Registry, File System access, Public Key Policies, Software Restrictions, IP Security, Wired Network Policies, Windows Firewall with Advanced Security, Network Access Protection, and Network List Manager to name the general categories. These settings are reapplied every 16 hours even if the GPO has not changed. You can modify this duration through the Registry.

Lastly, some policies are not applied if a slow link is detected. Specifically, application deployment, scripts, folder redirection, and disk quotas are not applied by default when a slow link is detected. A slow link is determined by the responsiveness of the domain controller delivering the policies to the targeted systems. By default, when processing a GPO client, operating systems prior to Windows Vista will try four times to ping a domain controller. If the average of the four ping attempts is greater than the default or than as set by the GPO, only Registry settings, security policies, EFS recovery policy, and IP security policies will be applied. Since Windows Vista, this has changed. Instead of pings, Vista uses the Network Location Awareness handler, which verifies whether a domain controller is available. If it is available and if it is needed, the GPO is applied and refreshed.

Manually Update Group Policy Settings

You may not be willing to wait for background policy processing. You can manually update Group Policy settings on targeted systems by running the command gpupdate.exe from the target system. When testing Group Policy, you should usually run gpupdate /force before logging off or rebooting the computer. This allows you to make sure that Group Policy settings are flowing down to the system. This simple command can save you time, especially when you are troubleshooting. You can run gpupdate.exe from a command prompt. The command has a few parameters (listed in Table 6.3) that make the tool very useful.

Table 6.3: gpupdate.exe

Command	Function
gpupdate	Reapplies just the policies that have changed since the last update for both computer and user settings
gpupdate /force	Reapplies all the policy settings for both computer and user settings regardless of whether they have changed
gpupdate /target:Computer or gpupdate /target:User	Reapplies only the computer or user settings as reflected by the choice you set in the command

Windows Server 2012 introduced PowerShell support for updating Group Policy. The new cmdlet Invoke-GPUpdate allows you to refresh Group Policy remotely. For example, the following forces a refresh of the policy on Desktop1.

```
Invoke-GPUpdate -computer Desktop1 -Force
```

To learn more about Invoke-GPUdate, use PowerShell's built-in help.

```
Get-Help Invoke-GPUdate.
```

If you choose to use remote updating functionality, you must make sure you have opened the following inbound ports on your firewall:

- TCP RPC dynamic ports, Schedule (Task Scheduler service) for Remote Scheduled Tasks Management (RPC) traffic

- TCP port 135, RPCSS (Remote Procedure Call service) for Remote Scheduled Tasks Management (RPC-EPMAP) traffic

- TCP all ports, Winmgmt (Windows Management Instrumentation service) for Windows Management Instrumentation (WMI-in) traffic

In Windows Server 2012, you will find a starter GPO named Group Policy Remote Update Firewall Ports that allows you to use Group Policy to make the proper changes to the firewall. You can learn more about starter GPOs in the "Work with Starter GPOs" section later in this chapter.

Manage Active Directory and Local Users

PART II

Learn How Group Policies Process on the Client Side

One last consideration you need to be aware of regarding Group Policy processing is how they are applied to the system. There are two types of Group Policy processing modes: synchronous and asynchronous. *Synchronous* processing occurs when a series of processes are handled and one process must finish running before the next one begins. *Asynchronous* processing, on the other hand, can run on different threads simultaneously because their outcome is independent of other processes.

Client-side systems (Windows XP, Windows Vista, Windows 7, Windows 8) process group policies asynchronously. The main reason for asynchronous processing on the client-side systems is fast logon optimization. Fast logon optimization is designed to enable the systems to quickly present the desktop to users. This can result in some policies not being applied initially to the targeted systems.

Server-side systems (Windows Server 2003, Windows Server 2008, Windows Server 2008 R2, Windows Server 2012) process group policies synchronously, which ensures the Group Policy settings are processed. With synchronous processing, all the Group Policy settings will be applied. You might notice a delay at logon; however, when you see the Logon screen, you will know the computer settings have been applied, and likewise when the desktop is displayed, you will know that all the user settings have been applied. Group policies are processed synchronously on Windows 2000 systems at startup and asynchronously during Group Policy refreshes.

As you can see, this is important to understand when it comes to maintaining and troubleshooting Group Policy. You can also control this setting on the client-side systems by modifying the Always Wait for the Network at Computer Startup and Logon setting; this will allow you to have the client-side systems process group policies synchronously. You can find this setting in Group Policy under `Computer Configuration\Policies\Administrative Templates\System\Logon` (accessed through the Group Policy Management Editor for a specific Group Policy Object), as shown in Figure 6.4. By enabling the setting, you control the processing behavior on the client-side systems.

Figure 6.4: Setting for synchronous processing

Service Running Group Policy Processing

On operating systems prior to Windows Vista, group policies were processed by the `winlogon` service. As a result, the `winlogon` service sometimes was the culprit for issues with Group Policy.

In later versions of Windows (Server 2008, Server 2008 R2, Server 2012, Windows Vista, Windows 7, and Windows 8), there is a dedicated service for Group Policy, aptly called the Group Policy Client Service. The service is responsible for applying settings configured through Group Policy.

This change is important because it offers better reliability for Group Policy, enables better efficiency, and reduces the resources required for background processing of Group Policy. The dedicated service provides the ability to read to new files and allows the Group Policy service to take on the workload provided by multiple services in other versions of Windows.

Administer Group Policy

Now that you have seen how group policies are processed, it is time to take a look at how to work with Group Policy. Managing Group Policy is straightforward after you have deployed your AD environment. To work with Group Policy, you will use primarily two tools: the Group Policy Management Console (GPMC) and the Group Policy Management Editor (GPME). In this section, you will take a look at both tools and see how to use them.

Use the Group Policy Management Console

The Group Policy Management Console is the main tool where you manage the deployment of Group Policy. This includes creating and linking your GPOs to the appropriate site, domain, or organizational unit. You also can manage security filtering, Windows Management Instrumentation (WMI) filtering, administration delegation of Group Policy, and various other tasks with the GPMC. In addition, you can also use it to gain access to the GPME to edit the settings for your GPOs (you will learn about the GPME in the next section). You can also view the settings for your various GPOs. You can find the GPMC in the Tools menu in Server Manager on your Windows Server 2012 server. Open Server Manager and then select Tools ➤ Group Policy Management to load the GPMC; your screen will resemble Figure 6.5.

Figure 6.5: Group Policy Management Console

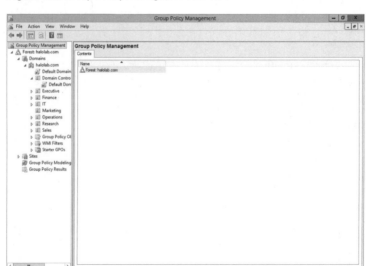

When you first open the GPMC, expand the management tree. You will see two GPOs that are configured by default: the Default Domain Policy and the Default Domain Controllers Policy. These two policies contain the default security policies for the domains. To view the settings of the default policies, follow these steps:

1. Open GPMC.

2. Expand the Forest container.

3. Expand the Domains container.

4. Expand a domain to view the Default Domain Policy. If you want to view the Default Domain Controllers Policy, continue in the domain you expanded, and expand the Domain Controllers container.

5. Click either Default Domain Policy or Default Domain Controllers Policy, depending on which you want to view.

6. In the Details pane to the right, click the Settings tab, and you will see a screen similar to Figure 6.6, which shows the Default Domain Policy.

Figure 6.6: Default Domain Policy

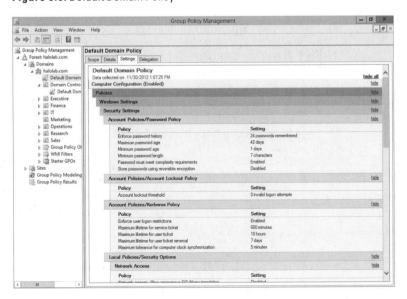

WARNING The Default Domain Policy sets the basis for security in your domain. Specifically, the Default Domain Policy sets the Default Domain Password Policy, Kerberos, and public key policies. They provide protection for your users' passwords. The Kerberos and public key policies help provide secure authentication mechanisms for your domain.

The Default Domain Controllers Policy sets the local security rights for the domain controllers. The rights govern the administrative access to the domain controllers in your domain. These rights help harden the server and keep it secure for the right people in your organization.

These default policies are designed to provide you with a solid, secure network; you should never change them. If you believe you need to change the default settings, seriously consider the repercussions before you do. Whether the change is an addition or a deletion, consider making separate policies rather than altering the defaults.

Work with Group Policies

Creating, linking, and setting security for group policies starts with knowing the scope (site, domain, or OU) and users to whom you want the policy to apply.

1. From the Group Policy management tree, select the scope for your GPO.

2. Right-click the scope, and you will see a screen similar to Figure 6.7.

Figure 6.7: Creating a GPO

3. Select Create a GPO in this domain and Link it here.

4. Enter the name for your GPO and select an appropriate starter GPO, if one exists. In the next section, you will take a look at starter GPOs. Click OK to finish creating your GPO.

You can also create a GPO without having the policy linked directly to a scope. Use the GPO container. After you create a GPO, you can easily link that GPO to a scope by simply dragging and dropping.

1. Click the Group Policy Objects container.

2. Right-click the container and select New.

3. Enter a name for the GPO and select an appropriate starter GPO, if one exists. Click OK to finish creating your GPO.

Work with Starter GPOs

Starter GPOs allow you to create a template for quickly creating new GPOs, with a predefined list of settings. They can save you a lot of time because part of the challenge of working with GPOs is the number of settings you can modify. There are literally thousands of settings you can manipulate with Group Policy. Learning which settings work best in your environment is key to using Group Policy effectively. By using starter GPOs, you can reuse a list of frequently used settings when you create new GPOs, which will save you time. It is important to note that starter GPOs contain settings only from the Administrative Templates section of Group Policy. You edit the settings in the GPOs just like any other GPO.

To create a starter GPO, click Starter GPOs in the GPMC tree. If this is the first time you have clicked Starter GPOs, you will see a screen similar to Figure 6.8.

Figure 6.8: Creating a starter GPO

Manage Active Directory and Local Users

PART II

You need to create a folder to store the starter GPOs, so click the Create Starter GPOs Folder button to create the folder. Once you create the folder, you will see a few starter GPOs provided by Microsoft by default. You'll see two acronyms with all the built-in starter GPOs, and they provide the key to what type of settings are in the policies. EC stands for "enterprise client" and provides basic security and power settings, among others, for your infrastructure. SSLF stands for "specialized security limited functionality," which provides robust security-enabled clients. Note this starter may cause compatibility issues with applications. To view the settings for any of these starter GPOs, select one and click the Settings tab.

In Windows Server 2012, you also have two new starter GPOs: Group Policy Remote Update Firewall Ports and Group Policy Reporting Firewall Ports. These two starter GPOs provide quick ways for you to configure firewall ports, not only for updating GPOs with Invoke-GPUdate but also for remotely accessing the RSOP. You will learn more about RSOP in the "Use Tools to See the RSOP" section of this chapter.

Work with Group Policy Object Links

After you create the GPO, you will see the link of the object associated with your container. Note that this is the link for the GPO, not the GPO itself. This is an important distinction to make, because there are different administrative tasks that you can perform for either the GPO link or the GPO itself. To see a list of all the GPOs in your domain, click the Group Policy Objects container located in your management tree.

Working with GPO links provides you with the ability to set the enforced setting, as mentioned earlier. You can also enable or disable the link on the scope. You also control all the filtering of the GPO by working with the link. To access and see the tasks you can perform on links, you can right-click the link and select the appropriate option (link enabled or enforced). You can also select the link and click the Action menu, and you will see same options (link enabled or enforced) to control the link.

Working with the GPOs provides you the ability to back up and recover them. You can also import settings from previously backed up items. To access these tasks, you can simply right-click the object, and you will see the various actions you can perform (backup, import, and so on), or you can highlight the object and then click the Action menu. Remember, you can link GPOs to more than one scope of management.

While viewing the objects, you can also link the GPO to other sites, domains, or OUs. To link a GPO to a scope, you can either drag and drop the object on the scope you want to target or right-click the scope and select Link An Existing GPO. When you edit the GPO, you are modifying the object, and all the changes you make will apply to all the scopes linked to the GPO.

There are a few common tasks that you can perform on both the links and the GPOs. You can access the Group Policy Management Editor by selecting Edit. You can also save all the settings to an HTML file (an example of the HTML file is shown in Figure 6.9) by right-clicking the GPO and selecting Save Report.

Figure 6.9: Settings report

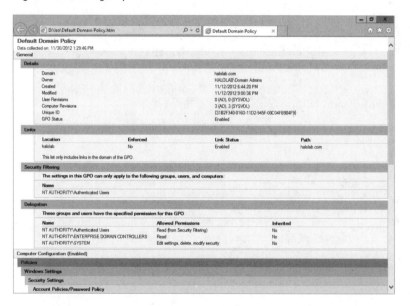

GPO Status

One of the special tasks you can perform on the GPOs is to control which sections of the GPO are applied. When you right-click the GPO (or select the GPO and click the Action menu), one of the items you can select is GPO Status, as shown here.

The GPO has four status options:

Enabled: Both user and computer settings are enabled.

User Configuration Settings Disabled: User settings are disabled, and computer settings are enabled.

Computer Configuration Settings Disabled: User settings are enabled, and computer settings are disabled.

All Settings Disabled: Both user and computer settings are disabled.

The purpose of these settings is for GPO processing efficiency. When you create a GPO, you can have both user and computer settings in the GPO. However, you may create a GPO without one of the two settings; if you do this, it is recommended that you disable the portion that has no settings. This will improve how the targeted systems process group policies.

Filter Group Policies with GPMC

When working with Group Policy links, you have additional control over the objects targeted by your GPO. Typically, when you link a GPO to an OU, for example, you want all the objects in the OU impacted by the GPO. However, there may be some scenarios where you want only some of the objects to have the Group Policy applied to them. In Group Policy, you have two main mechanisms for filtering GPOs. Two of the filters you can work with are Windows Management Instrumentation (WMI) filters and security filters.

WMI filtering provides a very powerful filtering tool that allows you to leverage WMI scripting to filter which objects are targeted by your GPOs. WMI scripting leverages an industry standard for how to work with systems across network infrastructures. In a nutshell, WMI scripting will allow you to find various inventory types of information about computers—from what OS they are running to what applications are installed to what type of hardware, and so on. What this provides for GPOs is the ability to target systems meeting very specific criteria. For example, you could use Group Policy to install a software application and then use WMI filtering to make sure only systems having the required amount of free hard drive space to support the application have the application installed on them. To see what WMI filters are currently installed on the system, look in the WMI Filters container in the GPMC. If no WMI filters are installed, this container will be empty. To see some examples of WMI, take a look at the following link. Although the article was written for Windows Server 2003, it is still applicable.

```
http://technet.microsoft.com/en-us/library/cc758471.aspx
```

Security filtering is another great way to filter objects. To access the security filter for a GPO link, click the link you want to view and make sure you are on the Scope tab for the GPO link. You can see the list of users and groups in the Security Filtering section. By default, the group Authenticated Users is added to the security for all GPOs. When you work with security permissions, two permissions are required for your users to process a Group Policy Object targeted on the OU:

- Read
- Apply Group Policy

You can use security filtering to prevent applying a GPO to security groups or users. For example, say you have an OU containing a group of people including Matt, and you want the policy to apply to everyone in the OU except Matt. You could simply add Deny access to either Read or Apply Group Policy for Matt. You can see an example of this in Figure 6.10.

Figure 6.10: Denying a user a Group Policy

You can view the security filtering for a GPO by clicking the GPO link for the targeted scope. On the Scope tab, you will see the current security filtering for the GPO in the Security Filtering section of the Details pane inside the GPMC. To modify the security filtering for a GPO, follow these steps:

1. Click the GPO you want to filter.

2. Click the Delegation tab.

3. Click the Add button to open the User/Group Selection dialog box.

4. Find or enter the group or user you want to work with, and click OK, which will bring up the Add Group or User dialog box, as shown in Figure 6.11. This dialog box allows you to choose the base security level for the user or group you have selected.

Figure 6.11: GPO base security filter

5. Choose the appropriate level from the three choices, and click OK. Read will give the ability to read and apply the GPO, Edit Settings grants the ability to modify the GPO settings themselves, and the last choice (Edit Settings, Delete, Modify Security) allows basic administration over the GPO link.

6. To further modify the security, click Advanced on the Delegation tab, which will bring up an advanced view of the security settings, as shown in Figure 6.12.

Figure 6.12: GPO advanced security filtering

7. Click the user you want to modify, and choose the appropriate security settings for that user. It is important to note that Deny permissions supersede any Allow permissions. In other words, if you have selected the user to have Allow for Read and Deny for Read, the user would have Deny permissions for that setting. In the example you saw earlier, if you did not want Matt to be able to have the GPO applied, simply select Deny for Read and deselect Allow for Read, as shown in Figure 6.13. When you are finished modifying permissions, click OK.

Figure 6.13: Denying Read for a GPO

Advanced Group Policy Management Tool

Another tool you may be able to take advantage of is the Advanced Group Policy Management (AGPM) tool. You can find this tool in the Microsoft Desktop Optimization Pack (MDOP); it's available only to volume license customers with Software Assurance as part of the licensing agreement. You can also download the evaluation version if you are an MSDN or TechNet subscriber. The tool provides some nice benefits to working with Group Policy, including change management, auditing, reporting, and offline editing of GPOs. To learn more and to see whether you can leverage this tool, refer to http://technet .microsoft.com/en-us/library/cc749396.aspx.

Use the Group Policy Management Editor

To access the Group Policy Management Editor, all you need to do is right-click the GPO link or GPO to edit, and select Edit. Whether you choose to edit from the link or from the GPO, they both will modify the GPO, meaning any other scopes linked to the GPO will be affected. When you edit the GPO, two main containers work with the settings: Computer Configuration and User Configuration. To work with a

Group Policy setting, open the appropriate container and click the setting you want to edit.

One of the great features in Group Policy is the built-in documentation. With every setting in the editor, you will see an explanation of what it does, and you can see the explanation as you are expanding the tree or double-clicking a setting to configure it. Figure 6.14 shows an example of a setting and the explanation. Notice that the setting will include the minimum required OS for the setting to be applied to the targeted system. This is important when you are working with a variety of OSs connecting to your domain.

Figure 6.14: GPO setting

As mentioned previously, you can configure thousands of settings. In this section, you will see the main areas explained and what types of settings you can expect to find. When working with the editor, the settings are broken down into two main containers, one for computers and one for users. Inside both User Configurations and Computer Configurations, you will see policies and preferences. Table 6.4 describes the computer and user policies you'll find in specific policy areas.

Table 6.4: Overview of Computer and User Policies

Policy Area	Description
Software Settings	In this section of Group Policy, you can configure installations of software packages to the targeted computers or users. Typically, the packages are in the Windows Installer (MSI) format. You can deploy applications by assigning or publishing them to the target. If you assign an application in the computer configuration, the application will be installed on the targeted system the next time the system reboots. If you assign the application to a user, the application will appear on the Start menu, and the first time a user clicks the icon or opens a file associated with the application, the application will be installed. Publishing an application is available only if the target is a user. Publishing an application will allow the application to appear in the Add or Remove Programs applet. The user will need to go into the Control Panel to install the application.
Computer Windows Settings	This contains several important Windows settings specific to the computer. This is where you configure your startup and shutdown scripts, networking Quality of Service (QoS) settings, and security settings. In the security settings, you can configure IPsec, wireless or wired network configuration and security settings, the firewall, and a variety of other security settings. You will also find a new policy in Windows Server 2012 called Name Resolution, which is used to configure DirectAccess, which only really applies to Windows 7 computers and DNS security settings.
User Windows Settings	This contains several important Windows settings that are specific to the user. This is where you configure your logon and logoff scripts, additional networking QoS settings, and security settings. The security settings for the users have two sections: Public Key Policies and Software Restriction Policies. Public key policies, commonly referred as PKI, are used to configure the client-side certificate security settings. Software restriction policies allow you to configure which applications are restricted on your client systems. You can also configure folder redirection for users' common directories, which is particularly useful when your users have roaming profiles.
Administrative Templates	This is where you find a majority of all the settings available for Group Policy and is where you can configure most of the aspects of the interface for users and computers. Administrative templates are also unique in that you can add templates you have created or get from other software applications. For example, Internet Explorer 8 has its own administrative template with more than 1,300 settings just for the browser. A new category (introduced with Windows Server 2008 R2) inside Administrative Templates called All Settings is very useful when you are using filtering to search for a particular setting.

You can also work with preferences in the Group Policy Management Editor. Table 6.5 gives you a quick reference for the type of settings you will find in the tool.

Table 6.5: Overview of Computer and User Preferences

Preference Area	Description
Window Settings	You can configure system-wide environment variables and modify Registry settings and INI files for any application. You can also work with the local file system by configuring files, folders, and network shares.
Control Panel Settings	You can configure local system devices, local users, and groups. Also, you can set power options here to help optimize the power consumption of your desktop operating systems. This is also where you can configure printers on the network and local-based devices. You also have the ability to work with services and the Task Scheduler.

These two tables are meant to give you just a brief glimpse into the setting areas. The best way to learn how to use the settings is to look through them and their categories; becoming familiar with the setting locations is worth your time.

Filter Group Policy with the Editor

Prior to Windows Server 2008, there was no built-in way to search through Group Policy settings. You had to work with the Group Policy settings reference file, which is a free downloadable spreadsheet. You can find the current Group Policy settings reference file at:

```
http://www.microsoft.com/en-us/download/details
.aspx?id=25250
```

In Windows Server 2008, Windows Server 2008 R2, and Windows Server 2012, you can filter the administrative template settings inside the Group Policy Management Editor. To work with the built-in filter, follow these steps:

1. Right-click Administrative Templates and select Filter Options. You will see a screen similar to Figure 6.15.

Figure 6.15: Filter options

2. You can filter based on several criteria including keyword filters and software requirements. Notice the two options to filter: Managed and Configured. Managed policies are true policies and are managed directly by Group Policy; unmanaged policies are persistent settings, sometimes referred to as *tattooing* the Registry. Configured is a useful option to allow you to quickly find only the settings you have configured. By default, all policies are marked as not configured; by setting the Configured option to Yes, you will find only the settings that have been configured.

3. After you're done setting the options, click OK to enable the filter. To turn the filter off, click the Filter icon.

Automate Group Policy Administrator Tasks

When you work with Group Policy, you should perform common administrative tasks such as backup and recovery on a regular basis. These tasks can be performed through the GPMC, as well as PowerShell. In Table 6.6, you can see a few general PowerShell commands to help you with working with Group Policy. To see the full list, go to this website:

```
http://technet.microsoft.com/library/hh967461.aspx
```

Table 6.6: Group Policy PowerShell Commands

PowerShell Command	Description
`Get-Help *-gp*`	Lists all the possible commands involved in working with GPOs. As you learned in Chapter 3, "Automating Administrative Tasks with Windows Server 2012," you can access help for individual commands listed by this command.
`Get-GPO -all`	Lists all the GPOs in your current domain.
`Backup-GPO -all -path 'c:\gpobackup\'`	Backs up all the group policies in the domain to the `c:\gpobackup` directory, as long as the `c:\gpobackup` directory exists. You can back up to any directory you choose.
`Import-GPO`	Is a useful command for importing GPOs from a backup server to a new server.
`Restore-GPO -all -path 'c:\gpobackup\'`	Restores all the group policies in the domain from the `c:\gpobackup` directory. Typically, you would use this command with the GUID for the GPO you are restoring to find the GUID. In GPMC, click the GPO located in the Group Policy Objects container, and click the Details tab or use `get-gpo` cmdlet.
`Get-GPResultantSetofPolicy -ReportType html -Path 'c:\rsop\rsop2.html'`	Generates an HTML report showing you the RSOP for the policy applied to a particular system. This is a particularly useful tool for troubleshooting.

Troubleshoot Group Policy

When you're working with Group Policy, which has several moving parts, learning some tools to troubleshoot the application of group policies will help save you administrative time and hassle. Understanding the processing covered in this chapter can offer a clue or two about why a Group Policy is not being applied. In this section, you will see some of the built-in tools designed to help you troubleshoot Group Policy.

The built-in tools focus on predicting how your policy settings will be applied and how to find the results on how the policy was applied. The tools are the Group Policy Modeling Wizard (GPMW) and three tools for generating the RSOP: the Group Policy Results Wizard (GPRW), GPResult.exe, and the RSOP snap-in. Ultimately, these tools will allow you to see the Group Policy order of precedence in action. You can see which policies were applied to the system and which policies "win."

In addition, because Group Policy relies on the network, all the tools you use to test the network — from ping to name resolution — still apply when troubleshooting Group Policy. For example, you can run the RSOP tool, which will inform you if a policy was not applied. If you check your GPO and it is all correct, this will generally indicate it's a network or replication issue.

Use the Group Policy Modeling Wizard

The GPMW allows you to preview your group policies. The tool models the results of group policies before they are deployed. This tool compiles reports based on what is configured at the site, domain, and OU levels for both computer and user objects. Based on the rules for applying group policies, the tool will give you a snapshot of what policies will be applied. GPMW can also show you how any security or WMI filtering will affect the application of group policies.

The GPMW is located in the GPMC, and you can find it under the Sites container. It is important to note that the GPMW evaluates only the theoretical RSOP based on all GPOs and filtering set via AD. It does not take into account any physical issues on the network that may affect GPO application.

To create a model, perform the following:

1. In the GPMC right-click Group Policy Modeling, and select Group Policy Modeling Wizard.

2. On the Welcome page, click Next.

3. Select the domain and the domain controller you will use to process the requests for modeling, and click Next.

4. Determine what you want to model. You can choose an individual user, individual computer, or a whole scope (domain or OU) for either a user or a computer. You can also model a combination of any of these. For example, you could model just one user for user settings and an entire domain for computer objects. After you have selected your target, click Next.

5. On the Advanced Simulation Options screen you have the ability to simulate a slow network, model loopback processing, and model the site you want to apply the GPO on; make any necessary selections, and then click Next.

6. In the Alternate Active Directory Paths dialog box, you have the ability to choose other locations for the simulation. (You may not see this dialog box option, depending on what choices you made in step 3.) Make your selection and click Next.

7. You can also simulate changes to a user's security group. After you make your selection, click Next.

8. As with users, you can also simulate changes to a computer's security groups. After you make your selection, click Next.

9. The WMI Filters For Users setting allows you to control which filters are used. After you make your selection, click Next.

10. The WMI Filters For Computers (if you have any installed) setting allows you to control which filters are used for your computer accounts. After you make your selection, click Next.

11. On the Summary screen, review your selections and click Next to create the model.

12. When the model is done being created, click Finish to see the report. The report will be saved under the Group Policy Modeling node. You can rerun the model at any time by right-clicking the model and selecting Re-run Query. Figure 6.16 shows an example of the report.

Figure 6.16: Group Policy modeling report

Use Tools to See the RSOP

Several tools will allow you to see the RSOP. One of those tools is built into the GPMC. The Group Policy Results Wizard is similar to the GPMW, and it is located in the GPMC. To run the GPRW, go the Sites container and perform the following steps:

1. Right-click Group Policy Results, and select Group Policy Results Wizard.

2. On the Welcome page, click Next.

3. You can select the local computer or a remote computer. Make your selection, and click Next.

4. Select the user account for which you want to see the RSOP, and click Next. It is important to note that you will see only users who have already logged on to the system.

5. Review the Summary screen and click Next.

6. After the wizard runs successfully, click Finish to return to the GPMC and view the report.

7. The report will be saved under the Group Policy Modeling node. You can rerun the model at any time by right-clicking the report and selecting Re-run Query. Figure 6.17 shows an example of the report.

Figure 6.17: Group Policy results report

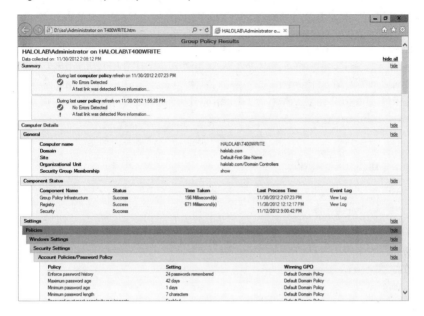

The second tool is a command-line tool called GPResult.exe. This tool will allow you to see the results of Group Policy either for the local system and current user or for remote systems and other users. As with many other commands, several switches/parameters are available providing additional information. You can pipe the results to a text file and utilize the command in batch files or scripts. You can also use the Get-GPResultantSetOfPolicy which operates very similarly to its command-line counterpart GPResult.exe.

If you choose to use the remote RSOP functionality, you will also need to make sure you open the following inbound ports:

- TCP SMB 445 All Services and Programs for Remote Event Log Management (NP-in) traffic

- TCP RPC dynamic ports, EventLog (Windows Event Log service) for Remote Log Management (RPC) traffic

- TCP port 135, RPCSS (Remote Procedure Call service) for Remote Event Log Management (RPC-EPMAP) traffic

- TCP all ports, Winmgmt (Windows Management Instrumentation service) for Windows Management Instrumentation (WMI-in) traffic

In Windows Server 2012, there is a starter GPO named Group Policy Remote Update Firewall Ports that allows you to use Group Policy to make the proper changes to the firewall. You can learn more about starter GPOs in the "Work with Starter GPOs" section of this chapter.

Lastly, the Resultant Set of Policy snap-in is available by loading the Microsoft Management Console (MMC) and adding it. You can also find the tool in the Active Directory Users And Computers tool, as shown in Figure 6.18.

Figure 6.18: RSOP in ADUC

This tool is similar to the GPRW, but it is able to display the results of multiple GPOs. This is a great tool to troubleshoot your GPOs if the GPMC is not currently available. The tool also has two modes: Planning mode and Logging mode.

The main difference between the modes is how the RSOP is provided. Planning mode, which is similar to the GPMW, simulates the processing of Group Policy. Logging mode queries a specific computer's WMI database, which is collected when Group Policy is applied. You can view user information with this tool only if the user has logged on to the system. Additionally, you will see only those policies that have been processed by the system.

Both modes have benefits. The main benefit of Planning mode is that it generates a report based on what settings will be processed before they are processed. Planning mode allows you to simulate behaviors and troubleshoot your group policies before you apply them into production. The main benefit of Logging mode is accuracy, because the report is based on what has actually been processed.

A Common Debate with GPOs

When you are working with Group Policy, one of the popular debates is how many settings to make per GPO. Do you create one GPO with all of your desired settings, or do you create more GPOs with a few settings? Well, the answer to the question is one of the favorites in all of IT administration: It depends.

Seriously, you do not want to create one GPO for every individual setting or create one massive GPO with all the settings. The answer lies in balance, performance, how often you make changes, and how you delegate administration.

Generally speaking, if your group policies do not change, you can consolidate them into fewer GPOs, which will increase client processing time. However, this method sometimes can be hard to track changes and troubleshoot. Another method is to create GPOs based on the settings they are processing and segment if they are computer-based or user-based settings. For example, create a GPO for just the security settings of a computer, and create another for the security settings for the users. Although this method will cause more client-side processing, it does help mitigate frequent changes to your group policies.

PART III
Data Access and Management

IN THIS PART ▶

Data Access and Management

PART III

7

Configuring Folder Security, Access, and Replication

IN THIS CHAPTER, YOU WILL LEARN TO:

Data Access and Management

PART III

A network of servers has one central purpose: to provide controlled access to resources that have been shared in that network. The resources could be files, folders, web pages, databases, printers, or a whole host of other things. The point of the servers is to provide access to all this "stuff." If there is no "stuff," then there is nothing to secure and protect and, therefore, no need for Windows Server. The need for Windows Server 2012 is greater now than ever before. The sheer amount of data you are storing in your networks is constantly growing, while the demand for methods to secure and access that data are keeping pace right along with amount of data.

Implement Permissions

By definition, a *file system* is a hierarchical structure of folders that house and secure files. Access control lists (ACLs) and access control entries (ACEs) define the type of permissions that are granted or denied to those same folders and files. This means that in the Windows Server 2012 world, the primary methodology for securing folders and their files is the use of permissions.

Permissions come in two varieties: share-level permissions and NTFS permissions. If you think about it, this makes perfect sense. When you create a file or folder in the file system, a default set of permissions is assigned to the file or folder. The system itself, the user who created the file or folder, and the local Administrators group on the server where the folder was created all need some level of access to the file or folder, as shown in Figure 7.1.

NTFS permissions are assigned when the file or folder is created, but they can be edited at any time by a user or group member who has the permission to change permissions on the folder.

NTFS folder and file permissions come in two types: *standard* permissions and *special* permissions. Standard permissions come in the form of Full Control, Modify, Read & Execute, List Folder Contents, Read, and Write. Each of these permissions can be either allowed or denied. Because you have the option to allow or deny permissions on a file or folder in an NTFS file system, you have incredible flexibility over the level of access on a given file or folder.

In addition to the standard permissions, there are special permissions that can be set on each folder or file. Special permissions do more than simply provide access to the folder on which they are applied. They provide the basis for folder ownership, as well as the ability to change permissions for a folder and the hierarchy that could exist beneath the folder in the file system.

Figure 7.1: Default NTFS permissions

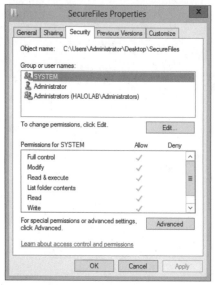

Set Standard NTFS Permissions

Setting or changing standard NTFS permissions is a straightforward process. Follow these steps to get started:

1. Open File Explorer.
2. Locate the desired file or folder.
3. Right-click the file or folder.
4. Choose Properties.
5. Select the Security tab.
6. Click Edit.

At this point, you can select an existing user or group from the list of users and groups that have existing permissions, or you can click the Add button to add new users or groups to which permissions may be assigned.

You can add users and groups from the local accounts available on the physical machine or from the Active Directory database if the folder resides on a server that is part of an Active Directory forest. In the event you are interested in removing permissions, you can simply select the user or group account from the list of users and groups and then click the Remove button shown in Figure 7.2.

Figure 7.2: Setting and removing standard NTFS permissions

Please keep in mind that not just anyone can add, change, or remove NTFS permissions. You need to have permission to change permissions or take ownership of a file or folder in order to change its permissions. These permissions are special permissions.

Set Special NTFS Permissions

As with standard permissions, adding or changing special permissions is a fairly straightforward process. Follow these steps to get started:

1. Open File Explorer.

2. Locate the desired file or folder.

3. Right-click the file or folder.

4. Choose Properties.

5. Select the Security tab.

6. Click the Advanced button.

At this point, the Advanced Security Settings dialog box for this folder will be displayed, as shown in Figure 7.3.

Figure 7.3: Advanced Security Settings dialog box

On the Permissions tab, you can click Change Permissions and add, edit, or remove the special permissions. The Disable Inheritance button at the bottom of the window disables inheritance. Also note the Replace All Child Object Permission Entries With Inheritable Permission Entries From This Object check box. NTFS file systems have a system of inheritance that is built into the file system. This means that permissions added higher up in the file system hierarchy can flow down to the folders that are beneath them in the hierarchy. This is valuable when you want to assign permissions to users or groups to a section of the NTFS file system. It can also present some interesting challenges when you are trying to figure out exactly what permissions a given user or group has been granted on a given folder. To help with this issue, you can use the Effective Access tab in the Advanced Security Settings dialog box shown in Figure 7.4.

Data Access and Management

PART III

Figure 7.4: Effective Access tab

View Effective NTFS Permissions

To view the effective NTFS permissions, follow these steps:

1. Open Windows Explorer.
2. Locate the desired file or folder.
3. Right-click the file or folder.
4. Choose Properties.
5. Select the Security tab.
6. Click the Advanced button.
7. Select the Effective Access tab.
8. Click Select A User (to select a user or group and view their effective permissions) or select a device (to choose a computer account and view its effective permissions). This is useful when you have computer roles, such as Hyper-V, that need to access files on your server.
9. After you decide which type of object you want to view, browse for the user, group, or device whose effective permissions you want to view. Click OK to return to the Effective Access tab.
10. Click View Effective Access to view the effective permissions, as shown in Figure 7.5.

Figure 7.5: Effective Permissions tab

Notice in Figure 7.5 that on the Effective Access tab you can view both standard and special permissions for the user, group, or device you selected. This can be a very valuable tool to aid you in determining the permissions on an NTFS folder.

Take Ownership of an NTFS Folder

By now you may have noticed that a set of default permissions is given to each folder created in an NTFS file system. A special set of permissions is given to the creator of an NTFS folder. These permissions can be defined as "ownership" of the folder. The owner of the folder has full control of the folder and both its standard and special permissions. The Administrators group is also given special permissions, including the permission to take ownership of the folder. This means that at any given point in time anyone in the Administrators group might choose to take ownership of an NTFS folder and thereby take control of its associated permissions. In order to take ownership of a folder, you need to have that special permission assigned to your user or group. If you do not have permissions to take ownership of a folder, you cannot

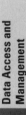

simply "force" your way to ownership. By the same token, if you are the owner, you can deny the ability to take ownership to all parties with the exception of yourself. Now, that's control!

If you have the permission to take ownership, the process works like this:

1. Open File Explorer.

2. Locate the desired folder.

3. Right-click the folder.

4. Choose Properties.

5. Select the Security tab.

6. Click the Advanced button.

7. On the Advanced page, you will see the current owner and a link labeled Change.

8. Click Change.

9. Select the user or group you want to be the new owner and click OK to change the owner. You'll see the result on a screen similar to Figure 7.6.

Figure 7.6: Taking ownership

It is important to consider the Replace Owner On Subcontainers And Objects check box. If you take ownership of a folder, you also have the option to take ownership of the folders beneath it in the hierarchy. This may be desirable if your intent is to take control of a section of the file system.

NTFS folder and file permissions are a great way to control permissions to a local resource. The problem you will have is that in a network environment the users are almost never sitting at the server where the resources are located. How do you provide access and permission controls for folders that are not on the same physical system the user is on? You share them!

Share Folders

Sharing a folder makes it visible and accessible to users and groups that have been granted share-level permissions across the network. Share-level permissions are different from NTFS permissions. NTFS permissions are rooted in the file system, while share permissions provide network accessibility to a folder. When you implement folder sharing, you also set permissions for each of the shares that are created in your network.

Create a Shared Folder

When you are ready to start making folders available across your network, do the following:

1. Open File Explorer.

2. Locate the desired folder.

3. Right-click the folder.

4. Choose Properties.

5. Select the Sharing tab.

6. Click Share. The File Sharing dialog box opens (see Figure 7.7).

Data Access and Management

PART III

Figure 7.7: File Sharing dialog box

7. Enter the name of the user or group with whom the folder will be shared, and click Add.

   By default, the user permissions will be assigned as Read unless you change them to Read/Write.

8. Set the desired permission level.

9. Click the Share button.

   The network path to the share will be displayed.

10. Click Done.

Once a folder is shared, it becomes accessible from other network locations. The permissions on the share provide some degree of control on the level of access to the folder.

Share permissions are implemented with either an Allow or Deny option. The levels of permission are Full Control, Change, and Read.

Implement Advanced Sharing

To implement advanced sharing, follow these steps:

1. Open File Explorer.

2. Locate the desired folder.

3. Right-click the folder.

4. Choose Properties.

5. Select the Sharing tab.

6. Click the Advanced Sharing button. The Advanced Sharing dialog box will open (see Figure 7.8).

Figure 7.8: Advanced Sharing dialog box

At this point, you have the option to select the box to share the folder. One of the great features of using advanced sharing is the ability to limit the number of simultaneous users on a shared folder. By default, only 16,777,216 users can connect to this share. That seems a little high to us. Change that to a number that is appropriate for your share.

7. Click the Permissions button.

8. Click Add to include users or groups for permissions to this share.

9. Click OK to close the Permissions dialog box.

10. Click OK to close the Advanced Sharing dialog box.

You may be wondering why that extra button labeled Caching was there. In short, caching can make the share available to users when they are not actually connected to the network. Offline file caching will be discussed in more detail later in the chapter.

Data Access and Management

PART III

Resolve Permission Conflicts

When you implement shared folders on an NTFS file system, two different sets of permissions are applied to each user or group that attempts to access the folder: NTFS permissions and share permissions. If these two types of permissions are *complementary*, meaning that they are both set to allow the same level of access, there will be no real issues to address. However, if there is a difference in the level of permissions assigned, the level of access will be limited.

When resolving disparate permissions in shared NTFS folders, a couple of simple rules make this process easy to understand:

Rule 1: Deny permissions always override Allow permissions.

Rule 2: When the share and NTFS permissions are different from one another, the most restrictive permission will be applied.

Let's say you had a shared folder that had a test user who was assigned Read permissions to the share. The same test user is also assigned Write permissions to the NTFS folder. The two permissions are not complementary, so the most restrictive takes precedent. The test user would have an effective permission of Read.

Let's say that test user 2 has Full Control permission on the same share and has been denied Read access on the NTFS folder. These permissions are definitely not complementary, and the Deny permission would override Allow Full Control. The effective permission would be Deny Read.

These two simple rules will suffice to handle the vast majority of cases in which permissions between NTFS and shared folders are not complementary. Make sure you plan carefully as you assign permissions to folders in NTFS and folder shares. Beginning with Windows Server 2012, when you add users to the share level, Windows Server 2012 automatically adds the users to NTFS security as well. This will help keep your permissions consistent and avoid security permission conflicts.

Windows Server 2012 Server Manager offers a couple of new features to make working with shares even more flexible in your environment. Server Manager now provides an easy way to make file shares for the variety of uses your organization needs. In Server Manager you have the ability to easily create shares in the following five profiles:

SMB Share - Quick: The basic profile allows you to make a general purpose file share

SMB Share - Advanced: This profile will allow you to set additional properties of the share, including quotas, folder owner, and default classification.

SMB Share - Applications: This will step you through the process of creating shares for applications such as Hyper-V and other server-based applications.

NFS Share - Quick: This profile allows you to create an NFS share, which is typically used for UNIX-based computers. NFS sharing will require the Server for NFS and File Server Resource Manager role services to be installed.

NFS Share - Advanced: This profile is similar to SMB Share - Advanced, allowing similar selections for the NFS Share. NFS sharing will require the Server for NFS and File Server Resource Manager role services to be installed.

To create a share, perform the following procedure:

1. Open Server Manager.

2. Click File and Storage Services.

3. Click Shares.

4. When a screen similar to Figure 7.9 opens, notice that Server Manager provides a new way to quickly view all of the shared directories on the current server. You can also see the storage the share is currently using, as well as the quota usage for the share. You will learn more about quotas in Chapter 9, "Managing Disks and Disk Storage."

5. Click Tasks, or right-click below the current list of shares and select New Share. You will see a screen similar to Figure 7.10.

6. Complete the wizard. Based on your selections, the wizard will offer you different choices. When you are finished, click Create.

7. Verify the results and then click Close.

Data Access and Management

PART III

Figure 7.9: Server Manager File and Storage Services

Figure 7.10: Share Profile Selection

Configure Offline File Caching

In today's business world, you'll need to access information from many different locations but you won't always be connected to the network that hosts your folders and file shares. If you take your laptop with you when you leave your network, why not take the essential files that you need with you too? With offline file caching, you can do just that.

Working with offline file caching is really pretty simple. You choose the files and folders that you want to make available offline. Windows Server will automatically create a copy of each file or folder as you connect to it and store it on your computer. These files are called *offline files*. The files can be opened, modified, and saved the same way as if you were connected to your network. This means that the caching is completely transparent to the user accessing the files. If the user accessed the files by going to \\fileserver\share when connected to the network, they could also type the same path when off the network and the files would still be accessible. When you are offline, any changes that are made to these files will be stored on your local computer and then will be synchronized the next time you connect to your network.

Before you can use offline files on your server, you must enable Desktop Experience under Features in Server Manager. Without this feature enabled, offline files will not be an available option for you to enable. Offline files must be enabled before they can be used. To enable offline files, follow these steps:

1. Go to the Start screen.

2. Type **manage offline files.**

3. Click the Settings Search category.

4. Click Manage Offline Files.

5. When the Offline Files dialog box (Figure 7.11) opens, click Enable Offline Files and then click OK.

6. If you are ready to restart your server, click Yes to restart the computer.

Data Access and Management

PART III

Figure 7.11: Offline Files dialog box

Once offline files have been enabled, you can right-click any shared file or folder and select the option to make the files always available. These files will be copied to your local machine for use offline. In the case of a shared folder, you can click the Caching button to enable offline files for the share. It is also possible to make offline files available through the use of Group Policy Objects (GPOs). If you had implemented folder redirection using GPOs, for example, those redirected folders would be made available using offline files.

When you use offline files, there is a potential for multiple versions of the same file. If you have a file and are working with it offline and another user in your network makes changes to the file in its online version, there is going to be a conflict. You can resolve such conflicts using a tool called the Sync Center. You can find the Sync Center in the Control Panel. The Sync Center is responsible for more than managing conflicts. It is responsible for keeping offline files synchronized with their online counterparts each time you connect to the network.

You can also access the Sync Center through the Manage Offline Files tool. The Manage Offline Files tool has a component that will allow you to view all your offline files. This allows you to see folders, mapped network drives, and shares that you are caching for offline access.

Secure Folders and Files

Files and folders contain data. That data may be innocuous data that you use regularly and that requires little or no protection, or it might be critically sensitive data requiring extensive protection. In either case, you will need to implement a strategy to protect your sensitive data. A strategy for protecting data will include, but not be limited to, a structured design for permissions, storage, encryption, and auditing. So far, this chapter has addressed permissions. Storage will be addressed in Chapter 8, "Backing Up and Recovering Your Server," and Chapter 9, which cover backups and disk management, respectively. That leaves encryption and auditing. You must understand both.

Configure the Encrypting File System

The Encrypting File System (EFS) is a feature of Windows that you can use to encrypt files and folders on your hard drive to provide a secure format of storage. EFS is a core file encryption technology used only on NTFS volumes. An encrypted file cannot be used unless the user has access to the keys required to decrypt the file. The files do not have to be manually encrypted or decrypted each time you use them. They will open and close just like any other file. Once EFS is enabled, the encryption is transparent to the user.

Using EFS is similar to using permissions on NTFS files or folders. However, a user who gets physical access to encrypted files would still be unable to read them because they are stored in an encrypted form.

You can encrypt or decrypt files or folders by setting the encryption property attribute for the file or folder. The encryption property is an attribute that is applied much like the attributes of read-only, compressed, or hidden files or folders, as shown in Figure 7.12.

Figure 7.12: Advanced Attributes dialog box

To encrypt a file or folder, follow these steps:

1. Select the file or folder you want to encrypt.

2. Right-click the file or folder.

3. Choose Properties.

4. On the General tab, click the Advanced button.

5. Select the Encrypt Contents To Secure Data check box, and then click OK to encrypt the file.

6. On the File Properties dialog box, click OK

7. If you see an Encryption Warning dialog box, review the message and click OK to complete the process. Click Cancel if you want to stop the process.

It is important to note that the attributes of compression and encryption are mutually exclusive. You cannot do both. If a file is compressed and you want to encrypt it, you must remove the compression bit before the file can be encrypted. Likewise, if a file is encrypted and you want to compress it, you must remove the encryption bit before the file can be compressed.

When you're using EFS, be sure to consider these additional points:

- Only files and folders on NTFS volumes can be encrypted. You can use Web Distributed Authoring and Versioning (WebDAV), which also works in NTFS volumes, to transfer encrypted files and folders in their encrypted form.

- Encrypted files and folders are decrypted if you move them to a volume that is not NTFS.

- Moving unencrypted files or folders into a folder that has been encrypted will result in the encryption of the moved files or folders; however, the reverse is not true. Files or folders that are moved from an encrypted NTFS folder to an unencrypted folder will *not* automatically be decrypted. Files must be explicitly decrypted.

- Files marked with the system files attribute and files residing in the system root directory structure cannot be encrypted with EFS.

- Marking the encryption attribute of a file or folder does not prevent a user with the appropriate NTFS permissions from deleting or listing files or directories if their NTFS permissions allow those functions. Use EFS in conjunction with NTFS permissions.

- You can encrypt or decrypt files and folders on a remote computer that has been enabled for remote encryption. When you do, the data is transmitted over the network in its decrypted form. Other protocols such as Secure Sockets Layer (SSL) or Internet Protocol Security (IPsec) must be used to encrypt the traffic.

As you would expect, you can also implement EFS through the use of Group Policy. (Take a look back at Chapter 6, "Maintaining and Controlling the Centralized Desktop," if you need a Group Policy refresher.) The settings are located in `Computer Configuration\Windows Settings\ Security Settings\Public Key Policies\Encrypting File System`.

Through these settings, you can choose whether you want to allow or deny the use of EFS for your entire network. You can also choose to allow or deny the use of Elliptic Curve Cryptography (ECC) encryption. ECC allows your network to comply with Suite B encryption standards. Suite B standards meet the Advanced Encryption Standard (AES) with key sizes of 128 and 256 bits for symmetric encryption, Elliptical Curve Digital Signature Algorithm (ECDSA) for digital signatures, Elliptic Curve Diffie-Hellman (ECDH) for key agreement, and Secure Hash Algorithm (SHA-256 and SHA-384) for message digest.

EFS is a great tool to help you secure files and folders. As you implement an EFS program in your network environment, you can provide access to files and folders while maintaining very good security for those same files and folders.

But what about those system files?

Configure BitLocker Drive Encryption

In the previous section, you learned that EFS will not provide encryption to any files marked with the system attribute or files located in the system root directory. So, what do you do with them? How do you secure the system files? The answer is to use a tool called BitLocker. BitLocker was designed to encrypt the partition on which the operating system files reside. Unlike EFS, which allows the user to pick and choose which files and folders to encrypt, BitLocker encrypts entire partitions or drives. BitLocker can be used to encrypt the locally attached drives, while a tool called BitLocker To Go can be used to encrypt devices such as USB sticks that may be temporarily attached to the system. If your drive were stolen and put into another machine, the data would be inaccessible. BitLocker utilizes a hardware module on the motherboard called a Trusted Platform Module (TPM) chip. BitLocker uses it to seal the keys that are used to unlock the encrypted operating system drive. When you start your operating system, BitLocker requests the key from the TPM chip and uses it to unlock the drive. If you do not have a system that supports TPM, you can use a USB key to support the BitLocker process.

When you are using a BitLocker-encrypted drive and add new files to the drive, they are automatically encrypted. Drives (fixed or removable) can be unlocked with a password or a smart card, or you can set the drive to automatically unlock when you log on to the computer.

BitLocker can be used in conjunction with EFS. Make sure you use a strategy that maximizes the security needs of your data, while minimizing the impact on the users who will need access to that data. Security measures like BitLocker are not one-stop shops for the security of your environment. You must approach security in a layers method. While BitLocker is a fantastic security measure, after the BitLocker drive is mounted, it is decrypted. Using EFS on a BitLocker provides another layer to security.

Install and Enable BitLocker

BitLocker sounds like a good idea, but how exactly do you turn it on? First, you need to turn on the TPM chip in your system BIOS. Having hardware with a TPM chip is highly recommended for BitLocker. However, if your hardware does not have a TPM chip, you can leverage a USB key to enable and leverage BitLocker. This section will show how to use a TPM chip in your BitLocker implantation. If you have to use a USB key, or want to have an additional layer of security with a USB key, please refer to this site:

http://technet.microsoft.com/en-us/library/hh831507.aspx

Next, you need to add the BitLocker feature through Server Manager and install it:

1. Open Server Manager.

2. Select the Dashboard.

3. Click Add Roles And Features.

4. On the Welcome screen, click Next.

5. On the Installation Type screen, select Role-based or Feature-based Installation and click Next.

6. On the Server Selection screen, select the server to use for the BitLocker installation and click Next.

7. On the Server Roles screen, click Next.

8. On the Features screen, select BitLocker Drive Encryption, as shown in Figure 7.13.

Figure 7.13: Installing BitLocker Drive Encryption

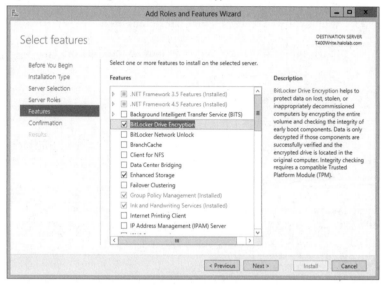

9. When prompted to add some required features (as shown in Figure 7.14), click Add Features.

Figure 7.14: Adding BitLocker required features

10. Once you are returned to the Add Features screen, click Next.

11. On the Confirmation screen, review your selection and then click Install.

12. After the installation is complete, review the results and click Close.

13. When you are ready, restart your computer.

After the computer has restarted, you can enable BitLocker.

1. Go to the Start screen.

2. Type **BitLocker**.

3. Click the Settings Search category.

4. Select Manage BitLocker, and you will see a screen similar to Figure 7.15.

Figure 7.15: Turning on the BitLocker Drive Encryption tool

5. Click Turn On BitLocker on the System drive.

Just after you add the BitLocker feature, only the system partition is enabled for BitLocker even though you may have multiple drives and partitions on your system. If you want to enable the other drives, you can select them in the BitLocker Drive Encryption screen.

6. Review the components you selected and click Next.

7. If you haven't turned on TPM in the BIOS, you will be prompted to do so now, and the process will be automated for you. Click Shutdown. (This is kind of cool.)

8. After you reboot your system, follow any on-screen prompts from the BIOS on your system to turn on TPM, and then log back on to your computer.

9. When BitLocker prompts you to encrypt the drive, click Next.

   At this point, BitLocker will ask how you want to store your recovery key (Figure 7.16). This is important! If your BitLocker drive becomes inaccessible, you are going to need this key.

TIP   Be sure to store this key on a drive other than the drive on which you are enabling BitLocker, in a location that you can easily access. We recommend a USB key or network location. The recovery key is not your typical password; it is 48 characters long.

Figure 7.16: Recovery key storage options

10. Pick the option that works best for you, and click Next.

11. Beginning with Windows Server 2012, you can choose from two different options for encrypting your drives, as shown in Figure 7.17.

    Encrypt used disk space only: the fastest option, typically used for new servers or new hard drives

    Encrypt entire drive: a slower option, but good for servers and hard drives already in use

    After you make your choice, click Next.

Figure 7.17: BitLocker encryption choices

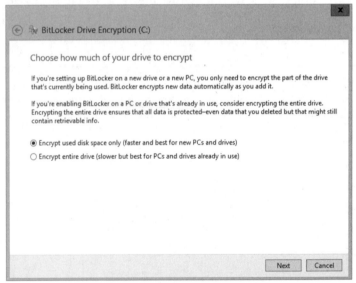

12. Select the box to run the BitLocker system check.

13. Click Continue to start encrypting. If the drive you are encrypting is the system drive, you will be prompted to restart the system to encrypt the drive and you will see a screen similar to Figure 7.18.

Figure 7.18: Begin the encryption process.

TIP Some words to the wise: Do not perform the initial BitLocker drive encryption on your key servers during peak operating hours. The initial encryption process takes time and will slow down your performance. Find a time when the servers are less busy and initialize BitLocker on them then.

---

14. When you're ready, click Restart Now to begin the process. At this point, the drive will begin its encryption process.

Once the encryption process is complete, BitLocker can be configured for other drives and partitions on your system using the BitLocker Drive Encryption tool.

Recover BitLocker

As you well know, things can go wrong with servers. What do you do if things go wrong with a server that is running BitLocker?

What if the TPM module that contains the keys necessary to start the operating system is unavailable? What if a user forgets the PIN? What if the hardware crashes on the box and you are trying to salvage the hard disk?

Luckily, there is a system for recovering BitLocker. The process relies on one very important component, the *recovery key*. When you turned on BitLocker, you were prompted for a location in which to store the BitLocker recovery key. If you have access to this key, you are well on your way to recovering the BitLocker drive. The process is simple and straightforward:

1. Boot the computer.

2. The computer will present a message indicating that it cannot locate the keys necessary to start decrypting the operating system. One of your options will be to recover BitLocker.

Data Access and Management

PART III

3. Type in the 48-digit (yes, 48 digits) recovery key.

4. The system will decrypt and start the operating system as normal.

At this point, you will need to make some decisions. If you still have the original key, you can reestablish connectivity to that key. If you do not have the original key, you will need to generate a new one by turning off BitLocker, which will decrypt the drive, and then turn BitLocker back on to create a new set of keys for the system.

Windows Server 2012 introduced a new feature to help with the recovery of BitLocker keys. Network Unlock provides an easy way to manage your BitLocker desktops in your Active Directory environment. This provides an automatic way for those managed desktops to be unlocked when they are connected to your corporate network. Network Unlock also provides a great mechanism for applying patches and updates to corporate desktops. Please refer to this article on how to enable the Network Unlock feature:

http://technet.microsoft.com/en-us/library/jj574173.aspx

Use the BitLocker To Go Tool

BitLocker To Go introduces the benefits of an encrypted partition to a removable drive. Instead of using a file encryption tool, you can use BitLocker to encrypt the contents of a removable drive. This drive could be a USB device, a memory stick, an SD card, or some other type of removable storage. The benefit of using BitLocker To Go is that you can enjoy the ease and portability of a USB storage device without worrying about the data on that device falling into the wrong hands. If someone were to steal the device, the data would be encrypted and, therefore, inaccessible.

Once you have added and enabled the BitLocker feature on your Windows Server 2012 machine, you will see the option in the BitLocker Drive Encryption tool called BitLocker To Go. If you insert a removable storage device, that device will be added to the tool as an additional drive under the BitLocker To Go section, shown in Figure 7.19.

Figure 7.19: BitLocker To Go tool

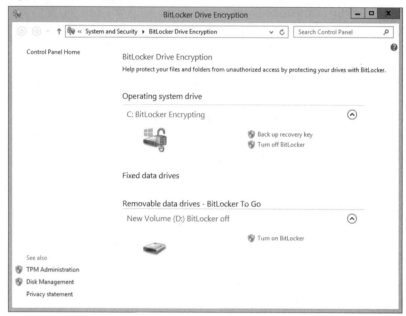

At this point, you can simply click the link to turn on BitLocker for the removable drive. The Setup tool will prompt you to start BitLocker setup for this drive.

BitLocker To Go is a little bit different from the traditional BitLocker tool in that there is no TPM chip to hold keys for BitLocker To Go. You will need to choose how you want to unlock the drive. It can be unlocked using a password that you supply during setup or through the use of a smart card and PIN.

Just as with traditional BitLocker, a recovery key is associated with BitLocker To Go. Save this file carefully to a location where you will not lose it, or better yet, print it and add it to your network log book. Remember, if the drive becomes inaccessible for whatever reason, the recovery key is your only ticket back to that data.

The drive will be encrypted in much the same way as your system drive was encrypted, albeit probably a little quicker because the size of the removable device is likely much smaller than your system drive. Once the drive is encrypted, when the user plugs the drive into a physical machine running Windows 7 or Windows Server 2012, they will be prompted for the password or smartcard PIN in order to unlock the

Data Access and Management

PART III

drive. Any files that are copied or moved to the drive will be encrypted. A BitLocker To Go Reader is available for use with Windows XP and Windows Vista systems. For older operating systems, files on the encrypted drive are not accessible and the OS will prompt you to format the drive.

BitLocker To Go provides excellent security to files and folders stored on a removable drive.

One of the cool things about BitLocker To Go is that you can use Group Policy to require BitLocker To Go in order to use thumb drives and require that the keys are stored in Active Directory.

Implement the Distributed File System

If you are trying to make data accessible, you have lots of options such as creating shared folders and using offline files. If you want to extend the availability of your files and folders, you might consider building more than one server to house the same data and then copying or replicating that data between the various servers so that it stays consistent. Replicating data to multiple servers increases data availability and gives users in remote sites fast, reliable access to files. Replication is configured via Distributed File System (DFS) namespaces. DFS namespaces allow you to group shared folders located on different servers by transparently connecting them to one or more namespaces. A *namespace* is a virtual view of shared folders in an organization. When you create a namespace, you select which shared folders to add to the namespace, design the hierarchy in which those folders appear, and determine the names that the shared folders show in the namespace. When a user views the namespace, the folders appear to reside on a single, high-capacity hard disk. Users can navigate the namespace without needing to know the server names or shared folders hosting the data.

The path to a namespace is similar to a universal naming convention (UNC) path of a shared folder, such as \\server1\shares\test. If you are familiar with UNC paths, you know that, in this example, the shared folder, Shares, and its subfolder, Test, are all hosted on the server called server1. Now, assume you want to give users a single place to locate data, but you want to host data on different servers for availability and performance purposes. To do this, you can deploy a namespace.

To build a namespace, you will need a namespace server. A namespace server hosts a namespace. The namespace server can be a member server or a domain controller.

To install DFS, you will need to add the DFS role located under File Services in Server Manager:

1. Open Server Manager.

2. Click Dashboard.

3. Choose Add Roles And Features.

4. On the Welcome screen, click Next.

5. On the Installation Type screen, select Role-based or Feature-based Installation and click Next.

6. On the Server Selection screen, select the server for DFS installation and click Next.

7. On the Server Roles screen, expand File And Storage Services, and then expand File and iSCSI Services.

8. Select DFS Namespaces and DFS Replication, add any required features for the roles to be installed, and click Next.

9. On the Features screen, click Next.

10. Review the Confirmation screen and click Install.

11. Review the Installation results and click Close.

Configure a DFS Namespace

After you install the DFS role service, you can begin the process of creating the DFS namespace and configuring the DFS root:

1. Open Server Manager.

2. Select DFS Management from the Tools menu.

3. Click New Namespace on the Actions pane.

4. Type the name of the server, or click Browse to select it from a list (see Figure 7.20) and then click Next.

Figure 7.20: Creating a new namespace

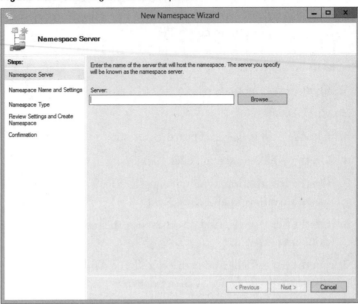

5. Type a name for the namespace. This is what users will see after the server name in the UNC path.

   You can click the Edit Settings button and set the drive location and security level of the DFS namespace. By default, all users have Read access.

6. Click Next.

At this point, you will be prompted to choose the type of namespace. You can choose either a domain-based namespace or a stand-alone namespace. The domain-based namespace begins with a domain name, and its metadata is stored in Active Directory. A domain-based namespace can be hosted on multiple namespace servers. Notice the check box for Enable Windows Server 2008 mode. This option provides additional security and increased scalability for your domain-based DFS namespaces. A stand-alone namespace is stored only on the namespace server, but it can be hosted on a server cluster. The path begins with the namespace server name. A dedicated namespace server should be used to host a namespace that contains more than 5,000 replicated folders. Figure 7.21 shows a summary of typical settings and the button you will use to create the namespace.

Figure 7.21: Reviewing the DFS settings and creating the namespace

You have just successfully created your first DFS namespace, which is called the *DFS root*. When you expand the DFS Management tool in the Server Manager and then expand Namespaces, you will see the existing namespaces. The namespace is really just the location that will be used to hold targets that will point to the location of resources located elsewhere on the network. A folder may have one or more folder targets that may be added using the Add Folder tool displayed in Figure 7.22.

Figure 7.22: Adding a new folder to DFS

This is where you start to see the real potential of DFS. If you have more than one target location that hosts shared data, you can configure multiple targets for the same folder in your DFS namespace. The namespace will route requests from users to the appropriate folder target based on the site information for that user. This way, you can maintain multiple shared folders containing the same data and maximize referrals to users using DFS namespaces. You may be wondering what happens if a user changes the contents of one of the shares? How will the other targets be updated? Not to worry, DFS has a built-in replication system called Distributed File System Replication (DFSR).

DFSR uses something called Remote Differential Compression (RDC), which replicates only the changes in files. In Windows Server 2012, DFSR can even replicate SYSVOL using RDC, resulting in a dramatic reduction in bandwidth consumption while maintaining the integrity of your folder targets.

Configure Replication Groups

Replication groups define the relationships that DFS will use to replicate data between partners in a DFS replication topology. You will choose the partnerships and the types of replication that occur between those partners.

1. Open the DFS Management tool, select Replication.

2. From the Actions pane, select New Replication Group.

3. Select the type of replication group. There are two choices:

    Multipurpose replication group: This group type allows you to control how replication occurs—from a full mesh (where all your servers replicate to each other) to your own custom topology. This option gives you the most flexible replication option, and it is the default selection.

    Replication group for data collection: This group type is useful in branch office scenarios where you want data from branch locations to be replicated to central servers. This is the preferred option for a hub-and-spoke topology, and it provides a good option for backup.

4. Click Next.

5. Type a name and a description, and select the domain for the replication group.

6. Click Next.

7. Click Add to select two or more servers to become members of the replication group.

8. Click Next. You may be prompted to start the Replication Service. An example prompt is shown in Figure 7.23. Click OK to continue the configuration.

Figure 7.23: Start DFS Replication Service.

9. Select a topology for replication.

10. Select a replication schedule. One of the coolest things about DFSR is that you can pick the amount of bandwidth that will be used by DFSR and the schedule for when the replication will occur.

11. Click Next.

12. Use the drop-down menu to select a primary member.

When you first set up replication, you must choose a primary member. Choose the member that has the most up-to-date files that you want replicated to all other members of the replication group, because the primary member's content is considered "authoritative." This means that during initial replication, the primary member's files will always win the conflict resolution that occurs when the receiving members have files that are older or newer than the same files on the primary server. After the initialization of the replicated folder, the "primary member" designation is removed. The member that was previously the primary member is then treated like any other member, and its files are no longer considered authoritative over those of other members who have completed initial replication.

Data Access and Management

PART III

13. Select the path to the folders you want to replicate.

14. Click Next.

15. Define the local path on the other servers for the folder you want to replicate on the other members of the replication group.

16. Click Next. You may see a Warning screen regarding the replicated folder. If a Warning screen appears, review the information and then click Yes to continue.

17. Review the Summary settings for the replication group, as shown in Figure 7.24, and then click Create.

Figure 7.24: Summary settings to create a replication group

18. Review the results of the wizard, and click Close.

Please keep in mind at this point that the replication will not start immediately. Based on the settings and schedule you provided during setup, the initial replication will proceed when DFSR is ready and only after the new configuration settings have been picked up by all the members of the replication group. This can take some time, depending on how your Active Directory replication occurs.

Enable Previous Versions of Files

Let's say you have been working for the past few hours modifying a file. Your boss calls and says he would like a copy of the same file you are working on but without all the current changes. If you were really lucky, you used Save As and started editing with a new file. (We know that's not very likely.) But if you had enabled previous versions, you could simply smile and say, "Sure, Boss! The file is on its way."

You can use the Previous Versions feature to allow users to access previous versions of their files and folders that they have stored on the network. The service that is working behind the scenes to make this all possible is called the Volume Shadow Copy Service. To use previous versions of files and folders, you will need to enable *shadow copies* of shared folders on the file server.

1. Open Server Manager.

2. Select Computer Management from the Tools menu.

3. In the console tree, right-click Shared Folders.

4. Go to All Tasks, and click Configure Shadow Copies.

5. Select the drive on which you want to enable shadow copies.

6. Click Enable.

   A notice (as shown in Figure 7.25) warning you of the potential problems of enabling shadow copies on servers that have high I/O loads will open. Heed the warning.

Figure 7.25: Shadow copies warning

7. Click Yes to enable shadow copies.

Now your enabled shares will maintain previous versions of files.

Restore a Previous Version

Restoring previous versions of files and folders is a pretty straightforward process:

1. Locate the file or folder you want to restore.

2. Right-click and choose Properties.

3. Click the Previous Versions tab.

4. Select the version of the file you want to restore.

    A warning message will appear about restoring a previous version of a file or folder.

5. Click Restore.

It is really important to understand this point! Restoring a previous version will delete the current version. When you restore the shadow copy, you will replace the current version with the file or folder at a previous point in time, and your changes since that point in time will be lost. To avoid losing your changes, you can choose to copy the previous version to a different location, thereby preserving your changes and allowing you to use the previous version as well.

When you are working with previous versions, you should also consider the following points:

-   If the Previous Versions tab does not appear in the Properties dialog box, shadow copies might not be enabled on that server. Remember that shadow copies are enabled on a server-by-server basis.

-   If no previous versions are listed on the Previous Versions tab, that file has not changed since the oldest copy was created. The Previous Versions tab shows only unique versions of the file.

-   When you restore a file to its existing folder, the file permissions will not change. When you copy a previous version to a new folder location, the files will inherit the permissions of the target folder.

- If you choose to restore a large folder, it will put a heavy workload on the file server and can result in previous versions being deleted. Best practice is to restore individual files instead of folders or directories.

- Previous files should not be used as a substitute for a good backup solution!

The Previous Versions feature is an excellent resource for your network. It enables users to manage basic recovery operations of shared files and folders.

Data Access and Management

PART III

8

Backing Up and Recovering Your Server

IN THIS CHAPTER, YOU WILL LEARN TO:

▷ **UNDERSTAND BACKUP AND RECOVERY** (Pages 262 – 270)
- Understand Backup and Recovery Terminology (Page 263)
- Use Backup and Recovery Tools (Page 264)

▷ **MANAGE BACKUP AND RECOVERY** (Pages 270 – 294)
- Back Up Your Server (Page 271)
- Recover Your Data (Page 282)
- Recover via Shadow Copy (Page 292)

▷ **PERFORM BACKUP AND RECOVERY WITH COMMAND TOOLS** (Pages 294 – 299)
- Use wbadmin.exe (Page 294)
- Use PowerShell (Page 297)

A ccidents happen. There are many scenarios in which data can get lost, deleted, infected, or corrupted; events can range from a user accidentally deleting a file to a hard drive failing to an operating system failing to a full disaster scenario during which Mother Nature decides to go after your data. When such scenarios occur, it is time for you to shine as the hero for your data and bring it back!

One of the most important tasks you need to perform as an administrator is backing up your server. Performing regular backups on your server is a necessity to help protect you from any number of potential problems. Backups can save you time and money, and, more important, they allow you to sleep well at night. If you have performed proper backups and are proficient in the proper procedures to restore your data, you can quickly identify the proper backup media to begin recovering data. No one wants to spend thousands of dollars to pay a recovery company to bring back data that you could retrieve yourself with the proper safety measures in place.

Backing up your data is just one part of the process. Learning recovery techniques is just as important. Understanding recovery techniques goes hand in hand with understanding backup solutions. Also, in certain situations you may be able to enable your users to help recover their own lost data. If you know your backup procedures backward and forward, you will be able to get your recovery operation under way quickly and properly.

Knowing the terminology and when and where to perform backups will allow you to perform the task of backing up and recovering your data efficiently and effectively. This will also allow you to establish proper policies and procedures to gain consistency in protecting your organization. In this chapter, you will learn the tools and terminology behind performing backups and recovery.

Understand Backup and Recovery

In this section, you will learn the terminology behind backup and recovery, as well as the many tools at your disposal to perform the tasks necessary to protect your data. The tools you will see in this chapter are all built in to your Windows Server 2012 server, so they will incur you no additional costs. In fact, not having your data protected using these simple tools can definitely have some cost consequences.

Beginning with Windows Server 2008 R2, Microsoft made several improvements to the Backup tool and provided the ability to back up specific files and folders. You can include or exclude folders or individual files. You can also exclude files based on the file types, and you can perform incremental backups of system state. Previously, you could perform a full backup of the system state only by using the `wbadmin.exe` utility. You can perform incremental backups of the system state by using the Windows Server Backup utility, the `wbadmin.exe` utility, or a built-in PowerShell cmdlet. You can also perform scheduled backups to volumes or network shares.

Windows Server 2012 has improved backup in some important areas. Hyper-V virtual machines can now be backed up individually. Prior to Windows Server 2012, virtual machines were backed up only as part of a volume. With the larger hard drives that are allowed, Windows Server 2012 now has support for larger volumes and is not limited to 2TB volumes. Lastly, Windows Server 2012 added support for Clustered Shared Volumes (CSVs). Backups of CSVs have the following limitations:

- Virtual machines hosted on CSVs cannot be added as part of backup configuration.

- Windows Server Backup must be configured on all nodes.

- Volume recovery is not supported.

- File recovery to the root of a CSV volume is not supported because security access control lists are not applicable on the CSV file service root.

Understand Backup and Recovery Terminology

When working with backup and recovery technologies in Windows Server 2012 or any Windows environment, you need to know the lingo used by the operating system. Table 8.1 defines some of the key terms you will see used throughout this chapter.

Table 8.1: Backup Terms

Term	Definition
Normal or full backup	Normal backups, sometimes known as full backups, are the slowest of the backup processes to complete. The time your backup will take is determined by how much data you are backing up. However, performing a normal backup every night and completing it during off-hours is the preferred way to protect your system. This is the default setting for Windows Server Backup.

Table 8.1: Backup Terms *(continued)*

Term	Definition
Incremental backup	Incremental backups are the fastest backup process because this type of backup tracks only the changes to your data since the last backup of any kind. Incremental backups control how your restore process will work. When you want to restore data with incremental backups, you first need to restore the latest normal backup followed by all the incremental backup sets in order. This method might impact your servers' performance.
System state	System state backups contain most, but not all the needed configuration for your system; you should always consider using this in conjunction with a full backup. The roles you currently have installed on a server will determine what components make up the system state. See the "Perform a System State Backup" section for more information about what is backed up.
Bare-metal recovery	A bare-metal recovery allows you to recover a full server environment without first installing an OS. It is based on a backed-up image you created previously. This allows you to recover a server that might otherwise have been inoperable because of any number of errors that a regular backup and recovery could not fix. Bare-metal recovery is one of your last lines of recovery to bring back a failed system.
Shadow copies	Shadow copies are point-in-time copies of data typically located on file shares. A shadow copy provides users with a self-service method of recovering files they have deleted or overwritten accidentally.
Volume Shadow Copy Service (VSS)	VSS is the master service inside Windows Server 2012 governing the majority of the backup infrastructure. It is the service that provides you with the ability to create shadow copies.

Use Backup and Recovery Tools

Three tools allow you to access the backup and recovery toolset in Windows Server 2012. You have a fully functioning GUI management tool called Windows Server Backup, you have a command-line tool called wbadmin.exe, and lastly you have PowerShell cmdlets at your disposal to perform these commands.

In addition to these tools, another valuable tool you can leverage to help protect data located in the file shares is Volume Shadow Copy Service. This tool creates point-in-time backup copies of your file on shared resources. This powerful utility gives your users the ability to protect themselves from accidentally deleting or overwriting files; it even allows them to compare versions of a file.

Install Windows Server Backup Tools on a Full Server

Before you can use any of these tools, you first need to install the tools on their respective server environments. Even though you will see the Windows Server Backup utility in the administrative tools on your Windows Server 2012 server, the feature is not installed by default; you will see a message similar to Figure 8.1 when you first try to run it.

Figure 8.1: Windows Server Backup message

To install the tools, you just need to install the built-in Windows Server 2012 feature:

1. Open Server Manager.

2. Open the Dashboard.

3. Click Add Roles And Features.

4. On the Welcome screen, click Next.

5. On the Installation Type screen, select Role-based or Feature-based Installation and click Next.

6. On the Server Selection screen, select the server where you want to install backup and click Next.

7. On the Server Roles screen, click Next.

8. On the Features screen, select Windows Server Backup, as shown in Figure 8.2.

Figure 8.2: Installing Windows Server Backup

The Windows Server Backup choice installs the GUI Management tool for your backup administration, the command-line tools, the wbadmin.exe command-line tool, and the PowerShell cmdlets.

9. Click Next.

10. Review the Confirm Installation Selections screen, and when ready, click Install to install the backup tools.

11. After the installation completes, click Close to use the tools.

Install Windows Server Backup Tools on Core Server

Windows Server Core has the same built-in backup tools and functionality as a full Windows Server 2012 server installation. Because of the nature of the Server Core installation, there is no GUI tool; however, you can install either the wbadmin.exe command-line tool or the PowerShell backup cmdlets. Just as with the Windows Server 2012 full installation, the backup tools are not installed by default.

1. Log on to your Server Core server.

2. Start a PowerShell session by typing **powershell**.

3. Type the following command and press Enter to see the current state of the backup tools (as well as other features installed on Server Core):

   ```
   Get-WindowsFeature
   ```

   You are looking for the feature called Windows Server Backup, and by default the current state will be not installed.

4. Type in the following command to install the backup tools on the Server Core server.

   ```
   Install-WindowsFeature Windows-Server-Backup
   ```

5. To verify that the tools installed properly, you can run the following command and press Enter.

   ```
   Get-WindowsFeature
   ```

   If the tools installed properly, you will see the current state of your backup tools as Enabled, and you will see a screen similar to Figure 8.3. Note the X next to Windows Server Backup.

Figure 8.3: Server Core backup tools enabled

Data Access and Management

PART III

Enable Shadow Copies

Shadow copies help protect data located in the file shares and drives of your Windows Server 2012 server. Shadow copies are point-in-time backup copies of your files on shared resources. They're enabled at the volume level. This means that when you enable this on a volume, you protect all the resources and shares residing on the volume. Although you cannot enable shadow copies for individual shares, you can recover information from individual shares when needed because the volume is protected.

When a shadow copy is created for a file, only the incremental changes are stored for the file. This means the amount of storage needed for your network could be minimal, based on how many files and changes are made to those files. The copies you create can be stored on the same volume where the data is stored. You can move the shadow copies to another volume, which will help the performance of the shadow copies and the volumes themselves. Before you enable shadow copies, you should also be aware you can have only 64 copies on the volume at one time. This will impact the schedule you choose as well, which is Monday through Friday from 7 AM to 12 PM (noon) by default. Shadow copies are run by the Volume Shadow Copy Service (VSS). When you enable shadow copies, a 100MB backup file is automatically created. Additionally, by default the maximum size used for the backups is set to 10 percent of the volume's total space. This means that if you run out of space, VSS will start deleting older versions of your shadow copies.

Allowing your users to work quickly with these volumes will save you from having to use your recovery media to help restore lost data. However, shadow copies are not a replacement for your current backup and recovery implementation. Rather, they provide a nice complement for your backup-and-recovery toolbelt.

Enabling shadow copies is just a matter of enabling the volume, and you can do this for both Windows Server 2012 full and Server Core installations.

1. Open Server Manager and select Computer Management from the Tools menu.

2. In the Computer Management tree on the left, right-click Shared Folders and select All Tasks ➢ Configure Shadow Copies. You will see a screen similar to Figure 8.4.

Figure 8.4: Enabling shadow copies

3. Select the volume that contains the shares you want enabled for shadow copies.

4. To modify the settings for shadow copies, click Settings; you will see a screen similar to Figure 8.5. The Settings screen allows you to control the storage location and schedule for the shadow copies. You can change the storage location for the shadow copies only when they are disabled on the volume. So, you want to make sure you change the location of the shadow copy storage before you enable shadow copies.

Figure 8.5: Shadow copy settings

Data Access and Management

PART III

5. After you have modified the settings, click Enable to enable shadow copies on your selected volume; you will see the warning shown in Figure 8.6.

Figure 8.6: Shadow copy warning

6. Click Yes to enable shadow copies. You can also select the Do Not Show This Message Again check box to keep from seeing the warning again.

Manage Backup and Recovery

Now that you have seen some of the tools for backups and recovery, it is time to put them to use. When you perform backups traditionally, you want to have the backups on a schedule so you are sure they occur at regular intervals. This will make finding the right media for recovery easy. Even though backup and recovery are performed separately, they are joined together in form and function. The type of backup you perform will always dictate the recovery options available to you. In reality, the backup strategy is determined by your recovery requirements and your service-level agreement with your users and business. Is it OK if a user has to wait 24 hours to recover a file? What if the user is the CEO? Is it OK to turn off a server during work hours? What if the server is mission critical to your organization? These and other key questions must be addressed when defining your policies and procedures and determining the best way to handle the needs of your organization.

Whether you choose to perform backup and recovery tasks with the GUI, the command-line tool, or the PowerShell cmdlets, you are essentially performing the same task. In this section, you will learn how to use the backup and recovery tools to perform your daily tasks. Note that to perform either backup or recovery, you do need to be a member of the Backup Operators or Administrators groups.

Back Up Your Server

After you have determined your backup strategy, it will be time to back up the server. When you back up your server, you want to make sure you schedule your backup times to minimize the impact on your network and your users. Try to schedule the backups after hours, when the system is used the least. You also want to make sure your backups complete in a timely manner; this is where knowing the difference between full and incremental backups can be valuable to you and your organization.

Configure Backup Settings

Before you perform your backup, you might need to define your backup settings. You have only a few selections to make. Specifically, you need to determine whether you want to perform a full/normal backup, an incremental backup, or a custom combination of both of these methods. To configure your server backup, perform the following steps:

1. Start Windows Server Backup by opening Server Manager and selecting Windows Server Backup from the Tools menu.

2. Click Local Backup on the left and in the right Actions pane, click Configure Performance Settings; you will see a screen similar to Figure 8.7.

Figure 8.7: Backup performance settings

Data Access and Management

PART III

The three options listed determine how the backup will be performed. Remember that the choices you make here will not be applied if you are backing up only the system state.

> *Normal Backup Performance* is the default method for Windows Server Backup, and this method performs a normal backup. All data is backed up.
> *Faster Backup Performance* performs an incremental backup for your system. Only data that has changed since the last backup is backed up.
> *Custom* allows you to choose a combination of the previous two options for your drives. For example, you could perform a full backup on your data volume but only an incremental backup on your system drive.

3. Select the setting for your system, and click OK.

Back Up Your Server

After you have installed the backup tools, it is just a matter of setting up the tasks to begin protecting your system. When you are ready to perform the backup and you know what files and folders you want to protect, you are ready to set up the backup test and schedule.

The first time you load the tool, you will see a message telling you no backup has been configured and you need to either set up a backup schedule or set up a backup once to begin protecting your system. Whether you choose to create a backup schedule or perform a backup once, the choices in the wizard are the same, with the exception of configuring the schedule:

1. Start Windows Server Backup by opening Server Manager and selecting Windows Server Backup from the Tools menu.

2. Launch the Backup Wizard. Click Local Backup on the left and, in the Actions pane on the right, select Backup Schedule to create a regular backup task, or select Backup Once if you just want to perform an immediate backup. For this set of tasks, you will see the Backup Schedule choice.

3. Review the Getting Started screen, and click Next to see a screen similar to Figure 8.8.

Figure 8.8: Configuring the backup

4. Select Full Server (Recommended) and click Next.

5. Set your schedule; the default is once a day at 9 PM. You can configure the system to perform backups multiple times a day. After you set your schedule, click Next.

6. On the Specify Destination Type screen, shown in Figure 8.9, you'll see three choices; they allow you to store your backup to a dedicated hard disk, to another volume, or to a network share. These methods provide flexibility for your backup process that did not exist in versions of Windows servers prior to Windows Server 2008 R2. If you choose to back up to another volume or shared network folder, make sure you make note of the performance costs to your additional volume or network. You will have to decide on the right balance for you and your organization. After you make your selection, click Next.

Figure 8.9: Backup destinations

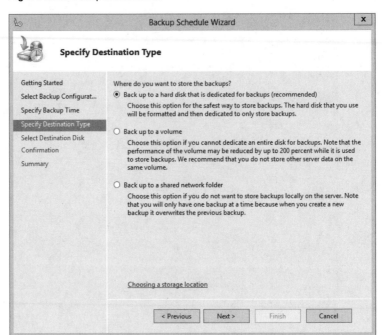

NOTE The first time you run the Backup Wizard, you may be asked to format the destination drive. When you select the default choice of Backup To Hard Disk That Is Dedicated For Backups, it will reformat the selected disk before the backup process begins. Make sure you have saved any necessary data off the drive. The format of the drive must be NTFS; also, make sure that the drive contains at least 1.5 times the free drive space when compared to the amount of data you are backing up.

7. On the Select Destination Disk page, select where you want to store your backups. For a scheduled backup, this can be another hard drive or a network share. After you make your selection, click Next.

8. If you are presented with a warning to format the disk and you are positive you want to use the selected disk, click Yes. Otherwise, click No, and select another drive to store your backup.

9. Review the Confirmation screen, and click Finish to create the scheduled task for backup and format the volume (if this is your first time using Windows Server Backup). If you chose Backup Once, you will click Backup to immediately perform the backup.

10. Review your Summary screen, and click Close.

NOTE   After you have run the Backup Wizard the first time, the next time you run it you will see a screen similar to Figure 8.10. You can use this screen to modify the existing backup or stop the backup process. You can still configure the Backup Once if you need to create new backups for different files or needs, such as bare-metal recovery.

Figure 8.10: Modifying the existing backup schedule

Back Up Specific Files

Windows Server Backup allows you to include or exclude folders or individual files from a backup. You can also exclude files based on the file types with filters. For this purpose, you will see how to modify an existing backup schedule.

1. Start Windows Server Backup by opening Server Manager and selecting Windows Server Backup from the Tools menu.

2. To launch the Backup Wizard, click Local Backup on the left. In the Actions pane on the right, select Backup Schedule.

3. On the Modify Backup Schedules screen, verify that Modify Backup is selected and click Next.

4. Select Custom, and click Next.

5. On the Select Items For Backup screen, you will see what you are currently backing up. If you want to add or remove items from the backup, click Add Items. You will see a screen similar to Figure 8.11.

Figure 8.11: Backup item selection

6. Select the items you want to add to or remove from the backup by selecting or deselecting the check boxes next to the items. If you want to select specific folders, expand the directory tree and then make your folder selections. When you are done selecting items to back up, click OK.

7. If you want to exclude certain file types from your backup, such as temporary files (*.tmp) or music files (.wmv, .mp3, and so on), click the Advanced Settings button.

8. Click Add Exclusion to select the drive or folders to which you want to apply your exclusions.

9. Select the drive you want to use. Typically, you will want your full volumes to have the exclusion applied. However, you can select individual folders or files to exclude directly. When you're done selecting your locations, click OK.

10. To exclude certain files, click in the File Type column, and type in your exclusion. You can also specify whether you want to apply the filter to the subfolders. For example, if you wanted to exclude .tmp files from your backup, type *.tmp. Your screen would look similar to Figure 8.12.

Figure 8.12: Backup exclusions

If you want to add more exclusions, click Add Exclusion and repeat the process. Likewise, if you want to remove the exclusion, you can select it and click Remove Exclusion.

11. When you are finished creating exclusions, click OK to proceed through the rest of the wizard.

12. Set or modify your schedule, and click Next.

13. Select your destination type, and click Next.

14. Select the destination disk, and click Next.

15. On the Keep or Change Backup Destinations screen, you will be presented with the choice to keep your existing backup destination, add additional destination drives, or remove destination drives. Make your selection and click Next.

16. If you choose a new destination drive, you will be presented with a warning to format the disk. If you are positive you want to use the selected disk, click Yes. Otherwise, click No and select another drive on which to store your backup.

17. Review the Confirmation screen, and click Finish to create the scheduled task for backup and format the volume (if this is your first time using Windows Server Backup). If you chose Backup Once, you will click Backup to immediately perform the backup.

18. Review your Summary screen, and click Close.

Perform a System State Backup

When you back up the system state, you are backing up a majority of the system configuration information. In Windows Server 2012, you can perform the system state backup from inside the Windows Server Backup tool; you do not have to rely solely on wbadmin.exe. If you have installed additional roles on a Windows Server 2012 server, your system state will contain more data. By default, on a server with no additional roles, the system state backup always contains the following components:

- Registry
- COM+ class registration database
- Boot files, including system files
- System files under Windows File Protection

If the system is a domain controller, in addition to the default system state data, a system state backup will include the following:

- Active Directory service
- SYSVOL directory

If you have installed clustering on the server, the system state backup data will include the clustering services information.

If you have installed a certificate services server, the system state backup data will include the certificate services database.

If you have installed IIS, the system state backup data will include the IIS metadirectory.

1. Start Windows Server Backup by opening Server Manager and selecting Windows Server from the Tools menu.

2. To launch the Backup Wizard, click Local Backup on the left. In the Actions pane on the right, select Backup Schedule to create a regular backup task, or select Backup Once if you just want to perform an immediate backup. For this set of tasks, you will see the Backup Schedule choice.

3. Review the Getting Started screen and click Next.

4. Select Custom and click Next.

5. On the Select Items For Backup screen, click Add Items.

6. Click System State, click OK and then click Next.

7. If presented with a Scheduling window, set or modify your schedule and click Next.

8. Select your destination type and click Next.

9. Select the destination disk and click Next.

10. If you are presented with a warning to format the disk and you are positive you want to use the selected disk, click Yes. Otherwise, click No and select another drive to store your backup.

11. Review the Confirmation screen, and click Finish to create the scheduled task for backup and format the volume (if this is your first time using Windows Server Backup). If you chose Backup Once, you will click Backup to immediately perform the backup.

12. Review your Summary screen and click Close.

Perform a Bare-Metal Backup

Another backup option that will provide you with a great recovery option in case of a catastrophic failure is a bare-metal backup. A bare-metal backup backs up your system state, your system volume, and the system reserved data. This backup set is unique in that you will need Windows Server 2012 installation media available during recovery. We recommend using a USB drive or another portable media to store this backup. The main reason is because to perform the restore, you need to boot the system into the Windows Recovery Environment using a Windows Server 2012 installation DVD.

Data Access and Management

PART III

1. Start Windows Server Backup by opening Server Manager, and select Windows Server Backup from the Tools menu.

2. To launch the Backup Wizard, click Local Backup on the left. In the Actions pane on the right, select Backup Schedule to create a regular backup task, or select Backup Once if you just want to perform an immediate backup. For this set of tasks, you will use the Backup Schedule choice.

3. Review the Getting Started screen and click Next.

4. Select Custom and click Next.

5. On the Select Items For Backup step, click Add Items.

6. Click Bare Metal Recovery and click OK; then click Next.

7. If presented with a Scheduling window, set or modify your schedule and click Next.

8. Select the destination type and click Next.

9. Select the destination disk and click Next.

10. If you are presented with a warning to format the disk and you are positive you want to use the selected disk, click Yes. Otherwise, click No and select another drive to store your backup.

11. Review the Confirmation screen, and click Finish to create the scheduled task for backup and format the volume (if this is your first time using Windows Server Backup). If you chose Backup Once, click Backup to immediately perform the backup.

12. Review your Summary screen and click Close.

Look at the Scheduled Tasks

Whenever you create a backup schedule, you may wonder where the task is stored. The task is stored in the Task Scheduler tool, and you can view your backup tasks there. You can also run the task directly from the Task Scheduler. The tasks in the Task Scheduler have several properties you can modify, as described in Table 8.2.

Table 8.2: Task Property Tabs

Property Tab	Definition
General	Contains the description, author, and what account will be used to run the command.

Triggers	Determines when the task will be performed. In the case of a backup, the trigger is date and time.
Actions	Determines what programs or commands will be run.
Conditions	Specifies additional options, combined with the triggers, that determine whether the task should run.
Settings	Controls additional behaviors of the task. An important setting here is Allow Task To Be Run On Demand. If you want to be able to run your tasks directly from the Task Scheduler, you have to select this setting to turn it on.
History	Shows the past history of the task when it was run.

To view the properties of the backup task, follow these steps:

1. Open Server Manager and select Task Scheduler from the Tools menu.

2. Expand the tree to view the backup tasks. Expand Task Scheduler Library ➤ Microsoft ➤ Windows, and then click Backup.

3. Double-click the task to view the properties of the backup task, and you will see a screen similar to Figure 8.13.

Figure 8.13: Backup task

Data Access and Management

PART III

You can also view the status of your backups and get more details on the main console page of the Windows Server Backup window, as shown in Figure 8.14.

Figure 8.14: Windows Server Backup

From the Main Console window, you can view the details, status, and next schedule for your backups and recovery processes. The Windows Server Backup tool will show all the events with your backups and restores in this Main Console window.

Recover Your Data

Recovering data is not a daily task. However, you should know how to recover data just in case. Fortunately, the Recovery tool is straightforward to use, presuming you have performed a proper backup. The method you use to back up your data will always determine what recovery method you will need to perform. Your desired outcome will impact what and how you need to perform your recovery.

Restore Specific Files or a Full Volume

If the time comes when you need to recover files, it is just a matter of knowing what files and what time frame you need to restore.

1. Start Windows Server Backup by opening Server Manager and selecting Windows Server Backup from the Tools menu.

2. To launch the Recovery Wizard, click Local Backup on the left and, in the Actions pane on the right, select Recover.

3. Select where you have stored the backup, and click Next. If the backup is stored locally on an internal hard drive or a connected external drive (this could be a USB 3.0 drive), verify that This Server is selected, click Next, and proceed to step 7. If the backup is stored elsewhere (for example, on a network drive), select A Backup Stored On Another Location and click Next.

4. Depending on the location of the backup, click Local Drives or Remote Shared Folder and click Next. If you specified Remote Shared Folder, you will need to type in the UNC name for the backup in the form of \\servername\sharename.

5. On the Select Backup Location screen, verify your backup set and click Next.

6. Select which server's data you want to recover, and click Next.

7. On the Select Backup Date screen, select the date and possible time for the backup set you want to recover from, and click Next.

8. On the Select Recovery Type page, select what you want to recover.

   - Select Specific Files Or Folders if you trying to recover a specific file or folder. When you select this option and click Next, you will see a screen similar to Figure 8.15. Using this option, you can expand the tree to locate and recover the file.

   - Select Volumes if you need to recover the entire volume from a backup set. When you select this option and click Next, you will be provided with a list of volumes that can be recovered.

   - Select System State if you want to recover the system state. (We'll provide more information about this option in the next section.)

Figure 8.15: Recovering a specific file

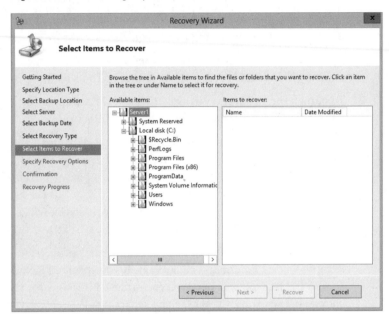

NOTE   You may also notice a choice called Applications. Depending on the applications you have installed on your server, some may be registered with Windows Server Backup. If they are registered, you can recover those applications as well. If you have installed the Hyper-V role on your Windows Server 2012 server, you might also notice a Hyper-V option. Choosing Hyper-V allows you to recover your virtual machines, virtual hard drives, and other aspects of the Hyper-V role.

9. After you make your selection for the recovery of files, click Next.

10. The Specify Recovery Options screen will look like Figure 8.16. This screen gives you a few options on how you want to recover the file. You can recover to the original location or an alternative location. You can also control whether you create a copy of the file to make sure you have both versions, overwrite any existing version of the file, or do not recover the file if one already exists. You can also bring back any security permissions on the file. After you make your selection, click Next.

Figure 8.16: Recovery options

11. Review the Confirmation screen and click Recover.

12. After the recovery process is complete, review the results and click Close.

Perform a System State Restore

When you want to recover system state data, you need to take an extra bit of precaution and planning when recovering this data. Because of the nature of the data being recovered, you have the potential to render your system unbootable. Specifically, when this restore process is started, it cannot be stopped or interrupted. If it is, this process could render your server unbootable. In other words, use caution when recovering the system state. Of course, if you are using this process, you probably are not too far from having to rebuild your server anyway.

1. Start Windows Server Backup by opening Server Manager and selecting Windows Server Backup from the Tools menu.

2. To launch the Recovery Wizard, click Local Backup on the left, and in the Actions pane on the right, select Recover.

3. Select where you have stored the backup, and click Next. If the backup is stored locally on an internal hard drive or a connected

external drive (this could be a USB 3.0 drive), verify that This Server is selected, click Next, and proceed to step 7. If the backup is stored elsewhere (for example on a network drive), select A Backup Stored On Another Location and click Next.

4. Depending on the location of the backup, click Local Drives or Remote Shared Folder and click Next. If you specified Remote Shared Folder, you will need to type in the UNC name for the backup in the form of \\servername\sharename.

5. On the Backup Location screen, verify your backup set and click Next.

6. Select the server data you want to recover, and click Next.

7. On the Select Backup Date screen, select the date and possible time for the backup set you want to recover from and click Next.

8. On the Select Recovery Type screen, select System State to recover the system state information and click Next.

9. Select the area you would like to recover your system state data to, either the original location or an alternative location. If you are trying to recover, make your selection and click Next.

10. On the Summary screen, review your selections and then click Recover.

11. After the recovery process is complete, review the results and click Close.

Recover System State Data Containing Active Directory Data

If your system state backup contains Active Directory information, you will not be able to recover the data via the Recovery Wizard unless you specify an alternative location to which to recover. If you try to recover the data in the Windows Server Backup tool, you will see an error message similar to the one shown in Figure 8.17.

Figure 8.17: System state with Active Directory data error

To perform a system state recovery of your Windows Server 2012 server containing Active Directory information, you need to boot the operating system into Directory Services Restore Mode (DSRM). Specifically, you will be performing an authoritative restore.

Before you can boot into DSRM, you need to configure your boot process:

1. Open the Start screen, type **msconfig**, and click the System configuration.

2. Click the Boot tab.

3. In the Boot Options section, select the Safe Boot check box, and select the Active Directory Repair option. Click OK. Your screen should look like Figure 8.18.

Figure 8.18: Booting into DSRM

4. Make sure you have the local administrator ID and the DSRM password and then restart the server.

5. Log on to the server with the local administrator ID and the DSRM password you created while installing the server.

6. Start Windows Server Backup by opening Server Manager and selecting Windows Server Backup from the Tools menu.

7. To launch the Recovery Wizard, in the Actions pane on the right, select Recover.

8. Select the location where you stored the backup and click Next. If the backup is stored locally on an internal hard drive or a connected external drive (this could be a USB 3.0 drive), verify that This Server is selected, click Next, and proceed to step 12. If the backup is stored elsewhere (for example, on a network drive), select A Backup Stored On Another Location and click Next.

9. Depending on the location of the backup, click Local Drives or Remote Shared Folder, and click Next. If you specified Remote Shared Folder, you will need to type in the UNC name for the backup in the form of \\servername\sharename.

10. On the Specify Backup Location screen, verify your backup set and click Next.

11. Select the server data you want to recover, and click Next.

12. On the Select Backup Date screen, select the date and possible time for the backup set from which you want to recover and click Next.

13. On the Select Recovery Type screen, select System State to recover the system state information and click Next.

14. Select Original Location, and select Perform An Authoritative Restore Of Active Directory files, as shown in Figure 8.19.

Figure 8.19: Authoritative restore

15. You will receive a warning noting that all replicated content on the server will be resynchronized and that this can cause potential latency on your server and network. Acknowledge the message by clicking OK.

16. On the Summary screen, review your selections and then click Recover.

17. You will receive another warning message stating that system state recovery cannot be paused or canceled once it has started. Click Yes to proceed with the recovery, or click No to complete the recovery at a later time.

18. After the recovery process is complete, review the results and click Close.

Before you restart the server, you need to turn off DSRM.

1. Go to the Start Screen, type `msconfig`, and click System Configuration under Apps.

2. Click the Boot tab.

3. In the Boot Options section, deselect the Safe Boot check box. Click OK.

4. Restart the server, and log on with your normal domain credentials.

5. If you see a Command Prompt window notifying you the status of your recovery, review the message and press the Enter key.

Perform a Bare-Metal Restore

Sometimes, you run into problems that a simple file restore or a system state recovery cannot fix. If you have created a bare-metal recovery image, you can recover your full server using the recovery process. This recovery process is different from recovering just files or the system state. The bare-metal recovery process is part of the Windows Recovery Environment; to get to it, you need a Windows Server 2012 DVD to boot the operating system and you need access to the drive containing the bare-metal backup. Typical USB drives can work really well in this scenario, presuming your BIOS supports USB at boot.

This recovery process is destructive; when you run a bare-metal recovery, all the data on your drives will be replaced with data from the system image. You also have the potential during the recovery process to partition and format the drives. In other words, you can restore a server completely to a previous working state.

1. Make sure your backup media is attached to the server, and insert and boot to your Windows Server 2012 DVD.

2. Select your language preferences and click Next.

3. On the Options screen, click Troubleshoot.

4. On the Advanced Options screen, click System Image Recovery.

5. On the Choose The Target Operating System For Windows Server 2012 screen, select Windows Server 2012.

6. In the Install Now window, click the Repair Your Computer option located in the lower left of the Installation window.

7. To recover from your bare-metal backup, select the Restore System Using A System Image You Created Earlier radio option, and click Next. You can also get to the image via the Recovery Tools option.

8. The system image will scan your system's drives for an image from which you to restore; you will see a screen similar to Figure 8.20. You can select the image provided (usually the most current), or you can select a different image by selecting Select A System Image. When you have the proper image selected, click Next.

Figure 8.20: Bare-metal image selection

9. On the Choose Additional Restore Options screen, you have the ability to control how your drives and partitions are handled, as shown in Figure 8.21. You can repartition and format the drives. You can also exclude drives from the partition, which is

particularly useful when you want to keep other drives intact. By clicking Advanced, you will see a window similar to Figure 8.22. This window allows you to control whether you want to restart upon completion. It will also allow you to perform a hard-disk scan to check and possibly repair errors. After you're done, select your options and click Next.

Figure 8.21: Bare-metal recovery options

10. Review your selections, and click Finish to begin the bare-metal restoration.

Figure 8.22: Advanced options

11. You will be presented with a warning reminding you that the process will replace existing data from the bare-metal backup image. If this is what you want to do, click Yes to finalize the restoration process. This process could take a long time to complete based on how much data you need to recover.

12. When the recovery is complete, you will prompted to restart, or the system will restart automatically (the default option).

Recover via Shadow Copy

Recovering files via a shadow-copied shared volume is something you can teach your users to do. It is very straightforward when it is enabled and as easy to access as right-clicking the file or folder you want to recover. To access the shadow copies on a Windows Server 2012 server, the users must be running an operating system that supports the Shadow Copy Client. Windows Vista, Windows 7, Windows 8, Windows Server 2003, Windows Server 2008, Windows Server 2008 R2, and Windows Server 2012 all have built-in support for the Shadow Copy Client. For Windows XP or Windows Server 2000 SP3 or later, you need to download the client located from this location:

http://support.microsoft.com/kb/832217

Using the Shadow Copy Client to recover a file is just a matter of knowing where the file is located and knowing how you want to recover the file. Shadow copies are great if a user has accidentally deleted a file or folder, or inadvertently overwritten a file, such as by choosing Save instead of Save As. You can work with the shadow copy files or folders just as you would any regular file or folder.

When restoring with shadow copies, you have three options, as listed in Table 8.3.

Table 8.3: Shadow Copy Options

Option	Usage
Open	Allows you to open a shadow copy of the file or folder to view any changes. You can copy and paste between the shadow copy and the original file or folder. This method is very useful when you want only to recover a file from a folder instead of the whole folder.
Copy	This will make a copy of the shadow copy and store it in a different location. This is also useful when you want to compare files or folders side by side.
Restore	This will restore the file in the original location. Be careful if you restore a folder with this method because it will restore all the contents of the folder.

You can access the shadow copies locally if the shadow copy has been enabled on your local volume or via a network share after you have opened the folder or share where you want to recover data from.

1. Right-click the file or folder you want to restore with the shadow copy. You can also right-click the whitespace of an opened folder.

2. Select Properties.

3. Click the Previous Versions tab; your screen will look similar to Figure 8.23.

Figure 8.23: Shadow copy restore

4. Select the shadow copy you want to use; they are stored by date and time.

5. Select Open, Copy, or Restore.

6. When you are finished, click OK.

NOTE If you do not see any shadow copies listed, the most likely cause is that the file has not changed. Remember, shadow copies store only the changes for the files; if no copies are listed, the file is the original.

You also need to know that shadow copy is not retroactive. The feature will not protect you until the feature is enabled. In other words, if a user makes changes to files or deletes a file prior to enabling shadow copy, the act of enabling shadow copy will not allow you to retroactively make copies of files and folders.

Perform Backup and Recovery with Command Tools

You may choose to back up and recover your systems with command-line tools. Specifically, in the case of a Windows Server 2012 Server Core installation, two options are available to you; they are the command-line tool wbadmin.exe (the command-line equivalent of the Windows Server Backup GUI) and PowerShell cmdlets.

Regardless of which tool you use, the techniques, terminology, and processes in this chapter still apply. These tools provide the same capabilities as the GUI for Windows Server Backup. Therefore, you do not need to relearn all the previously mentioned information—the command-line versions are just an alternative way to access the tools.

In this section, you will see how to back up and recover your systems with the command-line tools.

Use *wbadmin.exe*

Using the command-line tool wbadmin.exe provides you with a method to create scripts for backup as well as a method to back up servers like Server Core installations where there is no GUI present. Table 8.4 describes some of the common switches for the wbadmin.exe backup. For more information on how to use wbadmin.exe, in a command prompt, type the following command and press Enter:

```
wbadmin /?
```

Table 8.4: wbadmin.exe Common Switches

Switch	Explanation
enable backup	Allows you to modify or create a backup schedule
start backup	Performs a one-time backup
get disks	Lists the current disks available and online
start systemstatebackup	Allows you create a system state backup
start recovery	Begins the recovery process from an existing backup

wbadmin.exe Examples

Here are some examples of how you can use wbadmin.exe to perform the various tasks of backup and recovery.

Before you back up the systems, you will need to see what drives are available on the system. When you create a backup, you can use the drive letter if one exists, or you will need the disk identifier. To see what drives are available, run the following command:

    wbadmin get disks

Your output will look similar to Figure 8.24.

Figure 8.24: Available online disks

```
Volumes: <not mounted>[System Reserved],C:[]

Disk name: Hitachi HTS723232L9A360
Disk number: 1
Disk identifier: <116bb1aa-0000-0000-0000-000000000000>
Total space: 298.09 GB
Used space : 68.01 GB
Volumes: D:[New Volume]

Disk name: Seagate FreeAgent Go USB Device
Disk number: 2
Disk identifier: <a4b57300-0000-0000-0000-000000000000>
Total space: 232.88 GB
Used space : 143.10 GB
Volumes: E:[]

Disk name: Microsoft Virtual Disk
Disk number: 3
Disk identifier: <56ffea28-fdc6-4afa-ae75-0b416c3d4651>
Total space: 148.85 GB
Used space : 9.19 GB
Volumes: <not mounted>[]

C:\>
```

The following command will create a backup of the C: and D: drives, and the backup will occur daily at 4 AM and 10 PM. The backup will be stored on the disk {7caba166-0000-0000-0000-000000000000}.

```
wbadmin enable backup -addtarget:{7ca
ba166-0000-0000-0000-000000000000} -schedule:04:00,22:00
-include:c:,d:
```

If you want the backup to occur just once, the command should look like this:

```
wbadmin start backup -backuptarget:{7ca
ba166-0000-0000-0000-000000000000} -include:c:,d:
```

The following command will back up the system state to the disk {7caba166-0000-0000-0000-000000000000}:

```
wbadmin start systemstatebackup -backuptarget:{7ca
ba166-0000-0000-0000-000000000000}
```

To be able to restore items with wbadmin.exe, you need to know two things: the backup version identifier and what items are stored in the backup. Use wbadmin get versions to find out what backups you currently have available. Specifically, you are looking for the version identifier, which is formatted as a date and timestamp. Run the following command to see the items backed up on December 12, 2012, at 8:20 PM.

```
wbadmin get items -version:12/12/2012-20:20
```

The results would look similar to Figure 8.25.

Figure 8.25: wbadmin.exe get items

The following command restores the C: volume from the backup taken on December 12, 2012, at 8:20 PM:

```
wbadmin start recovery —version: 12/12/2012-20:20-itemType:Volume
-items:c:
```

Use PowerShell

Using the backup and recover cmdlets for Windows Server 2012, follow the same syntax and language used in Chapter 3, "Automating Administrative Tasks with Windows Server 2012." These cmdlets provide another tool to perform your server recovery. When you install Windows Server Backup, you will have access to the PowerShell backup and restore cmdlets as well.

Working with the PowerShell is quite a bit more complex than working with wbadmin.exe to perform backup tasks. You need to create a PowerShell script to accomplish your tasks. Although PowerShell can be more complex, it does offer some nice flexibility when performing backups. All the capabilities of PowerShell are determined by what backup policy you set. The backup policy for PowerShell is stored in an object called WBPolicy. The WBPolicy object contains all the settings for the backup, including the schedule, backup types, backup targets, and so on.

When working with PowerShell and backup, you need to understand how to set the values for the WBPolicy object. Table 8.5 describes some of the common PowerShell commands used for backup and recovery and how to set the parameters for WBPolicy. For a full listing of the PowerShell cmdlets for backing up the system, run the following cmdlet:

```
Get-Command *wb* -CommandType cmdlet
```

Table 8.5: PowerShell Backup Cmdlets

cmdlets	Explanation
Get-WBPolicy	Displays the current settings for the WBPolicy object on the server.
Set-WBPolicy	Allows you to set the parameters for the WBPolicy.
Add-WBVolume	Adds a volume to the WBPolicy object to be backed up.
Add-WBSystemState	Adds the system state to the WBPolicy object to be backed up.

Data Access and Management

PART III

Table 8.5: PowerShell Backup Cmdlets *(continued)*

cmdlets	Explanation
Set-WBSchedule	Sets the time for your daily backup schedule.
Start-WBBackup	Starts a one-time backup.
Get-WBJob	Shows the current status of a running backup job.
Start-WBFileRecovery	Starts a file recovery operation. For file recovery, you must specify the backup set from which to recover the file, along with the file that you want to recover.
Start-WBVolumeRecovery	Starts a volume recovery operation from a backup set. The operation will format the recovery target volume before recovery.

PowerShell Examples

As you can see in Table 8.5, only a few of the commands are available to work with PowerShell in Group Policy. This section gives a couple of examples to help you to get used to using PowerShell.

Back up a system with current policy settings.   The following two lines will back up your system with your current Backup Policy settings. You can create a PowerShell script to run these commands, or you can run each line separately by pressing Enter after each line:

```
$policy = Get-WBPolicy
Start-WBBackup -Policy $policy
```

The first line sets the $policy variable to the current settings in WBPolicy. The second line starts the backup process with settings currently in the WPObject object's $policy variable.

Back up volumes and system state to a specific drive.   The following script will back up the C:, D:, and system state on your system to your Z: drive. Notice you will be using a variety of the Add cmdlets to modify the value of the variable $policy, as well as variables for target and paths:

```
$policy = New-WBPolicy
$volume = Get-WBVolume -VolumePath c:
```

```
Add-WBVolume -Policy $policy -volume $volume
$volume1 = Get-WBVolume -VolumePath d:
Add-WBVolume -Policy $policy -volume $volume1
Add-WBSystemState -Policy $policy
$target = New-WBBackupTarget -VolumePath Z:
Add-WBBackuptarget -Policy $policy -target $target
Start-WBBackup -Policy $policy
```

Recover files to their original location.   This command recovers
the file at the path C:\Dir1 from the backup set named $Backup and
restores it to its original location. Because the command includes
the Force parameter, the backup proceeds without confirmation
prompts.

```
PS C:\> Start-WBFileRecovery -BackupSet $Backup
-FilePathToRecover C:\Dir1
-Recursive-FileRecoveryOption CreateCopyIfExists -Force
```

9

Managing Disks and Disk Storage

Data Access and Management

PART III

I n this chapter, you will learn some of the fundamentals of working with the hard drives on your system. You will get to see the basics of hard drive management and learn how to create, format, and delete your partitions. You will look at the tools needed to make sure your disks are running properly and are properly formatted.

You will also take a brief look at leveraging software RAID levels to provide your Windows Server 2012 server with some software-level redundancy, and you will learn what levels are supported by Windows Server 2012. You will also take a look at two additions: built-in deduplication and storage spaces.

This chapter will also introduce you to the built-in tools used to manage large hard drive arrays and volumes. You will learn that some built-in tools allow you to control how much space your users can use on your server, preventing them from taking over the hard drive space on your servers.

All of the tools in this chapter showcase Windows Server 2012 as a true storage server in your infrastructure. Windows Server 2012 storage services have become first-class citizens on the Windows Server platform and can save you time and money in your datacenters.

Understand the Basics

As you begin to manage the disks and storage for your Windows Server 2012 server, you will need to have a firm handle on the basic terminology used. We'll define some key terms and then go into how to work with storage, how to work with partitions, and how to use DiskPart.

Learn Disk Management and Storage Terminology

Before you start creating and working with the drives on your server, you need to have a solid understanding of the basic terminology associated with using the disk storage on your server. Table 9.1 defines some of the basic terms.

Table 9.1: Basic Disk Management Terminology

Term	Definition
Basic disk	These are the default disk types in a Windows environment and have been around since MS-DOS.

Dynamic disk	Dynamic disks are used to create volumes that span multiple hard drives. These drives can also be used for simple volumes.
Foreign disk	You will see a Foreign Disk option when you take a dynamic disk from one server and place it in another server.
Partitions	These define how you divide your physical drives into logical units. Partitions can be primary partitions, extended partitions, or logical drives.
Simple volume	This is the most basic type of volume and can be used to create a single logical drive and used only on one physical disk.
Spanned volume	Spanned volumes combine two or more physical disks and allow you to create a volume larger than a single physical disk on your system. The disks in a spanned volume need to be dynamic disks.
Striped volume	Striped volumes combine two or more physical disks. The data stored on these volumes is *striped*, which means when data is written to the drives, it is written alternatively in equal amounts across both physical drives. Striped volumes are faster than spanned or mirrored volumes; however, they do not provide any redundancy. The disks in a striped volume need to be dynamic disks. This is also known as RAID 0.
Mirrored volume	Mirrored volumes combine two disks that are duplicates of each other. This provides you with an identical copy of data stored on two different disks and, therefore, some protection against data loss. This is also known as RAID 1.
RAID	RAID stands for Redundant Array of Independent (or Inexpensive) Disks. RAID drives are broken into different levels and, with the exception of RAID 0, all levels of RAID offer data protection and redundancy from a failed drive or volume.
Master Boot Record (MBR)	The MBR is part of the hard drive system used by the BIOS. The MBR is used to store all the initial boot-processing information for performing the initial boot sequence of the operating system. The MBR has been around for a long time and is primarily used for smaller hard drives and is not recommended if your drive is larger than 2TB.
GUID Partition Table (GPT)	The GPT, like the MBR, is another system used by the BIOS to load the initial boot sequence of the hard drive. The GPT is a newer form of the MBR but utilizes the extensible firmware interface for working with the drives. GPT drives can have more than four partitions and are designed to work with large and small drives, particularly drives larger than 2TB. However, GPT drives are not recognized by all previous versions of Windows.

Data Access and Management

PART III

Table 9.1: Basic Disk Management Terminology *(continued)*

Term	Definition
Data deduplication	Finds duplications in your data storage and reduces the overall storage demand on your server.
Storage spaces	Allow you to combine locally connected physical drives into one virtual storage pool, where you can divide the space up any way that meets your needs.
Storage pools	These logical configurations of storage space allow you to combine physical drives into a virtual disk; once they are combined, you can provision volumes as you would any other physical drive.
Primordial pool	These are drives that are currently unallocated, normally new drives you have just added to your server. The drives in the primordial pool are generally going to be the drives you use in your storage pools.

The Resilient File System

As you work through the storage space exercises, you will have two choices to format a drive. The default, NTFS, has been the standard for Windows servers for years. NTFS should be your choice for a majority of your file system needs.

The other choice is ReFS (Resilient File System). ReFS is the new file system introduced with Windows Server 2012. It was designed to be self-tuning and correcting. Typically, it is used to handle large amounts of data that may be used by applications, such as database applications.

Although ReFS is an exciting new file system, it is designed for large volumes up to 1YB (yottabyte or one quadrillion gigabytes) and to be more resilient. Test this in your environment before you consider moving to ReFS. If you need use features like Disk Quotas or EFS, for example, then you need to stick with NTFS.

To learn more about ReFS, take a look here:

http://technet.microsoft.com/en-us/library/hh831724.aspx.

Work with Your Storage

Now that you understand the terminology involved, you need to learn how to work with your disks and create partitions. Although these may not be day-to-day activities, they will create the foundation for storing data on your server. To begin working with storage on your Windows Server 2012 server, you'll need to open the Disk Management utility for your server. This utility will work with your locally connected hard drives.

1. Open Server Manager.

2. In the Server Manager, select Computer Management from the Tools menu.

3. In Computer Management, click Disk Management, and you will see a screen similar to Figure 9.1.

Figure 9.1: Disk Management utility

Convert a Basic Disk to a Dynamic Disk

In the Disk Management tool, you will see your volumes and disks listed on your server. When you first put your physical disks on the system, they will most likely be basic disks. You can choose to leave them as basic or convert them to dynamic. You will want to convert these disks to dynamic disks when you need to create spanned and striped volumes. It is recommended that you convert these disks prior to creating partitions or placing any data on the volumes.

To convert a disk to dynamic, follow these steps:

1. Open Server Manager.

2. In the Server Manager, select Computer Management from the Tools menu.

3. In Computer Management, click Disk Management.

4. Right-click the disk you want to convert.

5. Select Convert To Dynamic Disk.

6. In the bottom window of the middle pane, select the disk or disks you want to convert and click OK.

Import a Foreign Disk

When you move a dynamic disk from one server to another server, the drive will be labeled as Foreign. You can see an example of a foreign disk in Figure 9.2.

Figure 9.2: Foreign disk

Before you can use the drive, you need to import it:

1. Open Server Manager.

2. In the Server Manager, select Computer Management from the Tools menu.

3. In Computer Management, click Disk Management.

4. In the bottom window of the middle pane, right-click the disk you want to import.

5. Select Import Foreign Disks.

6. On the Import Disk screen, select the disks you want to import and click OK.

7. In the Foreign Disk Volumes dialog box, you will see which volumes currently exist on the drive, as shown in Figure 9.3. Review the volumes and click OK.

Figure 9.3: Foreign volumes

WARNING   You might see a warning about some of your volumes losing data, as shown here. This typically occurs when you import disks and volumes that may have been part of a RAID volume. If you are ready to import and have reviewed the message about your volumes and data loss, click Yes.

Data Access and Management

PART III

Create Simple Volumes

Before you can use your disks for storage, you will generally need to create volumes on the drives for use within your server. Creating simple volumes is fairly straightforward:

1. Open Server Manager.

2. In the Server Manager, select Computer Management from the Tools menu.

3. In Computer Management, click Disk Management.

4. In the bottom window of the middle pane, right-click the unallocated space with which you want to create the volume.

5. Click New Simple Volume.

6. On the Welcome screen, review the message and click Next.

7. Select the size you want to make the volume, and click Next.

8. Select how you want to mount the volume. You can choose to mount to a drive letter, mount to a folder on an existing drive, or not assign any mount point. After you make your selection, click Next.

9. Next, you can select how to format the drive. After you make your selection, click Next. You will see a screen similar to Figure 9.4.

Figure 9.4: Format partition options

10. Review the Summary screen, and click Finish.

Create Spanned and Striped Volumes

Creating spanned and striped volumes is similar to creating simple volumes. These types of drives require your disks to be dynamic, and they require two or more drives to create. The ability to create these types of volumes is determined by the number of drives and amount of unallocated space available on your Windows Server 2012 server. When you right-click the unallocated space and the options are grayed out, as shown in Figure 9.5, you do *not* have the needed disks or unallocated space to create the volumes.

Figure 9.5: Grayed-out options

Creating a spanned volume is similar to creating a simple volume:

1. Open Server Manager.

2. In the Server Manager, select Computer Management from the Tools menu.

3. In Computer Management, click Disk Management.

4. In the bottom window of the middle pane, right-click the unallocated space of the disk where you want to create the volume.

5. Click New Spanned Volume.

6. On the Welcome screen, review the message and click Next.

7. On the Select Disks screen, as shown in Figure 9.6, select the disks you want to use for the volume, and click Add to place them in the Selected section.

Data Access and Management

PART III

Figure 9.6: Selecting disks

8. Select the size you want to make the volume, and click Next.

9. Select how you want to mount the volume. You can choose to mount to a drive letter, mount to a folder on an existing drive, or not assign any mount point. After you make your selection, click Next.

10. Next, you can select how to format the drive. After you make your selection, click Next.

11. Review the Summary screen, and click Finish.

12. You will see a Warning dialog box, as shown in Figure 9.7, if the drives need to be converted to dynamic drives for spanned volumes. After you review the warning, click Yes.

Figure 9.7: Dynamic disk conversion warning

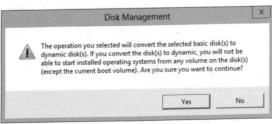

Creating a striped volume is similar to creating spanned volumes. Striping helps improve the performance of your hard drive; however, it does have one risk. If you lose one hard drive from the striped volume, you will lose all the data across the entire volume. Take a look at the "Work with RAID Volumes" section later in this chapter to learn more about RAID and how it functions.

1. Open Server Manager.

2. In the Server Manager, select Computer Management from the Tools menu.

3. In Computer Management, click Disk Management.

4. In the bottom window of the middle pane, right-click the unallocated space of the disk where you want to create the volume.

5. Click New Striped Volume.

6. On the Welcome screen, review the message and click Next.

7. On the Select Disks screen, select the disks you want to use for the striped volume (remember you have to select at least three drives), and click Add to place them in the selected option.

8. Select the size you want to make the volume, and click Next.

9. Select how you want mount the volume. You can choose to mount to a drive letter, mount a folder on an existing drive, or not assign any mount point. After you make your selection, click Next.

10. Next, you can select how to format the drive. After you make your selection, click Next.

11. Review the Summary screen and click Finish.

12. You will see a Warning dialog box, as shown in Figure 9.7, if the drives need to be converted to dynamic drives for striped volumes. After you review the warning, click Yes.

You can see an example of a striped volume in Figure 9.8.

Data Access and Management

PART III

Figure 9.8: Striped volume

NOTE When you create a striped volume, it will make the volumes on all disks the same size.

Work with Partitions

After you create the partitions, you can perform a variety of tasks on the drives, including reformatting, deleting, shrinking, and extending. All of these tasks are done in the Disk Management utility. In addition, you can perform almost all of these tasks by merely right-clicking the volumes.

Format a Partition

To prepare the drive for use, you will need to format a partition. When you format the partition, you will lose all your existing data, so make sure you have a backup of if you want to save any of the data on it.

1. Open Server Manager.

2. In the Server Manager, select Computer Management from the Tools menu.

3. In Computer Management, click Disk Management.

4. Right-click the volume you want to format.

5. Select Format.

6. Next, you can select how to format the drive. After you make your selection, click Next.

7. Review the warning about erasing the data on the volume, and click OK.

Delete a Partition

If you need to repurpose the drive or get rid of an existing partition, you can delete partitions. Remember, when you delete a partition, you will lose all your existing data, so make sure you have a backup if you want to save any of the data from it.

1. Open Server Manager.

2. In the Server Manager, select Computer Management from the Tools menu.

3. In Computer Management, click Disk Management.

4. Right-click the volume you want to delete.

5. Select Delete Volume.

6. Review the warning about erasing the data on the volume, and click Yes.

Extend a Volume

You may have an existing volume that is not large enough to meet your current needs for data storage on your server. In that case, you can extend the volume with disks that have unallocated space on them.

1. Open Server Manager.

2. In the Server Manager, select Computer Management from the Tools menu.

3. In Computer Management, click Disk Management.

4. Ii the bottom window of the middle pane, right-click the volume you want to extend.

5. Select Extend Volume.

6. On the Welcome screen, click Next.

Data Access and Management

PART III

7. On the Select Disks screen, select the disks you want to use to extend the volume, and click Add to place them in the selected option.

8. Select the size you want to make the volume. You can select a size for each disk individually. Click Next.

9. Review the Summary screen and click Finish.

10. You may see a Warning dialog box about the drives needing to be converted to dynamic drives. After you review the warning, click Yes.

Shrink an Existing Volume

If you have an existing volume you want to shrink, you can reduce the size through the Disk Management utility. After you shrink the volume, any space you removed from the volume will become unallocated space.

1. Open Server Manager.

2. In the Server Manager, select Computer Management from the Tools menu.

3. In Computer Management, click Disk Management.

4. In the bottom window of the middle pane, right-click the volume you want to shrink.

5. Select Shrink Volume.

6. You can select the size by which you want to shrink the volume; you will see a screen similar to Figure 9.9. This allows you to choose the amount you want to reduce from the volume. You cannot shrink the volume to a size that is smaller than the existing data on the volume. After you make your selection, click Shrink.

Figure 9.9: Shrinking a volume

Use *DiskPart*

You may want to use the command prompt to work with your drive partitions, and in the case of Server Core installation, you will *need* to use the command prompt to work with your partitions. Windows Server 2012 provides a command-line utility called DiskPart that you can use to work with disks and partitions. To access DiskPart, follow these steps:

1. To open a command prompt, move your mouse to the lower-left corner, right-click and select Command Prompt (Admin).

2. At the command prompt, type **diskpart** and press Enter. When you see a screen similar to Figure 9.10, the DiskPart utility will be loaded and waiting for you to enter commands.

Figure 9.10: DiskPart

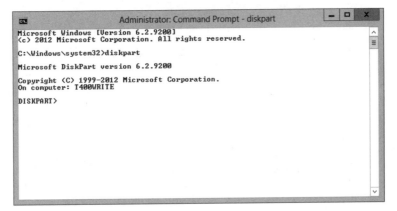

After you load DiskPart, you need to use commands to perform tasks such as creating volumes, formatting partitions, extending volumes, and so on. You can also take the commands, combine them in a script, and then use DiskPart to process the commands in the file. For example, typing **diskpart /s c:\diskscript.txt** will run DiskPart with the commands listed in diskscript.txt.

Table 9.2 describes some of the common commands used in DiskPart.

Data Access and Management

PART III

Table 9.2: DiskPart Switches

Switch	Description
select	This allows you to select the disk, partition, or volume. Using the select command allows you to access the information about the selected object with the detail or list command. Before you can use the detail or list commands, you need to use the select command to set the object with which you want to work.
detail	This displays detailed information about the object you have currently selected.
list	This displays existing information about your server's storage; you can list the disk, volume, or partitions.
create	This allows you to create volumes and partitions.
format	This allows you to format the partitions. This command's true power comes from using it in a script.
Extend	This allows you to use the command prompt to extend an existing volume.
Shrink	This allows you to reduce the size of the volume.
Delete	This can be used to delete a disk, partition, or volume.

NOTE   When you are working with disks and using the select command to target disks on your system, it is important to note how the drives are numbered. Drives are numbered beginning with 0. That means the first drive detected by your system in your system is drive 0. So, if you wanted to use the select command to select the first disk, the command would look as follows:

```
select disk 0
```

DiskPart Script Examples

Here are some examples of basic scripts you can run with DiskPart to help you see how you can utilize this powerful command. You can create simple script files using Notepad. If you have created the script file, you can type `diskpart /s <path and name of the script file>`.

Get detailed information.   The following script will select and list the partitions of disk 1 and output detailed information about partition 1:

```
select disk 1
list partition
select partition 1
detail partition
```

Create a new volume.   The following script will convert disk 2 to dynamic, format the disk with NTFS, create a new volume that's 1GB, assign a drive letter of G, and add a label of "New DiskPart Drive":

```
select disk 2
convert dynamic
create volume simple size=1000 disk=2
assign letter g
select volume g
format FS=NTFS label="New DiskPart Drive" quick
```

Create a mirrored volume.   The following script will convert disk 2 and disk 3 to dynamic, create a mirrored volume of 2GB, assign a drive letter of M, format the new mirrored volume with NTFS, and add a label of "New Mirrored Drive":

```
select disk 2
convert dynamic
select disk 3
convert dynamic
create volume mirror size=2000 disk=2,3
assign letter m
select volume m
format FS=NTFS label="New Mirrored Drive" quick
```

As you can see, `DiskPart` is extremely powerful, and it provides a great tool for scripting your disk management tasks.

Data Access and Management

PART III

Work with RAID Volumes

A Redundant Array of Independent Disks (RAID) is a special type of configuration that provides you with redundancy on your drives or volumes. RAID is designed to provide protection from failures of the drives on your server. RAID does not replace the need to perform regular backups of your systems; it offers an additional level of protection to your system and is designed to work in conjunction with regular backups. In most cases, RAID will tolerate a loss of one hard drive, meaning you will not lose any data; however, the performance of the RAID volume is reduced until you replace the failed drive. RAID is designed not only to help protect your data but also to help improve the performance of the overall drive system. RAID can be implemented via either hardware or software. In the next section, you will see how Windows Server 2012 implements RAID at the software level.

Understand RAID Levels

Essentially, RAID volumes (commonly called *arrays*) create duplicates of the data and spread the data over the drives in the volume. In the case of a RAID mirror, the data is completely duplicated in a one-to-one fashion across two drives. However, in other versions of RAID, a concept called a *parity bit* is introduced. One of the keys to understanding how RAID works is knowing how the parity bit works. The parity bit is the copy of the data; however, the parity is spread evenly across the drives.

When you begin to work with RAID, you need to know what the implications are for the chosen level of RAID for your server. Windows Server 2012 supports only RAID 0, RAID 1, and RAID 5 at the software level. Several of the more common RAID levels are listed in Table 9.3.

Table 9.3: RAID Levels

RAID Level	Description
RAID 0	RAID 0 is commonly known as *striping*. This is the only level of RAID that does not provide any protection from a failed volume. That means if you lose one drive, you will lose all of the data across your volumes. Striping is designed to provide improved drive performance.
RAID 1	RAID 1 is commonly known as *mirroring*. RAID 1 uses only two drives. As you write to one drive, a duplicate copy is written to the second drive at the same time. If you lose one drive in the mirror, the second drive contains the backup, and you will not lose any data unless you lose the second drive. This is also the slowest version of RAID.
RAID 5	RAID 5, commonly known as *striping with parity*, is a combination of performance and redundancy. RAID 5 requires three (or more) drives or volumes and provides protection if one of the drives fails. RAID 5 spreads the data and the parity (copy of the data) evenly across all three drives. If a RAID 5 volume loses a drive, the overall performance of the drive will be reduced until you replace the drive. Additionally, RAID 5 may cause a performance impact for your memory and I/O. This will occur with all writes, since the parity bit must be calculated and then written.
RAID 6	RAID 6 is commonly known as *striping with dual parity*. It is nearly identical to RAID 5, but it creates an additional copy of the parity information. This provides you with the additional ability to lose up to two drives without losing your data.
RAID 10	RAID 10, sometimes referred to as RAID 1+0, is a combination of striping and mirroring. RAID 10 is essentially a striped mirror, which offers a nice hardware-level version of RAID with performance and mirroring.

Say, for example, you create a RAID 5 volume with three hard drives of 100GB each. Your total available hard drive space for the volume would be 200GB. The reduced space is because of the parity bit, which is the copy of the data. When your data is written to this volume, it will be spread evenly across the drives, and during the write, a parity bit will be written to help maintain the copy of the data in case a drive is lost.

Figure 9.11 shows an example of a RAID 5 volume. Additionally, if you look at Figure 9.12, you will see the drive and how it appears in the file explorer. Note that the drive is only about 100GB even though three 50GB volumes were used to create the RAID 5 volume.

Figure 9.11: RAID 5 volume

Figure 9.12: RAID 5 drive properties

Implement RAID

The number of drives or volumes you have available to you will determine what level of RAID you can implement. In this section, you will see how to create a RAID 1 volume with two drives and a RAID 5 volume with three drives in the Windows Server 2012 software. If you want to use a hardware solution to create RAID 5, please consult the manufacturer of your system.

Create a RAID 1 or Mirrored Volume

Creating a mirrored volume is similar to creating spanned and striped volumes. Additionally, as with striped volumes, the partitions on the mirrored disks will be the same size. Figure 9.13 shows an example of a mirrored volume.

Figure 9.13: Mirrored volume

1. Open Server Manager.

2. In the Server Manager, select Computer Management from the Tools menu.

3. In Computer Management, click Disk Management.

4. In the bottom window of the middle pane, right-click the unallocated space of the disk where you want to create the volume.

5. Click New Mirrored Volume.

6. On the Welcome screen, review the message, and click Next.

7. On the Select Disks screen, select the disks you want to use for the mirrored volume, and click Add to place them in the selected option.

8. Select the size you want to make the volume, and click Next.

9. Select how you want mount the volume. You can mount to a drive letter, mount a folder on an existing drive, or not assign any mount point. After you make your selection, click Next.

10. Next, you can select how to format the drive. After you make your selection, click Next.

11. Review the Summary screen and click Finish.

12. You will see a Warning dialog box if the drives need to be converted to dynamic drives for mirrored volumes. After you review the warning, click Yes.

Repair a Mirrored Volume

If you lose a hard drive in a mirror, the mirror has failed redundancy. You will need to replace the failed drive, remove the existing mirror, and then re-create the mirror.

1. Open Server Manager.

2. In the Server Manager, select Computer Management from the Tools menu.

3. In Computer Management, click Disk Management.

4. In the bottom window of the middle pane, right-click the half of the mirror that is still working.

5. Select Remove Mirror; you will a screen similar to Figure 9.14.

Figure 9.14: Removing a mirror

6. Select the drive that failed and click Remove Mirror. When you remove the mirror for the failed drive, this will remove the mirror. Then you are ready to re-create the mirror.

7. To re-create the mirror, right-click the drive and select Add Mirror.

8. In the Add Mirror dialog box, select the new volume on which you want to create the mirror.

9. A Warning dialog box will appear if the drives need to be converted to dynamic drives for mirrored volumes. After you review the warning, click Yes.

10. The drive status will appear as Synching. When the drive has completed the sync, you will see a status of Healthy.

Break a Mirror

You may choose to stop using an existing mirror. Maybe you want to choose a different RAID level or need to repurpose one of your disks for additional storage. You can at any time break your mirror and do not need to worry about seven years' bad luck. Also, unlike when a real mirror breaks, you will not lose any data. In fact, you will have two copies of the data on two separate volumes.

1. Open Server Manager.

2. In the Server Manager, click Tools and select Computer Management.

Data Access and Management

PART III

3. In Computer Management, click Disk Management.

4. Right-click one of the mirrored volumes in the bottom window of the middle pane in the mirror.

5. Select Break Mirrored Volume.

6. Review the warning about removing the fault tolerance from the drive. Remember, you will not lose data, just the redundancy of the mirror. Click Yes to break the mirror.

Create a RAID 5 or Striped Volume with Parity

After you have determined which disks you are going to use for your RAID 5 volume, you will use Disk Management to create the RAID 5 volume:

1. Open Server Manager.

2. In the Server Manager, select Computer Management from the Tools menu.

3. In Computer Management, click Disk Management.

4. In the bottom window of the middle pane, right-click the unallocated space where you want to create the volume.

5. Click New RAID-5 Volume.

6. On the Welcome screen, review the message, and click Next.

7. On the Select Disks screen, select the disks you want to use for the RAID 5 volume, and click Add to place them in the selected option. Remember, you need at least three drives.

8. Select the amount of space to allocate on each disk selected, and click Next.

9. Select how you want mount the volume. You can mount to a drive letter, mount a folder on an existing drive, or not assign any mount point. After you make your selection, click Next.

10. Next, you can select how to format the drive. After you make your selection, click Next.

11. Review the Summary screen and click Finish.

12. You will see a Warning dialog box if the drives need to be converted to dynamic drives for striped volumes. After you review the warning, click Yes.

Repair a RAID 5 Volume

If you lose a hard drive in a RAID 5 volume, you will need to repair the volume. When you are working with Disk Management and see a screen similar to Figure 9.15, with the words *failed redundancy*, one of your hard drives may have failed. To fix the RAID 5 volume, you need to replace the failed drive and then use Disk Management to repair the volume and reestablish redundancy.

Figure 9.15: RAID 5 failure

1. Open Server Manager.

2. In the Server Manager, select Computer Management from the Tools menu.

3. In Computer Management, click Disk Management.

4. Right-click one of the volumes in the bottom window of the middle pane, in the existing RAID 5 set.

5. Click Repair Volume.

6. You will see a screen similar to Figure 9.16, asking you which disk you want to use to repair the RAID 5 volume. Select the new hard drive and click OK.

Data Access and Management

PART III

Figure 9.16: Repairing RAID 5

7. You will see a Warning dialog box if the drives need to be converted to dynamic drives for striped volumes. After you review the warning, click Yes.

Your drives will begin the process of resyncing. This process could take several minutes. During the resync process, you will see a screen similar to Figure 9.17.

Figure 9.17: Resynching RAID 5

Manage Disk Storage

One of the keys to working with drive storage is being able to manage how your storage is being used and how the data is being stored on the drives. With Windows Server 2012, you have the ability to create storage *quotas* for your drives. The quotas allow you to limit how much space users can use. In Chapter 5, "Directory Management and Replication," you saw a little bit about the File Resource Manager. In this section, you will learn how to enable and manage storage quotas that are natively part of the Windows Server 2012 disks.

Manage Disk Storage Quotas

Managing storage quotas is simply a matter of enabling quota management on the volumes you want to manage. Then, after enabling the management of the volumes, you can set a quota for everyone using the volume, or you can set individual entries for users or groups through the Quota Management utility. Normally, you will want to enable quotas on the drive before you enable access to your users. Before you can work with disk quotas, you need to enable them on the drives. You can enable them by accessing the properties for the drive or volume you want to manage. You can access the properties for the drive either through Windows Explorer or through Disk Management. For the steps you see here, you'll use Disk Management:

1. Open Server Manager.

2. In the Server Manager, select Computer Management from the Tools menu.

3. In Computer Management, click Disk Management.

4. Right-click the volume where you want to enable quotas, and click Properties.

5. Click the Quota tab. You will see a screen similar to Figure 9.18.

Figure 9.18: Quota properties

6. Click Enable Quota Management to turn on quotas.

7. Click OK to close the Properties window; you will see a screen similar to Figure 9.19, which tells you the drive will be scanned to verify and update current storage statistics. Click OK to turn on quotas.

Figure 9.19: Quota initial scan

If you want to turn off quotas, simply reverse the process you used to turn on the quota system.

After you enable quotas, you can choose the amount of space all the users are limited to on your server. You can also choose when they receive a warning—when quota limits are approached or when quotas are about be enforced. You can also enable individual quota entries for users or groups. This provides you with a tool to allow exceptions for certain users or groups. You can create exceptions that are less than your set default or exceptions exceeding your default. By default, the Administrators group does not have quotas applied to it.

1. After you have enabled quotas on the volumes, you will need to set defaults for all your users. Set the defaults by modifying the select default disk space and warning levels for your users. Figure 9.20 shows a quota limit of 100MB with a warning given to the user at 90KB of usage space. Always set the warning to be less than the limit. By default, this quota applies to all of your users.

Figure 9.20: Disk quota limit

2. If you want to enable individual entries on the Quota tab, click the Quota Entries button.

3. Click the New Quota Entry button, which looks like a blank piece of paper.

4. Type in your users or groups, or click the Advanced button to search. This process is similar to working with users and groups. When you're done adding users, click OK; you will see a screen similar to Figure 9.21.

Figure 9.21: Quota entry

5. Modify the limits for the user or group, and when you are finished, click OK.

6. When you are done adding entries, close the window to return to the Quota Management screen.

7. Click OK to close the volume's properties when you are finished.

After you have enabled quota management and added your quota entries, you have a choice to make. By default the quotas are *soft*, or unenforced, quotas, which means users can exceed the limits you have set. If you want to keep the soft quota, you should also enable logging by selecting the logging options on the Quota tab, as shown in Figure 9.22. This will allow you to track events in Event Viewer when your users receive warnings or exceed the limits.

Figure 9.22: Quota logging

However, if you want to enforce your quotas, select the Deny Disk Space To Users Exceeding Quota Limit box on the Quota tab. This will ensure users will not exceed the amount of space you have granted them. Also, when you enforce the quota, your users will see the visual notifications for warnings and when they exceed the limit. In Figure 9.23, you can see an example of a user who has exceeded the limit.

Figure 9.23: Enforced quota

Work with Data Deduplication

Simply put, data *deduplication* allows you to store more data while using less physical space. In prior versions of Windows Server, there were some mechanisms (single instance storage or NTFS compression) that offered similar benefits, but they were not nearly as efficient as Windows Server 2012 data deduplication. Data deduplication works at the block level on the physical disk while maintaining reliability and data integrity. Windows Server 2012 data deduplication has been built to handle several large volumes simultaneously without impacting the performance of other server workloads.

To use data deduplication, you must first install it, then enable it on the volume, and then lastly configure it. You can install data deduplication either in the Add Roles and Features in Server Manager, as shown in Figure 9.24, or in PowerShell. PowerShell provides a quicker alternative; using PowerShell, you can both install this powerful feature and enable it.

Data Access and Management

PART III

Figure 9.24: Data deduplication

In this section, you will see how PowerShell allows you to install and enable data deduplication. To install data deduplication:

1. Open Server Manager.

2. In the Server Manager, select Windows PowerShell from the Tools menu.

3. In PowerShell, type the following command and press Enter to install data deduplication.

   ```
   Get-WindowsFeature *Deduplication* | Install-WindowsFeature
   ```

When the installation is complete, you will see a screen similar to Figure 9.25.

Figure 9.25: Data deduplication Installed

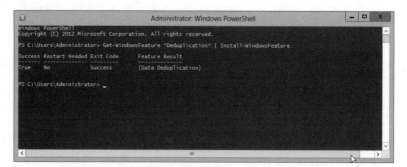

After you install data deduplication, you need to enable it on the volume or volumes you want to deduplicate. The following PowerShell command will enable data deduplication on the E: volume:

```
Enable-DedupVolume e:
```

After you enable data deduplication, you can view the status with the following PowerShell command. This example will check the status on the E: volume:

```
Get-DedupStatus e:
```

After you run the command, you will see a screen similar to Figure 9.26.

Figure 9.26: Enabling data deduplication

Even though you have enabled data deduplication on the volume, you still need to configure it. You can do this in Server Manager.

1. Open Server Manager.

2. Click File and Storage Services.

3. Click Disks, and then select the disk that has the volume where you enabled data deduplication.

4. In Volumes, select your drive.

5. Right-click the drive, and then click Configure Data Deduplication. On the Deduplication Settings page, you can configure the schedule, file exclusions, and folder exclusions. You will see a screen similar to Figure 9.27.

Figure 9.27: Data deduplication settings

6. After you configure your settings, click OK.

Data deduplication will run in in the background at its next scheduled increment, so you may not see the results immediately. You can also manually force data deduplication in PowerShell; the process can take some time. How long it will take depends on the drive size and amount of data currently on the drive. The following PowerShell example will run data deduplication on the D: drive:

```
Start-DedupJob -Type Optimization -Volume d:
```

To check the status of data deduplication, you can run the Get-Dedupjob command. A screen similar to Figure 9.28 will show the progress. After data deduplication has occurred, you can view the effectiveness of data deduplication in Server Manager.

Figure 9.28: Data deduplication job status

1. Open Server Manager.

2. Click File and Storage Services.

3. Click Volumes, and you will see a screen similar to Figure 9.29, where you can see the deduplication status of the volumes you have enabled. In Figure 9.29 you can see a deduplication rate of 64 percent and a savings of nearly 47GB.

Figure 9.29: Server Manager Data deduplication status

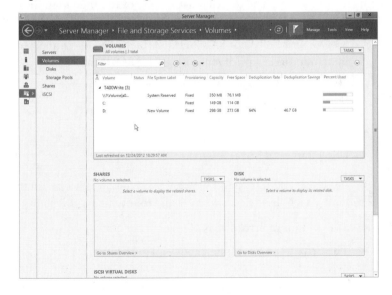

Work with Storage Spaces

Storage spaces are designed to combine your locally attached storage drives into a drive you can provision like any other volume. Storage spaces provide an easy-to-manage, highly cost-effective alternative to storage area networks (SANs). They leverage a new functionality in Windows Server 2012 called storage pools. *Storage pools* combine physical drives into a virtual disk, so you can provision volumes just as with any other physical drive. In this section, you will see how to configure and work with a storage space.

Understand Storage Spaces

The overall process to set up storage spaces is as follows:

- Create a storage pool.
- Create a virtual disk.
- Create volumes.

All drives in the pool need to meet some requirements. Based on your desired use for the storage space, you may have some additional requirements for the drives. The drives must be one of the following drive types:

- SATA (Serial ATA) or SAS (Serial Attached SCSI) connected disks in an optional just-a-bunch-of-disks (JBOD) enclosure
- SCSI (Small Computer System Interface)
- iSCSI (Internet Small Computer System Interface)
- SAS (Serial Attached SCSI)
- USB (Universal Serial Bus)

Although you could mix and match drive types, it is not recommended. Additionally, each drive needs to meet the following requirements:

- The minimum drive size is 10GB.
- The drive must be empty (raw)—no partition data can exist on the drive.

- The drive cannot be assigned to any other pool. (The primordial pool consists of physical disks that are not assigned to any existing storage pool.)

Storage spaces are supported with clustering services, but clustering adds some restrictions on the type of the drive you can use. See Table 9.4 for more details.

Table 9.4: Storage Space Requirements

Drive Type	Stand-Alone File Servers	Clustered File Servers
SATA	Supported	
SCSI	Supported	
iSCSI	Supported	Supported
SAS	Supported	Supported
USB	Supported	

When you create storage pools, you can configure data redundancy to meet your needs. The data redundancy options are listed and described in Table 9.5.

Table 9.5: Data Redundancy Options for Storage Spaces

Redundancy Type	Description
Simple	■ Data is striped across physical disks. ■ Maximizes capacity. ■ Increases throughput.
Mirror	■ Data is duplicated on two or three physical disks. ■ Increases reliability. ■ Reduces capacity by 50 to 66 percent.
Parity	■ Data and parity information are striped across physical disks. ■ Increases reliability. ■ Reduces capacity by 13 to 33 percent.

Data Access and Management

PART III

Create and Configure Storage Spaces

After you have physically attached the drives to your Windows Server 2012 server, you can create your storage space.

1. Open Server Manager.

2. Click File and Storage Services.

3. Click Storage Pools. You will see a screen similar to Figure 9.30. Notice the primordial disks under physical disks. These are the disks you will use to create the storage pool.

Figure 9.30: Primordial disks

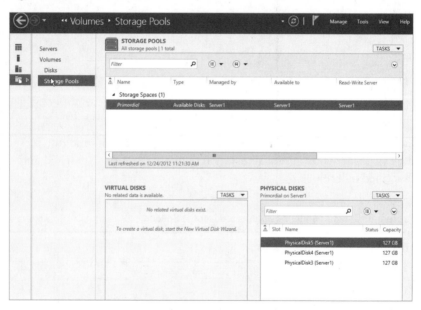

4. Under Storage Pools, click Tasks and then click New Storage Pool.

5. Review the Welcome screen, and then Click Next.

6. Provide a name and description for your storage pool, and then click Next. You will see a screen similar to Figure 9.31.

Figure 9.31: Selecting disks

7. On the Select Drives screen, select the drives you want to add to the pool. Storage pools also provide an option for you to configure a hot spare. If your physical drives support hot spare, select this option. (Contact your drive manufacturer to verify that your drives support hot spare.) After you select the drives you want to include in the pool, click Next.

8. Review the Summary screen and click Create.

9. After the storage pool is created, you will see a screen similar to Figure 9.32. Review the information and then click Close.

Figure 9.32: Created storage pool

After you create the storage pool, you will need to create a virtual disk and provision it to use a storage pool. In Windows Server 2012, you have a new option to provision your drives: Thin Provisioning. *Thin provisioning* offers you just-in-time allocations for your physical drive space. This allows your drive to be used efficiently. When you thin provision a drive, the drive will also have the trim functionality. *Trim* provides the ability to reclaim storage that is no longer needed. This provides Windows Server 2012 the ability to fully leverage your storage.

1. In the Storage Spaces screen, click the pool where you want to create a virtual disk. Then in Virtual Disks, click Tasks and select New Virtual Disk.

2. Review the Welcome screen and click Next.

3. Verify you have the correct storage pool selected, and click Next.

4. Provide a name and description for your virtual disk, and then click Next. You will see a screen similar to Figure 9.33.

Figure 9.33: Storage layout

5. In the Storage Layout pane, select how you want to configure your storage and then click Next. You will see a screen similar to Figure 9.34.

Figure 9.34: Virtual disk provisioning

6. On the Provisioning screen, choose Fixed (thick) or Thin provisioning and click Next.

7. In the Size screen, enter the size of the virtual disk you want to create and then click Next.

8. Review the Summary screen and click Create. The operation's progress will be reported a screen similar to Figure 9.35.

Figure 9.35: Virtual disk configured

9. Review the Summary screen; also note the check box (selected by default). Create a volume when this wizard closes. After you review the screen and click Close, the New Volume wizard will launch by default.

Before you can use the virtual disk created with the storage pool, you must create a volume on the storage pool. The New Volume Wizard should have launched after you created the virtual disk. If it did not, go the Disks section in your File and Storage Services. Then, in Volumes, click Tasks and select New Virtual Disk.

1. In the New Volume Wizard, review the Welcome screen and click Next.

2. In the Select Disk screen, select the virtual disk on which you want to create a volume and click Next.

3. Configure the volume size and click Next.

4. Assign a drive letter to the volume and click Next.

5. Configure the file system settings and click Next.

6. Review the Confirmation screen (your screen will look similar to Figure 9.36) and click Create.

Figure 9.36: Volume Creation summary

7. Review the results and click Close.

To view your newly created volume, you can open the file explorer and browse to your computer. You will see a screen similar to Figure 9.37. Notice that the storage pool appears as a single drive on the system, even though under the hood Windows Server 2012 combined multiple physical drives into one virtual drive.

Figure 9.37: Newly created drive

PART IV

Network Configuration and Communication

IN THIS PART ▶

Network Configuration
and Communication

PART IV

10

Maintaining Your Web Server

IN THIS CHAPTER, YOU WILL LEARN TO:

Network Configuration
and Communication

PART IV

I n this chapter, you will learn how to work with Internet Information Services (IIS). The IIS server role gives an environment the ability to have web services for both internal- and external-facing websites. IIS also provides several other key components that you will see in this chapter. IIS in Windows Server 2012 is a new version, labeled IIS 8.

In addition, IIS has several key improvements to assist administrators; it now includes PowerShell modules and supports the ability to install IIS on Windows Server 2012 Server Core. You will learn some of the key features for application support for IIS, including support for PHP applications. You will also take a look at installing IIS on a server.

Install Internet Information Services

In this section, you will learn how to install Internet Information Services. You will see how to install IIS on a full Windows Server 2012 installation and on a Windows Server 2012 Server Core installation. Being able to install IIS on Windows Server 2012 Server Core significantly benefits your IIS infrastructure without the operating overhead of the full graphical installation of Windows Server 2012. The ability to install IIS on Windows Server 2012 Server Core is available because of the .NET application framework provided by Server Core. You will also get a brief overview of the various components IIS can provide to your environment.

Understand Internet Information Services Role Services

When you install IIS on your server, you will see a screen displaying the role services you can choose to install, as shown in Figure 10.1. Understanding which components you need to install will help you support your web server requirements and any needed web applications. Prior to installing IIS, you need to talk with your web developers to make sure you provide the proper level of support for their applications.

Figure 10.1: IIS role services

The role services are divided into three main categories:

Web Server: This category contains all the components for your websites from basic HTML websites to complex web applications. This is the main role of an IIS server, and it has several components and capabilities to provide the web infrastructure your environment will need.

Management Tools: This category provides the tools necessary to manage and administer your web servers. You will also be able to select management tools for previous versions of IIS.

FTP Server: This category allows you to install and set up a basic FTP server for your infrastructure.

The Web Server role service is broken into five major sections.

Common HTTP Features   The first component is Common HTTP Features, which provides a web server with basic functionality. Primarily basic and static HTML pages are provided by these features, as described in Table 10.1.

Table 10.1: Common HTTP Features

HTTP Feature	Description
Static Content	This provides the support needed for HTML pages and graphics and provides the basic level of functionality for your IIS server. This feature is installed by default.
Default Document	This provides the web server with the ability to offer users of your website a default document when they reference your site without a specific file request. Essentially, the default document is the home page for your web server. This feature is installed by default.
Directory Browsing	This allows your users, if they have the proper permissions, to browse the directory for the contents on your web server. This feature is installed by default.
HTTP Errors	This provides the customizable error messages that users of your website will see. For example, when you see an error message like "Error 403: Access Denied/Forbidden," this is the service that provides the error message. This feature is installed by default.
HTTP Redirection	This provides the ability to redirect users of your websites to a different location. This is great to use when you want to send users to a different URL than what they typed. This is useful when you want or need to rename or change your domain for your website.
WebDAV Publishing	Web Distributed Authoring and Versioning (WebDAV) provides the needed capability to allow files to be published via HTTP to your web server. This is commonly used by web applications. Outlook Web Access is an example of an application requiring WebDAV.

Application Development   The second category is Application Development. This unlocks the true power of a web server by providing the web server with the necessary infrastructure to support web applications and in general extend the functionality of IIS. This component allows you to support the many different programming languages developers can use to write web applications. It is vital that you understand how these components are installed and configured. However, you may be wondering which of the components, listed in Table 10.2, you need to install. This is an important question, and generally speaking, your web developers can help you make the proper decision to support the applications they are programming. It is good to take some time and chat with the developers, so you can install the proper components. By default, none of the Application Development components are installed.

Table 10.2: Application Development Components

Component	Description
ASP.NET	ASP.NET is an object-oriented programming environment. Installing this component allows your web server to support sites built using managed code via the ASP.NET framework. If you install this component, you also need to install ISAPI Filters, ISAPI Extensions, and .NET Extensibility to properly support this environment.
.NET Extensibility	This allows your developers to change, add, and extend your web servers. This component provides the necessary framework to support ASP.NET.
ASP	Active Server Pages (ASP) is a scripting environment commonly used to build websites. ASP provides support for VBScript and JScript. This is primarily used for older application support, and your developers may be using ASP.NET for any new projects. Installing ASP requires that you install ISAPI Extensions.
CGI	Common Gateway Interface (CGI) is another scripting-based language commonly used to create websites. PHP applications typically require CGI to be installed on the IIS server. This component provides a key framework for interoperability for non-Microsoft-based applications.
ISAPI Extensions	Internet Server Application Programming Interface (ISAPI) provides support for dynamic content that is written using ISAPI.
ISAPI Filters	The ISAPI filters help determine how requests are processed by your web applications. The filters are files that allow you to change the functionality of IIS to support your web applications.
Server Side Includes (SSI)	SSI is another scripting-based language allowing you to dynamically include common web clients on other web pages in your environment. For example, if you wanted to have a common menu appear on all the web pages on your site, your programmers could use SSI to provide the menu.

Health and Diagnostics   Health and Diagnostics provides the basic functionality to monitor and tune your IIS server. Table 10.3 describes the features.

Table 10.3: Health and Diagnostics

Component	Description
HTTP Logging	As the name implies, with HTTP logging you can track website activity on your IIS server. The types of events logged are typically when an HTTP transaction occurs (such as a web page request). This feature is installed by default.
Logging Tools	This allows you to manage your logs, as well as provide the functionality to automate common logging procedures.
Request Monitor	This provides the ability to monitor the health of your web applications. This allows you to see when a process runs slowly or does not respond. Identifying the process helps to identify any issue. This feature is installed by default.
Tracing	This is another tool that allows you to monitor web applications. Tracing is typically used for hard-to-find problems, such as when your website times out or performs slowly because of poor performance.
Custom Logging	With this component installed, you can create or use your own logging components.
ODBC Logging	This component provides logging for the Open Database Connectivity (ODBC) activity generated by your web server when it connects to an ODBC-compliant database. Most modern databases are ODBC compliant. ODBC logging provides a framework for you to log web activity to those databases.

Security Security is vital in not only protecting your IIS servers but also protecting your applications and data. The Security section provides you with the ability to determine your level of secure authentication support in IIS. By protecting the authentication mechanisms, you can control how users access your web server environment. You need to speak to your web developers to determine which authentication mechanisms are supported by the applications they are currently writing and find the right blend of secure authentication, performance, and application compatibility. IIS has the capability to have multiple authentications supported on the server. In Table 10.4, you can find a list of the different authentication mechanisms and descriptions.

Table 10.4: Security Components

Component	Description
Basic Authentication	This method is the weakest of the authentication methods; this method stores passwords in an easily decrypted format during transmission. If you need to use basic authentication, make sure you also use SSL. Basic authentication is used generally when you need to offer compatibility to a variety of web browsers.
Windows Authentication	This is a secure authentication mechanism, allowing you to leverage your existing Windows Active Directory domain environment for authenticating your users. You should use this solution for internal websites only, not for users who access your website from behind proxy servers or firewalls.
Digest Authentication	This provides a more secure authentication methodology over basic authentication. This method will also leverage your Windows Active Directory domain environment, by sending a secure password hash to the domain controllers. This method should be considered if your users need to access your website and they are behind proxy servers or firewalls.
Client Certificate Mapping Authentication	This allows you to use client certificates to authenticate your Active Directory users, in a one-to-one mapping across multiple web servers.
IIS Client Certificate Mapping Authentication	This is a faster performance model than client certificate mapping but also uses client certificates to identify your users. This method can use either one-to-one or many-to-one mappings and is typically used in heterogeneous directory environments.
URL Authorization	This provides a security mechanism to prevent access to websites in your web servers. URL authorization gives you a tool to explicitly allow or deny access to a directory on your web server either by username or by role. You can use rules based on users, groups, or the header verbs of your HTTP pages.
Request Filtering	This method provides a layer of security at the web server to help prevent many common hacking attacks to your server. This helps filter attacks that may make odd requests or that may use long URLs to target your server. This method screens all inbound requests of your server. This provides you with a mechanism to help mitigate attacks on your server. This feature is installed by default.
IP and Domain Restrictions	This allows you to allow or deny access to your web content, based on the IP address or domain name of the requestor. This provides an additional layer of security to your groups, your roles, or even your NTFS permissions.

Performance   The last section is Performance. There are two choices in this section: Static Content Compression and Dynamic Content Compression. Static Content Compression is installed by default and provides your server with the ability to improve bandwidth utilization. As the name implies, this is useful only for static content on your web server, and it has the additional benefit of not affecting the CPU performance on your server.

Dynamic Content Compression also allows you to improve the bandwidth utilization of dynamic content for your web server. However, this method will also potentially have a negative impact on your server's CPU performance. If your Windows Server 2012 server is already heavily taxed for usage with your CPU, you should not install this component.

Install IIS on Windows Server 2012 Full Server Installation

After you determine which components you want to install for your version of IIS, you will need to install the IIS role with the required components. As with all the roles on Windows Server 2012, you begin the process in Server Manager:

1. Select the Server Manager icon from the taskbar.

2. In Server Manager, click Add Roles and Features.

3. Choose Role-based or Feature-based installation.

4. From the server pool, select the server to which you want to install.

5. On the Select Server Roles screen, select Web Server (IIS), as shown in Figure 10.2, and click Next.

6. There are no additional requirements to run IIS, so click Next on the Select Features screen.

7. Click Next on the Web Server Roll (IIS) screen.

8. Select the necessary role services to support your web application platform, or just use the defaults, and click Next.

9. Click Install.

10. Review the information on the Confirm Installation Selections screen, and when you are ready, click Install.

11. Review the Installation Progress screen, and click Close.

Figure 10.2: Installing IIS

Install IIS on Windows Server 2012 Core Server

The inclusion of the .NET Framework on Windows Server 2012 Server Core provides another platform to install web server roles. As with many other roles, you will use the Deployment Image Servicing and Management (dism) command-line tool on the server to install the IIS role. Because of the complexity and the numerous additional roles required, you will want to add the components separately as you build your IIS server, even though you can run this all in one command.

Network Configuration and Communication

PART IV

1. After you log on to Server Core, type the following command to install the .NET Framework:

   ```
   DISM /Online /Enable-Feature
   /Featurename:NetFx2-ServerCore
   ```

2. After the .NET Framework is installed successfully, you can install the IIS role on Server Core. To begin the process, type the following command. The name of the role, in this case WebServerRole, is case sensitive. This command will install IIS with all the default components on Server Core:

   ```
   DISM /online /enable-feature
   /featurename:IIS-WebServerRole
   /featurename:IIS-WebServer
   ```

3. To verify the installation and the necessary components, you can run the get-features switch for the dism command, as in dism / online /get-features. You will see a screen similar to Figure 10.3.

Figure 10.3: IIS Server Core role services

After you run the command, you will see all the IIS features (enabled or disabled) listed in the feature list. These are all the role services for IIS, and they all begin with IIS.

Before you install any additional features on your IIS server, it's important to install the prerequisite features. For example, if you want to install ASP.NET on Windows Server 2012 Server Core, you need to install the following features: ISAPI Filters, ISAPI Extensions, and .NET Extensibility. When you install these components on a Windows Server 2012 server with a GUI, the GUI wizard will handle the prerequisite installation for you. Figure 10.4 shows an example of what you will see on a Windows Server 2012 full edition server.

Figure 10.4: ASP.NET requirements

This is not the case for Server Core; you will need to install the required features prior to installing the main feature. For example, if you run the command to enable ASP.NET prior to installing the required features, you will see an error message similar to Figure 10.5.

Figure 10.5: ASP.NET error

The error message will inform you of the required features you need to install. In the example of installing ASP.NET on Server Core, you will need to run the following command prior to installing the ASP. NET feature:

```
dism /online /enable-feature
  /featurename:IIS-ApplicationDevelopment
  /featurename:IIS-ISAPIFilter
  /featurename:IIS-ISAPIExtensions
  /featurename:IIS-NetFxExtensibility
```

After the command runs successfully, you can enable the ASP.NET feature by running the following command:

```
dism /online /enable-feature /featurename:IIS-ASPNET
```

Manage Internet Information Services

After you install IIS, you will be able to access the default tool to manage the web server. This tool is the IIS Management Console. However, you may need to install additional components depending on the management needs for your Windows Server 2012 web server or web server farm. The IIS Management Console will also provide you with the ability to manage IIS 7.0 and 7.5 from Windows Server 2008 and Windows Server 2008 R2.

IIS also provides the ability for you to manage and support your previous IIS installations. If you need these capabilities, simply select them during the IIS server installation. This section will focus on managing IIS 8, which is built into Windows Server 2012.

Work with the IIS Management Console

You can access the IIS Management Console in any of three ways:

- Via Server Manager from the Tools menu
- Via the administrative tools
- Via Server Manager in IIS view by right-clicking a server

  To load the IIS Management Console from the Administrative Tools group, simply select Internet Information Services (IIS) Manager. To access the console, click the Server Manager icon on the taskbar. Select Tools ➤ Internet Information Services (IIS) Manager. When you load the console, you will see a screen similar to Figure 10.6.

Figure 10.6: IIS Management Console

The start page gives you some basic tasks, allowing you to connect to other websites and applications. You will also be able to access online websites and help files. One resource specific for IIS you will want to make note of is www.iis.net, which is a great website with tons of references and examples for you to use when maintaining your web server.

IIS Configuration Files

In prior versions of IIS, configurations were stored in a location called the *metabase*. You may have used this very unwieldy file. Now in IIS, the configuration is XML-based and is centralized on the server. Three main files make up the IIS manager configuration. The files, by default, are located in your Windows directory in the System32\Inetsrv\Config folder:

administration.config: This configuration file contains all the management settings for your IIS server and your management console.

applicationhost.config: This stores all the settings for the websites located on your web server.

redirection.config: This file allows you to have centralized settings. You can use this file to redirect the IIS server's configuration to a centralized server location.

These files create the main default settings for your web server. A good reference for you to learn more about the configuration files is at:

http://learn.iis.net/page.aspx/122/getting-started-with-iis-7-configuration/.

The true power in the IIS Management Console is available when you first click a server in your management console; you will see a screen similar to Figure 10.7.

Figure 10.7: IIS server tasks

As you can see, this screen is divided into three panes, which is typical of most Microsoft Management Consoles, with tree navigation on the left pane, details of the selected object in the middle pane, and actions in the far-right pane. As you navigate the tree or components regarding your website, your details and actions will change.

When you first click your server in the IIS Management Console, your IIS Management Console will show only the components currently installed for IIS. With a default installation of IIS only, your management screen will be divided into three areas: ASP.NET, IIS, and Management. (If ASP support has not been added, you will see only IIS and Management.) This allows you to navigate quickly around the areas on your IIS server you want to manage. You can also change the view to Category or just list the different areas for you to manage on your server. To change how the IIS management tasks are organized, you can click the Group By option on the toolbar in the console and select your desired view. In Figure 10.8, you can see an example of an IIS server with No Grouping tasks.

Network Configuration and Communication

PART IV

Figure 10.8: IIS tasks ungroup

When you click a site, you will see several of the same administrative tasks you can perform. When you are working with sites, selecting the proper level you want to administer is important. When you first select the server level, all the changes you make will impact the websites on the server. However, you can override the settings by making changes at the website level. The website level allows you to have customized settings of that website.

One of the things you will notice is the tasks all work the same way, and once you learn how to manage tasks at the server level, it is quite easy to apply the same knowledge to the website level. Table 10.5 describes some of the common tasks you can perform when managing IIS.

Table 10.5: Common IIS Tasks

Task Name	Description
Authentication	This allows you to control which authentication mechanisms are currently enabled. As you may recall, when you install IIS, you can have multiple authentication methods installed. With the Authentication task, you can control which sites use which authentication mechanism.

Default Document	Default Document is an important setting for you to use when users connect to a website or server but do not specify a specific page. The default document is what is displayed. You can list many default documents to be used, and they are processed in order.
Error Pages	When a user encounters an error on your web server or site, you can customize the error messages that users will see. This provides you with a tool to assist the user but also to assist your troubleshooting efforts.
Handler Mappings	Handler mappings work similarly to file extensions for documents. For example, when you double-click an .xlsx file, Excel opens. In the web server handler, mappings work with requests for applications. For example, if you open a web page, IIS will know to open the page and, if necessary, open the proper application as in the case of .php websites, for example.
Logging	If you have installed the logging role service, you will be able to control the default location, how log files are generated, and when logging will occur.
Management Service	If you have installed the remote management service, you will be able to configure the service with this task.
Request Filtering	Request filtering allows you to work with and filter content based on protocol or even IP settings. This essentially allows you to set what content will be served to users of your websites.

Work with Failed Request Tracing Rules

One of the tasks you can use to help troubleshoot errors on your web server is *failed request tracing*. To take advantage of failed request tracing, you need to install the Tracing role service of IIS.

1. To open Server Manager, click the Server Manager icon in the taskbar.
2. In Server Manager, click Add Roles and Features.
3. Select Role-based or Feature-based installation. Click Next.
4. Select the desired server from the server pool. Click Next.
5. Select Web Server IIS and click Next.
6. Click Next on the Select Features screen.
7. Click Next on the Web Server Role (IIS) screen.
8. Expand Web Server and then expand Health and Diagnostics.
9. Select Tracing, and click Next.
10. Click Install.
11. Review the installation summary, and click Close.

Once you have successfully installed the Tracing role service, you will be able to trace requests to websites that have failed. This allows you to set certain rules and conditions that, when met, allow you to see what happened and why the error occurred. You can then, ideally, track down the source of the error.

You can create failed request tracing rules at the server level or the site level. However, by default failed request tracing is not enabled at the site level. To enable failed request tracing, you need to modify the site settings:

1. To open the IIS Management Console, select the Server Manager icon from the taskbar and choose IIS Manager from the Tools menu.

2. In the navigation tree, click Sites.

3. Click the site on which you want to enable failed request tracing.

4. In the Actions pane on the right, click Failed Request Tracing; you will see a screen similar to Figure 10.9.

Figure 10.9: Enabling site failed request tracing

5. Click Enable, and set your directory for the log and how many trace files you want to maintain.

6. Click OK; you will be able to create tracing rules.

Creating tracing rules at the web server or site level follows the same procedures; the only difference is the scope of the rule. Creating failed request tracing rules follows a similar procedure to creating an email rule:

1. To open the IIS Management Console, click the Server Manager icon in the taskbar and then select IIS Manger from the Tools menu.

2. In the navigation tree, click the server or sites you want to manage.

3. Double-click Failed Request Tracing Rules in the center pane.

4. In the Failed Request Tracing Rules screen, click Add in the right Actions pane.

5. Select the content you want to look for, and click Next.

6. On the Conditions screen, set the conditions you are looking to trace; you can trace status codes, time-outs, and even the severity level. Before you can continue, you must select either Status Code or Time Taken. Even though these are check boxes that do not seem to be dependent on each other, one of the first two must be selected even if you just want the event severity. When you are done selecting your conditions, click Next.

7. In the Trace Providers step, you can select which providers you want to trace and what level of detail you want to see in your log. The more verbose your logs are, the bigger the files will be, but the better the chances will be for you to trace the error. When you are done, click Finish.

Remotely Manage IIS Servers

While you're using the IIS console to manage your local web server, you can also manage other IIS servers by using the IIS Management Console to connect to them. However, before you can remotely manage IIS on other servers, you have to configure remote management of the services. Specifically, you need to add the IIS management service and configure and start the service to be able to remotely manage your web servers.

First, you need to install the remote management component of IIS either via Server Manager or via the command prompt. To add the component in Server Manager, follow these steps:

1. Select the Server Manager icon from the taskbar.

2. Choose the IIS Manager from the left pane; you will see a menu similar to Figure 10.10. Select Add Roles and Features.

Figure 10.10: Adding role services

3. Select Role-based or Feature-based installation. Click Next.

4. Select the desired server from the server pool. Click Next.

5. Select Web Server IIS and click Next.

6. Click Next on the Select Features screen.

7. Click Next on the Web Server Role (IIS) screen.

8. Select the Management Service box to add the remote management service; you may also want to select the IIS Management Scripts And Tools box to provide management capabilities via the command prompt. You can see an example of these services being installed in Figure 10.11.

Figure 10.11: IIS remote management and scripting services

9. Click Next and then Install.

10. Review the Summary screen, correct any error messages, and click Close.

To add the IIS management service via the command prompt, as in the case of a Windows Server 2012 Server Core installation, type in the following command:

```
dism /online /enable-feature
/featurename:IIS-ManagementService
```

After you have installed the service, you will need to configure the Registry to enable the remote management service:

1. Start Windows PowerShell from the taskbar.

2. Type **regedit.exe** and press Enter.

3. In the Registry, open the following location: HKEY_LOCAL_MACHINE\ Software\Microsoft\WebManagement\Server.

4. Set the EnableRemoteManagement key to the value of **1**; you can see an example of this service enabled in Figure 10.12.

Figure 10.12: Enabling web management in the Registry

5. Close the Registry Editor.

After you enable the service in the Registry, you need to configure the service to start and run. You can configure the service in the Services Control Panel, or you can use the command prompt to start the service. To use the Services Control Panel, follow these steps:

1. Start Server Manager by clicking the icon on the taskbar. Select Services from the Tools menu.

2. Select Web Management Service. You will see a screen similar to Figure 10.13. If you want the service to start automatically, you can right-click the service and click Properties.

3. Use the Startup Type drop-down list box, set the service to start automatically, and click OK.

Figure 10.13: Web management service

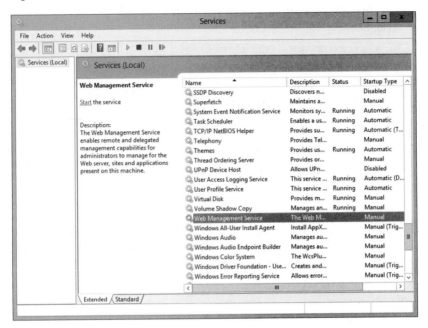

If you want to start the service temporarily or start the service from the command prompt, you can just run the following command. This will not change the startup properties of the service, and the service is only temporary, lasting until the service is stopped or the server is rebooted.

```
net start wmsvc
```

If you want the service started automatically—for example, when you are configuring Windows Server 2012 Server Core—you can type in the following command:

```
sc config wmsvc start= auto
```

After you follow those steps, you can remotely manage IIS web services from the IIS Management Console on a centralized workstation or server system. To connect to the remote servers, follow this procedure:

Network Configuration
and Communication

PART IV

1. Open the IIS Management Console by starting the Server Manager from the icon in the taskbar and choosing IIS Manager from the Tools menu.

2. On the tree root on the left side of the console, right-click Start Page, and click Connect To Server.

3. Type in the FQDN name or IP address of the server you want to remotely manage, and click Next.

4. If you are prompted for credentials, type in the necessary administrative credentials and click Next.

5. Give your connection a new name if you desire, and then click Finish.

After completing the connection, you will be able to manage the new web server from your centralized console. This will make working with your web servers, particularly your Server Core installations, easier and more efficient. The new servers will appear in the tree on the left side of the console. Remember that you can also manage other versions of IIS using this console.

Manage IIS with PowerShell

One of the great features of Windows Server 2012 is the support of PowerShell cmdlets and IIS. Managing IIS with PowerShell gives you another avenue to manage and maintain your web servers. Also, with the added PowerShell support to Windows Server 2012 Server Core, PowerShell provides an alternative for you to work with and configure IIS servers on Server Core installations.

1. Load PowerShell by selecting the PowerShell icon in the taskbar.

2. Run the following command:

```
Get-Module -all | Where {$_.moduletype -eq "Binary"}
|Format-List moduletype, name
Get-Module -all
```

Look for an entry that reads `Microsoft.IIS.Powershell.Provider` in your output list. By default, this provider is not loaded in Power-Shell; you can see an example of the command in Figure 10.14.

Figure 10.14: IIS PowerShell module

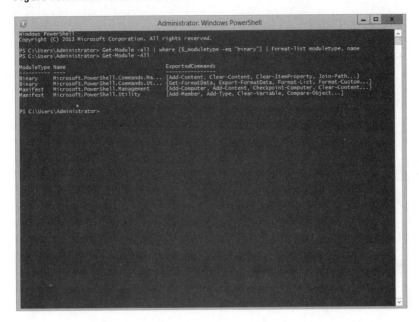

3. If you do not see the IIS PowerShell provider loaded, run the following command to load the IIS PowerShell module:

```
import-module WebAdministration
```

4. After you have loaded the IIS PowerShell module or verified that it is loaded, you can work with IIS Web Administration module.

After the module is loaded, you can manage several aspects of the IIS environment from within PowerShell; if you want to see all the commands, type the following command in PowerShell:

```
get-command -pssnapin WebAdministration
```

You will see a list of all the PowerShell commands, as shown in Figure 10.15.

Figure 10.15: IIS PowerShell cmdlets

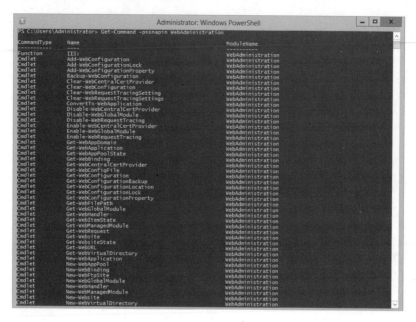

Table 10.6 describes some of the common cmdlets in IIS.

Table 10.6: IIS Cmdlets

Cmdlets	Description
get-website	This shows the basic configuration of the website, including the directory location for the web files, port bindings, and locations.
backup-webconfiguration	This backs up your existing web configuration information.
restore-webconfiguration	This allows you to restore the backup in case of an IIS failure.
stop-website	This stops the website. You can start, remove, or even stop websites from the PowerShell command prompt.
new-website	This allows you to create a new website with any settings you want to use.

If you want to create a new website called business portal on port 8080 with the website stored on the c:\bp drive, run the following PowerShell command:

```
new-website "business portal" -port 8080
-physicalpath "c:\bp"
```

You will notice there is one function listed, which is the IIS: function. This function allows you to navigate directly into the IIS configuration. When you enter the following command, you will be able to
navigate the IIS configuration using common commands:

```
cd IIS:\
```

You can then navigate three different areas of IIS configuration:
application pools, sites, and SSL Bindings. You can view or modify any
of those areas by using directory navigation commands, such as cd and
dir to view the information. For example, if you want to view some
basic information about all the websites currently on the IIS server, you
can perform the following steps:

1. Open PowerShell, and verify that the IIS administration module
   has been loaded.

2. Enter **cd iis:** and press Enter.

3. At the command prompt, type the following to navigate to the site
   information: **cd sites**. Then press Enter.

4. Your command prompt should read PS IIS:\sites>. Type in **dir**,
   and you will see basic information about your websites.
   Figure 10.16 shows an example.

Figure 10.16: Sites in IIS PowerShell

Work with Websites

After you have learned to work with the many tools in IIS to manage the environment, you will need to learn how a website is stored and how to work with the applications your website may need to support. In this section, you will learn how IIS can provide support for your websites.

Understand the Basics of IIS Websites

Before you can work with applications, you need to understand the basics of how websites are used in IIS. Even though your websites may have a combination of simple static web pages and complex applications, all websites have one thing in common. The files supporting the website are stored on the server. Being able to quickly navigate and work with these files provides you with a quick path to fix, replace, or even troubleshoot your applications.

Typically, before you start to work directly with your websites by looking into the directories, you will have a testing process in place. The testing process is essential so that when you modify the website currently in production, you do not crash the website or cause your users or even customers any issues.

By default, your website files are stored on your system drive under the inetpub\wwwroot directory. When your website programmers want to change the files, they can quickly navigate directly to the directory and work with the files on your websites. You can also view the website contents directly in the IIS Management Console. This is especially useful if the website is on a Windows Server 2012 Server Core installation. To view the content in the IIS Management Console, you need to be in the content view.

1. Open IIS Management Console by selecting the Server Manager icon from the taskbar and choose IIS Manager from the Tools menu.

2. In the navigation tree, click the server where the website you want to manage is located.

3. In the middle pane toward the bottom of the IIS Management Console window, click Content View.

4. Double-click the site you want to manage, and a screen similar to Figure 10.17 will appear.

Figure 10.17: Content view in IIS

5. From the Content View window, you can right-click any whitespace in the console and select Explore. This will take you directly to the Windows Explorer view of the directory where you can modify and work with your files.

One of the nice things about being able to work with your websites directly like this is that it does not require a lot of administrative burden when you need to move the application's files and settings. Even if the application is connected to a server, at the end of the day you are just moving files and not changing the configuration of the applications. You will still want to test and verify your applications prior to moving the files, however.

Moving the location of your websites from one physical location to another involves two steps. First, you configure the website's physical directory; and second, you copy/cut and paste the files into the new directory. Moving the physical path for your websites is the same procedure regardless of the application you are moving. You could be moving a .NET application or a PHP application. Keep in mind you are just changing the location of the files, not the configuration. Changing the physical directory is just a matter of modifying a setting inside the IIS Management Console:

1. Open Server Manager by selecting the icon from the taskbar, and then choose IIS Manager from the Tools menu.

2. In the navigation tree, click the server where the website you want to manage is located.

3. Double-click Sites in the middle Details pane, and click the site you want to change.

4. In the right Actions pane, click Advanced Settings; you will see a screen similar to Figure 10.18.

Figure 10.18: Website advanced settings

5. Click the physical path parameter, and either type in the new path location or click the ellipsis button to browse to the new location.

6. After you have configured your new directory, click Finish.

7. After you have changed the configuration in IIS, go to the original file location for the website, and copy and paste the contents to the new location.

Work with Applications

Most of your websites will contain some type of dynamic content, most likely generated from an application on your web server. One of the areas you need to understand is how IIS works with applications. Specifically, you need to understand the nature of application pools and how they provide your server stability.

Application pools allow you to separate running applications on your web server. Therefore, if one application crashes on your server, it will not impact any other applications currently running on your web server. Working with application pools allows you to configure how applications are run on your server. However, working with application pools means you need to understand how the applications need to run on your server. Often times, you will need to speak to a website developer to make sure you provide the proper support for the application.

When you create an application pool, you need to know a couple of aspects about the application you are going to support. First, you need to know whether the application is running using managed code; this typically means the application requires the .NET Framework to run properly. Second, you will want to know how the application pipe will be managed so you know if you should choose either Integrated or Classic. Classic is provided for backward compatibility for application support and simply means IIS will not use the IIS integrated pipeline for managed code. Again, take the time for a quick conversation to help provide adequate support to your web developers.

Recycle Applications

One last task you may need to perform from time to time is recycling your application pool. This will help free up resources on your web server in case an application encounters an error. Recycling your application pools periodically will allow you to maintain your applications and keep them running smoothly. You can set recycling to occur on regular intervals, or you can recycle an application pool immediately. When you recycle an application pool, you essentially clear up system resources and system state information. This could negatively impact users of your website, so you need to try to recycle the applications in off-hours. When you recycle an application pool on your server, all existing session state data will be lost on your server. If the application you are recycling depends on the session state data, any users with active connections may encounter problems when you recycle the application pool. This is why you should try to make sure you recycle the applications during downtime, if possible, to minimize the impact on users.

1. Start Server Manager by selecting the icon from the taskbar and then choosing IIS Manager from the Tools menu.

2. In the navigation tree, expand your server.

3. Click Application Pools.

4. Click the application pool you want to recycle.

5. If you want to recycle the application pool immediately, click Recycle in the Actions pane on the right. The recycle request will process immediately. If you want to set regular recycle intervals, click Recycling in the Actions pane on the right.

6. If you clicked Recycling, you will see a screen similar to Figure 10.19.

Figure 10.19: Recycling application pools

7. The recycling conditions will allow you to set a variety of conditions when you recycle. You can set the time intervals, number of requests, specific time, or even the memory usage of an application. When you are done selecting your conditions, click Next.

8. You can also create event log entries when a recycling process has occurred on your server. The choices you will see in the event logs will be based on the selections you made on the recycling conditions. When you are done selecting your logging options, click Finish.

Integrate PHP Applications in IIS

One of the tasks you may be asked to perform as a web administrator is to provide support of PHP applications on your IIS web server. IIS provides full support for working with PHP applications on the IIS platform. From an IT perspective, all you need to do is know how the components in IIS provide support for these applications and how you can maintain them. One of the great things about this support is that to IIS, whether the application is PHP or not, it is treated like any other applications. It will have application pools, and you will be able to support multiple versions of PHP on the same server.

Before you can begin working with your PHP applications in IIS, you need to make sure you have installed the proper IIS component to provide the PHP applications with the backend support they will need. In the case of IIS, you will need to install the CGI component located under the Application Development section of IIS. This component installs the underlying framework called FastCGI that provides the necessary support for PHP applications to run properly on IIS.

Install CGI on IIS

You can install CGI during the normal IIS installation or after you have already installed IIS. To install CGI if you already have installed IIS, you will need to install the additional role service.

1. Open Server Manager by selecting the icon in the taskbar.
2. Select Add Roles And Features.
3. Select Role-based or Feature-based Installation. Click Next.
4. Select the desired server from the server pool. Click Next.
5. Select Web Server IIS and click Next.
6. Click Next on the Select Features screen.

Network Configuration and Communication

PART IV

7. Click Next on the Web Server Role (IIS) screen.

8. Expand Web Server.

9. Select CGI in the Application Development section, and click Next.

10. Review the Confirmation screen and your selections, and when you are ready, click Install.

11. Review the Summary screen, correct any error messages, and click Close.

After you have installed CGI onto your IIS server, you will need to download the version of PHP required for your web server. You can find the latest version at http://windows.php.net/download/#php-5.4. When you go to download the PHP package, you will see two versions for Windows; one is titled thread-safe, and another is non-thread-safe. You want to download the non-thread-safe version of PHP for your IIS server on Windows Server 2012. The built-in FastCGI component will handle the necessary thread process checks for process integrity normally handled by the thread-safe version of PHP. This means better performance for the PHP applications loaded on your server.

Thread-Safe versus Non-Thread-Safe in IIS FastCGI

Using thread-safe PHP will typically ensure your applications' threads run properly, in order, and safely. Typically, this is a very good thing. Even though this may impact performance, making sure the applications run properly and smoothly is vital.

Non-thread-safe applications will try to execute the threads process as quickly as the threads can be called and executed. This sometimes means the threads bump into other threads or run improperly. The advantage of non-thread-safe applications is typically performance.

So, this is the age-old question of performance versus reliability and is why IIS is so special. The FastCGI component built into IIS on Windows Server 2012 will make sure the threads are executed safely. In a sense, it takes the place of the thread-safe version of PHP in regard to thread safety. You can expect the non-thread-safe PHP package to run faster with reliability on your IIS server.

You also need to make several changes to your PHP.ini file for the applications to run properly. You have to locate and uncomment the following sections in your PHP.ini file:

- Set fastcgi.impersonate=1.

- Set cgi.fix_pathinfo=1 .

- Set cgi.force_redirect=0.

- Set open_basedir to point to a folder or network path where the content of the website is located. By default, on a IIS server, this is c:\inetpub\wwwroot.

- Set extension_dir to the location where the PHP extensions reside. If you have installed PHP with the default settings, you would most likely set this parameter to extension_dir = "./ext".

Lastly, you need to set the application association for PHP applications when they are accessed by your web server. In IIS, this is called the *handler mappings* and is similar to mapping a file extension to a program such as .doc for Microsoft Word. The PHP applications will have the .php extension. IIS will need to know how to process the files when the requests come. With the newer PHP version (beginning at IIS 7) for Windows packages, this handler mapping is created; however, if it does not exist, you will have to configure the IIS handler mapping. This will make sure that when it processes a .php file, it passes the component to the FastCGI component.

1. Open IIS Management Console by starting the Server Manager from the icon in the taskbar and selecting IIS Manager from the Tools menu.

2. Click your server or website in the console tree on the left.

3. Double-click Handler Mappings in the center pane of the IIS console.

4. Look for an option in the Path column with a value of *.php. If one exists, double-click the mapping, and your settings should be similar to Figure 10.20.

5. If you do not see a *.php handler mapping, click Add Module Mapping on the right action list. Configure the mapping with the

Network Configuration and Communication

PART IV

following settings, which assume you used the default installation settings for PHP:

- Request Path: `*.php`

- Module: FastCGIModule

- Executable: Location of PHP installation (for example, `c:\program files\php\php-cgi.exe`)

- Name: Can be any value you want

Figure 10.20: PHP handler mapping in IIS

For more information on providing support for PHP applications, take a look at this website:

`http://learn.iis.net/page.aspx/246/`
`using-fastcgi-to-host-php-applications-on-iis-70`

11

Administering DNS

Network Configuration
and Communication

PART IV

N ame resolution services are critically important in every network. They provide name resolution for Active Directory, applications, and the Internet; they provide the mechanism for network connectivity. DNS is the service responsible for name resolution in Windows Server 2012. A clear understanding of DNS—and how to administrate it effectively—will ensure both internal and external connectivity for the users, computers, and applications in your network.

Add and Remove DNS Servers

Domain Name System (DNS) servers are used to provide name resolution services to your TCP/IP network. DNS is built on a client-server model where the server stores a database of records that maps TCP/IP addresses to the corresponding name type. Clients send queries to the DNS server in order to resolve names to their corresponding TCP/IP address. If your clients cannot resolve names to IP addresses, communication will be limited at best and nonexistent at worst because Windows relies on the name resolution services provided by DNS for the vast majority of its communications. If you can ensure that your clients have access to a DNS server, your ability to facilitate network connectivity increases.

DNS is very flexible; it can be run on a Windows Server machine in a stand-alone environment or as part of a domain-joined Active Directory (AD) network. If Active Directory is running in your network, you will want to add the DNS server role to your domain controllers. The really cool thing about this is that you can maintain the directory services database and the DNS database simultaneously. One option for DNS is to install what is called a *caching-only* DNS server. These servers simply perform name resolution and maintain a list of the results of the queries they receive. They do not have authority for any DNS zone. This option can be very desirable in situations where you have multiple sites connected by wide area network (WAN) links that have limited bandwidth.

There is no right or wrong way to deploy DNS; the key is that you understand the name resolution needs of your network and then deploy the DNS servers to meet your network's needs.

Add a DNS Server

As you install your first DNS server, begin with a simple configuration change. Whether you are planning to run DNS with Active Directory or will run it on a stand-alone server, you want to configure the local network adapter card with a static IP address. Please don't use a dynamically assigned IP address with a DNS server. The headaches are just not worth it.

The interesting thing about DNS is that it is required for Active Directory installation. If you are building a new AD forest, you actually need to configure DNS first. What if you didn't know you had to configure DNS before you ran DCPromo (dcpromo.exe) and installed AD? Not to worry. The AD Installation Wizard actually installs and configures a local DNS server for you. Although this process is certainly easy and it works just fine, we recommend you take the time up front to install your own DNS.

So, how exactly do you install DNS? First, you will need membership in the Administrators (or better) group in order to add DNS. Then follow these steps:

1. Open Server Manager by clicking the icon in the taskbar.

2. Choose Add Roles And Features.

3. Click Next on the Before You Begin, Installation Type, and Server Selection pages.

4. Select the DNS Server box, as shown in Figure 11.1.

Figure 11.1: Installing the DNS role

Network Configuration and Communication

5. Read the DNS info page. There is a lot of good information here.

6. Click Next.

7. Click Install.

8. Click Close.

Now that DNS is configured as a role service on the server, you need to configure the DNS server. You can do this with two different tools: DNS Manager, which is a GUI tool, or dnscmd, which is a command-line tool.

Configure a New DNS Server

When you install DNS on a server that is not an Active Directory domain controller, you will need to do three main things:

- Create a forward lookup zone to facilitate name resolution to IP address, and create a reverse lookup zone to facilitate IP address to name resolution, as shown in Figure 11.2.

Figure 11.2: Configured forward and reverse lookup zones

- Configure each zone for updates and determine how those updates will occur (secure or nonsecure).

- Define what happens when your server gets a query that it cannot solve. Usually, you will want to forward unsolved query requests to another DNS server.

To configure a new DNS server, follow these steps:

1. Choose the Server Manager icon from the taskbar and choose DNS from the Tools menu.

2. Right-click the name of the DNS server, and choose Configure A DNS Server.

3. Click Next on the Welcome page of the Configure a DNS Server Wizard.

4. Select a radio button to create the zones you desire. Typically, both forward and reverse lookup zones are created on an initial server. (Those are the standards.) Select both and then click Next.

5. Select the Yes radio button to create a forward lookup zone and a reverse lookup zone, and then click Next.

6. Select the type of zone you want to create, and click Next.

7. Type in a zone name. Typically, you want a zone name that is descriptive of the delegation for which the zone will work. For example, if you are creating a forward-lookup zone for xyz.com, you might simply name it **XYZForwardLookup**. Click Next.

8. Choose Create A New File With This File Name.

9. Choose the type of updates you will allow this zone to accept.

   If you are installing DNS on a DC, the option to allow only secure dynamic updates will be enabled. (Be sure to follow the on-screen prompts. Your process from here forward will be somewhat different.) Choosing to allow nonsecure updates could be a potential security risk because nonsecure updates come from nonvalidated servers. Be careful. If you choose to allow nonsecure updates, be sure that those updates are coming from trusted servers.

   When you are finished, click Next.

10. Choose to create a reverse lookup zone, and click Next.

11. Select the type of zone you want to create, and click Next.

12. Choose to create a reverse lookup for IPv4. You can come back and create a reverse lookup zone for IPv6 at a later time. Click Next.

13. Enter the network ID, and click Next.

14. Accept the new filename for the reverse lookup zone, and click Next.

15. Choose the type of updates you will allow for the reverse lookup zone, and click Next.

16. Choose whether you will forward unresolved queries. If you choose to forward, add the address of the server where queries will be forwarded and click Next.

17. Click Finish.

Of course, you could configure all this from the command line using the dnscmd tool. To view the options and syntax, open Windows PowerShell and type **dnscmd /config /help**.

Now that you have configured your initial forward and reverse lookup zones, have specified how updates will occur, and have chosen forwarders for unresolved DNS queries, your DNS server is ready to service host name resolution requests from clients. Of course, you will need to tell your clients that you have a DNS server for them to use. You can do this by directly configuring the DNS server entry on each network adapter card configuration, or you can build an option for DNS into your Dynamic Host Configuration Protocol (DHCP) server.

Once the clients know to look to the DNS server for name resolution, your DNS infrastructure is ready to go.

Add Query Forwarding

Once the DNS server is installed and configured, you will want to consider how to get name resolution when your DNS servers are not authoritative. If you think about the way DNS servers resolve names, you'll realize they use a process of recursive queries to find an authoritative server that will resolve a name to an IP address. Your DNS servers simply do not know all the possible host names and IP addresses in the world's networks. To resolve host names for domains that are outside your server's authority, you will need to configure *query forwarding*.

Your network will likely have several DNS servers. If you configure one of those servers to pass queries from inside your network to the Internet, you have really just designated that server as a forwarder. You would change your network firewall settings to allow DNS traffic from the forwarder through the firewall and out to the Internet. Queries will be returned from the Internet to the forwarder, and then the forwarder will pass those responses to the appropriate internal server. Do not host a local DNS zone on your forwarder! It is exposed to the Internet, and any zone stored on the forwarder will also be exposed to the Internet. You really don't want your internal DNS zone data to become available externally.

Maybe you don't want to simply forward all your unresolved queries through a single forwarder. Maybe you want to forward requests for certain domains through a specific forwarder. This concept of setting conditions under which queries are forwarded and through which server they are forwarded is called *conditional forwarding*. It offers a little more flexibility than traditional forwarding, and it can be far more effective than traditional forwarding if you are in a private network that hosts multiple domains, each with their own DNS zones. To add forwarders to your DNS architecture, use DNS Manager:

1. Click the Server Manager icon in the taskbar and then select DNS from the Tools menu.

2. Right-click the server name.

3. Choose Properties.

4. Select the Forwarders tab.

5. Click Edit. The Edit Forwarders dialog box opens, as shown in Figure 11.3.

Figure 11.3: Adding DNS forwarders

6. At this point you can add the desired server to your forwarders list.

Configure a Caching-Only DNS Server

All DNS servers resolve queries and then cache the results of queries for a limited time. They also perform other functions such as updating records and doing zone database maintenance. You might want a server that simply resolves queries and caches the results. A *caching-only server* is especially useful when DNS resolution is needed but when you don't want to create a separate zone for that location.

With a caching-only server, query information is gathered over time from other DNS servers as the caching-only server resolves client queries. That information is then stored by the caching-only server for future use. This process usually results in a decreasing amount of network traffic over time between the location containing the caching-only server and those other locations that contain full-version DNS zones. The benefit comes in the reduced use of the WAN link for DNS resolution while increasing name resolution performance for the local clients. The caching-only server does not perform zone transfers like other DNS servers, and so the WAN is not impacted by this traffic.

1. On the server where you want to configure the DNS caching-only server, open Server Manager by clicking the icon in the taskbar and choosing DNS from the Tools menu.

2. Right-click the name of the server you want to configure, and select Configure A DNS Server. Click Next at the Welcome screen.

3. Choose to configure the root hints only. Do not configure a forward or reverse lookup zone.

4. Click Finish.

This process really could not be much easier. You now have a caching-only DNS server that will take client requests and perform recursive DNS name queries. When the server resolves a query, it stores the answer locally. There are no zones to maintain or update. No zone transfers are necessary, and the clients get the benefit of a local DNS server.

Manage Root Hints

Some of you out there may be scratching your heads and thinking, "What in the world is a root hint?" By definition, a *root hint* is a piece of DNS data stored in the DNS database that identifies the authoritative servers for the root of a given DNS namespace. If you want to resolve a query for a namespace, you have to find the server responsible for resolving requests for that space. DNS names are hierarchical in structure, and each level of the hierarchy is separated by a period (or a *dot*). For example, if you had a client who was trying to resolve the hierarchical name www.microsoft.com, you would begin the process at the root, which in this case is com. Where is the com server? Wouldn't it be nice if you already had a list of commonly used roots (like com, mil, gov, edu, net, org, and so on) and their corresponding IP addresses? These are the root hints.

By default, DNS contains a standard list of commonly used root hints. The root hints contain the name server (NS) records and the host (A) resource records for the internet root servers. All of this works very well if you are on the Internet. What if you are on a private network and want to configure your own root servers? You can configure your own root zone and add the associated NS and A records to root hints as follows:

1. Open Server Manager by clicking the icon on the taskbar and then choosing DNS from the Tools menu.

2. Right-click the Root Hints and choose Properties, as shown in Figure 11.4.

Figure 11.4: Managing root hints

At this point, you can use the buttons and add, edit, or remove root hints, or you can choose to copy the root hints from another server.

Remove a DNS Server

There may come a time when you want to remove a DNS server from your network. When you remove a DNS server, it is important to remember that your DNS server is likely part of a larger DNS infrastructure, and it likely performs key functions and contains records referencing those functions to the other DNS servers and clients in your organization. You would not want to simply delete the server from DNS and remove the DNS server role from Server Manager without first making sure that there will not be an interruption of the name resolution service. As you remove a DNS server, make sure that its functions are being taken over by another server and that the records and references to those services have been updated in your DNS database.

This process consists of four steps:

1. Delete the host (A) record for the server.

2. Modify the NS records for the zone so that the server being removed is no longer included on the list of authoritative servers.

3. Modify the Start of Authority (SOA) record for the zone to point to the new server responsible for the zone. (If you are using an Active Directory integrated zone, this is not necessary.)

4. Use the NSLookup tool to verify zone delegation to be certain that the resource records used for delegation are functioning with the appropriate changes and that they no longer look to the removed server.

   a. Open Windows PowerShell.

   b. Type **nslookup** (**rootserveripaddress**), and press Enter.

   c. Type **nslookup**, and press Enter.

   d. Type **set norecurse** (this tells the root server not to perform a recursive query), and press Enter.

   e. Type **set q=ns** (this sends the query for name server records to the root server).

f. Type the fully qualified domain name of the domain you are testing followed by a period. A list of name servers will be displayed.

g. Verify the NS and A records for the existing name server in the domain.

Manage a DNS Server

After you have installed a DNS server, you might perform several different tasks to maintain or enhance the operation of DNS in your network. For example, you might need to make changes to the IP address of the server, change the way that DNS works with Active Directory, or maybe change the default settings of DNS to improve the security of your environment. Each of these tasks will change the function of DNS slightly, allowing you some flexibility in how you implement DNS in your network and, more important, how DNS operates within your network infrastructure.

Change the Address of a DNS Server

If circumstances arise that demand a change in the IP address of your DNS server, you will need to make a simple change to the A record. If the name of the server has not changed, then neither the NS record nor the SOA record will need to be changed. Make sure that you make the change in the zone records as well as check the records of the parent zone. Remember that your DNS server is updating records to zone database files. Therefore, a change in a single location does not guarantee updates to parents or other zones. Verify that these changes are made; otherwise, your zone updates may fail because of inconsistent records.

1. Choose the Server Manager icon from the taskbar and select DNS from the Tools menu.

2. Expand the server.

3. Expand the Forward Lookup Zones folder. Right-click the forward lookup zone you want to alter, and choose Properties.

4. Select the Name Servers tab.

5. Edit the IP address of the name server, as shown in Figure 11.5.

Network Configuration and Communication

PART IV

Figure 11.5: Changing the DNS server IP address

6. Click OK to accept your changes.

Configure a DNS Server to Listen Only on a Selected Address

Let's say you have a server that has more than one network adapter connected to your network. If the server is running DNS, you may want to configure the server so that DNS listens for queries on only a single network adapter. This can actually increase the security of your server by allowing DNS to listen to queries only on the network IP address that you have configured on the clients.

The process is fairly easy to complete:

1. Choose the Server Manager icon from the taskbar and then select DNS from the Tools menu.

2. Right-click the DNS server you want to configure, and choose Properties.

3. Select the Interfaces tab.

4. On the Interfaces tab, select Only The Following IP Addresses.

5. Select the check boxes for the addresses you want to use, as shown in Figure 11.6.

Figure 11.6: Configuring listening interfaces

6. Click OK.

By restricting the IP address that the DNS server listens to, you can effectively limit access to the single routed segment that your clients will be using to query DNS and eliminate potential threats or unwanted queries from other unrelated subnets.

Scavenge Properties for DNS

The DNS server performs queries and then stores the results of those queries as part of the zone database files. The size of a DNS database can really grow. Because of the nature of host name records, they will change over time. IP addresses are changed, names are changed, or both. It doesn't make sense to simply keep resolved queries in the zone database file indefinitely. Instead, it is desirable that you age records in the database and then *scavenge* them out of the database when they are no longer valid. This is where things get a little tricky. How long should a record stay in DNS? How old is too old? What is the usable life of a cached DNS record? Windows Server 2012 uses two values associated with aging and scavenging called the *refresh interval* and the *no-refresh interval*.

Network Configuration and Communication

PART IV

Refresh interval The refresh interval is the time between the earliest moment when a record timestamp can be refreshed and the earliest moment when the record can be scavenged. By default, this value is set to seven days. The question is, is seven days the right value? The answer is, probably! That is not really an answer, but in most cases seven days will work just fine. If you have a reason to change the value, you are more than welcome to do so. Do not feel like you have to keep the default value if something else will work better for your network.

No-refresh interval The no-refresh interval is the time between the most recent refresh of a record timestamp and the moment when the record can be refreshed again. This value is also set by default to seven days. Like the refresh interval, the no-refresh interval can be changed to suit the needs of your organization. In layman's terms, the no-refresh interval is really just a definition of how long DNS should wait until it refreshes a record. You want to make sure that your DNS server is not constantly refreshing records because it will slow down the response time of the server. Once a record is refreshed, the no-refresh interval defines how long to wait until the record is refreshed.

You can change both of these values using DNS Manager:

1. Choose the Server Manager icon from the taskbar and select DNS from the Tools menu.

2. Right-click the DNS server, and choose Set Aging/Scavenging for all zones.

3. Select Scavenge Stale Resource Records. (This is not enabled by default.) This way records that are not used will not remain in the database and slow down name resolution.

4. Change the no-refresh interval to your desired value.

5. Change the refresh interval to your desired value. Figure 11.7 shows the default settings, and click OK.

Figure 11.7: Changing the DNS aging and scavenging properties

Manage DNS Integration with Active Directory

One of the great things you can do with DNS is integrate it with Active Directory. As you might recall from earlier in the chapter, DNS is a requirement for installing AD. Active Directory has the ability to integrate DNS zone database information into the NTDS.DIT Active Directory database. This can have significant benefits for the security and replication of DNS data. In a typical Active Directory forest, there is more than one DC. When the AD database is replicated, the DNS database is replicated right along with it. This adds a degree of fault tolerance to the DNS data. Even if a server fails, you still have other DCs running DNS that can pick up the workload.

When you install AD and promote a server to a domain controller, you will be prompted to install DNS on the DC. This is the most common way of building DNS integration within AD. It is also possible to build something called Active Directory integrated zones that are not actually part of your AD namespace.

Integrate DNS with AD Domain Services

When you install Active Directory from Server Manager by adding the Active Directory role service, you will need to promote your server to domain controller status to complete the installation of Active

Network Configuration and Communication

PART IV

Directory. You will be given the option to install and configure a DNS server. If you choose to do this, the resulting server will be integrated with AD Domain Services. The nice thing about having your DNS integrated with AD is that when it comes to replication, the DNS zone information is going to be replicated along with the AD database. If you add DNS to the DCs in your network, you get a built-in secure replication topology for DNS and a built-in fault-tolerance strategy.

Build a DNS Application Directory Partition

The Active Directory database consists of partitions. Data from DNS zones can be stored in the domain partition or a partition called the *application directory partition*. If you store DNS zone data in the domain partition, it will inherit the replication parameters of the partition, which in short means you don't really control how the DNS data is replicated. The replication rules for the domain partition become the rules for the DNS zone. That is not necessarily a bad thing. If you want to control the replication parameters independent of the domain partition, you can build an application directory partition for DNS. By building an application directory partition, you have differentiated the DNS zone data from the AD domain data. In short, this gives you the opportunity to control the replication of the application directory partition without influencing or affecting the domain partition.

To create your own application directory partition for DNS, you will need two things. First, you will need membership in the Enterprise Admins security group; and second, you will need to know enough about dnscmd to enter a one-line command, where *servername* is the name of the DNS server on which you want to create the directory, and *FQDN* is the fully qualified domain name of the application directory partition:

```
dnscmd servername /CreateDirectoryPartition FQDN
```

Your server name can be specified by name or by IP address. If you are working from the local DNS server, you could simply use a period to indicate the local server. When you use this command, it is important to know that the FQDN will specify the name of the new application directory partition. You must use an FQDN, such as dnspartition.xyz.com.

With a DNS application directory partition, you have a great tool for managing replication and fault tolerance. When you create the partition, there is only a single DNS server that is part of the partition. If you want to have additional servers participate as part of the partition, you need to add them to the partition. The technical term for this process is *enlisting* a DNS server in an application directory partition. Much like creating the partition, enlisting servers requires that you use the dnscmd tool with the following syntax:

```
dnscmd servername /EnlistDirectoryPartition FQDN
```

The parameter requirements are similar to those you used in creating the application directory partition, where *servername* is the server name you are enlisting and *FQDN* is the fully qualified domain name of the application directory partition, such as the one you created earlier, dnspartition.xyz.com.

There is one last concept associated with application directory partitions that you need to be aware of before moving on to another topic. It is essential that, once you create your application directory partition and enlist your DNS servers in the partition, you verify the application directory partition and its enlisted members. Again, you will use the command line:

```
dnscmd /EnumDirectoryPartitions
```

When this command executes, it returns a display of all the directory partitions in which this server is enlisted.

The next command displays the information related to the specified directory partition. This way, you can verify your application directory partition and the enlisted members of the partition.

```
dnscmd servername /DirectoryPartitionInfo FQDN
```

Remove a DNS Server from an Application Directory Partition

As your network evolves and you add, modify, and remove servers, the situation may arise when you need to remove a server from your application directory partition. Remember that once a DNS server is removed from the partition, it will no longer participate in DNS replication. In other words, make sure you want the server out of the loop before you remove it from your application directory partition. Just as you used the dnscmd tool to create application directory partitions and enlist servers, you will also use dnscmd to remove a DNS server from an application directory partition. You will need DNS Admins or Domain Admins permissions to complete this configuration change.

```
dnscmd servername /UnenlistDirectoryPartition (FQDN)
```

Network Configuration and Communication

PART IV

Here again, *servername* is the name of the DNS server you want to remove, and *FQDN* is the fully qualified domain name of the application directory partition.

Finally, although you are free to enlist or unenlist DNS servers from application directory partitions that you have built, you *cannot* unenlist DNS servers from the DomainDnsZones or ForestDnsZones application directory partitions.

Change Security for a Directory Integrated Zone

As you can see in Figure 11.8, it is possible to change the security of a directory integrated zone in DNS. Each object in Active Directory has something called a *discretionary access control list* (DACL), which defines the users and groups that have access to the object. You can set the permissions of the DACL to allow specific users or groups to access and update your DNS zone database files.

1. Choose the Server Manager icon from the taskbar and select DNS from the Tools menu.

2. Find the zone you are interested in maintaining.

3. Right-click the zone name, and choose Properties.

4. Click the Security tab.

5. Edit the permissions as needed, as shown in Figure 11.8.

Figure 11.8: Changing DACL permissions for a DNS zone

Remember that this procedure works only for Active Directory integrated zones. If you have a standard primary, standard secondary, or other zone type, this procedure is not available.

Change Zone Replication

Controlling zone replication allows you to decide the parameters for replication for a DNS zone. These parameters are often called the *replication scope*. When DNS is integrated with Active Directory, it is replicated along with the other AD partitions between domain controllers. Active Directory consists of forest and domain structures, and there are domain controllers at both logical levels of this hierarchy. This structure lends itself to four replication scope options:

All DNS Servers in the Active Directory Forest   This scope option replicates DNS zone data to all DNS servers in the Active Directory forest. That's a broad scope, and depending on the size and physical layout of your forest, it could significantly impact replication.

All DNS Servers in the Active Directory Domain   This scope option replicates DNS zone data to all DNS servers that are running on domain controllers in the Active Directory domain. This seems like a tighter scope than the forest scope, but if you think about the size limitations on a domain (functionally, there really aren't any), this could present the same issues as the forest scope, albeit with the limitations of the domain.

All Domain Controllers in the Active Directory Domain   In this scope, you would replicate DNS zone data to all domain controllers whether they were DNS servers or not.

All Domain Controllers in a Specified Application Directory Partition   This scope allows you to replicate DNS zone data to the domain controllers that you have enlisted in the application directory partition.

Each of the scope options can be used effectively, depending on the network environment and DNS implementation in which they are implemented. If you had taken the time to create an application directory partition, it would make sense to change the replication scope to all domain controllers in a specified application directory partition. To make changes in replication scope, use the DNS Manager:

1. Choose the Server Manager icon from the taskbar and select DNS from the Tools menu.

2. Locate and right-click the zone, and then choose Properties.

Network Configuration and Communication

PART IV

3. On the General tab, locate Replication and click Change.

4. Select your desired replication scope; your choices are shown in Figure 11.9.

Figure 11.9: Configuring replication scope

Manage Zone Database Files

When you work with DNS, you have many files to manage. Each DNS server may be responsible for many different DNS zones. Each zone contains its own files and folders that will require some degree of effort in order to create, maintain, update, manage, and secure.

As you work with your DNS environment, you will likely break your forest into smaller segments that, in DNS, are referred to as *zones*. If the records in your DNS zone database are designed to allow the resolution of a name to an IP address, you would say the zone is *working forward*, and the zone database type you would create is called a *forward lookup zone*. If your object is to provide an option for finding names based on a provided IP address, then you would say your zone is *working in reverse*, and you would create a *reverse lookup zone*. What if you wanted a DNS server that only resolved the names of other authoritative DNS servers in your environment? You would create a *stub zone* to serve your purposes.

Each of the different zone types serves a particular purpose in DNS. You will likely want more than one server for each zone in order to maximize availability to your clients and to add some degree of fault tolerance to your network.

Create a Forward Lookup Zone

As you learned earlier, when you install DNS as part of Active Directory, the appropriate forward lookup zones for the domain are created automatically. If you choose to add zones or if you are not using DNS as an integrated part of Active Directory, you will use DNS Manager to create and manage forward lookup zones. Not all forward lookup zones are created equally; there are actually three different types, called *primary zones*, *secondary zones*, and *stub zones*.

Primary zones   Primary zones are zones that are created and stored on the local server. They can be updated and maintained directly on the server and can also receive replicated updates from other servers.

Secondary zones   Secondary zones are zones that are stored on the local server; however, all of their information comes from updates received from another designated primary server. Secondary servers are a good way to help share the workload that might otherwise be forced onto a standard primary server.

Stub zones   Stub zones create a copy of only the name server records for a given zone. This zone type is useful in helping clients find and query the appropriate internal DNS name server.

To create a new forward lookup zone, follow these steps:

1. Choose the Server Manager icon from the taskbar and select DNS from the Tools menu.

2. Right-click the name of the server you want to use.

3. Choose New Zone.

4. Click Next on the Welcome To The New Zone Wizard page.

5. Select the type of zone you want to create.

6. Choose whether you want the zone stored in Active Directory by selecting or not selecting the box at the bottom of the Zone Type screen, as shown in Figure 11.10.

Network Configuration and Communication

PART IV

Figure 11.10: Adding a new forward lookup zone

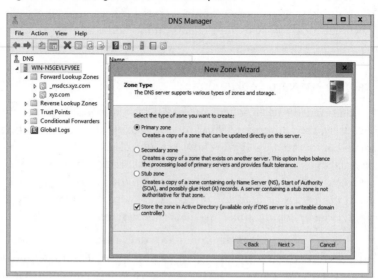

Depending on what type of zone you choose, the wizard will offer you the appropriate options from this point forward, including options for replication, zone name, and the types of updates you will allow.

Change the Zone Type

One of the nice things about DNS zones is that they are pretty flexible. If you needed, you could actually change a primary zone to a secondary or stub zone, or vice versa. Usually, you would do something like this if you were doing maintenance on a server and wanted to limit the effect on DNS or the clients that rely on DNS services. Changing the zone type is a simple procedure:

1. Choose the Server Manager icon from the taskbar and select DNS from the Tools menu.

2. Find the zone you want to change and right-click it.

3. Choose Properties.

4. Next to Type on the General tab, click Change.

5. Select the new zone type, as shown in Figure 11.11, and click OK.

Figure 11.11: Changing the DNS zone type

Manage Resource Records

DNS zones contain resource records of various types. These records are created as you create DNS servers, clients, services, and applications. Generally speaking, once a resource record has been created, there is not much you need to do to maintain these records. You may want to change the DACL security permissions if your resource records are part of Active Directory, or you may need to modify a record or even delete one.

You can manage records in the DNS zone using DNS Manager or dnscmd. You simply need to find the resource record in the designated zone.

If you are interested in changing the DACL for a resource record, follow these steps:

1. Choose the Server Manager icon from the taskbar and select DNS from the Tools menu.

2. Locate the zone that contains the resource record.

3. Right-click the resource record you want to change.

4. Choose Properties.

5. Select the Security tab.

6. Edit the permission to the resource record, and click OK.

Network Configuration and Communication

PART IV

If you want to delete the record, simply right-click the record and choose Delete. When the message asking you to confirm the deletion appears, simply click OK.

Configure Dynamic Update

When you work with DNS servers, it is ideal to have them update one another with their information. Windows Server 2012 allows the use of dynamic updates between configured DNS servers. This really eliminates the need for you to spend your valuable time administering zone databases. Clients who use DHCP can easily get access to an updated DNS server without having to call your help desk. You can configure each of your zones for dynamic updates. If you are using Active Directory integrated zones, you can also specify that the updates are done in a secure fashion and are based on the information in the DACL.

1. Choose the Server Manager icon from the taskbar and select DNS from the Tools menu.

2. Locate the zone where you want to enable dynamic updates.

3. Right-click the zone, and choose Properties.

4. On the General tab, open the Dynamic Updates drop-down list, as shown in Figure 11.12.

Figure 11.12: Configuring dynamic updates

5. Choose the type of updates you want to allow, and click OK.

As you probably noticed, dynamic updates can be configured as non-secure and secure. You may be wondering why you would ever consider using nonsecure updates. Imagine if all the DNS servers for the zone were residents of your own private network. You already have tight control over the servers, so you might not choose to enable secure updates only. If your DNS zones are not part of Active Directory, you will not have the option for secure dynamic updates only.

If you are using Active Directory integrated zones, it really does not make sense to use nonsecure updates. Nonsecure updates will expose your DNS servers to updates from unknown, disreputable, or downright malicious sources, and they will open your DNS infrastructure to potential threats. It just doesn't make sense to use anything but secure updates.

Zone Transfer Settings

DNS servers transfer zone data based on a schedule. You can control how the zone is transferred based on the zone transfer settings. Each of the settings can be changed or updated, so it is important to note that these settings will be limited if your DNS servers are Active Directory integrated. When working with the zone transfer settings you will have a number of different options and intervals that can be configured based on your network's DNS requirements.

- Whether the zone is transferred to any other server and to which servers it may be transferred

- The refresh interval, which describes how often the zone files will be transferred

- The retry interval, which describes how long a DNS server will wait to request a transfer after a transfer has failed

- The expire interval, which describes how long the DNS zone data is valid

- The list of servers that are notified when zone data changes

To configure zone transfer settings, follow these steps:

1. Choose the Server Manager icon from the taskbar and select DNS from the Tools menu.

2. Locate the chosen zone.

3. Right-click the zone, and choose Properties.

4. Click the Zone Transfers tab.

5. Select the box to allow zone transfers.

6. Specify the servers that you will allow transfers with, as shown in Figure 11.13.

Figure 11.13: Configuring the zone transfer settings

When you configure zone transfers, you can also build something called a *notification list*, which contains a list of servers that will be notified by the master DNS server in your domain when changes are made to the zone. Simply click the Notify button on the Zone Transfers tab to build a notification list.

The settings for Refresh Interval, Retry Interval, Expires After, and Minimum (Default) TTL are on the SOA tab.

1. Choose the Server Manager icon from the taskbar and select DNS from the Tools menu.

2. Locate the zone you want to configure.

3. Right-click the zone name, and choose Properties.

4. Click the Start Of Authority (SOA) tab.

5. Set the values for the selected interval or TTL, as shown in Figure 11.14.

Figure 11.14: Configuring the interval values

Secure a Zone

DNS provides name resolution services to clients. The information provided by DNS has a direct effect on the functional operation of your
network. You want to make sure that you take security into consideration for each of your DNS zones. Generally, DNS has two potential
security problems that you would worry about. First, you want to make
sure that the zone files are secured from unauthorized changes. If an
illicit source can update your zone database files, they could really cause
problems for your network. Generally, these attacks occur as dynamic
updates are pushed to your DNS servers from outside your organization. The easiest way to prevent this type of attack is to enable only
secure dynamic updates.

Second, you want to make sure you have taken precautions to prevent unauthorized access to your zone files. Imagine if someone outside
your organization set up a secondary server and managed to get updates
from your internal primary server. You would effectively be sharing
your DNS zone information with an imposter. The easiest way to prevent this type of attack is by configuring a list of servers to which you
will allow zone transfers.

If your zones are Active Directory integrated, you can, of course, use the DACLs associated with the zone to further control access to the files.

Beginning with Windows Server 2008 R2, security moves one step further when it comes to protecting the zone database files and adds something called Domain Name System Security Extensions (DNSSEC). DNSSEC allows the DNS zone and all the records in the zone to be cryptographically signed. When a DNS server receives a request for the signed zone files, it returns the files along with the digital signatures. By obtaining a public key, a resolver can verify that the files have not been tampered with.

As you will note, we discussed each of these topics in earlier sections of this chapter, and we demonstrated how to do the configurations. Much of securing a DNS infrastructure really comes down to the way it is configured.

Configure Single-Label DNS Resolution

The vast majority of networks use DNS as the primary name resolution system, but there are alternatives. For example, for many years Windows Internet Name Service (WINS) was used as an alternative; in many networks, it still is in use. Unfortunately, as you move forward to the next version of TCP/IP, which is called IPv6, there is no support for WINS. You will need another way to resolve single-label host names. If there is no WINS, a DNS client can still resolve a single-label name by appending a *dns* suffix to the name and trying to find it in DNS.

If you are planning to use IPv6, all name resolution will go through DNS. If you still have single-label names in your network, Windows Server 2012 uses a special zone called a *global names zone* (GNZ) to house these records and facilitate the resolution of those names through DNS. GNZ is not a replacement for WINS; instead, it provides an avenue for name resolution while you transition WINS out of your network. The GNZ is created and managed much the same as a standard primary zone. You should not enable dynamic updates for the GNZ to prevent its resource records from being registered into the zone.

Create the GNZ

The process of creating the GNZ begins with DNS Manager:

1. Choose the Server Manager icon from the taskbar and select DNS from the Tools menu.

2. Right-click the name of the server on which you want to create a GNZ.

3. Choose New Zone.

4. Click Next in the Welcome to the New Zone Wizard page.

5. Select the Primary Zone type, make sure the Store in Active Directory check box is selected, and click Next.

6. Select All DNS servers running on domain controllers in this forest.

7. Click Next.

8. Click Forward Lookup Zone.

9. Click Next.

10. Type `GlobalNames` in the Zone Name box, and click Next.

11. Select Do Not Allow Dynamic Updates, and click Next.

12. Click Finish.

It is also possible to enable GNZ from Windows PowerShell using the dnscmd tool and the following command:

```
DNSCMD servername /config /enableglobalnamesupport 1
```

Either method works for enabling GNZ; in both cases, you still need to configure the appropriate records for the zone.

After the forward lookup GNZ has been created, you need to add the alias resource records (called the *CNAME*) for each of the single-label clients in the network. This can prove to be a daunting task if you have lots of single-label clients, and it may provide the motivation necessary to quickly upgrade them to traditional DNS clients. To add new CNAME records for the single-label clients, follow these steps:

1. Choose the Server Manager icon from the taskbar and select DNS from the Tools menu.

2. Locate the GNZ.

3. Right-click the zone, and choose New Alias (CNAME).

4. Enter the alias name.

5. Enter the fully qualified domain name.

6. Click OK.

Troubleshoot DNS

DNS is an essential resource for name resolution. When something goes wrong with DNS, it can have far-reaching effects in your network. An understanding of how to troubleshoot DNS can be incredibly valuable. The thing you will love about DNS is that your ability to troubleshoot DNS is directly associated with your understanding of basic DNS operations and the specific DNS configuration with which you are working.

TIP   Read the DNS technical reference at http://technet .microsoft.com/en-us/library/cc732997(WS.10).aspx. Although it specifically references Windows Server 2008, it is the most current reference in the official Microsoft library and well worth the read.

With a good understanding of DNS and a strong understanding of your network, you are well positioned to deal with most of the issues that will crop up in DNS. One of the really good things about DNS is that, although there are occasional problems that fall outside the realm of what is considered normal, most of the problems are seen over and over again in networks that run DNS and are fairly easy to isolate and fix.

When you are troubleshooting a problem in DNS (or anywhere else in your network, for that matter), you should use a *root cause analysis* approach. What exactly is root cause analysis? It can be described with a single sentence:

Discover the problem before you "fix" anything.

When troubleshooting DNS, you will notice that problems seem to fall into four categories:

- DNS clients
- DNS servers
- Dynamic updates
- Zone problems

As you encounter an issue with DNS, begin by trying to isolate the source of the problem. You will find that the majority of the time the problem will easily fit into one of these four categories. If it doesn't, don't worry—all is not lost. You can keep working to identify the source of the problem.

The most common problems with DNS servers are actually not really problems with the DNS servers at all; they are generally hardware or network related. For example, say your users suddenly flood your help desk with calls indicating they cannot "find" anything on your network. Shares are unavailable, the Internet seems to be down, and some users cannot even log in. This sounds like a DNS problem. It is! Where does it fit among the four categories? It sounds like a DNS server problem. At this point, you can begin troubleshooting by checking the physical hardware that supports the DNS server. Is everything actually plugged in and working? You notice that the network cable that connects your DNS server and its network interface card has been laying across a sharp steel beam on top of your server rack, and the weight of the other cables has somehow managed to sever this one. You put in a new cable, and in minutes the network is up and running. Don't just assume that the hardware is fine and move on to other things. Check it out. Many, many times a simple hardware fix is all that is necessary.

If the hardware checks out, you can start going down your check list of items to identify the problem and then apply the solution. Microsoft maintains a troubleshooting tool specifically for DNS. It is excellent! Not surprisingly, it is broken down into four categories. The vast majority of DNS issues can be solved by using these simple troubleshooting tools. They provide a great level of detail and solutions at each step of the process to help you not only identify the problem but also fix the problem.

TIP   Use the troubleshooting DNS tools at http://technet
.microsoft.com/en-us/library/cc731991.aspx. Although it specifically references Windows Server 2008 and 2008 R2, it is still a good reference and the tools will assist you in your Windows Server 2012 environment.

The vast majority of DNS issues will be within your troubleshooting reach if you use the tools discussed in the previous section. If you run into a problem that you cannot solve quickly on your own using the troubleshooting tools, then use other resources at your disposal. The Internet can be a great source of information to help you isolate your problem and find a solution. If you have any kind of support contacts, use them. Support incidents that you initiate on the phone or in person may make sense if you have exhausted your knowledge without finding a solution. The key is not to give up. Use your root cause analysis skills and your understanding of the environment to find and fix the problem.

12

Troubleshooting TCP/IP

Network Configuration
and Communication

PART IV

The basis for all network communication is the network protocol, and no network protocol is more ubiquitous than TCP/IP. It is the core building block for all communication between network servers, clients, routers, switches, and even phones. If you understand how to troubleshoot TCP/IP, you will be able to solve many of the network communication problems that will arise in your networks.

Understand TCP/IP Basics

TCP/IP is a suite of protocols that have been the basis for network communication and traffic control for more than a decade. Although there are other network communication protocol suites, TCP/IP has emerged as the de facto standard in the vast majority of operating systems.

The TCP/IP suite of protocols has undergone a series of revisions. There are currently two versions of TCP/IP: IP version 4 (IPv4) and IP version 6 (IPv6). IPv4 has been popular as a network protocol since the early versions of Windows NT. It has a simple 32-bit addressing scheme that provides a relatively easily routed protocol for internetwork accessibility. The 32-bit address space offers a total of 2^{32}, or 4,294,967,296, addresses. Although that seems like a pretty large number, when you think about the number of client computers connected to the Internet, add the number of networked appliances such as switches and routers, then add the websites and web servers of the world, and finally add the servers of the world's businesses, it becomes glaringly apparent that just over 4 billion addresses is not nearly enough to meet the demand. The shortfall of IPv4 addresses was addressed (no pun intended) in the mid-1990s and resulted in the formation of a new suite of protocols called IPv6.

First supported in Windows NT 4, IPv6 offers some significant upgrades to IPv4, including but not limited to a much larger 128-bit address space. This means that the number of potential addresses in IPv6 is 2^{128}, an astonishing 340,282,366,920,938,463,463,374,607, 431,768,211,456 addresses. If you are wondering how you would succinctly express that number, you would say "340 undecillion," but we think it is much easier to understand the full impact and potential of the address space to see it listed in all its base-10, comma-separated, 39-digit glory. Now, 340 undecillion addresses should at least tide the world's IP address appetite over for a little while. That is a big number!

Even though IPv6 has been supported since the Windows NT days, few networks have adopted this new version of IP despite its potential benefits. As the old proverb states, the network world seems to believe "Better the devil you know than the devil you don't." Choosing between IPv4 and IPv6 is a topic that has engendered debate and even arguments in networking channels worldwide.

The question still remains, "Which IP version should you use?"

While Microsoft was developing the Windows Vista and Windows Server 2008 operating systems, its Windows Core Networking product team had a revolutionary idea. What if there were a protocol that understood both IPv4 and IPv6 natively? This idea resulted in the development of a protocol suite called the Next Generation TCP/IP stack. This stack represents a complete redesign of TCP/IP in both IPv4 and IPv6 and provides needed functionality to meet the communication, connectivity, and performance requirements of the modern network. This means you can have all of the well-known benefits of IPv4 and get all the cool new functions and features of IPv6. You don't have to choose one or the other. You can have both!

Be careful what you wish for, though. Before you begin the process of troubleshooting TCP/IP, it is a good idea to read one of the many books currently available on the inner workings of TCP/IP. The volume of information needed to fully understand TCP/IP will simply not fit into a single chapter, unless of course the chapter were 400 to 500 pages in length. The focus here is on troubleshooting TCP/IP. *Troubleshooting* is a broad term and could also cover hundreds of pages if we tried to cover every possible situation. Instead, this chapter will give you a good methodology to use to discover many of the standard issues associated with TCP/IP troubleshooting and point you to additional tools and resources to help you solve more isolated problems, as well.

Troubleshoot TCP/IP

To effectively troubleshoot TCP/IP, you need to have an approach to troubleshooting that will allow you to systematically identify the source of a problem and then, once the source is identified, allow you to take corrective action that will rectify the problem. This approach to troubleshooting is called *root cause analysis*. Do not simply "try something" to fix the problem. Often you will mask the problem with attempts to fix it and create a more complex environment for future troubleshooting scenarios. The old saying "If it ain't broke, don't fix it!" applies to troubleshooting.

You will want to employ a step-by-step approach to troubleshooting TCP/IP problems and utilize a number of different tools to help you in your quest for problems and the solutions to resolve those problems.

These are some common questions you might ask:

- What are the symptoms of the problem?
- What could cause these symptoms?
- What stuff is working?
- What stuff is not working?
- Is there any kind of relationship between the things that don't work?
- Is this a new problem or one that has persisted for a long period of time?
- Have any recent changes been made to the network or systems involved?
- What were the changes?
- What is the scope of the problem?
- Is one machine, a group of machines, or the whole network having problems?
- What do the machines that are having problems have in common?

Often if you can ask the right questions, the answers will lead you to the right place to start troubleshooting, or at very least they can help you narrow the possible problems to a manageable set of issues that you can begin testing in order to identify the culprit.

Understand Troubleshooting Tools

One of the best things about running Windows Server 2012 is that you have a full complement of tools that are included (or freely available to you) to help you troubleshoot TCP/IP. These tools are included with the installation of Windows Server or can be downloaded from the http://technet.microsoft.com website.

> **Event Viewer** The Event Viewer is found in the Control Panel and is likely the most valuable of the troubleshooting tools. Using the Event Viewer, you will find informational, warning, and error

events that will help you identify system problems and their associated causes. Remember that Event Viewer can display information and events about other systems in your network through the use of subscriptions; therefore, it can be used to monitor not just the local machine but many machines throughout your network. We recommend you begin your troubleshooting efforts with the Event Viewer, and when you have a good idea what you are really dealing with, then you can move to the tools listed next.

Performance Monitor   The Performance Monitor tool lets you configure hundreds of different functions of your systems, and it includes some great information related to TCP/IP and its associated traffic. If you are already capturing IP information in your network, you will likely want to view the results from captures before and after a problem is reported.

Command-line tools   There are also several Windows PowerShell command-line tools you can use, as shown in Table 12.1.

Table 12.1: TCP/IP Troubleshooting Command-Line Tools

Tool	Description	Common Commands
IPCONFIG	This command-line tool is generally the place where your troubleshooting begins. This command will display detailed information about the adapters attached to a system and the addressing information associated with each adapter. This command uses a series of switches that allow you to customize the output you receive and even do some basic address updates.	IPCONFIG /ALL
HOSTNAME	This command-line utility will display the host name of the local system.	HOSTNAME
PING	This command-line utility sends Internet Control Message Packets (ICMP) across an internetwork to verify connectivity. It is commonly used to verify the operation of TCP/IP at different levels of the TCP/IP protocol stack.	PING 127.0.0.1
PATHPING	This command-line tool allows you to see the path that an IP packet takes through an internetwork and will show you information about packet losses and where they occur.	PATHPING *xxx.xxx.xxx.xxx* (where Xs represent IP address)

(Continued)

Network Configuration and Communication

PART IV

Table 12.1: TCP/IP Troubleshooting Command-Line Tools *(Continued)*

Tool	Description	Common Commands
TRACERT	This command-line utility will display information about the network route taken from source to destination.	TRACERT *xxx.xxx.xxx.xxx* (where Xs represent destination IP address)
ROUTE	This command-line utility will display and allow the editing of routing table information in IPv4.	ROUTE PRINT
ARP	This command-line utility will let you view the Address Resolution Protocol cache.	ARP -A
NBTSTAT	This command-line utility can be used to display information about packets that running NetBIOS over TCP/IP.	NBTSTAT -C
NETSTAT	This command-line utility will show you information about current connections.	NETSTAT -A
NETSH	This command-line utility is not so much a troubleshooting tool as it is a configuration tool for TCP/IP and a whole bunch of other services. It uses something called a *naming context* and allows the configuration of items within its context. The command has a standard IP context, an IPv$ context, and an IPv6 context that can be used to fix configuration problems in TCP/IP interfaces.	NETSH INTERFACE IPv4
TELNET	This command-line utility will let you establish a TCP connection between two systems on your network.	TELNET

Each of these tools will allow you to identify, diagnose, change, or update the TCP/IP environment of your network. As you use the tools, you will find a methodology that works for you and, more importantly, gives you the right information about the critical segments of your TCP/IP configuration and management.

Troubleshoot IPv6

As you work with TCP/IP networks, you will probably run into some problems. Hardware fails, users make changes to their systems that inhibit communication, and applications or updates install with unintended consequences. Regardless of whether the changes are malicious or unintended, if they impact your TCP/IP infrastructure, you will need to troubleshoot the problems and find solutions quickly and efficiently. There is no one "right" way to do this. There are lots of tools and lots of methods of implementing those tools to help you discover the source of a problem and then craft a solution that will work for your environment. The best advice we can give you regarding your ability to troubleshoot TCP/IP problems doesn't include a troubleshooting methodology. It's this:

> Know your network!

If you clearly understand the operation of your network, it will be much easier to troubleshoot problems as they arise.

We have used a simple methodology for troubleshooting TCP/IP for a long, long time. We occasionally tweak it a little and add some new tools. Depending on the circumstance, we might change the protocol just a little bit, but the basic operations stay the same. Please keep in mind there is no one "right" way to do this; this just happens to be one of the ways we use.

The vast majority of problems that we have investigated related to TCP/IP have begun with the same complaint: "I can't connect to . . ."

Whether it is a network resource, the Internet, a printer, a file share, or any number of other things, when we hear that phrase, the TCP/IP alarm bells sound. If TCP/IP problems are primarily problems of connectivity, then you would be well served to make your primary efforts focus on discovering and resolving connectivity problems.

Verify Connectivity for IPv6

The first thing you will want to do when troubleshooting TCP/IPv6 is to verify that TCP/IP is actually set up and configured correctly. This is generally where you will find the cause and can implement a solution. Consider the following steps when verifying connectivity for TCP/IPv6:

1. Check the physical hardware. Check the network cable. Is it plugged in? Check the connections at switches, hubs, and routers. Don't laugh—you will solve a lot of TCP/IPv6 problems right here in step 1. You might even be well served to simply unplug the cable and plug it back in on the off-chance that the cable somehow became loose even if it looks connected.

2. Verify the function and configuration of the network interface, using the following commands:

ipconfig /all This command displays the status and configuration of the IPv6 interface. Verify that the interface has an address and is in fact enabled. Check the DNS settings for the interfaces to be certain that they are configured correctly.

netsh interface ipv6 show address This command shows you the TCP/IP address of the IPv6 interface, as shown in Figure 12.1.

Figure 12.1: Results of netsh interface ipv6 show address

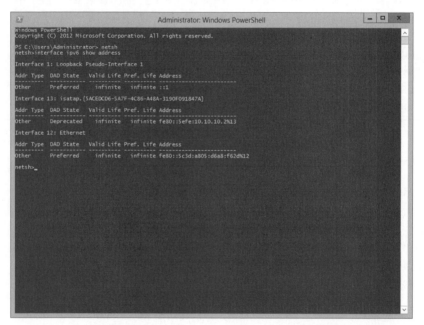

In the event that there is, in fact, a problem in the TCP/IP configuration, you can change the configuration using the netsh interface ipv6 set command.

We always start here because statistically we have found that many of the problems related to IPv6 have to do with configuration. Once you get the configuration right, TCP/IP works correctly, and your user's connectivity will be restored.

Verify Responsiveness

Of course, not every problem is going to be fixed with a simple check of the hardware and address configuration. Responsiveness is also important. Responsiveness takes into account the fact that communication takes at least two endpoints. If either of the endpoints fails to respond, then the communication cannot take place. If you have checked the local configuration and everything is in order, you should check to see if the machine is responding.

IPv6 uses something called a *neighbor cache* to store link layer addresses that have been resolved recently. If for some reason the neighbor cache holds incorrect information, it can impede connectivity. You can flush the neighbor cache with no negative effects to TCP/IP:

```
netsh interface ipv6 delete neighbors
```

If you are thinking to yourself, "Hey, that's a lot like the ARP cache from IPv4," you are right!

There is another cache you should check in conjunction with responsiveness, called the *destination cache*. The destination cache is used to maintain a list of next hop addresses for addresses recently used. As shown in Figure 12.2, you can view the contents of the destination cache using the following command:

```
netsh interface ipv6 show destinationcache
```

Figure 12.2: Results of netsh interface ipv6 show destinationcache

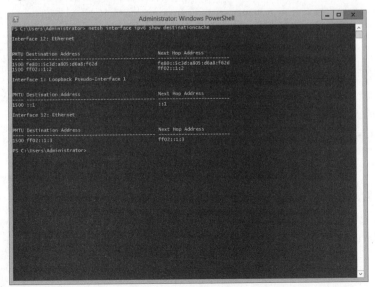

Network Configuration and Communication

PART IV

As shown in Figure 12.3, if you decide you want to delete the cache, you can do so with the following command:

```
netsh interface ipv6 delete destinationcache
```

Figure 12.3: Results of netsh interface ipv6 delete destinationcache

Both of the previous steps, deleting the neighbor cache and deleting the destination cache, act as preemptive actions to eliminate the possibility that your machine is being incorrectly directed to a link address that is not going to respond. To truly troubleshoot responsiveness, you will need to start sending packets onto the network and watching for responses. There are a couple of tools that are uniquely suited for this exercise.

PING uses the Internet Control Message Protocol to send echo request packets to a host and then measures the response time as the host responds to those echo requests. This tool can be incredibly valuable in verifying responsiveness in IPv6. Traditionally, when you use the PING tool, you begin with the process of pinging the local host address and then move on to the local IP address, then an IP address on the same subnet, next the default gateway of the local router, and finally an address on another network segment. You might have learned that you can skip right to pinging a remote host on another segment; if you get a response, you know everything in the cascade is working. As tempting as that is, in the event that you do not receive a response from the remote host, you really don't know anything about where your problem is located. Start with the local host, and work your way through the list. When you don't receive a response, you have reached the area that is having the problem.

One more very important point concerning PING is that ICMP packets can be considered a security risk, and often network administrators configure their computers to not accept or respond to ping echo request packets. If you ping a machine and get no response, make certain that the reason you are not getting a response is that there really is no connectivity, not that the system you pinged does not support ping packets. This process of removing or limiting response to specific packet types is often termed *packet filtering.* Packet filtering is a common reason for lack of responsiveness.

If you are confident that TCP/IP has been installed and is configured correctly and you are still not getting connectivity, it may well be an issue of filtering. Consider checking the following:

- Windows Firewall rules

- IPsec policies

- Remote access policies

- IPv6 packet filters

- Router policies

Check the Routing Table for IPv6

If you find yourself unable to connect to remote resources using IPv6, one of the things you will want to check is the routing table. Specifically, you will be looking for routes that have been incorrectly identified or erroneously entered into the routing table. Use ROUTE PRINT, as shown in Figure 12.4.

Figure 12.4: Routing table displayed using ROUTE PRINT

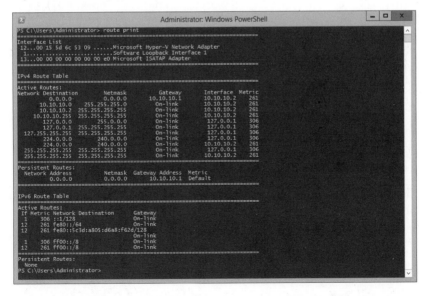

Network Configuration and Communication

PART IV

```
NETSTAT -R
NETSH INTERFACE IPv6 SHOW ROUTE
```

Each of these commands will show you the IPv6 entries on the routing table. To correct or enter a missing route, you will need to use the following:

```
NETSH INTERFACE IPv6 SET ROUTE, ROUTE ADD, or ROUTE CHANGE.
```

It is also possible to remove erroneous or incorrect routes using this:

```
NETSH INTERFACE IPv6 DELETE ROUTE command or ROUTE DELETE.
```

In each of these cases, it is important that you have a clear understanding of what the correct routing table entries should look like and that you are able to recognize entries that are not correct or are simply not there. As discussed earlier, you really need a good knowledge of the way things are supposed to work in your network infrastructure in order to troubleshoot them effectively.

Validate DNS Name Resolution for IPv6 Addresses

If the IPv6 addressing configuration and response checks out, move up and check on the resolution of host names to TCP/IP addresses, which means DNS. DNS resolves host names to IP addresses for both IPv4 and IPv6. You can perform some simple tasks to ensure that IPv6 host name to IP address resolution is occurring properly.

First, verify that your DNS server has been configured to resolve host names to IPv6 addresses and that it is acting upon name resolution requests that it receives. To begin, use the HOSTNAME utility to check the host name of the server and to check the DNS suffix.

Next, open the DNS Manager tool, and verify that all your configured DNS servers appear on the DNS Manager's list of authoritative servers. You can also use the DNS Manager to check the process of forwarding in the event that a host name cannot be resolved to an IP address on the local DNS server. If you need to make changes to the DNS suffix or to connection-specific DNS suffix information, you can do it using DNS Manager.

Flush the DNS Cache

Each IPv6 client maintains a list of recently resolved DNS-to-IPv6 addresses. This list is called the *DNS resolver cache*. If for some reason a record in the cache had an incorrect address for a given host name, it would limit connectivity. In cases like this, you can flush the contents of the DNS resolver cache using IPCONFIG /FLUSHDNS. See Figure 12.5.

Figure 12.5: Results of IPCONFIG /FLUSHDNS

This command will remove all entries from the cache and force the machine to resolve the address with recursive queries sent to the local DNS server hierarchy and get the correct host name to IP address information.

You can quickly check for the function of DNS resolution using the PING tool. PING can be used in conjunction with IP addresses, host names, or FQDNs. For example:

    PING Computer 1

or

    PING www.microsoft.com

Test IPv6 TCP Connections

So, what if everything works from an IP perspective, but you still cannot get a TCP connection to occur between systems? In the majority of cases, there is a problem with packet filtering. You learned earlier in the chapter about packet filtering locations for IP packets. You will need to check the same locations for TCP filtering. Because you will be checking your filters when you are validating IP connectivity, it makes sense to check for TCP filters at the same time. If you didn't check for TCP filtering earlier, it is time to do it now.

One of the easiest ways to check TCP connections is with the TELNET tool. TELNET is a command-line tool that establishes TCP connections between systems. TELNET uses a syntax similar to the PING command; simply use the TELNET command followed by the IPv6 address.

If the connection is possible, TELNET will create it. TELNET connects to a service, so once you connect to a machine, you can execute commands against the machine to test, configure, or view the contents of the remote machine. TELNET is sometimes seen as a potential security risk, so

Network Configuration and Communication

PART IV

don't be surprised if the local firewalls or security policies do not allow TELNET packets. If they do not, you may be able to test TCP connectivity with a tool called Test TCP (TTCP), which is available from PCAUSA at http://www.pcausa.com/Utilities/pcattcp.htm. This tool allows you to build TCP connections and also monitor for incoming TCP connection requests. You can configure a computer to "listen" for TCP connections on a specific port, which is good because you can test TCP connections without having any specific services installed or configured.

Troubleshoot IPv4

Troubleshooting IPv4 requires many of the same practices as trouble-shooting IPv6. Remember, TCP/IP is a stack of protocols working at different layers of the Open Systems Interconnect (OSI) model for net-work communication. There is no right way to go about troubleshoot-ing IPv4; you simply need to find a methodology that works for you. We encourage you to take a similar root cause analysis approach to trouble-shooting IPv4 as you did with IPv6. The goal of troubleshooting is to identify the reason or reasons preventing connectivity and then make the necessary adjustments to restore connectivity.

Use the Network Connection Repair Tool

When you find a problem with connectivity, it makes sense to begin your troubleshooting in some common areas. The Network Connection Repair tool will check for some of the most common connectivity prob-lems. If it finds them, it will make the necessary adjustments and recon-nect the system.

The Network Connection Repair tool automates a list of functions including the following:

- Checking that DHCP is enabled and refreshing the IP address lease
- Flushing the ARP cache
- Flushing the DNS cache using IPCONFIG /FLUSHDNS
- Reregistering DNS names using IPCONFIG /REGISTERDNS
- Flushing the NetBIOS name cache
- Reloading the NetBIOS name cache

The really cool thing about the Network Connection Repair tool is that the whole process is automated, and it can be initiated from the client and requires no administrative intervention. This means you can resolve the most common IPv4 problems with very little administrative effort.

To start the Network Connection Repair tool, you will need to go to the Network Connections folder. Right-click the connection you want to repair, and choose Diagnose.

Verify IPv4 Connectivity

If the Network Connection Repair tool does not fix the connectivity problem, you will need to dig a little deeper to identify and resolve your IP connectivity issues. We recommend you begin at the Event Viewer.

The Event Viewer shows events, warnings, and error messages from the local system or any system to which you have subscribed for event updates. This means the local Event Viewer will collect data about the local system and other systems you choose. You can effectively use the Event Viewer as a central resource to monitor key clients and servers throughout your network. The Event Viewer will likely display any related events that are affecting TCP/IP connectivity.

You will want to make sure the TCP/IP configuration is correct before you do anything else. Does the current configuration match the defined configuration for this network connection? Knowing your network and how the configurations are supposed to be will have tremendous value when you are troubleshooting.

1. Check the physical hardware. Check the network cable. Is it plugged in? Check the connections at switches, hubs, and routers. Don't laugh—you may solve a lot of TCP/IP problems right here in step 1.

2. Verify function and configuration of the network interface.

   Ipconfig /all displays the status and configuration of the IPv4 interface. Verify that the interface has an address and is in fact enabled. Check the DNS settings for the interfaces to be certain that they are configured correctly, as shown in Figure 12.6.

Network Configuration and Communication

PART IV

Figure 12.6: Results of `IPCONFIG /ALL`

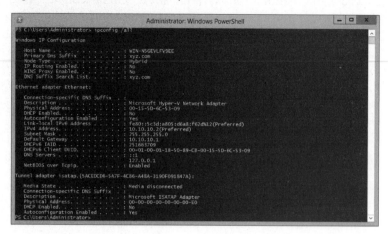

You can use the command-line tool `NETSH INTERFACE IP SHOW CONFIG` to display the configuration of the IP interfaces and to modify or delete incorrect configuration information.

Verify Responsiveness

As previously noted, not every problem is going to be fixed with a simple check of the hardware and address configuration. Responsiveness is also important. Responsiveness takes into account the fact that communication takes at least two endpoints. If either of the endpoints fails to respond, then the communication cannot take place. If you have checked the local configuration and everything is in order, you should check that the machine is actually responding to IP requests.

IPv4 uses something called an Address Resolution Protocol (ARP) cache to store IPv4 addresses that have been resolved to MAC addresses recently. If for some reason the ARP cache holds incorrect information, it can impede connectivity. You can flush the ARP cache with no negative effects to TCP/IP using this command:

```
ARP -D
```

If you are thinking to yourself, "Hey, that's a lot like the neighbor cache from IPv6," you are right!

The previous step, deleting the ARP cache, acts as a preemptive action to eliminate the possibility that your machine is being incorrectly directed to an IPv4 address that is not going to respond. To truly troubleshoot responsiveness, you will need to start sending packets onto the network and watching for responses. There are a couple of tools that are uniquely suited for this exercise.

PING uses ICMP to send echo request packets to a host and then measures the response time as the host responds to those echo requests. This tool can be incredibly valuable in verifying responsiveness in IPv4. Traditionally, when you use the PING tool, you begin with the process of pinging the local host address and then move on to the local IP address, then an IP address on the same subnet, next the default gateway of the local router, and finally an address on another network segment. You might have learned that you can skip right to pinging a remote host on another segment; if you get a response, you know everything in the cascade is working. As tempting as that is, in the event that you do not receive a response from the remote host, you really don't know anything about where your problem is located. Start with the local host, and work your way through the list. When you don't receive a response, you have reached the area that is having the problem.

IPv4 has a tool called Trace Route (TRACERT) that allows you to do exactly as its name suggests and trace the route from source to destination in a TCP/IPv4 connection. This tool will help you identify any routing issues that might exist on the route from source to destination computer. Its syntax is as follows:

```
TRACERT -D xxx.xxx.xxx.xxx
```

where x is the IP address of the destination computer.

One more very important point concerning PING and TRACERT is that ICMP packets can be considered a security risk, and often network administrators will configure their computers not to accept or respond to ping echo request packets. If you ping a machine and get no response, make certain that the reason you are not getting a response is that there really is no connectivity, not that the system you pinged does not support ICMP packets. This process of removing or limiting response to specific packet types is often termed *packet filtering*. Packet filtering is a common reason for lack of responsiveness. If you are confident that TCP/IP has been installed and is configured correctly and you are still not getting connectivity, it may well be an issue of filtering. Consider checking the following:

- Windows Firewall rules
- IPsec policies
- Remote access policies

Network Configuration and Communication

PART IV

- IPv4 packet filters
- Router policies

Although you are checking for IP filtering issues, you will also want to identify any potential TCP filtering issues. This will save you a troubleshooting step later if you happen to have a problem with TCP connectivity.

Check the Routing Table for IPv4

TCP/IP connectivity issues could be caused by incorrect entries on the IPv4 routing table. You can use the ROUTE PRINT command to show the IPv4 routing table. Here again you will need to be familiar with what the correct routes should look like and then check for any erroneous information on the routing table.

You can add new routes with the ROUTE ADD command. If you find erroneous routes and want to update them with correct information, you can modify the entries with the ROUTE CHANGE command. If you find entries that should just not be there, you can delete routes using the ROUTE DELETE command.

Although you are working with the router and routing table, it makes sense to trace a path through routers from source to destination. You can use the PATHPING *xxx.xxx.xxx.xxx* command to trace the route. Remember, this tool will display packet losses for each router along the path. Some administrators like to use the -d switch with PATHPING in order to speed up the display of results by preventing the reverse DNS lookup at the internal interface of each router on the path. We like the additional detail provided, and we don't mind waiting. You choose what works best for your situation.

Validate DNS Name Resolution for IPv4 Addresses

If the IPv4 addressing configuration and response checks out, you will want to move up and check on the resolution of host names to TCP/IP addresses, which means DNS. DNS resolves host names to IP addresses for both IPv4 and IPv6. You can perform some simple tasks to ensure that IPv4 host name to IP address resolution is occurring properly.

First, verify that your DNS server has been configured to resolve host names to IPv4 addresses and that it is acting upon name resolution requests it receives. To begin, use the HOSTNAME utility to check the host name of the server and to check the DNS suffix.

Next, open the DNS Manager tool, and verify that all of your configured DNS servers appear on the DNS Manager's list of authoritative servers. You can also use the DNS Manager to check the process of forwarding in the event that a host name cannot be resolved to an IP address on the local DNS server. If you need to make changes to the DNS suffix or to connection-specific DNS suffix information, you can do so using DNS Manager.

Flush the DNS Cache

Each IPv4 client maintains a list of recently resolved DNS to IPv4 addresses. This list is called the *DNS resolver cache*. If for some reason a record in the cache had an incorrect address for a given host name, it would limit connectivity. In cases like this, you can flush the contents of the DNS resolver cache using this:

```
IPCONFIG /FLUSHDNS
```

The command will remove all entries from the cache and force the machine to resolve the address with recursive queries sent to the local DNS server hierarchy and get the correct host name to IP address information.

You can quickly check for the function of DNS resolution using the PING tool, as shown in Figure 12.7. PING can be used in conjunction with IP addresses or host name or an FQDN. For example:

```
PING Computer 1
```

or

```
PING www.microsoft.com
```

Figure 12.7: Results of successful PING of the local computer Win-N5GEVLFV9EE .xyz.com

Network Configuration and Communication

Test IPv4 TCP Connections

What if everything works from an IP perspective, but you still cannot get a TCP connection to occur between systems? In the majority of cases, this is a problem with packet filtering. You learned earlier in the chapter about packet filtering locations for IP packets. You will need to check the same locations for TCP filtering. Since you will be checking your filters when you are validating IP connectivity, it makes sense to check for TCP filters at the same time. If you didn't check for TCP filtering earlier, it is time to do it now.

One of the easiest ways to check TCP connections is with the TELNET tool. TELNET is a command-line tool that establishes TCP connections between systems. It uses a syntax similar to the PING command; simply use the TELNET command followed by the IPv4 address.

If the connection is possible, TELNET will create it. TELNET connects to a service, so once you connect to a machine, you can execute commands against the machine to test, configure, or view the contents of the remote machine. TELNET is sometimes seen as a potential security risk, so don't be surprised if the local firewalls or security policies do not allow TELNET packets.

PART V
Manage Desktop and Server Virtualization

IN THIS PART ▶

13

Managing Remote Access to Your Server

IN THIS CHAPTER, YOU WILL LEARN TO:

I n this chapter, you will learn how to manage remote access to your server. Often when you think of remote access, you do not think about virtualization. However, remote access is another variation of virtualized access to your servers — whether that comes in the form of a remote desktop or application virtualization. They both factor into how you grant users on your network access to your servers remotely. You will see an overview of the new methods of configuration for Remote Desktop Services (RDS) in Windows Server 2012.

Understand Remote Desktop Services

Remote Desktop Services in Windows Server 2012 is designed and built to allow users to connect to virtual desktops, also referred to as Virtual Desktop Infrastructure (VDI), remote applications (RemoteApp), and virtual machine sessions called *session-based desktops*. Remote Desktop Services can provide access to each of these resources from within your local network or be used to provide access from the Internet. The tools and techniques used to provide and control access are configured as part of the Remote Desktop Services role in Windows Server 2012.

Microsoft calls Windows Server 2012 the Cloud OS because it has built-in components designed to work in cloud-based networks. Remote Desktop Services is one of the areas where this is particularly noticeable. While many services in Windows Server 2012 are deployed on a single server, Remote Desktop Services are intended to operate across multiple servers or virtual machines as part of a shared Remote Desktop Services infrastructure. If you have used Remote Desktop Services in the past, many of the terms and operations will be familiar to you; the methods of implementation may have changed.

Remote Desktop Services is deployed in either a VDI deployment or a Session Virtualization deployment (a single network may implement both deployment types). You will want to understand the individual component services used by Remote Desktop Services, what they do in the infrastructure, and how to work with each of them.

Understand the Remote Desktop Services Role

Windows Server 2012 Remote Desktop Services is made up of six role services that can be used to provide the desired level of remote access to VDI-, RemoteApp-, or session-based desktops. You can view each role and its description in Table 13.1.

Table 13.1: Role Services

RDS Role Service	Description
Remote Desktop Virtualization Host	This role integrates with Hyper-V to deploy pooled or personal virtual desktop collections using RemoteApp and desktop connection.
Remote Desktop Session Host	Enables a server to host RemoteApp programs.
Remote Desktop Connection Broker	This role service adds three functions. Allows users to reconnect to their session. Provides workload distribution between servers in a server collection. Provides access to virtual desktops.
Remote Desktop Gateway	Allows connections to internal resources from the Internet through the Remote Desktop Gateway.
Remote Desktop Web Access	Allows connections to RemoteApp or Desktop sessions using a Windows 8 or Windows 7 Start menu or a web browser.
Remote Desktop Licensing	This role manages the licensing for connections to VDI, session-based desktops, and RemoteApps.

Please note that although previous versions of RDS allowed installation on a domain controller, Windows Server 2012 does not. As with Windows Server 2008 R2, domain membership is required in order to install RDS components; Figure 13.1 shows the domain requirement reminder.

Figure 13.1: Domain requirement reminder

Install Remote Desktop Services Role Services

Remote Desktop Services are deployed using either a VDI deployment or a session-based deployment. These streamlined deployment methods ensure that the right roles are deployed in order to support either VDI or remote desktop sessions and RemoteApp. Now, to make matters even more interesting, Microsoft includes the option to deploy each of the two methods using two different architectural strategies called quick deployment and standard deployment.

A *quick deployment* is used to install all of the required role services on a single server for testing purposes. Quick deployments are recommended only for testing purposes and not for real-world deployments. *Standard deployments* are used for real-world Remote Desktop Services deployments and allow segmentation of roles among several different servers. Functionally, the two deployments are the same because they deploy the same role services. Architecturally, the standard deployment is far more capable of supporting an actual remote desktop infrastructure.

VDI Standard Deployment

Before you begin, it is important to note that the Hyper-V role is a required component for successful VDI Standard deployments.

1. Open Server Manager from the Desktop.

2. Select Add Roles and Features.

3. On the Before You Begin screen, click Next.

4. From the Select Installation Type screen, select Remote Desktop Services installation, and then click Next.

5. From the Select Deployment Type screen, select Standard Deployment and click Next.

6. Select Virtual Machine-Based Desktop Deployment and click Next.

7. Review the role services installed in this deployment (see Figure 13.2), and then click Next.

8. On the Specify RD Connection Broker server page, choose a server on which to install the RD Connection Broker role service. Select the computer from the list in the Server Pool box, and then click the arrow to move the server to the selected box. Click Next.

9. On the Specify RD Web Access server page, select the server on which you want to install the RD Web Access server role by selecting the computer from the Server Pool box and then clicking the arrow to move the computer to the selected box. (You could also choose to check the box to "Install the RD Web Access role service on the RD Connection Broker server," as shown in Figure 13.3.) Click Next.

Figure 13.2: VDI Standard Deployment Role Services

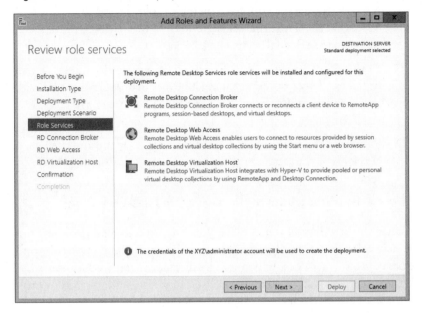

Figure 13.3: Install RD Web Access role service on the RD Connection Broker server.

10. On the Specify RD Virtualization Host server, select the desired server in the Server Pool pane on which to install the RD Virtualization Host role service and click the arrow to move the server to the selected pane. Click Next.

11. At this point, you will see a Checking Compatibility screen, which provides a list of criteria that must be met in order to proceed with the installation. Review the list and make sure you have met the requirements.

12. Review the contents of the Confirm Selections pane and then check the box to restart the destination server automatically if required. Click Deploy.

13. Review the results of the installation and then click Close.

Once the installation is complete, you may need to restart servers for the new role settings to take effect. You will also certainly want to configure collection services, which will be discussed later in the chapter, on the target servers. Configuring collection services allows you to provide access to virtual desktops using the RDS tools that were added to the Server Manager as part of the deployment.

Standard Session-Based Desktop Deployment

Session-based desktop deployments are used to establish remote connections for RemoteApp and for desktop sessions, both internally and from the Internet. The roles required for standard session-based desktop deployments are installed together during the deployment process.

1. Open Server Manager from the Desktop.

2. Select Add Roles and Features.

3. On the Before You Begin screen, click Next.

4. Select Remote Desktop Services Installation from the Select Installation Type screen, and then click Next.

5. Select the Standard Deployment from the Select Deployment Type screen, and Click Next.

6. Select Session-Based Desktop Deployment from the Select Deployment Scenario screen, and click Next.

7. Review the roles that will be installed and click Next.

8. Select a server on which to install the RD Connection Broker role from the server pool, click the arrow to move the server to the selected box, and click Next.

9. Select a server from the server pool on which to install the RD web access server, click the arrow to move the server to the selected box, and click Next.

10. Select a server from the server pool on which to install the RD Session Host server role, click the arrow to move the server to the selected box, and then click Next.

11. Review the contents of the Confirm Selections pane and then, if required, check the box to restart the destination server automatically.

12. Click Deploy.

The servers will restart after a standard session desktop deployment. Server Manager will start by default as Windows Server 2012 starts, and you will see the new Remote Desktop Services link in the left pane, as shown in Figure 13.4.

Figure 13.4: Remote Desktop Services in Server Manager

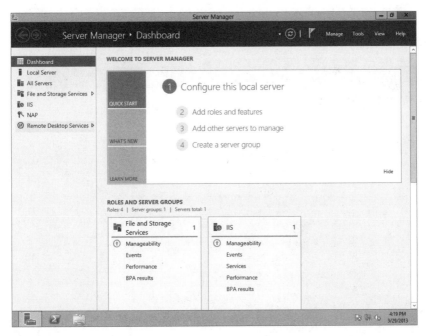

Manage Desktop and Server Virtualization

PART V

Remote Desktop Services in Server Manager is the primary tool for configuring and managing Remote Desktop Services operations.

Remote Desktop Services Tool

Server Manager in Windows Server 2012 has become the one-stop shop for most of your configuring, monitoring, and managing tasks. The integrated tools make this central console the powerful and easy way to get things done on your server. When you installed the Remote Desktop Services role, the tools for working with the various role services were added to Server Manager. One of the major improvements to Remote Desktop Services in Windows Server 2012 is the ease that this central Dashboard tool brings to managing a distributed Remote Desktop Services infrastructure.

When you click the link to open Remote Desktop Services, you will see an active architectural diagram like the one shown in Figure 13.5. The diagram depicts the various roles and services you have installed in your Remote Desktop Services deployment and suggests next steps for configuring your virtual machine-based or session-based desktop deployments. Each of the images in the diagram is linked to actual configuration and management tools to make administration of Remote Desktop Services easier.

Figure 13.5: Remote Desktop Services tool

The beauty of working with RDS in Windows Server 2012 is that the entire RDS platform is installed, configured, and managed through Server Manager. You could, of course, install RDS the "old-fashioned" way by choosing to Add Roles and Features and simply choosing Remote Desktop. This method requires a deeper understanding of the intricacies of each role and how the component pieces interact to provide the desired level and type of services required.

Manage Remote Desktop Services

In Chapter 2, "Adding Server Roles and Functionality," you saw a brief overview of how to install Remote Desktop Services. In this chapter, you will see a more detailed look at working with Windows Server 2012 RDS.

Administer Remote Desktop Session Host

The main component you will need to administer when working with RDS is the Remote Desktop Session Host.

Remote Desktop Session Host works with a series of collections, which are defined as a group of one or more session hosts configured to support a specific AD Group assigned permissions to access the collection.

Create a New RD Session Collection

Remote Desktop Services are managed and accessed throughout the use of collections. Collections define groups of resources and the users and groups that can access those resources. It is important to understand how to create and manage those Remote Desktop session collections.

1. A new collection is built by right-clicking the RD Session Host icon in the Remote Desktop Services tool in Server Manger and choosing Create Session Collection.

2. Read the notes on the Before You Begin page, and then Click Next.

3. Create a name for the collection and then click Next.

4. Choose a server (or servers) from the server pool to support the session collection, and click Next.

5. On the Specify User Groups screen, specify the Active Directory group that will have access to the collection. Click Next.

6. Select the box to enable user profile disks if you would like to use them.

NOTE One of the new features of Windows Server 2012 is the ability to run a single version of a session for all of the users who connect to the session. This saves a tremendous amount of disk resources and allows fast implementation of new session images. The drawback, of course, is that every user's session is exactly the same. Windows Server 2012 adds the ability to use user profile disks in conjunction with sessions to provide unique session content for each user while maximizing the session's performance and limiting the number of unique session images.

---

7. Review the Confirm Selections page, and then click Create.

After the collection is created, you will notice a new icon with the collection name on the hierarchy diagram in the Remote Desktop Services tool in Server Manager. If you click the New Collection link as it appears in the Collections menu to the left of the hierarchical diagram, you can configure the session collection by adding RemoteApp programs or host servers, or by adjusting the properties of the collection, as shown in Figure 13.6.

Figure 13.6: Configuring Session Collection

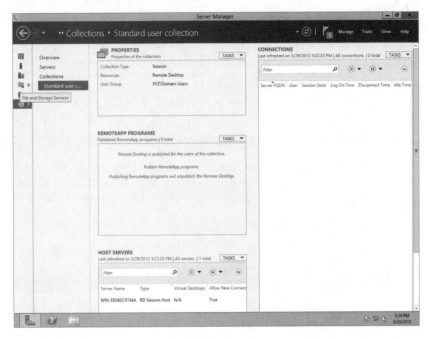

Publish RemoteApp Programs

Session collections can be used to publish RemoteApp programs. Just about any application that you want to run over Remote Desktop Services can be published as a RemoteApp program. To publish RemoteApp Programs, do the following.

1. Select a session collection in Remote Desktop Services in Server Manager.

2. In the Remote App Programs section, click the Publish RemoteApp Programs link, as shown in Figure 13.7.

Figure 13.7: Publishing RemoteApp programs

3. On the Select RemoteApp Programs page, select a program or click the Add button to add a program not on the list. The files you chose must be executable files. Click Next.

4. Review the information on the Confirmation page and then click Publish.

5. Review the information on the Completion page and then click Close.

Your application will appear in the RemoteApp Programs list, as shown in Figure 13.8. The right pane of the Session Collection pane also displays the current connections to the session.

Figure 13.8: Published RemoteApp program

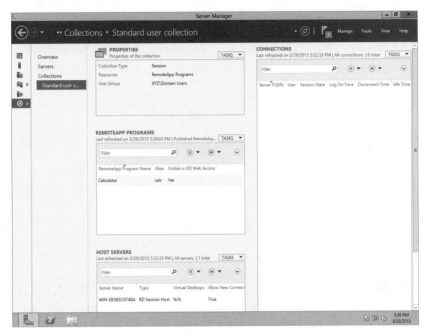

Activate Remote Desktop Licensing Server

The RD Licensing role of RDS plays a vital role in your network. This server governs the remote desktop client access licenses (RDS CALs) for your server. If a server is not properly configured or activated, your RDS environment could stop working and prevent connections to your RDS server. Install this role from Server Manager.

1. Open Server Manager from the Desktop.

2. Click Add Roles and Features.

3. On the Before You Begin page, click Next.

4. Choose Role-based or Feature-based Installation on the Select Installation Type page, and click Next.

5. Select your server from the server pool and click Next.

6. Expand Remote Desktop Services.

7. Choose Remote Desktop Licensing on the Select Server Roles page and Click Next.

8. If the Add Features Required for Remote Desktop Licensing box appears, choose Add Features and check the box to Include Management Tools (if applicable).

9. Click Next on the Select Features page.

10. Review your selections and click Install.

11. When the installation is complete, click Close.

Now that you have installed the Remote Desktop Licensing, you can manage the licenses issued in your environment. The RD Licensing Manager is opened by opening Server Manager and then choosing Terminal Services ➤ RD Licensing Manager from the Tools menu (it is called "Terminal Services" here, but everywhere else it is called RDS). The RD Licensing Manager tool lets you activate and distribute licenses for your Remote Desktop deployment.

You have two choices for the licensing mode of your RDS server. You can license the server per device or per user. *Per device* allows one device on your network to connect to the RDS server regardless of which user is logged on to the device. This licensing mode is useful when kiosk computers are used heavily in conjunction with RDS for your infrastructure. *Per user* allows a user to log on to the RDS services from any computer in your network. This mode is useful when you have users who use a variety of workstations to perform their tasks.

Configure Remote Desktop Gateway

The RD Gateway component of Remote Desktop Services provides a tool to allow users to access the RDS server in a secure fashion without using a VPN client. This is done by encapsulating Remote Desktop Protocol (RDP) inside Hypertext Transfer Protocol Secure (HTTPS) packets and using a certificate to validate the connection. You will need to add the Remote Desktop Gateway role to your RDS server.

1. Open Server Manager from the Desktop.

2. Click Add Roles and Features.

3. On the Before You Begin page, click Next.

4. Choose Role-Based or Feature-Based Installation on the Select Installation Type page and click Next.

5. Select your server from the server pool and click Next.

6. Expand Remote Desktop Services.

7. Select Remote Desktop Gateway.

8. Click the Add Features button to add features that are required for a remote desktop gateway.

9. Click Next.

10. On the Select Features page, click Next.

11. Read the Network Policy and Access Services page and then click Next.

12. Leave the box next to Network Policy Server checked and click Next.

13. Review the information on the Confirm Installation Selections page and then click Install.

14. When the installation completes, click the Close button.

After you have installed the role service, it is just a matter of working with your Connection Authorization Policy (CAP) and Resource Authorization Policy (RAP) to ensure the security of your server.

The Remote Desktop Gateway Manager allows you to monitor current connections to the service. You can also modify or create new policies; you just need to open the Remote Desktop Gateway Manager:

1. Open the Server Manager and select Terminal Services ➢ Remote Desktop Gateway Manager from the Tools menu.

2. In the RD Gateway Manager, click your server. A Dashboard screen similar to Figure 13.9 will appear. Even though the role has been installed, you still need to add a certificate. Click the link on the View or Modify Certificate properties. You also need to add Connection Authorization Policies and Resources Authorization Policies.

Figure 13.9: RD Gateway Manager

3. To create CAP policies, click Create Connection Authorization Policy. At this point, you can provide a name, requirements, device redirection, and time-out values for the policy. Click OK when finished.

4. To create RAP policies, click Create Resource Authorization Policy. Provide a name, user groups, network resources, and allowed ports for the policy, and then click OK.

The RD Gateway Manager can also be used to modify existing policies and monitor connections.

Configure Remote Desktop Connection Broker

In Windows Server 2012, the RD Connection Broker is responsible for allowing clients to reconnect to existing sessions, RemoteApp programs, or virtual desktops. The RD Connection Broker also balances the workload among RD session host servers to provide access and high availability. This role service relies on a SQL Server instance and maintains a database of connections.

> **TIP**   For detailed information on setup and configuration, refer
> to the following article:
> http://social.technet.microsoft.com/wiki/contents/
> articles/10391.installing-and-configuring-rd-connection-
> broker-high-availability-in-windows-server-2012.aspx

Configure Remote Desktop Web Access

One of the other avenues your users can use to access the RDS components on your Windows Server 2012 server is via their local web
browser. RD Web Access allows your users to log on to an RDS session via the browser. In RD Web Access, you can let your clients access
services from around the world. When you are configuring RD Web
Access, you need to understand how to configure applications to run via
the RDS components.

To configure RD Web Access, you first need to control how the website gets the applications you want to provide. In Windows Server 2012,
this is accomplished through the creation of session collections, as discussed earlier in the chapter. You can choose either a local RemoteApp
server or an RD Connection Broker to control your access. Your RDS
infrastructure will determine how your users receive applications via the
RD Web Access server.

1. Open Remote Desktop Web Access Configuration by starting
   Server Manager from the taskbar and then choosing Remote
   Desktop Services from the Tools menu.

2. Add a new collection for the RD Web Access Server by choosing
   Collections from the Actions pane on the left.

3. Select Tasks and choose Create Session Collection.

4. On the Before You Begin page, click Next.

5. Provide a name for the collection, and click Next.

6. On the specify RD Web Access Server page, select your server and
   click Next.

7. On the Specify Users and Groups page, select the users or groups
   who will have access to this session. Click Next.

8. On the User Profiles page, select a User Profile Location, or choose not to use User Profiles For This Session Collection, and then click Next.

9. On the Confirmation page, click Create. You will see a Progress screen like the one shown in Figure 13.10.

10. Once the process completes, click Close.

Figure 13.10: Progress screen

Connect with Remote Desktop Connection

In addition to using RD Web Access to connect to the RDS components, your users also have the ability to connect through programs located on the host computer. In the Microsoft OS, this connection program is called the Remote Desktop Connection. This connection tool allows you to connect directly to the RDS components and control many aspects of the connection.

1. Open Remote Desktop Connection by pressing the Windows key and then typing **Remote Desktop.** Choose Remote Desktop Connection.

2. If you do not want to modify any of the settings, you can enter the server name and your logon credentials. However, if you want to modify some of the settings, click Options, and you will see a screen similar to Figure 13.11.

Figure 13.11: Remote Desktop Connection

General: This tab contains the basic connection settings, the server name, and the username. You also have the ability to save these settings to your own RDP file.

Display: This tab controls the resolution and colors supported for the RDP session.

Local Resources: This tab allows the RDP session to leverage your existing local resources. Specifically, you can configure audio, keyboard, printers, and the Clipboard, as well as other local resources. These were new additions to Windows Server 2008.

Programs: You can specify which programs will load when the RDP session starts.

Experience: This tab allows you to make the RDP session appear very crisp and natural. The goal of these settings is to make the remote connection appear as close to a real desktop as possible.

Advanced: This tab allows you to control how server authentication failures are handled and also control the RD Gateway server, if configured, to allow a secure connection over the gateway.

3. When you are done modifying the settings, click Connect, and you will be connected to the RDP services, provided you have permissions and the server is available.

Work with Virtual Desktop Infrastructure

When you're using all the RDS components available to a Windows Server 2012 server, one of the key aspects you can take advantage of is the virtual desktop infrastructure. What this allows you to do, in a nutshell, is take a virtual machine created on your server using Hyper-V and enable remote desktop connections to the virtual machine. This provides a flexible desktop access solution for you and your users, and it gives you centralized management of the desktop sessions. Because the sessions are stored in a virtual machine, you can quickly manage these systems.

Under the covers, when the VDI user connects to the desktop, a connection with either RD Web Access or a Remote Desktop Connection file is initiated. The connection will be routed through the RD Connection Broker, with verification to AD and the RD Session Host, and then the client will be able to access the Remote Desktop Virtualization Host. As you may recall, the Remote Desktop Virtualization Host role service requires Hyper-V configured on the server. It is the Hyper-V virtual machines loaded on the Remote Desktop Virtualization Host that will provide the desktop to your users. Refer to the diagram in Figure 13.12 to see how this works.

Figure 13.12: VDI overview

There are numerous services to make this work from end to end. However, the RDS tools make this as straightforward as possible. After you create the virtual client machine to be used for VDI, you will need to configure the various components to properly handle the requests. A majority of your configurations will be completed in the RD Connection Manager. You will add the VDI components using the Remote Desktop Services Installation option under Add Roles and Features inside Server Manager.

Work with Remote Clients

In Windows Server 2012, in addition to the RDS components, the server can also be configured to provide powerful capabilities for remote clients to your network. Remote clients include your road warriors, telecommuters, and other users who are not connected to your network on a daily basis. In Windows Server 2012, you still have access to the Routing and Remote Access services that were available in Windows Server 2008. However, you also have a powerful alternative to a normal VPN with Direct Access. This section provides a broad overview of working with both solutions.

Install and Configure Windows Server 2012 VPNs

Creating a VPN on your Routing and Remote Access Service (RRAS) server provides secure remote access to private networks. When you decide to install a VPN and install the Routing and Remote Access role services, you get several capabilities for your network. RRAS can be used in a variety of configurations, as you can see in Table 13.2.

Table 13.2: RRAS Options

Component	Description
VPN Access	This allows clients to connect to your network across the Internet.
Dial-Up Access	This allows clients to connect to your network via a modem or other dial-in equipment.
Demand-Dial Connections	This allows your server to initiate and receive demand-dial connections. By dialing the connections only when needed, demand-dial connections allow your modem communications to be cost effective.

Table 13.2: RRAS Options *(continued)*

Component	Description
NAT	Network Address Translation allows the users on your network to share a single Internet connection. NAT translates between the public Internet address and your private network IP address scheme.
LAN Routing	This option allows your RRAS server to forward packets from one LAN segment to another.

Understand the Windows Server 2012 Role Services

When you install a VPN for your network, there are several core services you can choose to configure on a Windows Server 2012 server. Table 13.3 describes the role services and their functions.

Table 13.3: Network Policy and Access Role Services

Role Service	Description
Network Policy Server (NPS)	This role service gives you the ability to create access policies governing connection requests for authorization and authentication. This role service also allows you to install a client health enforcement tool called Network Access Protection (NAP).
RRAS Remote Access Service	The core RRAS services provide the VPN capability for your server. The connections can also be made with dial-up connections.
RRAS Routing	This role service will provide LAN and WAN routing services for your network as well as NAT, RIP, and IGMP proxy routers.
Health Registration Authority (HRA)	When you roll out your NAP solution, this is used in conjunction. The HRA will validate the health of remote clients connecting to the server by issuing certificates with the health status of the connection client. This role service will require the IIS Management tools, specifically, the IIS 6 WMI and Scripting tools.
Host Credential Authorization Protocol (HCAP)	This is another component for a NAP solution in your network; specifically, the HCAP component is designed to work with the Cisco Network Access Control. This role service will require the IIS Client Certificate Mapping Authentication and Digest Authentication components from the IIS services.

Install Routing and Remote Access Services

You install the Routing and Remote Access Services (RRAS) by adding the role services in Server Manager:

1. Open Server Manager from the Desktop.

2. Click Add Roles and Features.

3. On the Before You Begin page, click Next.

4. On the Select Installation Type page, choose Role-Based or Feature-Based Installation and Click Next.

5. Select your server from the server pool and Click Next.

6. In the list of roles, select Remote Access. Click Add Features to add the required prerequisites. Click Next.

7. On the Select Features page, click Next.

8. Review the Remote Access page, and then click Next.

9. On the Select Role Services page, select Direct Access and VPN (RAS) and click Next.

10. Review the Confirmation screen, shown in Figure 13.13, and click Install.

11. Review the Installation results, and click Close.

Figure 13.13: Installing Remote Access

Configure the VPN

After you have installed the RRAS solutions, you will need to enable and configure the role service. Windows Server 2012 has a wizard-driven utility designed to help you configure the VPN. You can simply click on the link to open the Getting Started Wizard from the RRAS Dashboard. Figure 13.14 shows the opening page.

Figure 13.14: The Getting Started Wizard

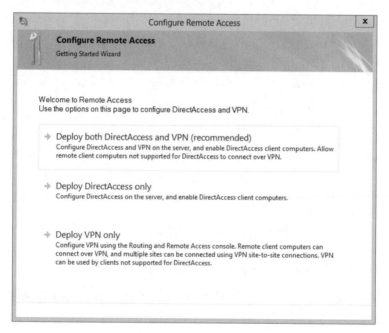

The Getting Started Wizard is the easiest way to configure and deploy VPN and Direct Access. The wizard recommends that you configure both of the services together because it is easier than configuring the VPN and Direct Access individually. You can, of course, choose to deploy each service on its own.

When you configure RRAS, you will have several choices. Follow these steps:

1. Open Server Manager and select Routing and Remote Access from the Tools menu.

2. Click your server in the tree on the left.

3. Select Action ➤ Configure And Enable Routing And Remote Access.

4. Review the Welcome screen, and click Next.

5. On the Configuration screen, select Remote Access (Dial-Up or VPN), and click Next.

6. The way your users will connect and the hardware you have on your server will determine whether you select VPN or Dial-Up. After you have selected your option, click Next.

7. Select the network interface you are using on your Windows Server 2012 server to connect to the Internet. After you have selected your Internet network interface, click Next.

8. Select the internal network adapter to which you want to assign your remote VPN users.

9. On the IP Address Assignment screen, you can use a DHCP server in your network, or you can create a specific range of IP addresses for the VPN connection. After you make your selection, click Next. If you choose your own range of addresses, you will have an additional step to configure the range.

10. On the next screen, you can choose to configure a Remote Authentication Dial-In User Service (RADIUS). You will see a screen similar to Figure 13.15. The RADIUS server is useful if you have several RRAS servers and you want to have a central authentication point. If you have only a single RRAS server, you can click No, as in this walk-through; then click Next.

Figure 13.15: RADIUS

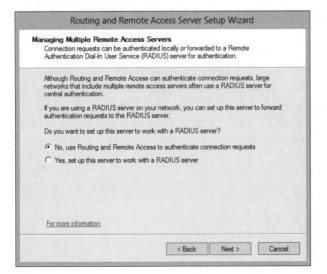

11. Review the Summary screen, and click Finish. You may receive a few additional warning prompts, which you will need to acknowledge before you can finish your setup. These additional prompts will be determined by the other options you may have configured during the setup of these services.

After you have completed enabling and configuring your RRAS server, your Routing and Remote Access management console will look similar to Figure 13.16.

Figure 13.16: RRAS configured

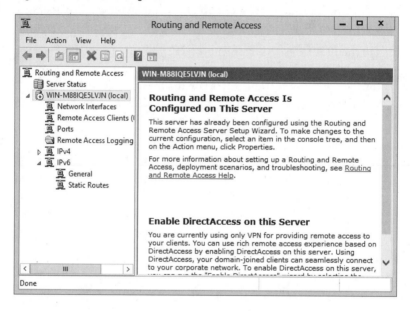

The completed console provides you with the ability to modify any of your VPN settings. Traditionally, once you have configured the VPN, you will not need to perform many day-to-day maintenance duties. However, the console does provide some nice monitoring tools to view server status as well as the ability to see which clients are currently connected to your server via VPN.

Network Access Protection (NAP)

One of the additional capabilities you have with RRAS is the ability to verify the health of your VPN clients to your network. NAP provides a method for you to quarantine your VPN clients before they are allowed to connect to your server. NAP can also be instrumental in providing remediation for clients not meeting the computer health requirements of your network. To learn more about configuring and working with NAP, please visit:

`http://technet.microsoft.com/en-us/library/dd314175(v=WS.10)`

Install and Configure DirectAccess

One of the coolest features in Windows Server 2012 is DirectAccess. In addition to requiring a Windows Server 2012 server, this feature is available only to Windows 7 and Windows 8 clients. This new capability allows IT administrators a great amount of control over remote clients. DirectAccess allows Windows 7 clients to always be connected to your corporate network regardless of how they are connected to the Internet. DirectAccess is a connection solution for Windows Server 2012 servers, as well as Windows 7 and Windows 8 clients, surpassing existing VPN solutions. Having your clients always connected provides a consistent management model for you. This provides you with a consistent way to manage, patch, and secure remote workstations that, in the past, may not have always been connected on a frequent basis. For your users, DirectAccess provides an "always-on" secure connection to corporate networks and resources.

The installation process for this toolset can be lengthy and complex, although in the end the work could be worth your time and effort if you have or are planning to have Windows 7 and/or Windows 8 clients in your environment. In this section, you will see an overview of the steps required to configure DirectAccess on your Windows Server 2012 server. There are also numerous prerequisites that need to be configured. Among many other things, DirectAccess requires an understanding of IPv6 (with IPv4 translation), Public Key Infrastructure (PKI), and the use of certificates, as well as a firm understanding of DNS to make this solution work. Microsoft created a nice step-by-step guide, which includes all the necessary prerequisites and the client-side configuration: go to `http://technet.microsoft.com/en-us/library/hh831416.aspx`.

Enable and Manage DirectAccess

When you need to configure DirectAccess, use the Routing and Remote Access tool to enable and manage Direct Access and its associated VPN components.

You can find the Routing and Remote Access management tool in the Administrative Tools group. When you open the tool, you can begin the process of setting up DirectAccess. When you first open the console, you will see a link in the center pane that says "Enable Direct Access on This Server." Clicking the link initiates the process of enabling and configuring DirectAccess. The Enable DirectAccess Wizard, shown in Figure 13.17, walks you through the simplified process of setting up DirectAccess for clients to connect securely to this server.

Figure 13.17: The Enable DirectAccess Wizard

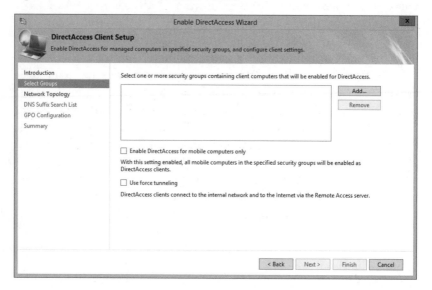

As you can see, the DirectAccess tool provides you visual step-by-step instructions to properly configure this powerful connection component. Each configuration step for DirectAccess can be modified after you have completed your initial configuration.

14

Maintaining Virtual Machines

IN THIS CHAPTER, YOU WILL LEARN TO:

Understand Virtualization with Hyper-V

Windows Server 2012 offers many opportunities for IT administrators to implement a virtualization strategy at the next level. Application Virtualization, Remote Desktop Gateways, and Remote Desktop all provide opportunities for virtualization. Although all these tools offer something uniquely valuable to the virtual environment, when we think of virtualization with Windows Server 2012, we think of Hyper-V.

Hyper-V enables you to create and host an entire virtualized environment in which you can host client and server operating systems. Hyper-V offers the benefits of running multiple operating systems simultaneously on the same set of physical hardware. The problem of ever-increasing numbers of servers (called *server sprawl*), and its associated costs in both implementation and administration, can be effectively controlled with a Hyper-V environment. There are also benefits related to the testing and development areas of IT because test machine and development environments can be easily built, maintained, and reused. On a system running Hyper-V, the hardware utilization typically goes way up while the hardware and administration costs go way down. These benefits have made Hyper-V a very popular addition to the Windows Server 2012 network.

Install Hyper-V

To install Hyper-V, your system must meet certain requirements:

- It must have an x64-based processor.

- The machine must support hardware-assisted virtualization.

- The processors must support Intel Virtualization Technology (Intel VT) or AMD Virtualization (AMD-V) enabled through the system BIOS.

- Your system must have hardware-enforced Data Execution Prevention (DEP) via a BIOS-enabled Intel XD bit or AMD NX bit.

- Your system must have Windows Server 2012 Standard edition or Datacenter edition installed.

Hyper-V is installed as a role in Windows Server 2012. You will use Server Manager to install Hyper-V components and the Hyper-V Manager tool:

1. Open Server Manager.

2. Select Add Roles and Features.

3. Select Role-based or Feature-based installation. Click Next.

4. Choose the destination server from the server pool where the role will be installed. Click Next.

5. Select the box for the Hyper-V role. See Figure 14.1.

Figure 14.1: Installing the Hyper V role

6. Click Next.

7. Click Next to verify the informational messages.

8. Select a network adapter to use with your virtual machines. (You can modify this later with the Virtual Network Manager.)

9. Check the box to allow the server to send and receive live migrations, as shown in Figure 14.2.

Figure 14.2: Enable live migrations.

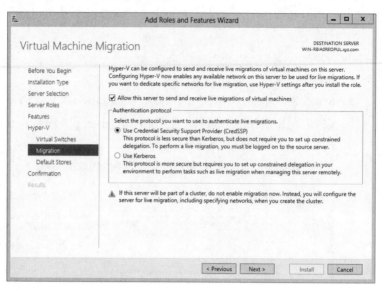

10. Click Install.

Once the installation of Hyper-V has completed, you will need to restart your computer.

After the restart, you can use a tool called the Hyper-V Manager to manage your virtual networks and virtual machines. You can open Hyper-V Manager from the Tools menu in Server Manager.

Hyper-V Manager consists of three panes, as you can see in Figure 14.3. The Tree pane is on the left side, the Details pane is in the center, and the Actions pane is on the right. As you select the server by its name in the Tree pane, the options available in the Details and Actions panes will update.

Work with Virtual Networks

The first things you will want to do after installing Hyper-V will be to build the virtual network infrastructure you will use to connect your virtual machines to one another and make them available to the rest of your network, or even the rest of the world.

You can build and manage virtual networks using the Virtual Network Manager tool in the Hyper-V Manager. When the Hyper-V server is selected, you will find the Virtual Switch Manager option in the Actions pane, as shown in Figure 14.4.

Figure 14.3: The Hyper-V Manager

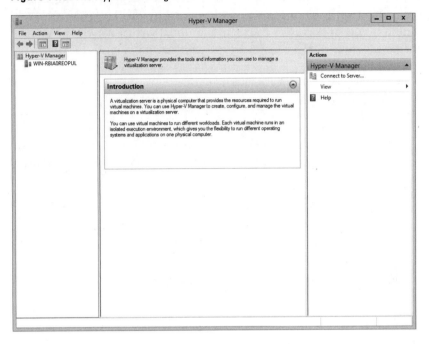

Figure 14.4: Virtual Switch Manager option

When you click the Virtual Switch Manager option, you will see the default network that was created when you installed Hyper-V, and you will have the opportunity to create additional virtual networks. Virtual networks come in three distinct types, as shown in Figure 14.5.

Figure 14.5: Create Virtual Network Wizard

External This type of virtual switch binds to the physical network adapter so that virtual machines can access the physical network.

Internal This creates a virtual switch that can be accessed only by the virtual machines hosted by the local Hyper-V server and the host physical server.

Private This creates a virtual switch that can be accessed only by the virtual machines hosted by the local Hyper-V server.

When you are working with virtual machines, you might want to have some machines connected to private virtual networks, such as in a testing environment—or you might want to have machines connected to the physical network, such as a hosted web server, or a legacy server running as a virtual machine. The cool thing is that Virtual Network Manager does not limit you to creating a single virtual network. You can build multiple virtual networks and link virtual machines to the various virtual networks based on your network needs.

To create a virtual network, follow these steps:

1. Open the Hyper-V Manager.

2. Select the server name in the Tree pane.

3. Click Virtual Switch Manager in the Actions pane.

4. Select the type of network you want to create (External, Internal, or Private).

5. Click Add.

6. Enter the name of your virtual network.

7. Enter any details or notes about the virtual network into the Notes field.

8. Under Connection Type, select the network interface (for an external network), or select the Internal Only or Private Virtual Machine Network radio button.

9. In the event that you are using an external network, you can also enable and use a VLAN ID in conjunction with this virtual network.

10. Click OK.

The nice thing about the Virtual Switch Manager tool is that you can easily add new virtual networks and make adjustments or changes to existing networks with relative ease. If you open the Virtual Switch Manager, the virtual networks you have already created are visible in the Details pane on the left. You can select them by name and make any changes, including removing the entire virtual network, by clicking Remove from Virtual Switch Properties.

Build Virtual Machines

A virtual machine is nothing more than an installed operating system. It is installed, and operates, inside a single special file called a *virtual hard disk* (VHD) file. The VHD file and the specific settings that define the hardware specifications combine to form the overall virtual machine. Windows Server 2012 introduces an additional hard disk type for Hyper-V called the VHDX (Hyper-V Virtual Hard Disk) file. This file type extends the size and functionality of virtual hard disks in Hyper-V. VHDX files are supported in sizes up to 64TB. The new format can store custom metadata and has the ability to increase the performance of applications on physical disks with sector sizes larger than 512 bytes. This format also provides support to manage virtual hard disks using PowerShell cmdlets. Windows Server 2012 can support both the traditional .vhd and the .vhdx format. The .vhdx format is not supported on Hyper-V versions before 2012.

Create a Virtual Machine

To create a virtual machine from Hyper-V Manager, click the New option in the Actions pane and select Virtual Machine. This will start the New Virtual Machine Wizard. This wizard will guide you through the rest of the process of creating a virtual machine. The process goes as follows:

1. Review the information on the Before You Begin screen and then click Next.

2. Provide a name for your virtual machine.

3. If you do not want the virtual machine stored in the default location, you will need to supply an alternative location.

4. Click Next.

5. Specify how many megabytes of RAM you will allocate to the virtual machine.

6. Click Next.

7. Choose which of your virtual networks you would like to connect to this virtual machine.

8. Click Next.

9. Specify the virtual hard disk. You can create a new one, use an existing one, or defer and attach a hard drive later.

10. Click Next.

11. Choose to install an operating system later, install from a DVD/CD, install from a boot floppy, or install an operating system from a

network installation server. This option is available only if you choose to create a new VHD. If you choose another option, you will be taken directly to step 13.

12. Click Next.

13. Read the summary information, and if it is correct, click Finish (see Figure 14.6).

Figure 14.6: Creating a virtual machine

Create Virtual Hard Disks

When you create a virtual machine, you will undoubtedly notice that it is possible to create a virtual machine and create the virtual hard disk (VHD) or Hyper-V virtual hard disk (VHDX) later. The virtual hard disk is the storage component for the virtual machine. It is the location where you will install the files for the operating system and applications.

Virtual hard disks have some degree of portability. It is possible to import and export VHD files using Hyper-V and "move" them from one server to another.

Not all VHDs are created equal. There are actually three different types. When you build a VHD, you will choose which type to create:

Dynamically expanding VHD   Dynamically expanding VHDs do exactly what the name suggests. The VHD starts relatively small and then dynamically increases in size to accommodate the storage needs of the virtual machine. It is important to note that although the disk automatically increases in size as new data is added to the VHD, it does not automatically shrink in size if data is deleted from the VHD. To resize the VHD file, you will need to run the Edit VHD Wizard.

Fixed VHD   A fixed virtual hard disk provides a specific amount of storage space that is defined at the time the hard disk is created. The size of the VHD will remain fixed regardless of how much data is added to the VHD. However, it is possible to use the Edit Virtual Hard Disk Wizard to increase or decrease the size of the fixed VHD should the need arise for additional storage space.

Differencing VHD   A differencing virtual hard disk provides storage to enable you to make changes to a parent virtual hard disk without altering the parent disk. The changes are actually made to the differencing disk while maintaining the original integrity of the parent disk. Both the parent and the child disks must be in the same format in order to function correctly.

Create a Virtual Hard Disk

To create a new VHD or VHDX, follow these steps:

1. Open the Hyper-V Manager.
2. Click New in the Actions pane.
3. Select Hard Disk.
4. Click Next on the Before You Begin page.
5. Select the type of VHD you want to create.
6. Click Next.
7. Name the VHD.
8. Click Next.
9. Specify the size of the disk, or copy the contents of a physical disk.
10. Review the settings you have made, as shown in Figure 14.7, and click Finish.

Figure 14.7: Creating a VHD

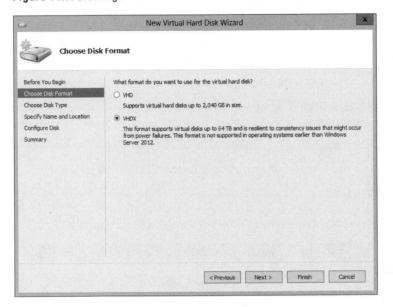

Note that these steps reflect the process of creating a virtual hard disk with either the fixed or dynamically increasing types. If you were to create a differencing disk to use in conjunction with an existing fixed or dynamically increasing disk, the process would be slightly different.

Use an Existing VHD or VHXD

The nature of the VHD and VHDX makes it relatively portable. As of this writing, Microsoft is providing VHD and VHDX files that can be used by individuals to evaluate Windows Server and other associated platform products. These VHD and VHDX files can be downloaded and used as the base of a virtual machine. You might create your own virtual machine files complete with operating system and applications and then export the VHD or VHDX file and use it on another Hyper-V server. The portability and versatility of the VHD and VHDX file make them very desirable. In fact, it is actually possible to deploy physical copies of Windows Server 2012, Windows 8, Windows Server 2008 R2, and Windows 7 from a VHD or VHDX file.

When you create a virtual machine, you have the option to create a virtual hard disk to go along with the virtual machine or wait until later to associate a VHD or VHDX with the virtual machine. If you select to associate the VHD or VHDX file later, you will need to modify the settings of the virtual machine you created.

To add a VHD or VHDX file to a virtual machine, do the following:

1. Open the Hyper-V Manager.

2. Select the virtual machine to which you want to connect the VHD or VHDX.

3. Click Settings in the Actions pane.

4. Select Controller IDE 0 or IDE 1, and select Hard Drive, as shown in Figure 14.8.

5. Click Add.

6. Click the Browse button, and locate the VHD or VHDX file.

7. Click OK.

Figure 14.8: Associating a VHD or VHDX to a virtual machine

Work with Virtual Machine Settings

Every virtual machine consists of two components: a virtual hard disk and the virtual machine settings. As you saw in the previous example, the settings are what tie the VHD or VHDX to the virtual machine. They define the operating environment of the virtual machine. You can manage the settings to maximize the performance of both the virtual machines and the physical server that is hosting the virtual machines.

The settings are broken down into two parts, the hardware settings and the management settings.

The hardware settings include the following:

Add Hardware The Add Hardware setting, shown in Figure 14.9, allows you to add a SCSI controller, a network adapter, or a legacy network adapter.

Figure 14.9: Add Hardware setting

BIOS Using the BIOS setting, shown in Figure 14.10, you can modify the order of the devices in the BIOS start order using the up and down arrows.

Figure 14.10: BIOS setting

Memory   Memory is critical to the operation of a virtual machine. The Memory setting, as shown in Figure 14.11, specifies the amount of physical RAM that is allocated to the virtual machine.

Figure 14.11: Memory setting

Processor   You can modify the number of virtual processors assigned to a virtual machine based on the number of physical processors and cores on each processor, as shown in Figure 14.12. You can also balance the usage of your processing resources between virtual machines. In addition, you can limit the processor features that a virtual machine can use to make it more compatible with different versions of processors, such as to make a processor more compatible with an older operating system like Windows NT.

Figure 14.12: Processor settings

Controller   The Controller settings, as shown in Figure 14.13, specify the IDE and SCSI controllers and what they are connected to. Traditionally, IDE 0 is connected to the VHD file that is the base of the operating system. IDE 1 is generally connected to the DVD drive, and you can define exactly what media you want to use with that DVD/CD drive; for example, you may have an ISO image of an operating system and want to install the OS using the image file. You can associate the ISO image with IDE 1.

Figure 14.13: Controller settings

Network Adapter The Network Adapter setting, as shown in Figure 14.14, allows you to define which of the available virtual networks you will connect to.

Figure 14.14: Network Adapter setting

COM settings   The COM settings, as shown in Figure 14.15, allow you to configure the virtual machine to communicate with the physical computer through a named pipe.

Figure 14.15: COM settings

Diskette Drive   Floppy disks are almost nonexistent in modern physical servers. However, they were commonplace in legacy hardware and often were the vehicle for delivering data, applications, and even operating systems. Should you need to use a floppy disk with a virtual machine, as shown in Figure 14.16, you will use this setting. A floppy disk is virtualized by using a virtual floppy disk file (.vfd).

Figure 14.16: Diskette Drive setting

The management settings associated with the virtual machine are as follows:

Name   Each virtual machine has a name, as shown in Figure 14.17. The name can be whatever you choose. We recommend you choose a name that allows you to easily recognize your virtual machines. The name of the virtual machine is not permanent. Like any other file, the virtual machine can be renamed.

Integration Services   Running a virtual machine can present some interesting challenges and opportunities for interaction between the operating system hosting the Hyper-V server and the virtual machines. These services are called the *integration* services, and you can adjust them based on need. Integration services, as shown in Figure 14.18, provide the ability for interactions between the Hyper-V host machine and the VM. They provide the ability for interactions between the Hyper-V host machine and the VM. This interaction allows simple transitions of the mouse pointer, access to shared drives, and the sharing of files and folders. You can also rename the virtual machine with the link in the Actions pane. It will update the value in the settings file.

Figure 14.17: Name setting

Figure 14.18: Integration Services setting

Snapshot File Location The Snapshot File Location setting, as shown in Figure 14.19, defines the physical location where snapshots of virtual machines will be stored. The snapshot allows the administrator to make a point-in-time snapshot of a virtual machine, and then if desired, the administrator can apply the snapshot file to return the virtual machine to the point in time when the snapshot was taken. You will learn more about snapshots later in this chapter.

Figure 14.19: Snapshot File Location specification

Smart Paging Windows Server 2012 introduced a new feature in Hyper-V: Smart Paging. *Smart paging* provides a disk-based failsafe in the event of a shutdown with insufficient memory resources. This paged memory is meant to be used in a temporary fashion for periods of less than 10 minutes. You will want to configure a file location for smart paging, as shown in Figure 14.20.

Automatic Start Action Automatic Start Action, shown in Figure 14.21, defines what you want the virtual machine to do when the physical machine is started. This setting makes it possible to start a virtual machine automatically each time its associated physical machine is started. You can also configure an automatic start delay so that the virtual machine is not competing with the physical machine for resources necessary to start up.

Figure 14.20: Smart Paging File Location specification

Figure 14.21: Automatic Start Action setting

Automatic Stop Action   The Automatic Stop Action setting, shown in Figure 14.22, defines what you want this virtual machine to do when the physical machine that is hosting it shuts down. The default value saves the virtual machine's state. You could, of course, shut down the virtual machine or let it turn off (not recommended because this is the equivalent of pulling the plug).

Figure 14.22: Automatic Stop Action setting

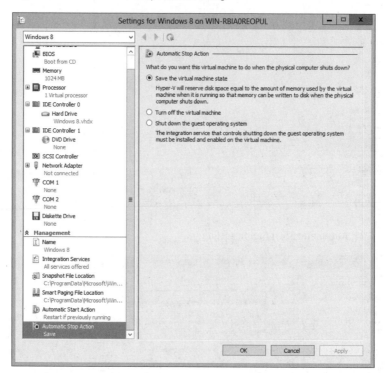

Install an Operating System

The whole point of virtual hard disks, virtual machines, and Hyper-V is to let more than one operating system run on a single set of hardware. When you build the virtual machine and its associated hard disk, the operating system is not included. You will still need to acquire and install the operating system of your choice. Hyper-V is very versatile, allowing you to run Windows operating systems and even SUSE Linux if you so desire. The process of installing an operating system on a virtual machine is very much the same as installing to physical hardware, with a few exceptions.

You will recall from our earlier discussion that a VHD or VHDX file is an allocation of disk space used to install operating systems and applications and to store data. When you install an operating system, you are actually installing to the VHD or VHDX.

Manage Desktop and Server Virtualization

PART V

Install from DVD

One of the most common methods used to install an operating system is to install it directly from the DVD/CD media. Each virtual machine has a setting for the DVD/CD drive. This setting can be configured to capture the physical DVD drive:

1. Set a controller to capture the DVD/CD.

2. Set the boot order to ensure that the DVD/CD is first.

3. Insert the DVD/CD into the physical DVD/CD drive.

4. Start the virtual machine.

5. When prompted, press a key to boot from DVD/CD.

At this point, the install will proceed as normal.

Install from ISO

DVD/CD is a great methodology for installations, but it is certainly not the only option. In fact, many in the IT world have picked up a subscription to TechNet or MSDN that will allow them to download an ISO image of a DVD that can be used to burn a physical DVD. In this case, it can actually be used to install the operating system directly to the virtual machine. The process is similar to a traditional install with one simple setting change:

1. Set a controller to capture the DVD/CD.

2. Select the DVD/CD drive.

3. In the Media section, select the Image File option.

4. Browse to the location of the ISO file, as shown in Figure 14.23.

5. Click OK.

You can get the same effect by using the connection window for the virtual machine. You can use the Media menu, select DVD Drive, and use the Insert Disk option.

When you install an operating system to a virtual machine, remember that all the files are being installed to the virtual hard disk. Using the operating system is no different than if it were installed to the local hardware. There are no different versions of operating systems for the virtual world. They are the same installs and have the same operational capacity as any other operating system installation.

Figure 14.23: Capturing an ISO image

Connect to a Virtual Machine

Once you have created a virtual machine and the operating system is installed and functional, there is one remaining obstacle. The operating system is running in an environment that is essentially invisible to the user. There is no default video output in Hyper-V. You will need to connect an application to the video output of the virtual machine in order to interact with the VM and to see what's going on. The application you will use to connect to the virtual machine was installed automatically when you installed Hyper-V. The application is called the Virtual

Machine Connection tool. Using this tool, you can connect to the virtual machine, control the state of the virtual machine, take snapshots of the virtual machine, and modify some of the settings of the virtual machine.

When you connect to a virtual machine using the Virtual Machine Connection tool, it will automatically use the credentials that you used to log in to the physical machine to establish the connection to the virtual machine. If you want to use other credentials, you can configure those in Hyper-V. By default, Administrator permissions are the minimum required permissions necessary to connect to the console. Please note that this does *not* mean that the Virtual Machine Connection tool will log you on to the virtual machine. The credentials supplied are simply used to connect to the virtual machine. You will still need to supply the appropriate credentials to log on to the virtual machine.

To connect to a virtual machine, you can open the Hyper-V Manager and locate the desired virtual machine. Double-click the virtual machine, and the Virtual Machine Connection tool will start. You can also right-click the selected virtual machine and choose Connect.

Use Snapshots

The coolest thing about virtual machines is that they *are* virtual machines. You are probably thinking, "Duh!" So, what's the big deal? Virtual machines are really compact. The operating system is located in a VHD file and the settings that go with it. This makes it really easy to take a point-in-time picture of the state of the operating system and the settings associated with the virtual machine. This process is called taking a *snapshot*. The value in this is that you can take a snapshot, work away making changes and updates to the virtual machine, and then (and this really rocks) apply the snapshot to take the virtual machine right back to the state it was in when you took the snapshot.

Virtual machine snapshots are file-based snapshots of the state, disk data, and configuration of the virtual machine. The snapshot creates a file called an AVHD file. You can take multiple snapshots of a single virtual machine, and you can even take a snapshot while the virtual machine is up and running. You can revert or apply snapshots to get to the virtual machine configuration you desire.

You can create snapshots using the Hyper-V Manager or the Virtual Machine Connection tool. Applying snapshots, listing available snapshots, and editing snapshots are tasks available through the Hyper-V Manager only.

Snapshots can help you create specific environments such as those needed in validation and testing. It is easy to reproduce the same environment and settings over and over again. Snapshots are perfect for building a staging server to test hotfixes, patches, and updates before deploying them to your network.

The things we love about snapshots can also be the things we hate about snapshots. When you take a snapshot, all the data and settings are in the snapshot. Anything you create, delete, save, or install will be reverted to the snapshot state when you revert or apply a snapshot. This means if you create a bunch of documents and then revert to a previous snapshot, all the data created since the snapshot was taken will be gone. If you know this ahead of time, it is not a big deal because you can simply take another snapshot to maintain the current data and state. If you didn't know this ahead of time, it could be really painful.

To make a snapshot of a virtual machine, follow these steps:

1. Open the Hyper-V Manager.

2. Select the virtual machine you want to snapshot.

3. Click Snapshot in the Actions pane, as shown in Figure 14.24.

Figure 14.24: Taking a snapshot

The snapshots will show up in the Snapshots pane in the center of the screen. It is important to note here that when you take a snapshot of a running virtual machine, the performance of the virtual machine will be impacted as the snapshot file is made. Snapshots are stored in a hierarchy. This means that the snapshot contains only the changes made to the VM since the snapshot was taken. Any previous changes are contained within the previous snapshot. In order for the VM to operate effectively in a multi-snapshot environment, each snapshot must be present. As you create additional snapshots, you will see them show up in the Snapshots pane of the Hyper-V Manager.

After a snapshot is taken, it is labeled with the virtual machine name and a date and timestamp. This is an easy, logical way to keep track of snapshots. If for some reason you want to change the name of a snapshot, you can do so using the Rename option in the Actions pane while the snapshot is selected.

To apply a snapshot, you will also use the Actions pane with the snapshot selected. This will allow you to apply the snapshot directly to the virtual machine.

It is possible to export the snapshot for use with a virtual machine using the Export option in the Actions pane.

Finally, it is possible to delete a snapshot, or a snapshot subtree, from the Actions pane with the snapshot selected. When you delete a snapshot, be aware that although the snapshot is no longer listed in the snapshot tree structure, the AVHD file is not deleted until the virtual machine is shut down. When a snapshot is deleted, the data and settings that were stored in the snapshot are merged, and this process can be very time-consuming.

One final note concerning snapshots is that although snapshots can be used to make a point-in-time picture of a running virtual machine, they do not use the Volume Shadow Copy Service (VSS) and, therefore, are not a substitute for a permanent backup system. Snapshots can make a great temporary backup. However, you should still configure a backup structure to protect your virtual machines.

Import a Virtual Machine

One of the things you will love about virtual machines is that they are really pretty portable. When it comes right down to it, a virtual machine and a virtual hard disk are easy to move. It is easy to see some of the reasons you might want to import virtual machines. Imagine Microsoft is releasing a new operating system. You decide you would like to try it before you buy it. What if Microsoft made a VHD file available for you to load in Hyper-V so you could try the new operating system? This is actually happening today. Or, imagine a situation where you are a software developer, and you have a standard development environment you use for testing. Why not build that environment in Hyper-V, export those files from the machine where they were built, and then import them on other machines throughout your development network?

You can import virtual machines using two different methodologies. The method you choose really depends on what you have to work with to begin.

If you have a .vhd or a VHDX file and no settings information, you will create a new virtual machine using the New Virtual Machine Wizard. When you are given the option to create a virtual hard disk or use an existing virtual hard disk, simply locate the VHD or VHDX file and create the virtual machine.

Now if you are lucky, you will have more than just the VHD or VHDX, and you might have the settings files associated with the virtual machine as well. If this is the case, you don't need to create a new virtual machine. You already have the virtual machine, so you just need to get that virtual machine and its settings associated with Hyper-V Manager and running on this server. It is important to remember that virtual machines can be reused or imported to more than a single Hyper-V server. To import a virtual machine more than once, it is important that when you import, you make a copy of the virtual machine files so that the VM can be imported again elsewhere. To accomplish this task, use the import tool in the Actions pane.

1. Open the Hyper-V Manager.

2. Click Import Virtual Machine in the Actions pane.

3. In the Import Virtual Machine Wizard, shown in Figure 14.25, browse to the location of the virtual machine.

4. Select the desired import settings.

Figure 14.25: Importing a virtual machine

Remember that a virtual machine will stay in the directory from which it is imported. If you want the virtual machine to be housed in a specific location on your server, you need to copy it there before you import it to Hyper-V. Remember that a VM is made up of the VHD or VHDX, the config.xml files, the binaries, and the snapshots. Once you have imported the VM, it cannot be moved. Importing a virtual machine is a great way to configure a virtual machine with limited up-front configuration work. If you have taken the time to build a great virtual machine and want to save it so that it can be used again, perhaps on another server in your network, you will want to export that virtual machine.

Export a Virtual Machine

The process of exporting a virtual machine is really the process of saving the name, configuration, VHD or VHDX, and snapshots associated with a virtual machine. You have already seen how virtual machines are named, how the virtual hard disks are created, and how to make snapshots. Although each virtual machine has a canonical name that you configured, each virtual machine also has a globally unique identifier (GUID), and each snapshot that you make also has its own unique

GUID. Armed with this information, you can begin the process of exporting a virtual machine.

1. Open the Hyper-V Manager.

2. Select the virtual machine you want to export.

3. Click Export in the virtual machine section of the Actions pane.

4. In the dialog box (shown in Figure 14.26) that opens, provide a directory location to save the virtual machine.

5. Click Export.

Figure 14.26: Export directory location

Depending on the size of the virtual machine and its contents, this process can take some time, so be patient. There is no status bar to tell you how much of the export has completed.

During the export process, a new folder will be created in the directory you chose for the export directory. The new folder will be named with the name of the virtual machine. Inside the new folder will be a series of subfolders:

Virtual Machines   This folder contains an export (.exp) file named for the GUID of the virtual machine. There is an additional folder here that can be used for an additional .exp file for machines that were exported in their saved-state configuration. If you are working with VHDX files, you will also have .xml files here.

Virtual Hard Disks This folder will contain a copy of each of the virtual hard disks associated with the virtual machine or VHDX files.

Snapshots This folder will contain an .exp file for each of the snapshots you created in the virtual machine. There are some additional folders here named after the snapshot IDs for any saved state snapshot data and a folder named after the virtual machine ID that will contain the AVHD files for the snapshots.

Once the export has completed, you can use the files in the export directory at will. You can copy them, move them, save them to DVDs (if they are small enough), compress them (if they are not small enough), and of course import them.

While talking about importing, we said that if you want to import a virtual machine more than once, you need to copy all the associated files. The reason for this is that during import Hyper-V will delete the EXP files and replace them with XML files. If there are no EXP files, the virtual machine cannot be imported. If you plan on using a virtual machine more than once, you will need to copy the exported virtual machine and its associated EXP files to be certain it can be imported again.

Replicate a Virtual Machine

One of the new features added to Hyper-V in Windows Server 2012 is called *virtual machine replication*. Replication is designed to produce a copy of a running virtual machine that is stored on a separate Hyper-V host and regularly updated from the source VM. In the event that there is a problem with the source VM, a process of failover can be initiated to provide near continuous operation of the VM. For more information on this feature, please see http://technet.microsoft.com/en-us/library/hh831716.aspx.

PART VI

Server Tuning and Maintenance

IN THIS PART ▶

Server Tuning and
Maintenance

PART VI

15

Tuning and Monitoring Performance

IN THIS CHAPTER, YOU WILL LEARN TO:

We all want our servers to run faster and perform at their peak capabilities. However, how do you make your server perform faster without adding hardware? In this chapter, you will see many of the powerful tools designed to help you improve your Windows Server 2012 server. You will see how the built-in Best Practices Analyzer will help you improve the server roles currently installed on your server. You will also learn how the Best Practices Analyzer provides feedback for your environment.

In addition, you will see the Performance Monitor and several of the tools designed to help you maintain and improve the health of your server.

Finally, you'll learn how to read and use the information your Windows Server 2012 server provides via system-wide events, and you will get an overview of the built-in Event Viewer.

Analyze Server Roles

Installing server roles, with proper planning, on a Windows Server 2012 server can be a fairly straightforward process. But even with the proper planning, sometimes your server roles can be made to run more efficiently. You might also want to make sure your servers and the roles installed on the servers are running properly.

When you install a server, you usually have planned how it will fit the needs of your business and your network infrastructure. However, what happens when you are not in control and you "inherit" servers from a new customer, from an acquisition, or because you took a new role in your organization? How do you know if the servers and roles are running properly? In the following sections, you will learn about a tool called the Best Practices Analyzer (BPA), which will provide you with guidance to help run your servers more efficiently.

Understand the Best Practices Analyzer

For several years, Microsoft has provided the Best Practices Analyzer for the various server platforms currently available. These analyzers are available through a free download from the Microsoft site. With Windows Server 2012, the Best Practices Analyzer is now built into the server platform and is available for you to use when you install certain roles on your server. The BPA in Windows Server 2012 includes the ability to run multiple BPA scans simultaneously and on multiple different servers. Currently in Windows Server 2012, the BPA is provided for many of the roles that you will install and for infrastructure workloads you may run on the Windows Server platform, including:

- Active Directory Certification Services (AD CS)

- Active Directory Domain Services (AD DS)

- DNS

- Remote Desktop Services (RDS)

- Internet Information Services (IIS)

- Hyper-V

- File and Storage Services

- Exchange

- SQL

- SharePoint

The BPA is like a mini IT consultant running around your Windows Server 2012 server and checking your roles to make sure the ones on your server are running properly. This tool provides you with the ability to manage your servers proactively and get in front of any potential issues or concerns before they happen. The BPA helps you make sure your configurations are good and helps reduce the amount of troubleshooting you have to do when issues do occur.

When you use the BPA, it will analyze your current environment and compare this against common best practices for the particular role. What makes the guidance from the tool unique is that Microsoft is not the only one providing feedback; the feedback comes from IT administrators and customers like you, from support professionals, and even from the many folks in the field working for Microsoft.

When you invoke a BPA scanner against one of your server roles, you start the BPA runtime. The *runtime* is the main process responsible for collecting and comparing the configuration settings on your Windows Server 2012 server. Regardless of which role you are currently scanning, the BPA follows the process illustrated in Figure 15.1.

1. The BPA scans and verifies the current role configuration settings.

2. As the BPA service scans and verifies, the BPA runtime uses a BPA Windows PowerShell script to collect configuration data and store it in an XML document.

3. The BPA runtime then validates the XML document against an XML schema. The schema defines the format and structure of the XML document.

4. The BPA runtime then applies the BPA rules (these are the best-practice configurations) for the environment against the XML document.

5. From there the guidance is used to produce the BPA report. The report is used to help make adjustments to your environment if needed.

Figure 15.1: BPA process flow

When you first review a report, you may see violations in the BPA report. You do not need to panic when you see them. These violations do not always indicate a major problem for your server. Remember, the BPA tool is trying to help identify server configurations that can result in poor performance, poor reliability, unexpected conflicts, increased security risks, or other potential problems.

Although the guidance the tool provides can be a tremendous help in reporting your actual configuration versus known best practices, you should always look carefully at the suggestions. The best practices are sound; however, sometimes based on your business rules and the demands of your infrastructure, they may not improve your configuration. Make sure you review the recommendations very carefully.

Use the Best Practices Analyzer

The BPA is located in Server Manager and becomes available after you install the supported roles. You will find the BPA on the Dashboard screen in the associated tile for the supported roles on your server. The Summary screen for the roles provides a wealth of information for your server; if the role has a BPA available, you will see it there.

1. Open Server Manager by selecting the Server Manager icon in the taskbar.

2. Identify the chosen Role box at the bottom of the main screen.

3. Select the BPA Results Option in the associated Role box; it will be similar to Figure 15.2.

Figure 15.2: Server Manager Dashboard screen

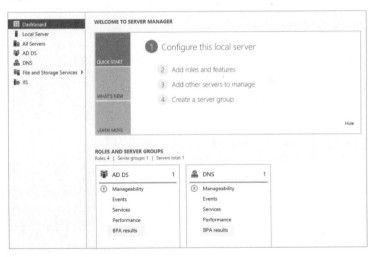

4. When BPA Results is selected, you will be presented with the option to configure the severity level, servers, and categories to be displayed in the report, as shown in Figure 15.3.

Figure 15.3: BPA results configuration

Understand the BPA Report

When you create a BPA report, the report provides an analysis of several factors for your server role. For example, when you run an AD DS BPA scan, the analyzer checks these aspects of your configuration:

- DNS rules
- Operation master connectivity rules
- Operation master ownership rules
- Number of controllers in the domain
- Required service rules
- Replication configuration rules
- W32time configuration rules
- Virtual machine configuration rules

You can view all the rules scanned for the different roles at:

http://technet.microsoft.com/en-us/library/hh831400.aspx

As you can see, the scan is very thorough. Regardless of what scan you run, you will see several aspects of the report on the BPA Results Detail View screen. Your report will have one of three severity levels for each rule. The three levels of severity for the scanned rules are as follows:

Error   Error results are returned when a role does not satisfy the conditions of a best practice rule, and functionality problems can be expected.

Warning   This means your current role is compliant, but your current configuration of the role does not meet all the conditions specified by the rule. In general, this means your role will work; however, there may be indications the role is not fully functional or may have operational problems.

Information   Information results are returned when a role satisfies the conditions of a BPA rule. In addition to the severity level, each rule is categorized into one of eight categories. The categories are designed to help you further target and work with the BPA report. In a sense, the categories, as listed in Table 15.1, help you prioritize the tasks you will need to address.

Table 15.1: BPA Rule Categories

Category	Definition
Security	These rules help you examine the areas of your server with potential security risks; you'll want to pay close attention to them.
Performance	These rules are designed to help you tune or improve the performance of your servers. These rules help to make sure your server can perform the appointed tasks properly.
Configuration	These rules allow you to verify the configurations of certain roles on your server. They help the role(s) run properly and free of configuration errors.
Policy	These rules identify which areas in the Registry or Group Policy need improvements to make sure your role is running in a secure and best-possible fashion.
Operation	These rules will identify whether a role is failing and how to correct the role to get it up and running properly.
Pre-deployment	These rules allow you to identify any issues or possible errors prior to the deployment of a particular role in the enterprise.
Post-deployment	These rules allow you to identify any issues or possible errors after the role has been deployed to the enterprise.
Prerequisites	These rules are for the BPA scanner. In order for certain BPA rules to be included in a report, there may be some prerequisites that need to be met in order for a rule to be scanned. If you have a BPA prerequisite error, this simply means the BPA tool could not scan your role with a particular rule.

Server Tuning and Maintenance

PART VI

Work with the BPA Report

Now that you understand how the report is categorized, you will want to see how to fix any issues the BPA scan detected for you. After the report is processed and you have identified the events you want to view, you will start to see the power behind the BPA reports. Each event generated by BPA will have additional information and detailed resolution procedures, which can be accessed by selecting the event and then choosing the "More information about this best practice and detailed resolution procedure" link at the bottom of the BPA screen.

1. In the BPA report, click the event you want to view.

2. To view the additional information and resolution procedure, click the link at the bottom of the BPA window shown in Figure 15.4.

   The More Information link will take you to an online TechNet Library of information on problems, impacts, and resolutions.

You also have the ability to exclude your BPA rule information from future reports. With a rule highlighted, you can right-click and select Exclude Result, and it will be removed from the report. It will be moved to the Excluded tab of the report.

As you can see, the BPA reports provide some excellent analysis for your server. After you have viewed the error messages and corrected any errors, you should also consider rerunning the BPA for the role to verify the issue has been properly resolved.

Figure 15.4: BPA events and the More Information link

Use PowerShell with the Best Practices Analyzer

The BPA tools also have full PowerShell cmdlet support. You can accomplish the BPA tasks in PowerShell as well. The BPA PowerShell cmdlets are also built into the server and do not require any additional tools or packages to be installed to use them. The PowerShell tools also provide you with the additional capability to run BPA scans of multiple roles at one time. One of the cool features of Windows 2012 and PowerShell is the BPA module is loaded automatically the first time you use one of the associated cmdlets.

There are really four commands you will need to learn, as shown in Table 15.2.

Table 15.2: BPA PowerShell Commands

Command	Usage
Get-BPAModel	This command allows you to view the roles installed on the server where you can run BPA scans; this tool also shows you when the last scan on a particular role was created.
Get-BPAResult	This command allows you to view the results for any given BPA scan you have performed.
Invoke-BPAModel	This command allows you to run a BPA scan on your server for a particular role you want to scan.
Set-BPAResult	This command allows you to filter the BPA report from the Get-BPAResult command to allow you to see only the information you want to view in the report.

BPA PowerShell Examples

To determine which roles are currently installed on the server that you can run a BPA scan against, or to see if a BPA scan has been run, you can use the following command:

```
Get-BPAModel
```

You will see results similar to Figure 15.5.

Figure 15.5: Get-BPAModel sample results

The important parts of the Get-BPAModel command are the model IDs displayed in the results. The model IDs are used in the other BPA commands to perform designated tasks. To scan the Internet Information Services role on your server, run the following command:

```
Invoke-BPAModel -id Microsoft/Windows/WebServer
```

The command will complete and display the information shown in Figure 15.6.

Figure 15.6: Results of Invoke-BPAModel

To view the BPA report for the Internet Information Services BPA scan, run the following command, and you will see results similar to Figure 15.7:

```
Get-BPAResult -id Microsoft/Windows/WebServer
```

Figure 15.7: Get-BPAResult sample results

Although you can view the results in the PowerShell window, remember that you can always view the results in the Server Manager interface, regardless of where you ran the scan from (the GUI or PowerShell). So, if you want to view the full report, we recommend using the Server Manager interface. If you want to filter results, you can do this in PowerShell with the Set-BPAResult command or with the Where clause.

If you want to view a BPA report for Internet Information Services but only with the rules in the Security category, you could run the following command:

```
Get-BPAResult -id Microsoft/Windows/WebServer
| Where { $_.Category -eq "Security" }
```

View Server Performance Data

Working with your performance data is part science and part art. Windows Server 2012 has thousands of performance counters with which you can view, track, and perform analysis. Part of the trick to doing analysis is to understand how the different counters work together to give you an overall picture of the server.

In the following sections, you will see some of the tools in Windows Server 2012, such as the system health report, that will provide you with some excellent pictures of your server from the hardware and software perspectives.

You will also see the basics of how to work with the Performance Monitor and the built-in reliability tools on your server to keep your server running properly.

Create a System Health Report

One of the tools you can use to help troubleshoot problems is the system health report. The system health report includes suggestions to help improve the overall health and performance of the Windows Server 2012 server. The report provides suggestions based on the performance of your server across many aspects:

- Software configuration
- Hardware configuration
- CPU
- Network
- Disk
- Memory

The system health report is also a handy report if you have no knowledge about a server and want to learn more about it quickly. When you run the report, it will take some time to generate information you will be able to use improve the performance. You will need to be a member of the local Administrators group to generate the report. The system health report is located in the Control Panel on your server.

1. Press the Windows key from the keyboard, type **Control Panel**, and then press Enter.

2. Click System and Security.

3. Click Generate a System Health Report, which is located in the Administrative Tools section.

   After you click Generate a System Health Report, you will see a screen similar to Figure 15.8; the report will take up to 60 seconds to generate.

Figure 15.8: Generating a system health report

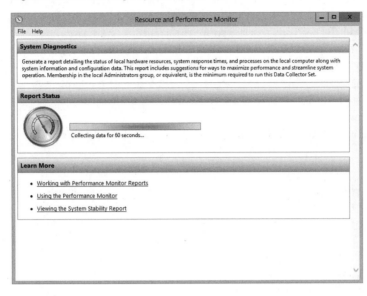

After the report is generated, you'll see a screen similar to Figure 15.9.

Figure 15.9: System Diagnostics Report

When you start looking at a report, you will notice the several categories and the arrows next to the category headings to allow you to expand the sections to view more information about the report. You may also notice in the middle of each heading bar there is an icon that looks like a three-column table. This icon allows you to open the table of contents for the report. When you click one of the icons, you will see a screen similar to Figure 15.10.

Figure 15.10: Diagnostic results

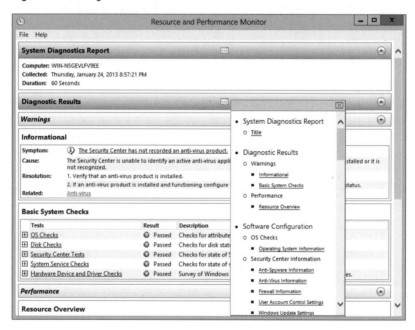

The Contents screen will allow you to quickly view any portion of the report. In addition to the individual categories you see in the report, you'll see a wealth of summary information for your server. There is also one area that will provide a quick snapshot of the overall performance of your server. This area is called the *resource overview*, and you can see an example of it in Figure 15.11.

Figure 15.11: Resource overview

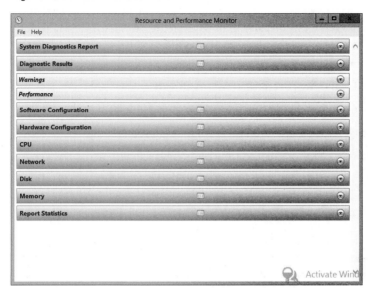

This report not only gives you a general utilization of your server but also tells you which areas of your server are being the most utilized. For example, when you look at the network utilization, the report tells you what the most utilized network adapter on your server is.

If the report has warnings, you will see a screen similar to Figure 15.12.

Figure 15.12: System health report with warnings

As you can see, the warnings tell you the issue and give you steps for resolution. Depending on the nature of the warning, the resolutions may be basic. For example, if you have a hardware warning because of a faulty driver, the system health report will tell you what to do, but the advice is fairly generic:

1. Verify that the correct driver is installed.

2. Try updating the drivers using Windows Update.

3. Check with the manufacturer for an updated driver.

4. Attempt to uninstall and then reinstall the device using the Device Manager.

Understand Performance Monitor

When you look at all the tools on your Windows Server 2012 server that provide you with performance data, you'll see they are all derived in some fashion from the same data you can generate in the Performance Monitor. As your server's operating systems become more sophisticated, you have many new and useful tools like the system health report that allow you to make sense out of the performance data on your server. This section will give you a brief look at how to leverage the data in the Performance Monitor.

When you look at the reports you can generate, you may want a more detailed picture of what is going on under the hood of your server. This is where the Performance Monitor can help you get into the details of all the data. You can use it to see how many of the different performance data points relate to each other and get the bigger picture. Learning to use the Performance Monitor is a combination of knowing what you are looking for, knowing how to use the tool, and knowing what counters can help you find the areas for improvement.

For example, if you want to monitor memory usage on your system, it is not enough to just look at the counters on the Memory object in the Performance Monitor. You may also want to look at disk I/O. You may be wondering why disk I/O is important. Remember, part of the memory on your system is used by the paging file on your system. For example, if you notice that memory is not performing optimally, you may decide to add more RAM to your server but then still see some of the same issues. Your problem really could have been because of slow reads and writes for the page file because of a slow or faulty hard drive. In other words, you had a false positive test, but you only looked at one portion of the story to determine your issue. The moral is simply that there are many factors to help you determine the performance of your server, and you need to try to do your best to look at as many factors as you can.

You also need to have some historical perspective when you are using the Performance Monitor. What does this mean to you? It offers you a baseline. Sure, you can turn on the Performance Monitor any time you want to peek at the system data. However, factors such as the time of day, the current workload on the server, the number of users logged on, and many other factors could skew your results. Normally, when you run the Performance Monitor, you want to run the counters before, during, and after the workload you are testing on the server. This will give you the most accurate and thorough results. This will also allow you to put your results in context. More important, the Performance Monitor will also allow you to save your results and compare them to a report run several months after you ran the original report.

Work with the Resource Monitor

To begin using the Performance Monitor, you can load the tool via Server Manager and use the Performance Monitor located under Tools. You can also load the Performance Monitor, shown in Figure 15.13, by starting Server Manager and selecting Performance Monitor from the Tools menu.

Figure 15.13: The Performance Monitor

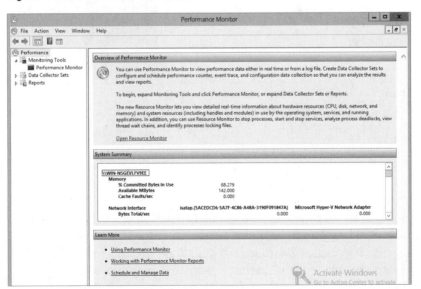

Before you start to add your own Performance Monitor counters and build your own data collector sets, you need to look closely at the System Summary screen when you first load the tool. You have a nice collection of summary information provided for you initially. From the Base Summary screen, you can gain some nice summary information about the four main resources on your server: memory, CPU, hard drive, and network.

You will also find a tool in Windows Server 2012 called the Resource Monitor. In the top section of the Overview of Performance Monitor screen, you will see a link called Open Resource Monitor. When you click the link, you will see a screen similar to Figure 15.14.

Figure 15.14: The Resource Monitor

You can also load the Resource Monitor directly. The Resource Monitor is part of your system tools. Start Server Manager, and then select Resource Monitor from the Tools menu.

The Resource Monitor is similar to Task Manager; however, the Resource Monitor has been greatly enhanced. Just as with Task Manager, you get real-time information about what processes, disk resources, network performance, and memory resources are currently being used by your server. The Resource Monitor offers much greater detail and access for you to see what is happening under the hood on your server. You will also have the ability to stop processes and start and stop services by simply right-clicking a service and choosing the action you want to perform. You can also get even more valuable information to help the developers in your organization debug applications. In the Resource Monitor, you get debuggers to diagnose application hangs and deadlocks. One option for working with application problems is by looking at a wait chain. Essentially, a *wait chain* is the order in which your threads of process execution occur. Each thread in a chain will wait for the additional threads following the initial thread; by analyzing the wait chain, you can potentially discover what is causing your application to have delays or not function.

Run Windows Memory Diagnostics

One of the more frustrating issues you may run into is memory issues. There can be many issues with memory, including poorly written applications, insufficient memory, or even a possible faulty memory chip. How do you know what could be the cause? You generally want to rule out a faulty chip. In Windows Server 2012, you have the ability to run the Windows Memory Diagnostics tool; start Server Manager, and then select Windows Memory Diagnostics from the Tools menu. You will be presented with a choice to restart your server and check your memory or schedule a memory check for the next time you reboot your system. Whichever choice you make, when your server is rebooted, your physical memory will go through several checks to ensure the integrity of your memory chips.

When your system reboots, you will see a screen similar to Figure 15.15.

Figure 15.15: Windows Memory Diagnostics tool

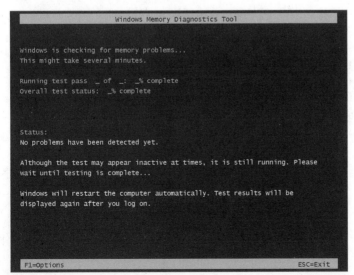

Server Tuning and Maintenance

PART VI

When you press F1, you will be given a choice to perform a basic, standard, or extended test. Each of these levels builds on the tests completed at the previous level by adding additional memory tests. Each test will perform a series of tests on your server's memory. The more memory you have, the longer the test can take. When the tests are complete, your server will be rebooted automatically. To view the report, you need to open the Event Viewer:

1. Open the Event View by starting Server Manager, and then selecting Event Viewer from the Tools menu.

2. In the Event Viewer, expand the following tree location: Applications and Services Logs ➤ Microsoft ➤ Windows ➤ MemoryDiagnostics-Results.

3. Click the event to see any errors that may have been reported.

Work with the Performance Monitor

Utilizing the Performance Monitor will allow you to see a variety of system aspects of your server. When you load the Performance Monitor, your first task will be to load counters to begin measuring and testing your server.

When you add counters to measure, you have a variety of choices to add. First, you will be able to choose which systems you want to measure; by default, your local computer is selected. You can also add counters from several main categories such as Processor, Memory, Network, and Disk, as well as many more. In addition to each counter, there may be several instances you can monitor. For example, when you measure the processor, you will be able to monitor your processor cores, or if you measure physical disks, you will be able to measure the physical drives on your system.

As you look into the sheer volume of counters and instances in the Performance Monitor, this may be a little overwhelming. Try not to get overwhelmed by the data by trying to understand each and every counter. More important, inside the Add Counters dialog box, there is an option to show a description that will explain the counter and, in most cases, explain what values the counter should be if it is running healthy.

1. Open the Performance Monitor by starting Server Manager, and then selecting Performance Monitor from the Tools menu.

2. Expand Monitoring Tools.

3. Click Performance Monitor; by default you will have one counter being measured, your %processor time.

4. Click the green + sign in the Performance Monitor toolbar to add counters you want to measure. You will see a screen similar to Figure 15.16.

5. To add a counter, click the category, click the counter, select the instance you want to monitor, and then click the Add button. Your counter will show in the list to the right, called Added Counters. Likewise, you can also remove a counter by selecting the counter and clicking Remove.

6. When you are done adding counters, click OK to begin monitoring the selected data. You will see the monitor begin; your screen may look like Figure 15.17.

Figure 15.16: Performance Monitor's Add Counters dialog box

Figure 15.17: Counters in Performance Monitor

Now, sit back and wait for the data to populate. You may want to also start the applications you are monitoring here to see how certain applications impact your system. You can save your Performance Monitor counters for future logging use.

1. Inside the left pane of the Performance Monitor, expand Data Collector Sets.

2. Right-click User Defined, and then select New ➢ Data Collector Set.

3. Provide a name for your data collector set, click Next, and then select a template for use.

4. Select a storage location, and then click Next.

5. Verify the creation of the set and click Finish.

Use Data Collector Sets

Using the Performance Monitor to measure data by adding counters one at a time is a very reactionary way to measure your server's performance. In the Performance Monitor, you can save your existing counters into a *data collector set*. Data collector sets are another built-in feature allowing you some proactive measurement for your server.

Data collector sets allow you to organize multiple performance counters and data collection counters into one logical object. This allows you to easily access and work with frequently used object counters. With data collector sets, you can create log files to track up to three areas for your performance:

Performance Monitor   This selection allows you to log data about your selected performance counters.

Event Trace Data   When you choose Event Trace Data, you can log data about various service providers on your server. For example, you can track the performance of built-in services.

System Configuration Information   This selection allows you to log data to reflect changes to your configuration. For example, you can modify specific Registry keys.

Additionally, you can also use data collector sets to proactively measure data by creating Performance Monitor alerts. An alert will fire a set of actions you determine when a counter meets a certain threshold.

1. Inside Performance Monitor, expand the data collector sets, and right-click User Defined in the tree on the left.

2. Select New ➤ Data Collector Set.

3. You can use predetermined templates from previous collector sets. Select Create Manually (Advanced), and then click Next. You will see a screen similar to Figure 15.18.

Figure 15.18: New data collector set

4. Select Performance Counter Alert, and click Next.

5. Add the performance counters on which you want to set the alert, set your threshold (either above or below) for the alert, and then click Next.

6. Verify the creation of the set, select Start this Data Collector Set (to start the set), and click Finish.

To view the logs or reports created by the data collector set, you need to look for the name of your data collector set in the Reports section of the Performance Monitor tree. For more information on configuring and using data collector sets in Window Server 2012, please see the information at http://technet.microsoft.com/en-us/library/cc749337.aspx.

View Server Events

The ability to look at the events occurring on your server has always provided useful information to help you find the source and resolution for any issues your server may encounter. The Event Viewer is one of the more powerful troubleshooting utilities you can use on your server. More importantly, the tool has been built into Windows-based operating systems for years and years. This tool keeps getting more robust and easier to use with each new version of Windows. In the following sections, you will take a brief look at the Event Viewer and how this tool can help manage your environment.

Work with the Event Viewer

The Event Viewer provides a wonderful utility that enables you to view and track system-wide events on your server. You can view events from all aspects of your server. You can view the traditional Windows logs (such as Application, Security, Setup, and System). Also, since Windows Server 2008, the Event Viewer provides a method to view events for individual applications and services.

Before you start working with log files in the Event Viewer, you need to know a couple of things. Every log entry and file is stored in an XML format, which helps keep the log files small and streamlined. However, log files can take up space on your server, and you need to know how to control the size the log files can become. By default, each log file takes up to 20MB of space. You can also control what happens when the log file reaches the space limit; you have three choices:

Overwrite Events As Needed   This overwrites events; the oldest events will be overwritten first.

Archive The Log When Full, Do Not Overwrite Events   This takes your full log, saves it to disk, and clears the log.

Do Not Overwrite Events (Clear The Log Manually)   This forces you to clear the log when it becomes full. Before you can see any more events, you must clear the log.

You can change the Log Retention Policy by going into the properties of the log file (right-click the log file and select Properties) and setting the option for retention. Figure 15.19 shows a picture of the log properties.

Figure 15.19: Log properties

Log Properties - Application (Type: Administrative)

General | Subscriptions

Full Name:	Application
Log path:	%SystemRoot%\System32\Winevt\Logs\Application.evtx
Log size:	3.07 MB(3,215,360 bytes)
Created:	Tuesday, December 4, 2012 9:45:22 PM
Modified:	Friday, January 18, 2013 10:01:37 AM
Accessed:	Tuesday, December 4, 2012 9:45:22 PM

☑ Enable logging

Maximum log size (KB): 20480

When maximum event log size is reached:

⦿ Overwrite events as needed (oldest events first)

◯ Archive the log when full, do not overwrite events

◯ Do not overwrite events (Clear logs manually)

Clear Log

OK | Cancel | Apply

If you choose to clear the log manually, you will want to save the log file. Additionally, saving a log file will also provide you with a way to share data with another administrator or support professional who may be assisting you with your problem. To save the events to a log file, simply right-click the log file and select Save All Events As. This will allow you to save your event log to a file and archive it to a file share or other archival method.

When you look at the many different events located in the log file, they will have been assigned one of the following four levels:

Critical Critical events represent a failure of a service and normally result in the service being shut down or crashing.

Error Events assigned this level result from some application error or other fatal software issue on your server.

Warning This level indicates potential events that can occur on your server.

Information This level includes general events about tasks, normally along the lines of a service turning on successfully or a process starting.

In addition to the four levels, there are two additional event types that are specific to the security log file: audit success and audit failure. These allow you to see which tasks were audited on your server. For example, the Security log could show you when a person is successful in logging on to your server or accessing an audited file.

To work with the Event Viewer, you need to load the tool and go to the log to review the events for a particular log:

1. Open the Event Viewer by starting Server Manager, and then selecting Event Viewer from the Tools menu.

2. Click the log you want to view, and you will see events in the pane to the right of the tree; your screen will look similar to Figure 15.20.

3. To view an event, double-click the event (or right-click the event and select Event Properties); you will see a screen similar to Figure 15.21.

Figure 15.20: Event Viewer

Figure 15.21: Event properties

When you view the properties of the event, you can view all the details of the event, the source of the event, the event ID, the classification, and a variety of other information. Looking at the event properties arms you with the information needed to troubleshoot the problem, either by researching help or by performing a search on the Internet.

Filter Events and Creating Custom Views

One aspect of the Event Viewer you may have noticed is that there is a lot of server noise. In other words, there are thousands of events, so how do you find the one event or group of events that will be of the most use to you when you are trying to solve a problem? In the Event Viewer there are two ways to do this. You can either filter an existing log or create a custom view for the events.

You can filter on a variety of criteria: date, level, event ID, source, computer, user, keywords, and tasks. This allows you to reduce the amount of event noise and quickly get to the events that interest you.

Both of these filter mechanisms utilize very similar steps and procedures. The difference is when you filter a log, you are filtering a specific log. With custom views, you can create a custom filter that will span multiple log files on your server. To filter an event log on your server, perform the following:

1. In the Event Viewer, select the log you want to filter.

2. Click Filter Current Log (either in the Action pane on the right side of the console or from the menu if you right-click the log). You will see a screen similar to Figure 15.22.

Figure 15.22: Filtering an event log

3. Select the criteria you want to filter, and when you are finished, click OK.

Once you create a filter for a log file, the filter stays on until you turn it off. To turn off the filter, select the log and click Clear Filter in the right Actions pane of the console, or right-click the log you want to clear the filter.

Creating a custom view follows a similar process to filtering a file:

1. In the Event Viewer, click Create Custom View, and you will see a screen similar to when you filtered a log file. The only difference between a log filter and a custom view is that a custom view provides you with the capability to span multiple logs, as shown in Figure 15.23.

Figure 15.23: Custom view of all logs

2. After you select your options, click OK.

3. Name your view, choose a location to store the view in your management tree, and click OK.

4. If you want to use your view, click the view in your management tree. By default, the views are stored under the management tree in Custom Views.

Save Event Logs

One other aspect of working with logs is saving them for future performance, analysis, and archival. You can save individual logs or even custom views you have created to files. This allows you to open logs from your own server as well as have another administrator send logs from another server for you to review. To save a log file or a custom view, you just need to right-click the log or the view.

1. In the Event Viewer, right-click the custom view or the log you want to save.

2. When you are saving a log, select Save All Events As.

   When you are saving a custom view, select Save All Events in Custom View As.

3. Enter a name, and select a location for the file. After you have named the file and selected a location, click Save.

4. You will see a dialog box asking you to save display information for proper viewing. This is important if you need log files to be viewed in alternative languages from your own. After you have made your selection, click OK.

You can also open saved log files or custom views by right-clicking the custom view or log files in the tree and selecting Open Saved Log.

Subscribe to Events

The Event Viewer also provides you with the ability to subscribe to events on your server or other servers. Subscribing to events allows you to see particular events as they occur. By subscribing to events, you can also view events from multiple servers in one view, since you can have events sent to one central location. Subscribing to events provides you with a similar filter mechanism as you used to create custom views.

To create a subscription on your server, you need to have the Windows Event Collector Service running on your server. The Event Viewer will help turn on this service for you. The first time you click Subscriptions in the Event Viewer management tree, you may see a screen similar to Figure 15.24. You must click Yes to take advantage of Event Viewer subscriptions.

Figure 15.24: Event collector server

1. In the Event Viewer, click Subscriptions.

2. If prompted to turn on the Windows Event Collector Service, click Yes.

3. Click Create Subscription in the right Actions pane; you can also right-click Subscriptions. You will see a screen similar to Figure 15.25.

4. After you set the computers and filter criteria, click OK; your subscription will be complete.

Figure 15.25: Creating a subscription

Subscription Properties	x

Subscription name: |

Description:

Destination log: Forwarded Events

Subscription type and source computers

● Collector initiated — Select Computers...

This computer contacts the selected source computers and provides the subscription.

○ Source computer initiated — Select Computer Groups...

Source computers in the selected groups must be configured through policy or local configuration to contact this computer and receive the subscription.

Events to collect: <filter not configured> — Select Events...

User account (the selected account must have read access to the source logs):
Machine Account

Change user account or configure advanced settings: Advanced...

OK — Cancel

Server Tuning and Maintenance

PART VI

Attach a Task to an Event

One of the more proactive capabilities you can do in the Event Viewer is to attach a task to a particular log or event. Normally, you attach tasks to specific events. When you attach a task to an event, you can perform one of the three following actions: start a program, send an email, or display a message. This allows you to be notified if a certain event occurs or run a program that will fix the issue. You can also assign a task to a custom view you may have created.

1. In the Event Viewer, right-click the event or log you want to create a task for and then choose Attach Task to this Event.

2. Give your task a name and description, and when you are done, click Next.

3. Review the event you have selected, and click Next.

4. Select an option; the default is to run a program. Then, click Next.

5. Depending on the action you have chosen, you may need to find a program or set up an email or message.

6. When you are done, click Next.

7. Review the summary, and click Finish. You will see a screen informing you that the task was created in Task Scheduler, as shown in Figure 15.26. Click OK to clear the message.

Figure 15.26: Task Scheduler

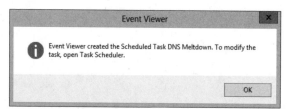

The Event Viewer has a significant number of options and settings that can be configured and used to provide you with incredible insights about your Windows Server 2012 servers. For more information on Event Logs in Window Server 2012, see http://technet.microsoft.com/en-us/library/cc722404.aspx.

16

Keeping Your Servers Up-to-Date

Work with Windows Updates

Windows Server is interesting from a product evolution standpoint. When a server product is "released," it is really just a point in time where Microsoft burns a DVD with the current operating system files from that designated point in time. In actuality, Windows Server is constantly being monitored through various customer and community tools that provide feedback, and Microsoft is constantly writing new updates, hotfixes, and patches for Windows Server. This process has been going on so long that there is an established rhythm of updates often referred to as *Patch Tuesdays,* because the updates are released on Tuesday mornings. This ecosystem of regular monitoring and regular updating creates two unique situations.

First, because the Windows Server operating system is being updated at regular intervals, the further removed in time you are from the Windows Server release to manufacturing (RTM) date, the more updates you will need to apply after installation to get that server up-to-date.

Second, because the Windows Server operating system is being constantly monitored and updates are being released at regular intervals, there is really no such thing as a completed installation of Windows Server. Windows Server 2012 machines are really only as good as the most recent updates that are installed on the servers. This means you will be updating your Windows Server 2012 machine on a regular basis throughout its usable life cycle. There are a couple of methods that you can use to do this and a number of methods to put these updates into production on your Windows Servers.

Find Out What Updates Are

When you consider that Windows Server is constantly being monitored, reviewed, and updated, it is important to consider what exactly is defined as an update. *Updates* are additions to software that can fix or prevent problems, enhance security, or even improve performance. In the help files for Windows Server 2012, Microsoft makes the following recommendation:

> We strongly recommend that you turn on Windows Automatic Updating so that Windows can install security and other important or recommended updates for your computer as they become available.

This recommendation provides insight into the paradigm that Microsoft uses in regard to updates, and it allows you to see the reality of the frequent changes and updates being made to Windows Server. These updates can be in the form of operating system updates, hotfixes to operating systems or applications, or patches to adjust operations of the operating system or applications.

Use Windows Update

Microsoft has been updating client and server operating systems for the last couple of decades. The company pretty much has the process down to a science. As of this writing, Microsoft makes its updates available publicly at http://update.microsoft.com. You can use this Windows Update site to install a simple application to your server that will review the status of the local server and then compare it to the currently available updates on the website. The administrator can then install the desired updates directly from Windows Update. Each copy of Windows Server 2012 has a built-in link to Windows Update, as shown in Figure 16.1. You can access this link by opening the Control Panel, choosing System and Security, and then selecting Windows Update.

Figure 16.1: Accessing Windows Update through the Control Panel

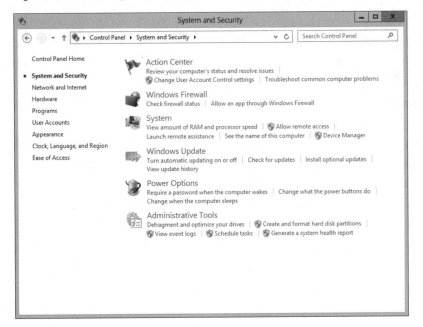

Server Tuning and Maintenance

PART VI

As you can see in Figure 16.2, the Windows Update tool allows you to check for updates, change settings for updates, view update history, restore hidden updates, and link to frequently asked questions about updates.

Figure 16.2: Windows Update

When working with Windows Update, you can specify several settings for your updates. If you click the Change Settings option in Windows Update, you can choose one of the following settings to meet your network needs:

Install Updates Automatically   This setting allows the server to download and install updates automatically. This setting removes much of the administrative effort necessary to keep a Windows server up-to-date. In addition to this setting, you can also define the frequency and time to install new updates. The default setting installs new updates daily at 3 AM. You will learn about additional options for setting up your automatic update configuration in the next section.

**Download Updates But Let Me Choose Whether To Install
Them** This option ensures the most current updates are downloaded to the local server but are not actually installed until you choose to allow them. This option is beneficial in an environment where you want to test and validate updates before deploying them to your servers.

**Check For Updates But Let Me Choose Whether To Download
And Install Them** This option further segments the server from the updates by giving you the opportunity to review the available updates online before downloading or installing the updates.

Never Check For Updates This option is self-explanatory. It is not recommended for the seemingly obvious reason that, if you never check for updates and thus never install updates, your servers will likely be out-of-date. Before you dismiss this setting altogether, though, consider that this setting would not necessarily be a bad thing if you were using some other system outside Windows Update to provide updates to your Windows Server and simply did not want the additional network traffic of having the servers check for updates they should already be receiving from another source.

Note that these settings are only for updates that Microsoft has deemed "important." There are also "recommended updates," which can be configured the same way as important updates. There are also optional updates that will be downloaded and installed based on administrative input. Of course, you can also configure Windows Update to provide updates for additional software running on your Windows Server, such as Office, Exchange, SQL Server, and so on.

Enable Automatic Updates

Windows Update provides a convenient location and process for keeping your Windows server up-to-date. Windows Update is a great tool, but to make the process even more effective, you can automate it by enabling automatic updates. By using automatic updates, you can eliminate the necessity of going to Windows Update and checking for updates, downloading, and then installing by hand. Depending on the settings you choose, you can automatically download and install, download only, or download and install updates at a specified time (by default at 3 AM), as shown in Figure 16.3. All of this can be configured to be totally automated by using the settings in Windows Update. It is worth noting here that although automatic updates can simplify the process of installing updates to a server, there is also the possibility that, as the updates are installed, the server may reboot if the update requires an operating system restart. Consider the implications of that before you enable automatic updates on your servers.

Figure 16.3: Enabling automatic updates with Windows Update

You can also enable automatic updates by using Server Manager, which was installed as part of the initial installation. When you install Windows Server 2012, you will see the Server Manager tool automatically start. When it does, you can choose the Windows Update option from the Domain properties of the local server, as shown in Figure 16.4.

Figure 16.4: Windows Update property for a local server in Server Manager

When you enable automatic updates, you will be given the opportunity to enable fully automatic updates or to configure the settings for manual updating. Notice that you also can download and install updates using this tool.

Whether you choose to configure automatic updates using Windows Update in the Control Panel or during the initial setup of the server using the Initial Configuration Tasks tool, Windows Server will still check for, download, and install updates using the online Windows Update site. You will not have to manually check to see which updates are available or which updates have or have not been installed. The updates are installed based on the schedule you define when you set up the automatic updates.

View Installed Updates

With automatic updates enabled, it is easy to forget that the process of updates is occurring in the background. You may want to check periodically which updates have been installed:

1. Start the Control Panel.

2. Select System And Security.

3. Click Windows Update.

4. Select View Update History.

Figure 16.5 shows the View Update History screen. After updates have been installed, when you view the update history, you will see the names of the updates that have been installed, their unique identifiers in parentheses, the status of the install, the importance of the update, and the date each update was installed. Each update can be right-clicked to view details. One of the cool features of Windows Update allows you to right-click any update in your update history and copy the details of the update to the Windows Clipboard so you can save them to your network log file or print them for your network logbook.

Figure 16.5: Viewing the update history

Remove an Update

Not all updates are created equally. There are updates for drivers, security, Internet Explorer, Windows Defender, and a whole host of others. Operating system updates for Windows Server 2012 are shown in the Windows Update history; however, they are also shown in another interface utility called simply Installed Updates inside Windows Update. This tool not only allows you to see which updates have been installed, but also allows you to select any of the installed updates and uninstall them by simply selecting the update and choosing to uninstall it.

Once you remove an update from your Windows server, it is highly probable that you will see it on the list of recommended updates again. To avoid this problem, you will need to go to the list of available updates and right-click the update. At this point, you can choose Hide Update so that it will no longer be presented to you as a recommended update.

But what if you were to remove an update and then hide it, only to find out that you actually do want it installed on your server? The process couldn't be easier, as shown in Figure 16.6:

1. Open Control Panel ➤ System and Security ➤ Windows Update.

2. Select Restore Hidden Updates.

Figure 16.6: Restoring hidden updates

Please keep in mind that when Microsoft addresses an issue with an update, it may address the same or similar issues again with future updates. Sometimes when you restore updates, you may not see all the updates you had previously hidden, especially if Microsoft has released another more recent update that addresses the same problem. You will only see the newest update in the list.

Install Automatic Updates Between Scheduled Times

Automatic updates are great if your computer is up and running all the time. In today's world of green computing and as businesses attempt to save money by minimizing power consumption, it is possible that a scheduled update may occur at a time when your computer is powered off. If this should occur, you have a few options.

When you boot the computer, it will check for available updates and, if configured to do so, will download them. At this point, you will be prompted to install the updates or to postpone the installation to a future time. The updates will automatically be installed with other available updates when the next configured installation time is reached.

If you choose to shut down the computer and updates are waiting to be installed, you will notice the option to install updates and shut down. At this point, you can choose to install the updates and then shut down the server.

Use Group Policy to Configure Automatic Updates

Automatic updates are great, because you really don't want to go from server to server checking for updates and then installing those updates manually. You probably would much rather let the server take care of that. In addition, you won't need to go to each server in your network to enable the automatic updates on that server in the first place. Group Policy is a great resource that allows administrators to enforce configurations for automatic updates not only on a single server but on groups of servers and clients in your network.

To configure Group Policy to enable automatic updates, you will need to do the following:

1. Open the Group Policy Management console.

2. Select the policy you will edit (or create a new one).

3. Right-click the policy, and choose Edit.

4. Expand Computer Configuration.

5. Expand Policies.

6. Expand Administrative Templates.

7. Expand Windows Components.

8. Select Windows Update, as shown in Figure 16.7.

9. You will notice that there are 16 options having to do with Windows Update in this policy container. When working with policies, remember that policies have three possible states: enabled, disabled, and not configured. To configure automatic updates using Group Policy, you will need to select the policy called Configure Automatic Updates, as shown in Figure 16.7. Double-click the policy, and then choose Enabled.

Figure 16.7: Group Policy Management Editor for Windows Update

The Configure Automatic Updates policy setting has four different values that you will need to choose from when you enable this policy. They are numbered from 2 through 5, as shown in Figure 16.8:

2 This setting notifies you before downloading any updates and notifies you again before installing any updates.

3 This is the default setting. Updates are downloaded automatically; you are notified when they are ready to be installed.

4 This setting automatically downloads updates and then automatically installs them based on a time scheduled in the Configure Automatic Updates policy setting.

5 This setting allows local administrators to select the configuration mode for automatic updates. This means the local administrators can choose when the updates will be installed by using their local Windows Update; however, they cannot turn off automatic updates.

Once you have selected one of the four options, you will likely need to establish the scheduled install day and time. There are eight options labeled 0 through 7. Don't ask us where the crazy numbering comes from—first, 2 through 5, and now 0 through 7. Just smile and configure the settings.

Figure 16.8: Configure Automatic Updates policy options

If you want the updates to install every day, choose option 0. If you want the updates to be installed only once a week on a given day, then choose the number assigned to the day you want the updates to install:

0 = Every day

1 = Sunday

2 = Monday

3 = Tuesday

4 = Wednesday

5 = Thursday

6 = Friday

7 = Saturday

You will also need to establish a time for the updates to be installed on the scheduled day. The default here is 3 AM. This setting uses a 24-hour clock. If you want to have updates installed after noon, you will have to add 12 hours to the time—for example, for 11 PM, you should select 23:00. Once this policy is set, you can apply it to servers in your network's sites, domains, or organizational units.

There is an additional checkbox setting here that will make automatic updates immediately install. When this setting is configured, it will allow an update to install immediately if the update does not require a restart of the Windows operating system or the interruption of Windows services.

By default, Windows Server 2012 checks for updates using an automatic update detection frequency of 22 hours. If you want to change that frequency, you can do so using the Automatic Updates Detection Frequency policy setting. When enabled, this setting specifies the number of hours between automatic update checks. The setting is interesting because the server will actually choose a value located somewhere between the actual setting in hours and 20 percent less than its value. This means that if you use a value of 20 hours, the server will check for automatic updates every 16 to 20 hours. This policy works in direct conjunction with Configure Automatic Updates and with Specify Intranet Microsoft Update Service Location.

The Specify Intranet Microsoft Update Service Location policy is used to enable Windows Update from a server within your corporate network. This means you can define which server in your network will provide centralized updates to the other clients and servers inside your network. This can be very desirable in many cases, because your server and clients are not getting their updates from an Internet property, but rather from an internal network location that can be tightly monitored and controlled.

The desire to move to an even more automated system of updating servers located inside the corporate network and to provide as much automation as possible for Windows Updates will eventually lead you to a group of resources called Windows Server Update Services.

Work with Windows Server Update Services

Windows Server Update Services (WSUS) is a comprehensive resource to help you deploy updates to the servers and clients in your network. This tool is now a server role that can be added to Windows Server 2012. The WSUS server role is also compatible with existing WSUS deployments and can be used in conjunction with the stand-alone editions of WSUS running on Windows Server 2008 R2. It is incredibly flexible and can be used in very small to very large network environments. WSUS is installed on a server or group of servers in your network and acts as an intranet-based Windows Update server.

Do a Simple WSUS Deployment

In its most basic form, a WSUS deployment consists of a single server on the local intranet inside the DMZ (perimeter network) and inside the Internet firewall. This server will be used to connect to Microsoft Update and download available updates in a process that is called *synchronization*. You will synchronize the WSUS server with the Windows Update servers on a regular basis, and the WSUS server will verify that available updates have been synchronized to the WSUS server. The initial synchronization will take an extended period of time if your Internet connection speed is good—longer if it is not. Subsequent synchronizations will be faster because the WSUS server will only synchronize new updates that have been made available.

To install the WSUS server role on your Windows Server 2012, do the following.

1. Start the Server Manager tool from the desktop.

2. Select Add Roles and Features from the Dashboard.

3. Click Next on the Before You Begin page.

4. Select Role-based or Feature-based installation. Click Next.

5. Select your server from the Server Pool. Click Next.

6. Check the Windows Server Update Services box. Click Next.

7. Accept the recommended prerequisites by clicking Add Features.

8. Click Next on the Select Server Roles page.

9. Click Next on the Select Features page.

10. Read the information and then click Next on the Windows Server Update Services page.

11. Accept the defaults and click Next on the Select Role Services page.

12. Choose whether you want to store updates locally or use Windows Update to download updates as needed. If you choose to store the updates, provide a location for storing the updates. Click Next.

13. Review the Confirmation page and then click Install.

14. When the installation completes, review the Installation Progress screen and click Close.

Once the WSUS server role has been added to your server, you will need to open WSUS in Server Manager and configure the WSUS role to work in your organization.

1. Open Server Manager from the desktop.

2. Choose the WSUS tool from the left pane of the Dashboard.

3. Choose More on the top right of the window.

4. Choose to run the initial configuration tasks. The server will be automatically configured based on the settings you chose during the addition of the role.

5. When the configuration completes, close the server Details pane.

6. Right-click the server name in the WSUS Servers list and choose Windows Server Update Services. You will see the Update Services pane similar to Figure 16.9.

From the Update Services pane, you can customize the operation of your server in the broader WSUS environment of your network.

Figure 16.9: WSUS Update Services

WSUS uses standard HTTP ports 80 and 443 to access and download the updates from Microsoft Update. These ports are likely already open on your firewall; if they are not, you will need to open them in order to use the WSUS server. It is possible to change the default communication ports to meet your network's specific needs.

Depending on the size and structure of your network, you may choose to add additional WSUS servers to your network. These additional servers can be configured to get their updates from the existing WSUS server. This process is called *chaining* servers together. As you chain more and more WSUS servers together, the WSUS deployment can become quite complex.

Automatic Updating is the client-side part of WSUS deployments. The service has to use the port assigned to the WSUS website in IIS. If no websites are running on the server where you install WSUS, you can choose to use the default website (port 80) or a custom website (ports 8530 or 8531).

Use Computer Groups

One of the coolest things about WSUS deployments is the use of computer groups. Computer groups allow you to target updates to specific groups of computers on your network. There are two default computer groups called All Computers and Unassigned Computers. Each computer that is added to WSUS is added to both of these two groups. Using the Actions pane in WSUS, as shown in Figure 16.10, you can create additional groups so that WSUS can target updates to specific groups of computers. You can also add computers to your new groups from the Unassigned Computers group. Note that you cannot remove computers from the All Computers group.

Figure 16.10: Adding computer groups

Computer groups allow you to structure your machines in such a way that you can test updates on a small group of machines before deploying those same updates on a broader scale to the rest of your network. If the testing works well, then broad deployment can be easily accomplished. However, if there is a problem in testing, you have limited the scope of the problem to a small computer group instead of the whole network. For additional information on installing and

configuring WSUS on Windows Server 2012, visit http://technet
.microsoft.com/en-us/library/hh852345.aspx.

Use WSUS Server Hierarchy

As mentioned earlier, it is possible to chain WSUS servers together.
There are two ways to build those links:

Autonomous mode   In *autonomous mode*, the upstream server,
or the server connected to Microsoft Update, shares synchronization information with its downstream partner but does not share
its computer group information. This way, the available updates are
passed from WSUS server to WSUS server while maintaining the
integrity of the individual computer groups.

Replica mode   In *replica mode*, the upstream server shares its
synchronization information and its computer group information
with its downstream partners. The downstream partners hold the
same information and are, therefore, functional replicas of the
upstream WSUS server.

We do not recommend that you do not create hierarchy beyond three
levels deep. At that point, the synchronization lag time introduced to
the process becomes prohibitive.

Get WSUS Updates on Disconnected Networks

It is sometimes necessary to operate servers and clients on a network
that is not connected to the Internet or to other networks. Servers and
clients operating in isolation still need updates. WSUS makes it possible to supply updates to isolated network segments through a simple
process:

1. Connect WSUS to Microsoft Update on a connected network.
2. Synchronize the available updates to the WSUS server.
3. Export the updates to media using the WSUS server.
4. Hand carry the media to the isolated network segment.
5. Import the updates to the isolated WSUS server using WSUS.
6. Deploy the updates to the isolated servers and clients.

This method not only makes it possible to deliver updates to isolated or disconnected networks but can also be used to limit the bandwidth in traditional connected WSUS deployments. For example, you might choose to have a single WSUS server synchronize updates with Microsoft Update and then export those updates to DVDs; then you can send the DVDs to be imported to each of your other WSUS servers instead of downloading the same information and slowing performance on the WAN.

Use WSUS with Branch Cache

One of the features of Windows Server 2012 is BranchCache. This feature can improve WAN performance by caching content on branch servers in order to make that content available to local clients without the need of constant WAN access. If the BranchCache feature is installed on Windows Server 2012, it can be used to cache the WSUS synchronization and computer group information. This can really improve the responsiveness of your WSUS servers that are located in branch-office locations. When you are using BranchCache with the WSUS role, it is important to know that the WSUS servers at the remote offices can only be configured as downstream servers in the Update Services tool; however, this benefit is significant in providing updates to the remote sites.

Learn Where to Store the Updates

The ideal place to store the updates from Windows Update is on the local WSUS server. This saves the network bandwidth of clients accessing the WSUS server only to be pointed to another network location to download the updates. There is one caveat here: the updates are going to take up a fair amount of space. Microsoft states that you should have 20GB of local storage at a minimum and actually recommends 30GB. Keep in mind that these numbers are only estimates and could go higher than 30GB, depending on your network needs and number of updates necessary for your particular client and server situation.

It is possible to use WSUS to approve updates for your network and then store those updates remotely. The most extreme example of this design would be to use the WSUS server to approve updates for your local clients and then point them to the Internet-based Windows Update servers for the updates. This effectively eliminates the requirement to store updates locally while still allowing you to test and approve the updates coming into your network.

Server Tuning and
Maintenance

PART VI

WSUS uses the Background Intelligent Transfer Service 2.0 (BITS 2.0) protocol for all of its file transfer needs. When time files are downloaded from servers to clients, they are moved using "spare" bandwidth. This technology also makes it possible to continue downloads, even if the computer is shut down in the middle of a download, once the computer is restarted.

Learn the WSUS Requirements

To run WSUS, your servers must meet the following minimum requirements:

- **CPU:** 1GHz minimum. 1.5GHz or better is recommended.
- **Graphics card:** 16MB hardware accelerated or better is recommended.
- **RAM:** 1GB minimum; 2GB or better is recommended.
- **Page file:** At least 1.5 times the physical memory is recommended.
- **I/O:** Fast ATA/IDE 100 hard disk or equivalent SCSI drives are recommended.
- **Network adapter:** 10MB minimum; 100MB or better is recommended.
- The system partition and the install partition for WSUS must be formatted with the NTFS file system.
- 1GB minimum free space on the system partition is recommended.
- 2GB minimum free space on the volume on which the database files will be stored is recommended.
- 20GB minimum free space on the volume where the content will be stored; 30GB is recommended.
- WSUS cannot be installed on compressed drives.

The current hardware requirements for WSUS should be easily met if you are running Windows Server 2012. If you are not running Windows Server 2012 as your WSUS machine, it is possible to use Windows Server 2003 SP2 or later as your WSUS server and install WSUS 3.0 SP2.

Get More Information on WSUS

WSUS is a great tool for controlling the update process in your network. To understand its true potential and the details associated with deploying and using WSUS, you will want to get the WSUS 3.0 SP2 deployment guide, as well as the WSUS step-by-step guides, available at http://technet.microsoft.com/en-us/wsus/default.aspx.

The information provided there will provide a strong base for using WSUS in your network.

Index

Note to the Reader: Throughout this index **boldfaced** page numbers indicate primary discussions of a topic. *Italicized* page numbers indicate illustrations.

D